GERMANS AND JEWS
SINCE THE HOLOCAUST

GERMANS AND JEWS SINCE THE HOLOCAUST

The Changing Situation in West Germany

EDITED BY
ANSON RABINBACH AND JACK ZIPES

HM
HOLMES & MEIER
NEW YORK · LONDON

First published in the United States of America 1986 by

Holmes & Meier Publishers, Inc.
30 Irving Place
New York, N.Y. 10003

Great Britain:
One Hallswelle Parade
London NW11 ODL, England

Library of Congress Cataloging-in-Publication Data
Main entry under title:

Germans and Jews since the holocaust. The changing
situation in West Germany.

   Bibliography: p.
   1. Jews—Germany (West)—Addresses, essays,
lectures.   2. Germany (West)—Ethnic relations—
Addresses, essays, lectures.   3. Holocaust (Television
program)—Addresses, essays, lectures.   4. Holocaust,
Jewish (1939–1945)—Public opinion—Addresses, essays,
lectures.   5. Public opinion—Germany (West)—Addresses,
essays, lectures.   6. Antisemitism—Germany—Addresses,
essays, lectures.   I. Rabinbach, Anson.   II. Zipes,
Jack David.
DS135.G332G42   1986   305.8'924'043   85-14036
ISBN 0-8419-0924-5
ISBN 0-8419-0925-3 (paper)

Book design by Ellen Foos

Manufactured in the United States of America

for George Mosse
mentor and friend

Contents

GERMANS AND JEWS
SINCE THE HOLOCAUST

1

INTRODUCTION

REFLECTIONS ON GERMANS AND JEWS
SINCE AUSCHWITZ

Anson Rabinbach

It is a commonplace that historical events force us constantly to reevaluate the past. But the impact of the Holocaust on the history of European culture, and on Jewish history specifically, has been so profound that it almost defies conceptualization. To invoke the Holocaust as an explanation is almost to have recourse to myth rather than to history. Overnight, as it were, the entire history of the Jews and their place in European culture had to be rewritten. This reconsideration of the place of the Jews in the history of Europe has been a central preoccupation of historians and philosophers since 1945. This book, since it focuses on the relationship between Germans and Jews after 1945, is necessarily part of that process. But at the same time it provides testimony to the difficulties of the undertaking. Instead of clarifying the relationship between the Germans and the Jews, the Holocaust has only sharpened our recognition of its complexity and opacity. To discuss the problem of Jewish identity and self-consciousness in the post-Holocaust age is to unravel the contradictions and vicissitudes of Jewish existence without arriving at a predictable destination.

Especially the post-Enlightenment German-Jewish tradition that produced the great cultural and intellectual achievements of the Wilhelminian and Weimar epochs was called into question. It is now almost two decades since the great scholar Gershom Scholem pronounced his verdict on the Jewish-German "symbiosis": "The love affair of the Jews and the Germans remained one-sided and unreciprocated."[1] The enthusiasm for German culture that had stamped his and earlier generations of extraordinary German-speaking intellectuals and artists was misguided. The Jews, he said, had unfortunately been dwelling at the wrong address, and that address had always been on a one-way street. The relationship of Germans and Jews was "never anything else than a fiction" ultimately "drowned in blood."[2] It was poisoned from the outset by what Scholem called "the price of Jewish emancipation," for which "the Germans demanded a resolute disavowal of Jewish nationality—a price the leading writers and spokesmen of the Jewish avant-garde were only too happy to pay."[3] Even the much envied "preeminence" achieved by the Central European Jewish cultural renaissance of the late ninteenth and early twentieth centuries was never truly appreciated by their German contemporaries. The very success of those Jews stoked the fires of *ressentiment* and anti-Semitism. They became a "source of irritation" and their "preeminence turned into disaster for them."[4]

Scholem's repudiation of the German-Jewish intellectual synthesis that nurtured so many important thinkers and artists seemed to many excessively harsh. It immediately became the subject of much controversy from both the German and the Jewish sides.[5] Scholem's critics called for a new dialogue, some even arguing that the assimilation of German Jews could not be judged through hindsight. Despite the persistence of anti-Semitism in the Kaiserreich, Peter Gay contended, "Germany's Jews . . . had good reason to feel themselves, or to aspire to feel themselves, to be Jewish Germans."[6] Gay's point that German history, especially in the nineteenth century, should not be read solely as "clues to a crime to come" was an important counterweight to Scholem's grim reappraisal. George L. Mosse has also emphasized the fact that the German-Jewish dialogue was a reciprocated cultural phenomenon that took place within the terms of the Enlightenment and later, among the intellectual advocates of socialism. The dialogue, he claimed, was "built on that culture into which the Jews were emancipated."[7]

A more balanced view suggests that the German-Jewish symbiosis was neither a one-way street nor a smooth path obstructed only by the accidental arrival of Hitler and his Third Reich. Significantly, there continues to be a German-Jewish symbiosis, perhaps not at the level of a German-Jewish *presence* in contemporary Germany—though this too must be taken into account—but at the level of an intellectual and cultural tradition that resonates and thrives beyond the historic boundary of 1945. It may in fact be impossible to resolve the question of what is ultimately meant by the German-Jewish symbiosis—especially since the Nazis in one stroke leveled *all* Jews, Eastern and Western, assimilated and unassimilated, to a democratically shared fate.

Until only recently much of the debate and discussion about the German-Jewish symbiosis has focused on the period before 1933. This seems only natural, since before that *caesura* Jews were integrally a part of German culture and society, if not German politics. Yet, what neither Scholem nor his interlocuters chose to consider was the possibility that they were part of the continuation of the dialogue in the postwar era. What has not yet been explored is the ways in which that relationship between Germans and Jews has been perpetuated, either in the real sociological sense, or perhaps more importantly, spiritually and intellectually.

One of the consequences of Nazism is that the German-Jewish symbiosis now transcends the physical territory of Germany and can be understood only in terms of a much broader notion of European cultural identity that left its trace on the French as well as on the Anglo-Saxon intellectual world. The extraordinary impact of the German émigré intellectuals of the 1930s and 1940s, who were mostly, but not entirely Jewish, underscores this conclusion.[8] Finally, we must also attempt to explain the German side of the equation—the persistence of the fate of the Jews in their attitudes, beliefs, and prejudices. If it is no longer possible to speak of a German-Jewish symbiosis, it is, ironically, still possible to speak of a "Jewish question" in Germany today.

There continues to be a German-Jewish dialogue, even if it is in large part a dialogue about a dialogue. Clearly, it is not the same one that existed before 1933, and certainly it is now marked by the abyss that separates the modern world from the one that antedates Auschwitz. Scholem's conclusion that there can be no German-Jewish dialogue after Auschwitz was premature. Certain features of a German-Jewish relationship can be discerned after 1945. To illuminate that relationship is the purpose of this book.

Most conspicuous, at the level of politics, is the ongoing connection between the postwar German states and the legacy of the Holocaust. The German Federal Republic's efforts to find absolution in reparations and an official policy of philo-Semitism must be seen in the context of its relative silence about the Nazi past, its myth of the "zero hour" of 1945 as a historical tabula rasa, its tolerance of former Nazis, and its unwillingness, at least until recently, to press for war-crimes trials of Nazi criminals still at large. As recently as 1979 the German parliament actually considered extending the statute of limitations on murder (thirty years according to the Federal Republic's Constitution) to Nazi war crimes, a move thwarted only by eliminating *any* statute on murder. Chancellor Helmut Kohl's decision to make a U.S. presidential visit to the site of Waffen-SS graves at the cemetery in Bitburg the price of support for the deployment of U.S. Pershing and Cruise missiles, and for Ronald Reagan's "Star Wars" program, is the most recent and glaring example of this tendency to publicly undermine their own protestations of sincere reparations.

The political culture of the Federal Republic has been characterized by what a recent commentator has called "the Caesar's wife syndrome," the need to be above suspicion in the eyes of the world.[9] All too often contemporary German efforts to assume a posture of moral responsibility for the Holocaust have revealed a deep-seated resentment at having to pay such a high price, which leads to default. Here again, the Bitburg affair provides an apt illustration. What led to Chancellor Kohl's fateful decision and implacable stand that a U.S. President visit a cemetery of German war dead—even after the revelations about the SS graves—was an effort to remove, once and for all, the image of Germany as the *Heimat* of Nazism and to bring it into the community of nations symbolically as well as diplomatically. German irritation at reminders from abroad about the German past, especially from the United States, produced a growing desire for a tangible symbol of the normalization of German history. Since World War II Germany has indeed suffered from a deficit of such positive historical symbols, which could be, if not celebrated, at least commemorated. This explains the inordinate importance accorded to the fortieth anniversary of the surrender of Nazi Germany on May 8, 1945. Whether this date was to be commemorated as a "defeat" or as a "liberation" remained unclear. What was clear, however, was that it was to symbolize a new phase in German national self-consciousness, give the Western alliance a shot in the arm, and shore up Kohl's own weakening position domestically.

For German conservatives there was, at least at the outset, a consensus that to finally overcome the abyss between past and present represented by the "zero hour" of German history, in which the historical past was buried under the ashes of defeat, the participants of the Nazi era must first be turned into its victims. While right-wing intellectuals who crudely whitewash the Holocaust have been scarce, German neo-conservatives have in the last few years begun to rewrite German history from the standpoint of national traditions and national honor, usually bracketing the crimes of the Nazis as a particular aberration. They represent the intellectual side of a popular tradition which sees the question of historical responsibility far more narrowly than non-German public opinion—or historical conscience, for that matter—would find reasonable elsewhere.

One important mechanism of this historical normalization has been the growing "Hitlerization" of Nazism, epitomized by the "Hitler-wave" of the mid-1970s, the cult-like insistence on the equation of Hitler and Nazism (the "Hitler diaries" scandal was an important example of this process), and even more pervasively, by the tendency to draw the circle of guilt ever more tightly around the Führer and his inner group so that even the Waffen-SS could be classified among the "victims of National Socialism." Another part of this normalization has been the simultaneous "Napoleonization" of Germany's role in World War II, in which the crimes of the SS are separated in the public mind from the heroic and tragic exploits of the Wehrmacht and the Waffen-SS.

It is above all this aspect that contributed most to the shocking distance between the German government's perception of Bitburg and the American public's response. The view that most Germans, including the military, were also victims of Nazism, having suffered so much during the last years of war and the Allied bombing, has long been a deeply felt part of the popular German psyche. But the inclusion of the Waffen-SS in this picture, its public avowal by the nation's leader, and its reaffirmation by Ronald Reagan was a different matter. For Reagan, the politicization of the Holocaust led to his greatest foreign policy debacle and the worst media performance by an American President once considered invulnerable in that sphere. For Kohl, the rush to reconciliation, a symbol of independence, in fact mortgaged his government even more deeply to U.S. interests.

In Germany, public reaction to Bitburg divided largely along generational lines. For Kohl, as well as for most conservative Germans of the generation over fifty, the Bitburg visit was to represent the symbolic nationalization of the entire German military in World War II, something which apparently many younger Germans were not willing to accept, at least publicly. While the older generation largely supported Kohl's efforts and resented the protests of American Jews, veterans, and Congressmen, Germany's younger generation seems to have found their Chancellor's premature attempt to count the Waffen-SS among the victims of Hitler a historical travesty. But because of the American public's outrage at the visit, especially among the Jewish community, and the widespread perception of Reagan as a "hostage" of foreign policy imperatives, many Germans who initially sympathized with the Chancellor's aims found the results distasteful. In the end the "gesture of reconciliation" turned into a gesture of division, opening the Holocaust issue to public debate precisely when it was supposed to disappear from view. Whether Bitburg will ultimately intensify rather than diminish the desire for the still-missing symbol of historical normalization is unclear. Nevertheless, the Bitburg affair points yet again to the significance of the Holocaust and the decisive character of the "Jewish question" in contemporary German politics.

Another case in point is the sharpening of tensions between the Federal Republic and Israel during the past half decade—a "special" relationship that provided much of the needed capital for the building of the Israeli economy in the postwar era—which has permitted the German left, including the Social Democratic Party (SPD), to become increasingly pro-Arab. By removing the mantle of responsibility toward Israel, still another step toward normalization can be taken. Chancellor Kohl's 1984 visit to Israel enraged both the Israelis and the German Jewish community because of his insistence that the postwar generation was less culpable for the crimes of the Nazis than their elders.

Certainly, the Federal Republic has no monopoly on the Holocaust issue in contemporary politics. It should not be forgotten that the German Democratic Republic's official ideology of anti-Fascism, though less lenient toward former Nazis, has all but obliterated the relationship between Nazism and anti-Semitism in the public mind. By making "capitalism" responsible for all evil, including Nazism itself, the East Germans have erased the specific issue of genocide from consciousness. The GDR then, has been alone in reclaiming the German past, first the heritage of Marx, Engels, Liebknecht, and Rosa Luxemburg, then Münzer, Goethe, Schiller, Hegel, and Kant, and most recently Martin Luther. Yet this picture of a "German heritage" makes capitalism the perpetrator of Hitler's crimes, and completely ignores those against whom they were actually committed. Whereas the Federal Republic of Germany suffers from a deficit of German history and a desire for normalization, the normalization of history in the GDR has resulted from a deficit of any real historical responsibility. On both sides of the wall the historical *presence* of the Holocaust is a decisive force shaping the development of public policy. In each case the official ideology of the German state is formed as a preemptive reaction to the Jewish question.

To understand the "Jewish question" in contemporary Germany, it is important to begin with the very small Jewish community that exists in Germany today. Of the more than 20,000 Jews who remained in West Germany after 1945, less than half were German Jews with prewar roots.[10] As of 1980 there were about 28,000 registered Jews in the Federal Republic of Germany (with only 650 in the GDR), comprising 0.2 percent of the world Jewish population. Jews in Germany after 1945 largely fell into two categories: émigrés from "other" nations (Eastern Europe, the Soviet Union, Israel) and the "official" German-Jewish community, composed of survivors or those who returned after the war. Until only recently, this official community pursued a quietistic policy of un-critical support for Israel and affirmation of the postwar West German pro-Israel policies. It even went so far as to oppose the prosecution of former Nazis accused of crimes, as in the famous "Filbinger Affair" of 1978, when the Christian Democratic Union (CDU) minister president of Baden-Württemberg was accused of sentencing a soldier to death for an anti-Nazi utterance after the surrender in 1945.[11]

In the past five years, however, there has been a growing tendency among younger Jewish intellectuals living in Germany to express their views on the failure of the Federal Republic to make good on its claims to eradicate the residues of anti-Semitism and Nazism. The demonstrations against the Bitburg visit and the violent protests against the reunions of the SS veterans organizations in Bavaria in May 1985 were outgrowths of a new and stronger sense that the Jewish community in Germany could no longer maintain its low profile and passive image. Even more significant has been the independent voice of younger Jewish intellectuals, mostly on the left, who have publicly taken stands against both the official govern-ment attitude toward the Holocaust, and against the mindless left-wing identification with the Palestinians, while remaining critical of Israel. This development was prompted not so much by the changing foreign policy of the Federal Republic, or by the attitudes of the official Jewish organiza-tions, as by a complex reaction to the German New Left of the 1960s and 1970s.

While the German New Left emerged in the mid-1960s as a student movement concerned with the silence of the postwar generation about the entire complex of Nazi crimes, the decisive turn against Israel and away from the politics of responsibility for the Holocaust took place in the period after 1967–68. In the context of growing opposition to the war in Vietnam and with the attraction of Third World revolutionary move-ments, Israel no longer appeared as the consequence of the Nazi catastro-phe. After the 1967 Arab-Israeli War, which released so much perverse German public enthusiasm for Israel's successful "Blitzkrieg" tactics, the German New Left increasingly viewed Israel as the product, not of Nazi genocide, but of "the political economy of Imperialism."[12] For the new German generation of the 1960s and 1970s, which was even more influ-enced by the New Left than was its American counterpart, it seemed that the legacy of the Holocaust could be overcome only by turning the victims into the oppressors and by total absorption into the Palestinian cause. This tragic course, which once again so markedly underscored the persistence of the Holocaust in German political reality, reached its most grotesque and destructive consequences in the training and support of German leftists for the RAF (Rote Armee Fraktion) in Palestinian camps and in the participation of Germans in the "selection" of "Jewish passengers" in the airplane hijacking at Entebbe in 1976.

By the early 1980s, however, the decade of hyperidentification with the Palestinians, symbolized by the unisex fashion of Palestinian shawls, was showing signs of wear if not farce. The broadcast of the television program "Holocaust" in January 1979 unleashed an enormous public debate on the "Jewish question" that coincided, ironically, with a new period of uncomfortable relations between the West German government and Israel. For the first time since 1945 the Holocaust loomed large in the public consciousness, as opposed to scholarly discussion. Two Jewish writers living in West Germany, the journalist Henryk Broder and Lea Fleischmann, author of a powerful autobiographical statement, *Dies ist nicht mein Land* (This Is Not My Country), emigrated to Israel while publicly condemning their colleagues on the left for historical amnesia and lack of compassion for their "own" Jews.[13] Even before the Lebanon invasion in 1982 a "Jewish Group" opposed to both the militarism of the Israeli government and the slavish identification of the Left with the Palestinians had already become active.[14] But the invasion brought about a dramatic change in the situation. At a Peace Congress held in Frankfurt in the summer of 1982 outrageous posters by left-wing sects condemning the "Final Solution of the Palestinian People by the Jewish State," and pamphlets denouncing "Zionist genocide," led to a strong public repudiation of this grotesque equation of Jews and Nazis.

The result was the emergence of a new German-Jewish political consciousness in the Federal Republic for the first time since 1945. Jewish and non-Jewish critics articulated the fundamental truth that the seamless identification of the German New Left with the Palestinians originated not so much in a sense of solidarity with the oppressed, but out of a need for a "giant exculpation."[15] The German New Left, they argued, was imprisoned by a distorted perception of Israel born of a need to exorcise German guilt. Ironically, they also pointed out, the Israelis too viewed all reality through the lens of the Holocaust, one-dimensionally casting the Palestinians in the role of yet another demonic force threatening the very existence of the Jews. Begin's crude comparison of Arafat with Hitler in the last days of the fighting over Beirut had its parallel in the Frankfurt posters.

As a result of this new German-Jewish "dialogue" the German New Left has also begun to find its own response to the criticisms that their Jewish critics (who often came from their ranks) leveled against them, though with rather ambiguous results. In 1983 the West Berlin journal *Ästhetik und Kommunikation (Ä&K),* one of the most influential organs of the post-1960s Frankfurt School of critical theory, published a controversial issue entitled "Germans, Leftists, Jews." The immediate response was far greater than any that journal had ever received. There were weeks of reaction in the press, much commentary in the periodicals, and even a television debate.[16] While most critics excoriated *Ä & K* for its purposefully naïve ignorance of historical facts and its unabashed hostility to contemporary German Jews—especially Broder and Fleischmann—for making them uncomfortable, some even found the journal anti-Semitic and accused the editors of harboring desires to "return home as in the Reich.[17] Nevertheless, the *Ä & K* issue clearly marked a new and important dimension in the postwar German attitude toward the Jewish question. Embracing neither the philo-Semitism qua silence of their parents, nor the anti-Semitism qua anti-Zionism of the student movement, the editors directly articulated for the first time the anger and resentment of their "second generation" for having to bear the full responsibility for the past. For them, the tragedy of postwar German culture is that they have been denied their legitimate right to a "normal" relationship to the previous generation, the generation of silence. In other words, the Holocaust sits at the gate blocking a reconciliation with their parents' generation like the doorkeeper in Kafka's famous parable "Before the Law." Because there can be *no* authentic rapprochement with *their* past, the anger is directed not at the Nazis but at the Jews, as if they posed the obstruction to a reconciliation with their own parents. Thus the theme of reconciliation and the repudiation of responsibility has recently appeared at the center of the new German-Jewish dialogue. Since it emerged in the form of a debate among "marginal intellectuals," it might seem as if it does not reflect wide "public sentiment" in contemporary West Germany. But, as so often in German history, it is precisely marginal intellectuals like the *Ä & K* editors who articulate what is a critical though largely unspoken component of German political culture.

Somewhat earlier, Martin Walser, the well-known West German writer, also expressed a similar sentiment. To be German today, Walser complained, is to display one's German-ness *(Deutschsein)* reluctantly, and when he tries to do this "even a little bit positively" he "immediately activates resistance." What is the cause of this dilemma? For Walser, "Auschwitz" is the answer: "Only when we can overcome Auschwitz," he said, "can we return to national tasks."[18] In other words the obstacle to German-ness itself is Auschwitz and its consequences.

Recently elements of the German peace movement, in their own efforts to exorcize the Holocaust demon, have occasionally turned to vulgar anti-Semitism as a way of justifying their political stance—even suggesting that the unconscious resentment of American Jews for the Jewish fate at the hands of the Germans and their secret desire "to turn Germany back to the level of an agrarian nation" has been the unconscious motivation for the powerful influence they exercise on behalf of the deployment of U.S. missiles in Germany.[19] An even more disturbing manifestation of the linkage between a sense of German national identity and national consciousness and the politics of anti-Semitism on the left was the scandalous "fact-finding" visit of a group of Greens to Israel in December 1984, prefaced by the publication of a supposedly confidential "working paper" outlining the purposes of the trip as the revelation of Israel's "terror policies" and "full responsibility for the impending blood bath in the Middle East."[20]

Moreover, Rudolf Barho, a former GDR dissident and most recently the apostle of the radical "fundamentalist" ecological wing of the Green Party, noted in a speech about the German alternative to Western capitalism, technology, and environmental destruction that Hitler was a great German mystic, who mobilized and instrumentalized the dark, aggressive, and repressed part of the "Genotype Human." "The next time we will win," Barho assured his audience, "because the power relations between authoritarianism and anti-authoritarianism have changed."[21] Though some Greens, notably Otto Schily, a prominent attorney and member of the Bonn Parliament, withdrew from the Israel trip and repudiated Barho, it is unlikely that this and future absurdities of the West German political landscape will disappear. For the Green fundamentalists, like the conservatives on the far right, German national identity can come about only through an at least partial reconciliation with the national tradition that includes the Nazi epoch. As Alfred Dregger, the Chairman of the CDU's Parliamentary Fraction, and one of Kohl's chief supporters throughout the Bitburg affair, said in a phrase echoing Barho's: "In the West a coming to terms with the past *(Vergangenheitsbewältigung)* has taken place which frequently has not been concerned with restoring to their purity the fundamental values perverted and misused by Hitler."[22]

Such statements not only affirm the permanence of the Holocaust in present-day German politics, but they point to its centrality in the current political situation of the Federal Republic itself. In a real sense the Bitburg visit was not simply about the Nazi past but about the role of the Holocaust in the present. For the Greens, and perhaps for the entire German generation born after 1945, the issue of national identity and national independence has taken on a critical significance. Although the SPD electoral slogan, "In the German interest," found little resonance in 1980, the issues of German national identity, anti-Americanism, and the Holocaust have become entwined since then. Although the Greens remain the only German political party to have opposed the Bitburg visit, their own politics have taken the traditional path of the German New Left of the 1960s and 1970s—identification with the Palestinians and anti-Americanism. But more important, the Greens have provoked a resurgence of national themes in German politics since their astonishing success in the 1980 elections. The new neutralism of the German Greens, with its emphasis on a reconstituted *"Mitteleuropa"* divorced from the imperatives of the superpowers, has rearranged the priorities of West German politics. The Greens are no doubt a potential but distant threat to the NATO alliance. But their success in mobilizing a popular feeling of resentment at the limited sovereignty that Germany enjoys in matters of defense and military policy has reopened the repressed issue of the status of the German nation. Appeals to German national identity, often combined with the rhetoric of anti-Americanism, made neo-nationalism a crucial component of the peace and alternative movement, and has caused concern in both the SPD and the CDU/CSU camps. In order to steal the thunder of nationalism from the pacifist left, it was necessary for the parties of the German center and right to find their own symbols of German national sovereignty. In the case of the SPD, regional elections in the Saar and elsewhere have shown a clear drift toward a more critical stance toward military preparedness and NATO support, while the CDU/CSU has tried to link its own defense of German traditions with a vigorous reassertion of the primacy of the American alliance. For neither the left nor the right, however, could reconciliation with German national traditions be achieved without some form of repudiation of German complicity in the Holocaust.

The contemporary German-Jewish "dialogue" is not limited, however, to these political controversies in West Germany. It also includes, as we have already noted, the broader intellectual and cultural continuity that transcends the existing German states. The influence of the German refugee intellectuals in spreading their intellectual heritage to the Anglo-Saxon world cannot be underestimated. And, it should be pointed out, their ideas returned to influence the postwar generation in Europe as well. This cross-fertilization is as true for those German intellectuals who found an untarnished tradition in the left-wing Jewish intellectuals of the Frankfurt School as it is for those non-German intellectuals (many of whom were Jewish) who rediscovered the German-Jewish symbiosis in the same thinkers abroad. The impact of the Frankfurt School on the generation of American intellectuals who came out of the student movement of the 1960s and founded in the 1970s such journals of contemporary critical theory as *New German Critique* and *Telos* is only one example of this ongoing relationship between Germans and Jews. The influence of Hans Gerth, who helped bring Max Weber and the Frankfurt School to the attention of American social scientists, or the more extraordinary impact of Hannah Arendt and the émigré social scientists in a wide variety of disciplines must also be included in this aspect of the postwar dialogue. As contemporary Germans must be concerned, consciously or unconsciously, with the fate of the Jews, the allure of the German-Jewish intellectual tradition continues to have a profound influence on contemporary non-Germans.

The German-Jewish symbiosis is, therefore, still of paramount importance for us, as the heirs of the historical relationship that was so damaged by the efforts of the Nazis to end it forever. This volume is less concerned with the role of the Jews in pre-1933 Germany history than it is with the fate of the symbiosis in the contemporary world. It asks a question different from the one posed by Scholem twenty years ago. Instead of wondering whether a German-Jewish dialogue did exist in the past, or whether it might exist in the future, it asks about the German-Jewish relationship in the present: What is the impact of the Holocaust on contemporary Germans? What is the impact of the German-Jewish experience on those who feel themselves to be part of the German-Jewish tradition, either as part of the small "return" of the Jews to Germany after 1945, or in the larger sense of the intellectual current that was brought to the English-speaking world by the great sea change of intellectual emigration after 1933? What is the state of the German-Jewish dialogue today?

We are concerned not so much with the failure of the German-Jewish identity before 1933 as with its *aftereffects* on a generation that did not experience firsthand the fruits of cultural emancipation or the horrors of destruction. In short, we are interested in what has become of "Germans and Jews" after Hitler, after Weimar, and after the eclipse of the great Jewish erudition of the nineteenth-century Central European cities.

It is self-evident that the Holocaust has not removed the dilemmas faced by Jews in the modern world. Until 1933, it appeared that European, and especially German, Jews could choose the alternatives of assimilation, socialism, and Zionism as the paths to modernity open to them. Though these have hardly been exhausted today, all of them have become far more problematic, more fragile, and more tenuous than they might have seemed to earlier, more optimistic generations. For many Jews the Holocaust destroyed the basic premise of nineteenth-century assimilationism. The identification of European Jews with liberalism and with the values of the Enlightenment—tolerance, reason, and cosmopolitanism—was experienced as a betrayal. The rise of Nazism made it clear that this tradition was not shared by the vast majority of Germans and that it was no longer possible to refer to Judaism as the religion of reason or to find solace in the human community idealized as secular habitus of faith. The idea of the nation, which many Jews considered the territorial substratum of both morality and identity, also suffered a considerable decline in fortune. Social revolution, once the spiritual homeland of what Isaac Deutscher aptly named the non-Jewish Jew, that curious and dedicated species that included Rosa Luxemburg, Leon Trotsky, and even Karl Marx, has become tainted with the memory of a different kind of death camp.[23] What all these secular Jewish visions of utopia had in common was the idea of the universal human being as the embodiment of Reason, of national, civic, or social *Virtu*—and all of them foundered on the horrors of the twentieth century.

The crushing blow delivered by the Holocaust to the Jewish ideal of a social path to emancipation, to the legacy of the French Revolution, and to the Enlightenment has been often noted. Its impact received one of its first and most systematic expositions by the theorists of the Frankfurt School in the 1940s, when they experienced Enlightenment universalism in all its guises as a cultural dead end. If, at the outset, critical social theory was based on the Marxist idea that dialectic is secularized hope, the translation of the desire for transcendence into history, and the identification with the suffering of past generations, the theory underwent a profound change in the 1940s. The characteristic motifs in the critical theory of the 1930s still owe a great deal to the Jewish Messianic idea with its emphasis on redemption, utopia, and the radical negation of the existing order of things. In its original conception, the Jewish Messianic impulse in critical theory was, as Herbert Marcuse put it in his appreciation of Walter Benjamin, conceived in primarily Marxian terms. Of course, critical theory replaced ideas of fate or myth with social domination as the roadblock to emancipation. But the "truth of critical theory" remained its belief in the possibility of a radical "overcoming" of what was perceived as history that had become reified as "second nature." Liberation was considered not in terms of planned economies, egalitarianism, or even greater democracy, but in terms of what Benjamin referred to as "exploding the continuum of history." Only when the history of domination abruptly and radically ceased could "freedom and justice begin."[24]

After the war, however, this original Messianic impulse in critical theory was altered by a very different vision. It was Theodor W. Adorno who was the first among the Frankfurt émigrés to place the experience of the Holocaust at the center of his philosophical concerns. For him, it became a central event, not only for Jews, but for all European culture, a paradigm of the modern experience. For Adorno the word "Auschwitz" signified the failure of a culture grounded in the bedrock of science and rationality, the irrational core of the technological epoch. Modern civilization, he argued, could not come to terms with *difference,* with that which could not readily be absorbed into a system of universal values and rules. The inability of society to find a place for the Jew "as the embodiment of a negative principle" within its perceptual framework paved the way for the ultimate irrationality, the attempt to do away with the problem through murder.[25]

In the *Dialectic of Enlightenment,* first published in 1947, Adorno and Max Horkheimer saw both the relatively benign anti-Semitism of the nineteenth-century bourgeoisie and the malignant and genocidal racial anti-Semitism of the Nazis as two sides of the same problem: the inability of modern society to come to terms with the paradox of Jewish identity. In their view, a simplistic social-psychological theory that takes for granted the *arbitrary* character of the Jew as victim in the psychology of anti-Semitic projection is mistaken. The Jews were not randomly chosen as the scapegoat for projecting social discontent onto an easily identifiable and vulnerable target. The Jews are the representatives of the paradox of modernity itself, of the inability to tolerate difference, even in the idea of tolerance itself. The repression of difference is the underside of Enlightenment, its authoritarian face. For the critical theorists, the conformist uniformity of modern mass culture has its roots here as well.

Since Enlightenment assumes not the acceptance or recognition of difference but its elimination, the only vehicle of acceptance for bourgeois society was the self-negation of the Jews as a collectivity and their assimilation into the social community as individuals. For the racists and the nationalists, on the other hand, the image of the Jew was permanently alien, a nonorganic other whose power was manifested in all forms of social organization (in capitalism, communism, and liberalism). In biological terms, the Jew as the carrier of abstract values was the polluter of the national and racial community. For the Nazis, therefore, only a biologically "pure" community could ensure the elimination of the Jews. In the first case, the Jew is an outsider to be taken into the culture; in the second, the Jew is an insider to be exorcised from it. To be both an outsider and an insider, to borrow Peter Gay's terms, is the essence of the Jewish dilemma. The very existence of the Jew is thus "the Jewish problem" for both the defenders and the irrationalist opponents of the Enlightenment.

As a consequence of this discourse on the Jews, two very real mental images of the Jewish threat, two competing stereotypes emerged, each corresponding to two very real social groups. The *"Ostjuden"* or Eastern-European ghetto Jews were perceived as the embodiment of the Jew's fundamentally unassimilable character, while the bourgeois Western Jews were seen as the powerful and assimilated Jewish capitalists and Communists who had irreparably infiltrated the community. In the anti-Semitic worldview, the Jews symbolized *both* the triumph of Enlightenment as civilization, modernity, abstraction, and its absolute nemesis, the primitive and unassimilable other.

The conclusion that Adorno drew from his reflections on anti-Semitism was a radical one. The Holocaust, he thought, called into question all metaphysical totalities, especially rationalism, nationalism, and Marxism. As the Lisbon earthquake of 1755 "sufficed to cure Voltaire of the theodicy of Leibniz," it was the Holocaust that cured Adorno of the theodicy of Hegel: "The visible disaster of the first nature was insignificant in comparison with the second social one, which defies human imagination.[26] His pessimistic belief that "whatever is, is *not* right," reflected the impact of what Hannah Arendt called "dark times" on his thought.[27]

This reading of Adorno and Horkheimer places the experience of the German Jew at the center of the recasting of their social theory by 1947. Martin Jay's "Jews and the Frankfurt School," included in this volume, provides an extensive account of the growing importance of the Jewish dimension for the Frankfurt theorists during the war, and of the abandoning of their initial tendency to see anti-Semitism as a secondary by-product of capitalism.[28]

As early as 1946, Jean-Paul Sartre also commented on the meaning of the Holocaust for all the once comfortable myths that no longer survived the ashes. Jewish authenticity, he claimed, "had to consist in *choosing oneself as Jew,* or the authentic Jew must abandon the myth of universal man."[29] His resistance is born of self-knowledge as "a historical and damned creature," not out of ideology or idealism. But, as Ferenc Feher points out in his essay on Istvan Bibó's theory of anti-Semitism, Sartre's standpoint corresponds to a particular historical moment, that of the Warsaw Ghetto Uprising.[30] It is not otherwise immediately clear what general relevance the idea of abandoning the idea of universality has apart from Zionism, which is clearly not Sartre's concern.

What these reflections point to is the conclusion that the problem of secular Jewish identity, or more precisely, the Jewish mode of being in the world has become completely problematic in the post-Holocaust epoch. These problems clearly cannot be resolved at the level of social theory or philosophy alone. The theoretical problems of universality and the place of the Jews in Western culture must first be considered in light of the major concerns facing not only German Jews, but most Jews in the contemporary world. How can the myth of universality be overthrown without succumbing to the equally distasteful appeals of ethnic particularism and national chauvinism? Can shamelessness be disassociated from arrogance, authenticity from self-righteousness? Can the historic burden of Jewish suffering be freed from its misuse as licence to moral absolutism or a grandiose equanimity in the face of the suffering of other victims? From a historical point of view, the "Final Solution" may have been unique, yet the view that Jewish suffering is also unique is not a corollary. If it is false to construct an abstract ideal of Jewish identity out of the historical experience of the Holocaust, is it not equally abstract to ignore its role in the political arrangements that grew out of it?

These questions all touch on the issue of the relationship of contemporary Jews to Zionism. The rise of Zionism is above all explicable in terms of the European catastrophe and its antecedents. To attribute Zionism to colonialism or imperialism, as anti-Zionist critics argue, is unhistorical at best. But one can clearly accept the legitimacy of the Zionist project without accepting the view that the nation-state is the only path to Jewish emancipation in modern history. The issue ultimately revolves around the meaning of the Holocaust for the present: What role do we ascribe to homelessness in the fate of the Jews? For the early Zionists the most dangerous of all states was statelessness, and that presumption led to the view that Jewish existence cannot be guaranteed without territory and arms. This may be the most telling argument in Scholem's 1966 essay "Jews and Germans." He points out that the fact that the "homelessness" of the European Jews was falsely glorified and taken "as an image of the *condition humaine,*" rather than seen as an indictment of the old status quo, and forces us to see the negative consequences of outsiderness. But, even if we concede the dark side of homelessness, is not the desire for a homeland also suspect for its association with those whose single-minded desire for territory blinds them to the fate of the dispossessed? More important, Margarethe Susman's statement that "the vocation of the people of Israel as a people [e.g., not as a state. A.R.] is not self-realization, but self-surrender for the sake of a higher, transhistorical goal"—which Scholem finds so shocking and self-destructive—is also a true rendering of the price of nonsurrender, the abandoning of the intellectualist mission of the Jews and their reentry into the conflict of nations.

Nor does the "non-Jewish Jew" whom Deutscher so eloquently described and embodied hold much promise for Jewish identity today. The "non-Jewish Jew" has learned, perhaps all too painfully and much too late, that so-called revolutionary and Communist nations have been among the most barbarous, not only in cultivating anti-Semitism, but in eliminating all traces of "universality" in the interests of false "internationalism." The recognition that socialism was as powerless as capitalism in the face of the Holocaust, disillusion with communism, and the decline of working-class radicalism has all but destroyed the historic affinity between socialism and secular Judaism.

Thus, neither secular universalism, nationalist and statist identification, nor socialist internationalism have been kind to the modern Jew. And yet, none can be ignored in understanding the different paths of Jewish existence today. In the long run, both territoriality and cultural extraterritoriality have failed to encompass Jewish aspirations. Scholem notwithstanding, homelessness remains a Jewish condition despite, and in part because of, Israel. The pariah people has been redefined as the pariah nation, with global consequences.

The recognition of the immensely dense tangle of meanings that have been attached to the German-Jewish experience in the modern epoch brings us to another theme that is central to this volume: the problem of Jewish identity. The second part of this volume is devoted to some personal responses by contemporary German and American Jews raised by these broader issues. In the wide range of these reactions we can see how complex the problem has become. They also provide testimony of the inadequacy of all easy generalizations in regard to the postwar fate of the German-Jewish symbiosis.

This volume is based on a project first developed by the journal *New German Critique* in three special issues designed to explore the problematic relationship of Germans and Jews in the postwar years. In the interest of clarification we have divided our book into four parts: a section on historical background; a series of Jewish (German and American) responses to the contemporary situation, including essays and statements by authors from different generations and life situations; a section on the public response to the television film "Holocaust"; and a reassessment of the problem of anti-Semitism. In the first part, Jack Zipes provides an overview of the multileveled Jewish community in Germany today, focusing on the relationship between the "resettled" Jewish community in West Germany (which is only in small part made up of German Jews who survived the war and the Holocaust) and government policies and attitudes in the Federal Republic. Zipes's essay documents the vicissitudes of Jewish identity in West Germany, in particular the emergence of a critical voice in a new generation that has become a thorn in the side of both official policy and the established Jewish community in the 1970s. Detlev Claussen, in an essay quite atypical of the attitude of most German intellectuals of the sixties generation toward the Jewish question, describes the fatal turn of the student movement away from the "hard" questions about Auschwitz and Nazism to a delusional reality that evaded them entirely. He also describes the difficulties encountered by younger, more critical Jews when confronted with the unconscious but impenetrable anti-Semitism of the New Left.

Jewish identity is also the problem explored through the short autobiographical essays and statements that have been collected for this volume. Our purpose is not to be representative but to find those German-Jewish intellectuals (including some born in America) for whom a sense of identification with German culture has been essential for self-definition. By no means are these individuals seen as exemplary, but rather they have been chosen to provide a broad spectrum of reflections on the problem. Ironically, the older generation, Manès Sperber, Jean Améry, and Toni Oelsner,[31] question the validity of the Jewish pariah status in prewar Germany, and Dan Diner and Yudit Yago-Jung, both of whom spent their youth in West Germany, underscore the importance of remaining a conscious pariah in a situation that threatens total absorption and the eradication of identity. Even more remarkably, Dan Diner's odyssey demonstrates his difficulties in remaining a Jew first in Germany and then in Israel, especially in light of the different heritage of the Holocaust in both settings. Finally, we have tried to consider what Germany and the German-Jewish tradition mean for American Jews who studied in or about Germany, and for whom the cultural heritage has maintained a paramount hold on their ideas and interests. Paul Breines and Atina Grossmann illustrate the problems that arise from being at once American, Jewish, and "on the left" in a German-Jewish milieu, whether it be Madison, Wisconsin, or Berlin.

These reflections would remain one-sided if the German response to the Jewish tragedy were not also presented. In order to achieve this we have focused on a single event, the Holocaust dramatization that was aired on West German television in December 1979. By analyzing the public response to the drama in the press, mass media, and public opinion we have been able to offer some insights into the attitudes of the postwar West German generation toward the history they inherited but often did not directly experience. It has become a banality of contemporary West German culture to speak of the necessity of "coming to terms with the past," and the ritualistic avowals of concern, the extensive commercialization of atonement, and the gross oversensationalism and political misuse of the Holocaust could easily result in a "flattening out of experience." On the other hand, the spontaneous reaction to the Holocaust drama, precisely because of its mass cultural appeal, was in many ways a Rorschach test of public response on a wide scale, though the sense of shock and shame that the series unexpectedly produced may have been short-lived. Jean-Paul Bier's essay, "The Holocaust, West Germany, and Strategies of Oblivion," discusses the manner in which the Holocaust was repressed in West German consciousness, producing a kind of national amnesia. Jeffrey Herf's essay on the media and political responses to the program demonstrates how few German journalists were willing to directly confront the issues raised by the series. Andrei Markovits and Rebecca Hayden discuss why such a popular, soap-opera presentation so deeply disturbed West German viewers, while the traditional documentary and literary attempts to educate the public about the Holocaust produced no similar effect. Siegfried Zielinski, taking a different view, questions whether the show had any long-term consequences, arguing that it aestheticized and senti- mentalized an event that demanded a less trivializing form of elaboration.

Despite the enormous amount of literature devoted to this subject over the past forty years, there is a shared sense among the authors of this volume that modern anti-Semitism has not yet been fully understood. While Marxist historians of National Socialism in both East and West Germany have often ignored anti-Semitism and the Holocaust, submerg- ing those events in an amorphous and often apologetic theory of fascism, liberal historians have contented themselves with the view that the Jews were the scapegoats, and that anti-Semitism was essentially a social-psy- chological response to structurally produced social conflicts and displaced aggression. Since neither of these approaches has led to a reexamination of the problem of anti-Semitism, a reappraisal is long overdue.

For this reason we conclude the volume with three original and thoughtful essays that point to new avenues of investigation. Martin Jay's essay on the Frankfurt School shows how the experience of the German- Jewish intellectuals formed the basis of such major works on the subject as Erich Fromm's *Escape from Freedom,* Horkheimer and Adorno's *Dialectic of Enlightenment,* and Paul Massing's *Rehearsal for Destruction.* In Jay's view, anti-Semitism and the fate of the Jews played an increasingly central role in the development of critical theory (despite the often considerable dif- ferences among the major protagonists), by moving the Frankfurt School away from the traditional Marxist belief in the proletariat as the agent of social change toward a pessimistic conclusion that at best one could hope for only islands of freedom and "negation" in the face of an increasingly one-dimensional world. Moishe Postone, following Adorno and Horkheimer's analysis, also places the problem of anti-Semitism at the core of his analysis of Nazi ideology: To the extent that the Nazis upheld the biologically concrete as opposed to the alien, abstract, and above all capitalist world of exchange and commodities, the Jew became the symbol for the real social evil. In his view Auschwitz and not 1933 was the real German Revolution—the overthrow of the existing social structure. Like the Frankfurt theorists, and Postone, Ferenc Feher's remarkable discus- sion of the Hungarian writer Istvan Bibó's little-known essay on anti- Semitism also places the problem in the context of the struggle between universalist and nonuniversalist social systems and values. Feher's essay is much more than a commentary on Bibó, it is a major reconceptualization of the problem of anti-Semitism in theory and practice, with a characteristic focus on Eastern rather than Western Europe. Feher, too, concludes pessimistically that the selection of the Jew as the "victim *par excellence*" in a secular age has deep religious as well as sociological roots. "The moderate hopes [that] great analysts of the Jewish question such as Bibó or Sartre raised more than thirty years ago have altogether waned," he notes, and "unfortunately, we are living in historical times in which there is once again a 'Jewish question.'" For Feher the contemporary world has brought about a new and fundamentally dangerous upsurge of anti-Semitism: in the Soviet bloc anti-Semitism has become official policy, while in the Islamic world it has appeared with a new virulence in the form of religious fundamentalism. In this multidimensional situation Israel, for which Feher is no apologist, has become a cipher of "an old-fashioned anti-Semitism *à rebours*. Feher's essay is wide-ranging and demands a careful reading, which will be highly rewarding.

It is our hope that this book will provoke readers to rethink their own attitudes about Jews, Germans, anti-Semitism, and the German-Jewish symbiosis. The three special issues of *New German Critique* called forth an unusually strong response, and it is our hope that this book will continue to do so. To encourage further reflection we include a selected bibliography of relevant books and articles.

NOTES

1. Gershom Scholem, "Jews and Germans," in *On Jews and Judaism in Crisis: Selected Essays* (New York, 1976), p. 86.

2. Gershom Scholem, "Against the Myth of the German-Jewish Dialogue," in *On Jews and Judaism*, p. 63.

3. Gershom Scholem, "Jews and Germans," in *On Jews and Judaism*, p. 75.

4. Ibid., p. 86.

5. Scholem's first statement appeared in 1964. Two subsequent contributions, "Once More: The German-Jewish Dialogue" and "Jews and Germans," appeared in 1965 and 1966 respectively. All three are collected in *On Jews and Judaism*.

6. Peter Gay, *Freud, Jews and Other Germans: Masters and Victims in Modernist Culture* (New York, 1978), p. 19.

7. George L. Mosse, "Gedanken zum deutsch-jüdischen Dialog," *Chronik der Ludwig-Maximilians-Universität München 1982/83* (Munich, 1983), p. 48.

8. Cf. Anthony Heilbut, *Exiled in Paradise: German Refugee Artists and Intellectuals in America from the 1930s to the Present* (New York, 1983); Lewis A. Coser, *Refugee Scholars in America: Their Impact and Their Experiences* (New Haven, 1984).

9. Timothy Garton Ash, "Which Way Will Germany Go?," *The New York Review of Books*, vol. XXXII, no. 1, January 31, 1985, p. 33. The relationship between Germans and Jews since 1945 is explored in Andrei S. Markovits, "Germans and Jews: An Uneasy Relationship Continues," *Jewish Frontier*, April 1984, pp. 14–20; also see Lily Gardner Feldman, *The Special Relationship Between West Germany and Israel* (Winchester, Mass, 1984).

10. See the essay by Jack Zipes in this volume.

11. Ibid. Mischa Brumlik, "Begin und Schmidt—oder: Die Unfähigkeit zu trauern," *Die Verlängerung der Geschichte: Deutsche, Juden und der Palästinakonflikt*, ed. Dietrich Wetzel (Frankfurt am Main, 1983), p. 95.

12. Horst Stemmller, Walmot Falkenberg, "Der Konflikt im Nahen Osten," *Neue Kritik* 42/43, August 1967, p. 68. A notable exception is the remarkable "Joint Declaration by 20 Representatives of the German Left, Concerning the Middle East Conflict," (1967) drafted by Ernst Erdös and Michael Landmann and signed by Ernst Bloch, Iring Fetscher, Helmut Gollwitzer, Walter Jens, Alexander Mitscherlich, Uwe Johnson, Martin Walser, Günter Grass, Ludwig von Friedeburg, and others.

13. Lea Fleischmann, *Dies ist nicht mein land. Eine Jüdin verlässt die Bundesrepublik* (Hamburg, 1980); Henryk M. Broder, "Ihr bleibt die Kinder Eurer Eltern," *Die Zeit*, no. 10 (February 27, 1981). Also see Michael Wolffsohn, "Leben im Land der Mörder: "Deutschlands Juden im Spannungsfeld zwischen Israel und Diaspora," *Die Zeit* 72 (May 27, 1983), pp. 9, 10.

14. Among the most prominent members of this group are Mischa Brumlik, Detlev Claussen, Dan Diner, Susann Heenen, Cilly Kugelmann, Moishe Postone, Hanna Salomon, Dina Stein, Khalil Toama, Dietrich Wetzel. Daniel Cohn-Bendit has also often played an important role. The most important publication to date is Dietrich Wetzel, ed., *Die Verlängerung der Geschichte*.

15. Susann Heenen, "Deutsche Linke, Linke Juden und der Zionismus," *Die Verlängerung der Geschichte*, p. 109.

16. "Deutsche, Linke, Juden" *Ästhetik und Kommunikation* 51 (June 1983); and the subsequent discussion in *Heft* 52 (September, 1983), pp. 115–130; *Heft* 53/54 (December 1983), pp. 242–256. For some responses see Jessica Benjamin and Anson Rabinbach, "Germans, Leftists, Jews," *New German Critique* 31 (Winter 1984), pp. 183–193; Marion Kaplan, "To Tolerate is to Insult," Ibid., pp. 195–199; Jack Zipes, "The Return of the Repressed," Ibid., pp. 201–210.

17. The most extreme attack was Eike Geisel, "Familienzusammenhänge," *Tageszeitung* (July 7, 1983).

18. Martin Walser, "Händedruck mit Gespenstern," *Stichworte zur "Geistigen Situation der Zeit"* I. Band: *Nation und Republik*, ed. Jürgen Habermas (Frankfurt am Main, 1979), pp. 47, 48.

19. This remarkable document by two peace activists, Peter Rubeau and Wolfgang Westermann, argues that American Jews—who traded revenge for money in the form of reparations—harbor an unconscious desire to punish Germany through their control over American foreign policy via the Zionist lobby. The Jews, who followed their financial

interests rather than their desire for revenge, now "regret that it was advantageous not to punish the Germans," and have become the prime movers of American foreign policy directed against Germany. The article appeared in the popular German magazine *Psychologie Heute* under the title "Asche auf unser Haupt—was schulden wir Amerika?" (Ashes on our head—what do we owe America?). See the discussion by Mischa Brumlik, "Antisemitismus wieder salonfähig," *Jüdischer Presse Dienst*, Nr. 1/2 (1984), p. 35. On the latest Green Party activities vis-à-vis Israel see "Israel Bars a Member of the German Green Party," the *New York Times*, December 18, 1984, p. A15.

20. "Israel Bars a Member of German Green Party," *New York Times*, December 18, 1984, p. A15.

21. "Bahro in Baden-Baden," *Tageszeitung*, April 3, 1985, p. 9.

22. Dregger's remark was made in 1977. Cited in Norbert Seitz, "Die Unfähigkeit zu Feiern," *Pflasterstrand*, May 17, 1985, p. 25.

23. Isaac Deutscher, *The Non-Jewish Jew and Other Essays* (London, 1968).

24. Herbert Marcuse, "Nachwort," in Walter Benjamin, *Zur Kritik der Gewalt und andere Aufsätze* (Frankfurt am Main, 1965), p. 104.

25. Theodor W. Adorno, *Negative Dialectics*, trans. E. B. Ashton (New York, 1973), pp. 362, 363; Max Horkheimer and Theodor W. Adorno, *Dialectic of Enlightenment*, trans. John Cumming (New York, 1972), p. 168.

26. Adorno, *Negative Dialectics*, p. 361.

27. Hannah Arendt, *Men in Dark Times* (New York, 1968).

28. Martin Jay, "The Jews and the Frankfurt School," in this volume.

29. Jean-Paul Sartre, *Anti-Semite and Jew*, trans. George J. Becker (New York, 1965), p. 136.

30. Ferenc Feher, "'The Jewish Question' Reconsidered: Notes on a Classic Essay by Istvan Bibó," in this volume.

31. To our sorrow, Manès Sperber, Jean Améry, and Toni Oelsner all passed away before this volume went to press.

Historical Background

2

THE VICISSITUDES OF BEING JEWISH IN WEST GERMANY

Jack Zipes

The favorable reception accorded such interesting studies as Fredric Grun-feld's *Prophets without Honour: A Background to Freud, Kafka, Einstein and Their World* (1979) and Anthony Heilbut's *Exiled in Paradise: German Refugee Artists and Intellectuals in America from the 1930s to the Present* (1983) indicates that there is still a great interest outside Germany in the German-Jewish symbiosis. Yet, this persistent fascination with Germans and Jews is concentrated largely on the pre-1945 period in Germany or on the fate of Jewish refugees in exile. Contemporary American and British readers, whether Jewish or Gentile, know very little about the situation of the Jews who decided to remain in Germany after 1945 or who emigrated to West Germany after 1949. It is almost as though it has been impossible to imagine how Jews could continue to live in the country of their murderers. But they have, and not only have they managed to rebuild diverse Jewish communities on a small scale, there has also been a new generation of younger German-Jewish intellectuals who have shed light on just how difficult it is to live as a Jew in the reconstructed Jewish communities or in the larger West German society.

Most of the Jews who have recently been critical of the new Jewish communities and the West German state were born after 1945 and have political and religious persuasions very different from those of their parents. As nonconformist, assimilated Jews, they form a distinct but vocal minority within Germany and have raised issues that have been disturbing

for Germans and Jews alike and even for the countercultural segment of
German society to which they belong. In many respects the new, critical
Jews point to the ambivalent nature of the role played by assimilated
intellectual Jews from the Weimar period to the present. To understand
this ambivalence and the vital role these Jews play as critics in contemporary West Germany, it is important to review some of the historical and
demographic data that have a bearing on the vicissitudes of being Jewish
in West Germany.

The Rise of the "New" German Jew

If we look merely at the statistics (and not at the accomplishments) of the
German Jews before and after the Holocaust, the reduction of Jewish
prominence and presence in Germany is striking. In 1933 there were
502,799 registered Jews living in Germany in addition to nonreligious
Jews.[1] They formed less then 1 percent of the German population but over
3 percent of the world Jewish population. After 1945 approximately
15,000 Jews survived in Germany, either in mixed marriages or in the
underground. By 1949, when the Federal Republic was constituted, there
were approximately 23,000 to 26,000 Jews. They formed one-twentieth
of 1 percent of the German population, or 0.2 percent of the world Jewish
population. This depletion of Jews in Germany has led to the transformation of the role played by assimilated Jews and has altered the basic
conditions for defining Jews in Germany.

Of the 15,000 German Jews who survived World War II, only 8,000
remained in Germany. The rest emigrated mainly to America and Israel.
Mass emigration was also typical for the majority of the 200,000 Eastern
European Jews who had been liberated from the concentration camps or
who had survived in the Soviet Union. Between 1945 and 1952 the Allied
Forces in the occupied zones of West Germany and the United Nation's
Relief and Rehabilitation Agency set up camps for those 200,000 East
European Jewish refugees, who eventually found homes for themselves in
the United States, Canada, South America, and Israel. Practically all the
Jews who were in these camps for displaced persons wanted to emigrate,
and there was also great pressure on the part of Zionist organizations
urging Jews to leave Germany. However, because of old age, sickness,
personal ties, and financial difficulties, more than 15,000 East European
Jews stayed in West Germany, and they, along with 8,000 German Jews
and 2,000 to 3,000 returnees and nonregistered Jews, formed the basis of
the "new" Jewish communities in West Germany. As Monika Richarz has
remarked:

This group of DPs who remained together with the remainder of the German Jews made up the membership of the new Jewish communities. Both groups differed greatly in their culture, language, mentality and also in the experiences they went through in the Nazi period. The German Jews were very assimilated, were for the most part married to German Gentiles and had ambivalent feelings toward Germany. The Eastern European Jews were on the average younger, spoke Yiddish, came mostly from a strong Jewish background and had had their first experiences with Germans during the "Selektionen" in the concentration camps. These differences were bound to lead to difficulties and disagreements in community life, expecially as religiousness and the type of religious service varied greatly.[2]

Despite the seventy-three Jewish congregations established in West Germany by 1963 and organized around the Zentralrat der Juden in Deutschland (The Central Council of Jews in Germany), one cannot speak about a unified Jewish community in West Germany. In addition to the profound differences between German and Eastern European Jews, there were other groups that began to return or emigrate to Germany, particularly after 1952 when the Federal Republic signed the Luxemberg Agreement with Israel that guaranteed Jews restitution of property and offered pensions. For example, numerous German Jews who were Socialists and Communists returned from exile to participate in the antifascist reconstruction in both parts of Germany or to pursue interrupted university and government careers. Some of the key figures in academic life in the West and in the East German political establishment belonged to this group.[3] However, the largest group of Jews—there were over 6,000—who returned to West Germany during the 1950s were older Jews of East European origin who were unable to adapt to conditions in Israel, the United States, and South America. In the 1960s and 1970s they were joined by different waves of immigration: approximately 1,300 Iranian Jews settled in Hamburg; 9,000 to 10,000 Israeli citizens came to West Germany to study or to pursue business careers, and many remained, although they retain Israeli citizenship; 3,000 Soviet Jews established new homes for themselves, largely in West Berlin.

Today there are approximately 28,300 registered Jews in West Germany, which means that they officially declare their religion to the government and that some of their tax money is given to Jewish synagogues. In addition, there are another 5,000 unregistered Jews who are citizens of the Federal Republic, and approximately 7,000 Israelis. The average age of the Jews ranges from forty-five to fifty, much higher than the average for the rest of the population. Most Jews live in large cities: there are 6,500 in West Berlin, 4,800 in Frankfurt, 1,400 in Hamburg, and 1,300 in Cologne. In addition, there are 5,400 Jews in Bavaria, 3,600 in North Rhine

Westphalia (not counting Cologne), and 2,000 in Baden-Württemberg. Though most register as members of the Jewish community, they do not tend to be religious. In fact, very few have religious knowledge, nor do they have roots in German culture. Significantly, only 10 percent of the Jews who live in Germany are of German-Jewish descent.

It is extremely difficult to describe a "Jewish way of life" in West Germany, since most Jews belong nominally to their congregations but have developed nonreligious and nontraditional life-styles. During the last ten or fifteen years there has also been a strong tendency to marry outside the faith, and thus an important part of the work of the Central Council of Jews and other official Jewish agencies has been to maintain and cultivate Jewish traditional beliefs and customs. In Frankfurt there is an elementary school for Jewish children that is also attended by Gentiles. The *Allgemeine Jüdische Wochenzeitung* (Düsseldorf) and the *Neue Jüdische Nachrichten* (Munich), two weeklies, endeavor to inform Jews about social and political events that are pertinent to their lives as Jews in a religious and, to a degree, Zionist sense. The Gesellschaft für Christliche-Jüdische Zusammenarbeit, founded in 1948, and the Deutsch Israelische Gesellschaft, founded in 1955, have enabled Jews and Gentiles to meet and to increase understanding between the different groups. The Institut für die Geschichte der deutschen Juden was founded in Hamburg in 1963 and has developed a program of instruction and research in the area of German-Jewish history, and the Hochschule fur jüdische Studien, established in 1979 in Heidelberg, trains future rabbis and cantors as well as researchers in the field of Jewish studies.[4] Yet, despite all these efforts, the number of young Jews who participate actively in these institutions is very low, and this nonparticipation in Jewish life is due in part to the formation of a "new Jew" in Germany. Monika Richarz has concluded that

(1) The Jewish communities in West Germany today are primarily immigration communities. Their members are extremely nonhomogeneous. (2) The Jewish communities in the Federal Republic cannot be considered a continuation of German Jewry. In the not too distant future there will be no German Jews, but only Jews in Germany. (3) The strong fluctuation of the Jewish minority which is also constantly overaged shows that up till now no really permanent new settlement of Jews in Germany has taken place. The readiness to emigrate is still a factor of Jewish life in Germany.[5]

In addition to these factors that have prevented the continuity of German-Jewish tradition, one must also consider the generation gap within the Jewish communities and the conditions of assimilation in West German society. Most Jews born after 1945 and educated in the Federal

Republic have a greater and more critical understanding of contemporary West Germany than their parents. On the one hand, this understanding enables them to find more acceptable positions in the society, but, on the other, it has created gaps between them and their parents that make the younger generation of Jews feel uneasy—both in the larger German context and in the smaller Jewish subtext. The differences between the older, more conservative Jews and the younger, more progressive Jews can best be grasped by focusing on the role played by the West German state and citizenry. In many respects the older generation of Jews allowed the Germans to define the Jewish role in the Federal Republic. The "new German Jew" appears to be resisting those roles and categories imposed on them by both the conservative Jewish communities and the German state.

The Role of the West German State

Ever since the establishment of the Federal Republic in 1949, the policy of the state toward Jews has generally been supportive.[6] The obvious reason for this support was to make clear to the world that Germany wanted to overcome its anti-Semitic past. Not only did the government extend financial aid to rebuild the Jewish communities and to enable victims of Nazi persecution to maintain themselves, but it sent millions of dollars in aid to Israel in military and economic assistance. Whenever possible, or necessary, the West German government cooperated and continues to cooperate with the Central Council of Jews to combat anti-Semitism and promote goodwill through educational and cultural programs. In return, the Central Council has rarely opposed the government, no matter which political party has been in control. As the official representative of the Jewish congregations in Germany, the council has been staunchly pro-Israel and sees its role mainly to safeguard the perpetuation of the traditional Jewish way of life. By adopting a less than critical role vis-à-vis the government, however, the council has often enabled West Germany to repress contemporary manifestations of its anti-Semitic past. As Andrei Markovits has remarked,

> The Federal Republic's main mode of distancing itself from the Nazi past was to cast this episode as a unique and aberrant period of brutal anti-Semitism. Once the Federal Republic and its leading political actors could establish themselves as *bona fide* philo-Semites, the most heinous ties to the Nazi past would automatically be severed while the more "innocuous" ones could continue more or less unabated. Thus, just as East Germany "instru-

mentalized" the Holocaust by simplifying it for its own legitimation purposes, the West Germans did the same. To the latter, the Final Solution was
a singular political construct of evil men. . . . By dividing the Germans into
"good" and "bad"—not like in East Germany along "capitalist" and "proletarian," but rather along "Nazi" and "non-Nazi" lines—the Federal Republic could once again claim respect for Germany and Germans if it could
only emphasize the "good" and at least contain, if not extirpate, the "bad."[7]

Given the expectations of the outside world, the government, which
was not free of anti-Semitism itself, had to control and temper the persistence of anti-Semitism among postwar Germans. For example, in the
early 1950s the majority of Germans opposed restitution for Jews and
payments to Israel. Thus, the government, which itself was divided on this
issue, had to legislate correct behavior. Though there is no doubt that
many Germans truly felt committed to creating better understanding
between Jews and non-Jews, and some wanted to atone for the past,
official state policies were often hypocritical, especially since denazification
was largely hollow and ritualistic: War criminals were not actively prosecuted in West Germany until after the Eichmann Trial of 1960–1961, and
numerous former Nazis and even some criminals continued to hold important positions in civil service and the government.[8] Right from the
beginning, the Adenauer administration enacted the infamous Law 131,
which allowed civil servants and officials who served under the Nazis to be
reinstated. Governmental policies were designed to grant concessions to
Jews in Germany and to provide support for Israel; at the same time
nothing substantial was undertaken to reeducate the German people about
the Nazi treatment of the Jews or to punish thousands of war criminals.

Instead of fostering democratic reeducation and exploring the links
between German fascism and anti-Semitism, most of the teachers and
professors, who had been notoriously sympathetic to the Nazis, retained
their posts, and the school system remained extremely rigid and authoritarian up through the late 1960s. Incidents of anti-Semitism were
common in schools, especially where they could embarrass Jews, as noted
by Dan Diner and Lea Fleischmann.[9] Jewish students did not take mandatory religious lessons with Gentile students and thus were made to
appear different from other pupils, who often resented them. For most
Jews, the school atmosphere appeared to be charged with latent anti-
Semitism that could explode at any moment. For both Jews and non-Jews
of the younger generation, silence about the Holocaust and the Nazi past
was the rule for the most part in the family and public school system. Since
neither side, Gentile or Jew, wanted to rock the boat, there was no
pressure on elementary and high schools to deal with modern history past

1933. Nor did the universities really address problems of anti-Semitism and Nazism until the student revolts of the late 1960s.

In essence, then, the West German state's efforts to create a deeper understanding between Jews and Germans and to probe German history have been cosmetic: The state has publicly taken the "correct" position by financially aiding the Jewish communities in Germany and establishing strong ties to Israel while neglecting the deep-rooted problems that had brought about Germany's unique kind of virulent anti-Semitism. For many Germans, the image of Jewry was and still is connected to Israel. Thus, even with official recognition and the establishment of regular diplomatic relations with Israel in 1965, the Jews/Israelis (Jews and Israelis are often collapsed together in the term *Israelit*) were still considered victims—strange, mysterious, powerful, but helpless creatures, only interested in financial gain. This image was altered greatly following the Six Day War in 1967. As Markovits points out,

> There occurred a nearly 180-degree turn in the way West Germans related to Israel and the Jews. Suddenly the political right, whose moderate faction had previously maintained a silent philo-Semitism and whose more radical wing still came out with periodic anti-Israeli statements bordering on anti-Semitism, rejoiced at Israel's "supermanlike" victory over the lazy and cowardly Arabs. Led by the very influential Springer Press, which enjoys near monopoly status among daily newspapers in large areas of the Federal Republic, the panegyrics regarding Israel's accomplishments often reached orgiastic dimensions.[10]

Although the increased "respect" for Israel generated stronger commercial and diplomatic ties and greater philo-Semitism in West Germany, the image of a strong "Jewish" state also led ironically to a gradual distancing from Israel in the 1970s. Here a threefold reaction can be discerned: (1) Christian Democratic voters and business leaders developed growing sympathies for the Arab states, which were becoming more important economically, especially during the oil crisis of 1975. (2) The Social Democrats have been more supportive of Israel, but while in power they have played the Israelis against the Arabs in the armaments industry, especially under the administration of Helmut Schmidt from 1979 to 1983. Begin's hostile reception of Schmidt in 1981 was a low point in postwar German-Israeli diplomatic relations. (3) Finally, the independent Left switched from a position of admiration of Israel's socialist tendencies to a position that condemned Israel for its Zionism and "imperialist" expansionist policies.

Since the welfare of the Jewish communities within West Germany is directly linked to the strength of Israel, the Central Council of Jews and the majority of Jews have identified themselves closely with official Israeli policies. This close identification further obfuscates the distinctions that are to be made among the Jews in Germany. It has also been pivotal for the younger Jews who grew up in Germany and who, in a manner of speaking, live on the border between the German society and the Jewish communities.

The Dilemma of the "New" Jewish Intellectuals

For Jews born after 1945, the complex psychology of post-Holocaust German life led to strong feelings of shame and depression, often linked to their parents, who were perceived as weak and helpless victims. In this situation Israel became extremely important as a counterimage to the fate of European Jews and enabled young Jews in Germany to function in troubled circumstances at home and in the society at large. Most Jews born after 1945 were introduced to Zionist views at an early age. Many of them participated in Zionist youth meetings and outings, and trips to Israel were organized so that German Jews could gain firsthand experience of their "true" homeland and might be induced to leave Germany at the proper time. Israel as homeland allowed young Jews to believe that Germany was only a transitory place of residence. By imagining that one was an Israeli because one was Jewish, a Jew in Germany could find an honorable way to deal with the past and to be proud of being Jewish.[11] We must recall that international Zionist organizations had frowned upon Jews who remained in Germany after World War II and that it was not until 1959 that the Zionist World Organization finally established the Zionist Youth of Germany. The purpose of the Zionist program in Germany was to make young German Jews aware of the fact that, if the Jews had all left for Israel in the 1930s, they would have avoided the gas chambers. The Holocaust provided the single lesson that Israel was the only country in which a Jew could be free and could live without fear.[12]

The period of strongest identification with Israel coincided with the Eichmann trial, growing protests against old Nazis in the Adenauer administration, and a more intensified prosecution of Nazi war criminals. In the early 1960s there was a growing awareness portrayed through such plays as Max Frisch's Andorra (1961), Rolf Hochhuth's The Deputy (1963), Peter Weiss's The Investigation (1965), and Heinar Kipphardt's Joel Brand (1965) that most older Germans knew all about the atrocities committed against the Jews and should share in the guilt.[13] From 1959, the period when Zionist organizations became more active in West Germany and recognized the existence of Jews in Germany, until 1967, the younger generation in Germany, Jew and Gentile alike, became obsessed with the problem of "responsibility" for Nazism and the Holocaust, and this concern led to an expansion of sympathy for Israel. In fact, after 1959, when the Zionist Youth organization was formed in Germany and, for the next decade, when it facilitated trips to Israel for young people of all religious denominations, hundreds of Germans traveled to Israel. Thus, younger Jews and non-Jews found common ground on which to base their criticisms of the authoritarian and Nazi tradition in Germany: moral protest about the repression of the past that had not been confronted and overcome in contemporary West German society. Many young Germans saw signs of continuity between the Federal Republic and Nazi Germany and sought greater democratic change in the state institutions. Moreover, for many, there was a sense that Israel represented a type of socialist model. It is hardly surprising, then, that, when the Six Day War erupted in June of 1967, numerous Jews and Gentiles in Germany tried to join the Israeli army and to protect the "model" state of Israel. However, the so-called *Blitzkrieg* prevented them from helping Israel, and the Israeli victory and expropriation of Arab territory soon led to marked dissension between Jews and Gentiles of the younger generation in Germany.

It must be pointed out first of all that after 1967 the majority of West Germans found a new admiration for Israel for the wrong reasons: The Israeli army was now a powerful force, and the Israelis were suddenly "adopted" by the Germans as "their" Jews, who recalled the German *Blitzkrieg* of 1940, or Rommel's early desert campaigns. German Jews were simply thankful that Israel had survived and had served warning to the rest of the world that a future Holocaust would not be tolerated. Another important consequence of the Six Day War was that the German New Left moved from support of "socialist" and "democratic" Israel to principled opposition to "imperialist" Israel, which was perceived as a puppet of American foreign policy.

Thus, for those Jews who had identified with Israel and Zionism and who had accepted the New Left as an "antifascist" movement, the situation after June 1967 brought about new difficulties that were to increase in the years to come. Psychological conflicts arose because Jewish criticism of Israel in the country of the former persecutors of Jews was bound to be misunderstood. In fact, when younger Jewish students publicly questioned the motives and tactics of the Israeli government, they were soundly criticized by the conservative Jewish congregations as traitors. On the other hand, as the German New Left began to withdraw its support from Israel and, by 1969, gave unqualified support to the Palestinians, the small group of younger Jewish intellectuals within the New Left were forced into isolation. With the exception of a Joint Declaration by twenty representatives of the German Left calling for a sober appraisal of Israel's right to exist (signed by such notable figures as Ernst Bloch, Iring Fetscher, Helmut Gollwitzer, Walter Jens, and Alexander Mitscherlich), the appeal for Arab-Jewish coexistence and a democratic Palestine went unheeded. In general, the growing radicalization of students after 1969 left the small minority of Jews who were aligned with the New Left in a great predicament: It seemed that the more the German New Left sought to overcome the Nazi past, the more the students reproduced some of its ugly manifestations. Above all, they lost sight of one of its most significant slogans, "Nie wieder Auschwitz" or "Auschwitz Never Again." At the same time, German students began to question "fascism" openly as part of a generational conflict with their families and with the German authoritarian tradition. By turning to Marxism and the philosophies of other radical critics who had been silenced after 1933, the students literally blew the lid off many subjects that had been taboo in their homes and schools. Whereas the more critical Jews endeavored to unite with the New Left in its struggle for a radical democratization of West German society, the Left splintered in the 1970s and became more one-dimensional in its support of the Palestinian cause.

The 1970s witnessed a series of developments that prompted most Jews, whether they were on the Right or the Left, to become even more wary of German attitudes toward Jews and Israel. It should be noted that these developments are being presented in capsule form and provide the background for understanding the quandary of the generation of critical Jewish intellectuals that has recently emerged.

1. In the 1970s there was an upsurge of new publications and films about Hitler, as well as new histories that played down the extermination of the Jews. The two most notorious examples were Joachim Fest's 1973 biography and film about Hitler and Helmut Diwald's 1979 history of the Germans, both of which painted a benign picture of Nazism and ignored the extermination of the Jews.[14] Because of such books and films, it became common to talk about a "Hitler-wave," which had even greater ramifications in everyday life. Aside from the cultural trend to minimize Hitler's role in the German atrocities against Jews, teen-agers made a new, grotesque fashion out of sporting Nazi emblems that they bought in secondhand stores and at flea markets, and some found it suitable to join the neo-Nazi Viking organization in the late 1970s.[15] Moreover, studies of pupils in junior high schools and gymnasiums revealed that they were abysmally ignorant about Jews, anti-Semitism, and German history in general.[16]

2. After a period of deep concern about the fate of Jews—largely during the 1950s and 1960s—radical students demonstrated a crass anti-Zionist position, which contributed to anti-Semitic sentiments in West Germany. After the 1979 telecast of "Holocaust" in West Germany, there were signs that the Left had once again become more sensitive to Jewish problems in West Germany. Yet, in 1983, the journal *Ästhetik und Kommunikation* provoked a debate about "Germans, Jews, and Leftists," which demonstrated that German sensitivity toward Jewish concerns is meager.[17] The Left still talks about fascism and capitalism while remaining silent about anti-Semitism and Nazism and is still reluctant to educate itself about German-Jewish history.[18]

3. The West German government and general public continued to harbor, tolerate, and support prominent ex-Nazis as important political leaders. The two most recent cases—and we must remember that this was a trend set at the very beginning of the Adenauer administration in 1949 with former Nazis such as Hans Globke and Heinrich Lübke established in important posts—reveal how "thoroughly" Germans have shunned their past. Hans Filbinger, who was minister president of Baden-Württemberg, resigned his position reluctantly and without contrition in 1978, when it was discovered that he had condemned soldiers to death for anti-Hitler sentiments after the war ended. Many people were disturbed by the fact that the playwright Rolf Hochhuth had brought Filbinger's case to light. In contrast, West Germans for the most part were not at all disturbed when Karl Carstens became president of the Federal Republic despite his own Nazi past.

4. Finally, the role played by the conservative Jewish community leaders in West Germany must be taken into account. The elected officials of the Central Council of Jews such as Heinz Galinski, Werner Nachmann, and others have continually supported the philo-Semitic positions of the state, despite evidence that these positions were hollow. The official Central Council has followed a policy of appeasement established in 1950,[19] and some of its members have publicly defended ex-Nazis. Though these "professional Jews," as they are called by their critics, seek to appear in public as representing all Jews in Germany, they rarely take into consideration the varied opinions of their constituency. Many assimilated Jews do not feel represented by the official organs of the Jewish communities, and the "silent" progressive Jews have rarely made themselves heard. That is, until recently.

The above sociopolitical developments in the 1970s—and there are other important factors such as the *Radikalenerlass* (professional proscription) of the mid-1970s, designed to exclude leftists and progressives from civil service, that created a McCarthylike climate during this period—give some indication as to why numerous Jews, toward the end of the 1970s, began making public declarations and announcements concerning their identity, their relationship to Germany, and their politics. What must also be made clear is that the TV film "Holocaust," produced in the United States in 1978, did *not* serve to generate those Jewish public pronouncements and publications that were conceived well before "Holocaust" was shown in West Germany. Obviously, the TV film did indeed stimulate more Jewish intellectuals to ponder their social and political situations.[20] But, by the end of the 1970s, there had already been several incidents that indicated anti-Semitism was still a strong undercurrent in West Gerrman society. In 1970 a Jewish old age home was bombed in Munich. In 1972, Israeli athletes were murdered in Munich. In 1976, two German terrorists of the RAF organization selected Jewish passengers as hostages in the Entebbe highjack attempt. In 1979 a Jewish teacher was slandered by anti-Semitic pupils, and shortly before the "Holocaust" film was to be telecast there was an attempt to destroy the TV transmitter. All these events, along with more blatant efforts by neo-Nazi organizations to recruit disenchanted youth and to heroize the old "martyrs," frightened Jews in Germany, and their relations with Germans have become more uneasy than in the 1950s and 1960s. This concrete "Jewish fear" was manifested time and again in statements made by younger Jewish intellectuals, even when some of them no longer lived on German soil. But it was not only fear that prompted numerous Jews to speak out about their experiences in and with Germany. By the late 1970s the first generation of "new" German Jews, all born after 1945, had begun establishing themselves in West Germany, and there was a small, critical, and vocal group that was bent on distinguishing itself from the older Jews, their own conservative Jewish peers, and most Germans. To a certain extent, it is in their attempt to define themselves that one can glimpse the potential for a new kind of German Jew who resists easy categories.

Speaking Out

Between 1978 and 1980 four books appeared that testify to a new expression of self-consciousness about the postwar German-Jewish symbiosis. Two of the books, *Mein Judentum* (1978) edited by Hans Jürgen Schultz[21] and *Die Zerstörung einer Zukunft* (1979) edited by Mathias Greffrath,[22] are largely essays and interviews with Jewish emigrants from Germany who reflect upon their unique experiences as assimilated Jews, and who had never made much of their Jewishness. The basic theme in the majority of writings is that Nazism and the Holocaust compelled them to take stock of their Jewishness. For the most part, these Jews had been assimilated intellectuals in Germany or Austria, and the Jewish religion and tradition had become distant in their lives. However, with the rise of Nazism and the effect of the Holocaust, there was a shift in their attitude toward their Jewishness so that the overall concern in these two books could be summarized by the statement: "You can save a Jew from the concentration camp, but you can't take the concentration camp out of a Jew."[23]

This theme is an underlying motif of two other significant books, *Fremd im eigenen Land* (1979) edited by Henryk M. Broder and Michel Lang[24] and *Dies ist nicht mein Land—Eine Jüdin verlässt die Bundesrepublik* (1980) by Lea Fleischmann,[25] which document more current attitudes toward West Germany. Since they reveal a great deal about conditions under which Jews live in contemporary West Germany, I want to discuss them in more detail than the books that contain the memoirs of émigrés.

The future of Germany and the German-Jewish critical tradition are the central themes in Broder/Lang's collection of essays in *Fremd im eigenen Land*. Broder and Lang explain that the idea to publish their book originated in 1978 right after Werner Nachmann, president of the Central Council of Jews in Germany, defended Hans Filbinger, the former minister president of Baden-Württemberg, whose crimes as a Nazi judge had recently been exposed. Nachmann's statement in behalf of Filbinger was considered by the German public as the "official position" of all Jews living in Germany. However, in discussions with many Jewish friends, Broder and Lang discovered that most of them did not feel represented by Nachmann and the council and particularly took offense at Nachmann's defense of a man like Filbinger, who declared in defense of his crimes that "what was right yesterday cannot be wrong today." Thus, Broder and Lang decided to gather as many personal statements as possible from those Jews who were normally not outspoken about how they felt about living in the Federal Republic. They wanted variety in profession, age, and politics. In their short introduction they assure the reader that they had not censored any of the manuscripts nor prescribed a position. Yet, when one looks at the thirty-seven contributors, it becomes apparent that Broder and Lang are not entirely honest. First, they omitted some contributions for obscure reasons. Second, almost all the Jews who were requested to write about their experiences in West Germany are from the educated middle class and represent political viewpoints primarily left of center. Most are professional writers, educators, or cultural workers. Almost all have a pronounced dislike for the Council of Jews and the general conservatism of official Jewish organizations. Twenty-three were born before 1930 and eleven were born in the 1940s. Almost all live permanently in West Germany and feel tension with governmental policies concerning Jews. Though it is true that Broder and Lang did not seek out "prominent" intellectuals of the Weimar period, it is clear that the Jews who aired their opinions in this volume represent a distinct minority, and, if there is variety here, it consists of variations based on a common political theme.

The polemical thrust is made clearer in Bernd Engelmann's introduction to the volume. As author of the important book *Deutschland ohne Juden*,[26] Engelmann was evidently chosen to provide the editors' political framework for the collected essays, and he develops a thesis directed at both a Jewish and a non-Jewish audience in West Germany: Historically, Jews were always fellow-sufferers of other German oppressed groups, and thus they were basically Germans. Their common enemy is the German state and upper classes that have defined their roles. The exploitation and mistreatment of socially underprivileged groups were general phenomena, and Jews differed from other "oppressed, exploited, and persecuted" groups only because of their religious adherence. Once the religious adherence weakened toward the end of the nineteenth century, Jews became essentially Germans. This thesis shows a lack of understanding of German historical research devoted to this topic during the last decade. It is an inaccurate historical representation of German-Jewish relations to equate Jewish harassment, suffering, and attitudes with those of other minority and underprivileged groups in Germany.[27] Engelmann does this because he wants to stress a point also shared by Broder/Lang:

> The great majority of Jewish Germans had taken an antisocialist and then strong anticommunist position before 1933. This corresponded to their prevailing membership in the bourgeois middle class. Also, the fact that there were a great many individuals of Jewish origin among the theoreticians and leading politicians of the German working-class movement did not change a thing in regard to the basic position of bourgeois liberalism and conservatism of the majority of the Jews in Germany. Many of them would have probably been ready to vote for the parties on the Right during the Weimar period instead of the middle or the moderate Left if the anti-Semitic harassment had not deterred them.[28]

All this is not only speculation, but it is also wrong. The facts are, as Monika Richarz has documented in *Jüdisches Leben in Deutschland. Selbstzeugnisse zur Sozialgeschichte 1918–1945*,[29] that the majority of the Jews voted for the liberal Deutsche Demokratische Partei, which generally stood left of center, until 1930, and another 20 percent voted for the

Social Democratic Party. When the DDP united with the more conservative Young German Order and formed the German State Party, most Jews switched to the SPD. It is certainly not appropriate to equate Jews with conservative, middle-class Germans and distort the facts about the political role of Jews in Germany as Broder and Lang do, especially since the series of books on German-Jewish history edited by Arnold Paucker and Werner E. Mosse reveal quite different trends.[30] To maintain that there were no differences is incorrect. It would be more worthwhile to pursue and analyze the specific ways and means that German Jews cultivated while they harbored the *illusion* that they were Germans and tried to be more German than the Germans themselves. Assimilation did not mean acceptance in Weimar Germany, nor does it mean full acceptance today.

If Engelmann had endeavored to elaborate on this distinction between assimilation and acceptance, then his criticism of "Jewish Germans" might have produced more results. As it is, his analysis does not enable us to understand the conservatism of Jews living in Germany today. If he means to draw a parallel with the Weimar Republic, then this parallel must be qualified by the fact that *most Jews living in Germany today are not of German origin* and their conservative outlook must be examined in depth as a reaction to the Holocaust and traumatic uprooting. Also, it is not established fact that most of the approximately forty thousand Jews living in Germany are antisocialist, support the hypocritical philo-Semitism of the government and Springer Press, demonstrate unqualified support for Israel, and follow a general policy of appeasement with ex-Nazis. Engelmann's terminological usage of "Jewish-Germans" is irritating and extremely provocative, and ironically it appears to stem from a deep-seated belief that Jews are indeed special and that they should play a "chosen" role in each and every society by not becoming like their alleged enemies.

By questioning the appeasement and conservatism of Jews in Germany, Engelmann himself writes in the tradition of what Hannah Arendt has called the Jewish pariahs.[31] Such Jews, according to Arendt, uphold basic nonmaterialistic and humanitarian Jewish values in a critical spirit and take a stand for universal suffrage while pursuing messianic ideas. In fact, many writing in this volume fit into this category of Jewish pariahs by assuming a marginal position *vis-à-vis* the established Jewish and German communities. Almost all define themselves and describe their experiences as if dedicated to this pariah role which constitutes part of their Jewishness.

It is difficult to summarize the remarks made by those Jewish intellectuals who voice strong dissident opinions in *Fremd im eigenen Land* about the nature of being Jewish while living in Germany.[32] However, there are common points that enable us to gain more insight about conditions under which Jews live in West Germany. Almost all the contributors base their definition of their Jewishness on their alienating experiences with West Germans and other Jews living in Germany while trying to establish the lessons of the Holocaust and to act upon them. They are oriented toward the present and the specifics of being Jewish in a country where the political shift to the Right has given rise to their fears of neo-Nazism. In the process of discussing their fears and paranoia in relation to the Holocaust and West Germany, they express some of the following general views:

Many of the older Jews find meaning as Jews in consciously dedicating themselves to living in West Germany, working to "demystify" the image of the Jew, and countering anti-Semitic tendencies (Abosch, Bornemann, Carlebach, Frei, Gingold, Goral, Rewald). Most of the intellectuals are not religious and adhere to Sartre's view of Jewishness as a sociohistorical designation, and they openly declare themselves committed to a secular notion of Jewishness that has been heavily defined by the Holocaust and its consequences (Bernstein, Merz). All return to the notion of the Holocaust as living history.

> ABOSCH: One can repress this period, one can want to forget it. However, such an attempt will not succeed. This period will always remain present. And rather than make the meaningless and useless effort to repress everything, it is better to declare one's allegiance to this heritage of the past which has become a component of one's identity.[33]
> GORAL: I am Jewish because of Auschwitz. I live my Jewishness with Auschwitz. By this I don't mean a life of passivity and tolerant acceptance or the attempt to give everything a theological, fatalistic, metaphysical meaning along irrational lines. No, when I say "I live my Jewishness with Auschwitz," I mean a constant confrontation in theory and praxis with the causes and conditions which led to Auschwitz, that is, a permanent struggle against open and concealed starts to initiate a new Auschwitz.[34]

Almost all see themselves as affected by the political repression and conservatism of the German state and people. They voice harsh criticism of the measures taken by the state to strengthen its authoritarian control which they see as part of a continuous *German* tradition that manifested itself strongly in the fascist period. In this regard most are incensed by the appeasement policies of the professional Jews and the Jewish communities and tend to dissociate themselves from the mainstream Jews who have become too German. Broder's summary of different incidents revealing German injustice and repression reflects most of the contributors' attitudes toward the German people. He regards the resurgence of reactionary currents as emanating from the correct German formalism which manifests itself everywhere and introduced racist genocide with the decree of the Nuremberg Laws in a very correct way. It is the German burgher who has never been a "citoyen" and takes pleasure in regulating his own humiliation by himself, in denouncing himself and playing warden. It is the conceit of the German bureaucrat who despises human beings and tramples over corpses if he can justify this with a legal paper; it is the continuous German notion that the burgher owes loyalty and gratitude to the state instead of viewing the state as a service organization for the burgher which can be made use of whenever necessary. It is the German compulsion for cleanliness, elimination, and extermination, the effort to arrive at a social consensus about what should be permitted and not permitted, not to appear visible and to deter all dissenters because they disturb the harmony. It is the German arrogance which is hardly restrained by even an ounce of tactical consideration.[35]

Most condemn the hypocritical German philo-Semitism.

BRANDT: As a Jew I did not expect brotherly love in Germany, but I did hope for tolerance. Philo-Semitism as an expression of German guilt complexes is repulsive to me because it imposes the status of "being special" on me, because it limits my freedom to feel free as equal among equals, and because it continually causes me to be influenced by the nasty saying that "the Germans are breathing down my back or are after me."[36]

Most of the feelings for Israel are positive, though many disagree about the politics of the Israeli government and the collusion between West Germany and Israel. Some of the writers feel that the professional Jews use the cause of Israel and Zionism to advance their careers, while many younger members attack the German Left for its indiscriminate anti-Zionism. All have experienced anti-Semitism in various forms in West Germany and believe that it would continue to exist even if Jews no longer existed at all.

The different voices in *Fremd im eigenen Land* are not unanimous on all issues, but they do enable the reader to understand the complex situation of the Pariah Jew in West Germany. It is significant that, despite their feelings of alienation, all, with the exception of Broder, have decided to remain in West Germany. Another exception is Lea Fleischmann, whose book *Dies ist nicht mein Land* is an autobiographical account of why she felt it necessary to leave West Germany and settle in Israel. Fleischmann is different from most of the authors in *Fremd im eigenen Land* insofar as she did not identify with the German Left in West Germany. This fact also makes her book an important companion piece to *Fremd im eigenen Land,* for it provides a picture of German society from the viewpoint of a Jewish woman who eventually left Germany not for ideological reasons but because of daily experiences that threatened her existence as a Jew. She recalls how her father and mother were broken by their experiences in concentration camps and never established a foothold in German society; she writes about how she spent most of her time with Jewish friends and how the past was always kept hidden from her. The major portion of her book, however, is devoted to her experiences as a teacher, and she compares the adherence to regulations by the teachers, the conformism, the intolerance, and the strict enforcement of meaningless rules with the experiences that Jews must have suffered in the concentration camps. Fleischmann's decision to emigrate to Israel is not entirely based on anti-Semitic experiences. Rather, she asserts that it is the intolerant way Germans treat each other which ultimately drove her to make her decision.

> The Germans forget to ask themselves why they are so anxious, pedantic, and stubborn when the matter concerns adherence to laws, and why they construct such a thick network of laws, decrees, rules, and instructions and systematically limit their own freedom. Schiller said, "Humans are created free, are free." That is true, but German education makes slaves out of them, orderlies and subservient underlings (*Untertanen*). And since the slave needs instructions and the orderly needs orders, they slobber for new roles so that they don't have to be responsible for their actions. Year after year, day after day, hour after hour, they learn to behave and keep order.[37]

In sum, Fleischmann's depiction of the German school system resembles a training camp for the banality of evil. Perhaps there are too many generalizations and stereotypes in her description of German schools and the Germans, but they must not be discounted. That is, they must be counted as the way a Jewish woman of the younger generation sought to develop her identity as someone who was other and wanted to be other.

Fleischmann's decision to emigrate in 1980 did not start a wave of German-Jewish emigration to Israel. However, Henryk Broder, who wrote the afterword to her book, and who was one of the most outspoken critics of the official Jews in West Germany, also decided to emigrate in 1981. Broder's reasons were different from Fleischmann's and caused a sensation in the press because he attacked the Left for being anti-Semitic. In a book and a series of articles and interviews Broder maintained that even the leftists were repeating the behavior and thought patterns of their parents and that there could not be normal relations between Jews and Germans.[38] Broder declared that the growing anti-Zionism in West Germany was nothing more than a perverted form of anti-Semitism. In an interview with *Der Spiegel* in 1981, he told a reporter that he would not mind debating the intolerance of Israeli policies with him. However, he said:

> I don't believe that this plays a role for the Left. There is a strong sympathy among leftists for very intolerant states and regimes such as Libya, Iraq, Cambodia. As far as Israel is concerned, the issue is the existence of a Jewish state that is an enormous provocation for the occidental mind which still lingers in each and every leftist who still needs the Jew who is a coward—the Jew as scapegoat as well as victim. There is plenty to criticize about Israel, but I ask myself why the suppression of the Palestinians by the Jews causes more commotion for example than the suppression of the Kurds by the Turks, Persians, and Arabs.[39]

For most Jews living in Germany, Israel still remains, along with Germany, pivotal for their identity. The invasion of Lebanon in 1982 and the massacres in the camps that ensued led to great debates between Germans and Jews of different political persuasions. Small groups of Jewish leftists protested in Bonn in front of the Israeli Embassy, and at the same time, these very same Jews were confronted with anti-Zionist protesters who carried anti-Semitic signs linking the Jewish people as a whole with the militaristic policies of the Israeli government and accusing Israelis of becoming like their murderers. The official Jews, on the other hand, backed the Israeli government and placed pressure on the German government to continue unequivocal support of Israel.

The events in the Middle East do indeed bring out the negative sides of both anti-Semitism and philo-Semitism in Germany. In the minds of Germans and German Jews, Israelis as Jews have been expected to be superhumans since 1948. They have been expected to create miracles in the desert, to defend themselves, conquer all enemies, and remain pure and democratic. The fact that Israel has shown in the last fifteen years that it can be as callous, ruthless, and "imperialist" as any other state has allowed critics and even admirers to vent their anti-Semitism. For many Jews in Germany, it has created another alternative with regard to their identity: Israelis are not the measure of their identity nor is allegiance to the state of Israel necessarily a measure of their identity. As Michael Wolffsohn has remarked:

> It can be basically ascertained that Israel has been a false idol for the German Jews, the Diaspora Jews. Gradually they have awakened from their wishdream. On the other hand, Israel is certainly not the ridiculous caricature of the professional murderer, which many of its critics and enemies have made out of it. The serious reflection about the causes and consequences of the Lebanon War is a propitious condition for Israelis, Di-

aspora Jews and non-Jews alike throughout the world to recognize Israel for what it actually is: a country in which human beings are living and not superhumans.[40]

To a certain extent, the present dilemma faced by Jews in West Germany is similar to the one faced by the Israelis with whom they identified closely at one time: The Jews have been expected to be superhuman. However, the pressures placed on the Jews in West Germany are different from those placed on the Israelis. The Gentile German world expects them to forget the Nazi atrocities, to forgive, and to be thankful for the opportunity to live and work in a philo-Semitic society. The different Jewish communities in West Germany expect West German Jews to remain true to the Jewish tradition, to provide a link to the alien German society, and to uphold the name of Israel, no matter what actions the Israeli government undertakes. Finally, the New Left and its heirs in the Green party expect the younger, more critical Jews to be anti-Zionist and to support notions of an ecologically "pure" Germany without considering that there are strong anti-Semitic undertones in the anti-Zionism of the New Left and dangerous chauvinist implications in the new nationalism of the Greens. To resist these pressures, the critical Jews, particularly those in Frankfurt and Berlin, have joined together and held meetings during the past five years in an effort to define their position against the various pressures they have experienced. And, in defining themselves, they have demonstrated how they, largely nonbelievers, have endeavored to keep the faith with their heritage more than the official Jewish organizations and conservative members of the Jewish communities—and certainly they have confronted the state's false, philo-Semitic policies. In the process there is a touch of tragic irony in the vicissitudes of being Jewish in West Germany especially if one has developed a critical spirit, for the "new" critical German Jews aim to break from the traditional community while keeping the Jewish messianic spirit alive. By refusing to conform to the more conservative policies of the Jewish communities, they also reject the control of the West German state. It is here that the critical Jews play a vital role in West Germany. They are no longer the Germans' Jews, they are their own Jews. And, as long as they want to stay in Germany and claim German citizenship, they are German Jews of a new kind, who insist on the right to define themselves and also to define Germany according to their post-Holocaust experience. Such an act of self-definition may disturb many Germans and Jews as well, but it has proved to be a substantial mode of demonstrating how one can survive the vicissitudes of being Jewish in West Germany.

NOTES

1. The statistics for this essay have been gathered largely from the following sources: Leo Katcher, *Post Mortem.* *The Jews in Germany Today* (New York, 1968); Leo Sievers, *Juden in Deutschland* (Munich, 1979); Monika Richarz, "Jüdische Kultur," in *Bundesrepublik Deutschland/Deutsche Demokratische Republik im Vergleich,* ed. Wolfgang R. Langenbucher, Ralf Rytlewski, and Bernd Weyergraf (Stuttgart, 1983), pp. 347–351; Michael Wolffsohn, "Leben im Land der Mörder," *Die Zeit* 22 (May 27, 1983), pp. 9–10.

2. For the situation of Jews in the German Democratic Republic, cf. Monika Richarz's essay "Jews in Today's Germanies" given as a talk at the Leo Baeck Institute in New York in December 1983. She points out that, excluding those Jews who returned for political reasons and remained dedicated to the Party, most German Jews left East Germany because of political persecution or inadequate reparations.

The membership in the eight Jewish communities of the German Democratic Republic dropped to about 1500 at the time the wall was built in 1961. During the following 20 years the overaged membership was further reduced to the 400 members who live there today. The Jewish community organisations can only survive with the generous financial help of the government. As far as the nonmembers are concerned, there are still a significant number of them who make up part of the political and cultural elite in the GDR; however, as their children intermarry, their complete absorption is only a matter of time. (p. 5 of Richarz's manuscript, "Jews in Today's Germanies")

3. Ibid.

4. See Jean-Baptiste Neveux, "Hochschule für jüdische Studien à Heidelberg," *Revue d'Allemagne* 13 (July–September 1981), pp. 597–600 and Peter Freimark, "Das Institut für die Geschichte der deutschen Juden in Hamburg und die deutsch-jüdische Geschichtswissenschaft heute," *Revue d'Allemagne* 13 (July–September 1981), pp. 589–596.

5. "Jews in Today's Germanies," ms., p. 7.

6. See Alfred Grosser, *Germany in Our Time* (New York, 1971), pp. 210–255 and Andrei S. Markovits, "Germans and Jews: The Continuation of an Uneasy Relationship," *Jewish Frontier* LI (April 1984), pp. 14–20.

7. "Germans and Jews," p. 15.

8. Cf. Grosser, *Germany in Our Time,* pp. 220–227.

9. See Dan Diner, "Fragments of an Uncompleted Journey," *New German Critique* 20 (Spring/Summer 1980), pp. 57–70, republished in revised form in this volume, and Lea Fleischmann, *Dies ist nicht mein Land* (Hamburg, 1980).

10. "Germans and Jews," p. 17.

11. Cf. Susann Heenen, "Deutsche Linke, linke Juden und der Zionismus," in *Die Verlängerung von Geschichte,* ed. Dietrich Wetzel (Frankfurt am Main, 1983), pp. 103–112.

12. Cf. Markovits, "Germans and Jews," pp. 17–20 and the various essays in *Die Verlängerung von Geschichte.*

13. See Jean-Paul Bier, *Auschwitz et les nouvelles littératures allemandes* (Brussels, 1979), pp. 30–31.

48   JACK ZIPES

14. See Fest's *Hitler: Eine Biographie* (Munich, 1973) and Diwald's *Geschichte der Deutschen* (Frankfurt am Main, 1979).

15. See Henryk M. Broder, *Deutschland erwacht* (Cologne, 1978); Aktion Sühnenzeichen/Friedensdienste e. V., eds., *Rechtsextremismus unter Jugendlichen* (Berlin, 1979); Alwin Meyer and Karl-Klaus Rabe, *Phantomdemokraten oder die alltägliche Gegenwart der Vergangenheit* (Reinbek, 1979); Werner Habermehl, *Sind die deutschen faschistoid?* (Hamburg, 1979).

16. See Dieter Bossmann, ed., *Was ich über Adolf Hitler gehört habe. Auszüge von Schülern und Schülerinnen aller Schularten der Bundesrepublik* (Frankfurt am Main, 1977).

17. See "Deutsche, Linke, Juden," *Ästhetik und Kommunikation* 51 (June 1983) and the subsequent discussion in vol. 52 (September 1983), pp. 115–130 and in vol. 53/54 (December 1983), pp. 242–256. In addition, see the following essays about the debate surrounding the *Ästhetik und Kommunikation* special issue, all of which appeared in *New German Critique* 31 (Winter 1984): Jessica Benjamin and Anson Rabinbach, "Germans, Leftists, Jews," pp. 183-194; Marion Kaplan, "To Tolerate Is to Insult," pp. 195–200; Jack Zipes, "The Return of the Repressed," pp. 201–210.

18. See Detlev Claussen, "Im Hause des Henkers" in *Die Verlängerung von Geschichte,* ed. Dietrich Wetzel (Frankfurt am Main, 1983), pp. 113–125. This essay has been translated and reprinted in the present volume.

19. See the discussion of the council in Leo Katcher's *Post Mortem: The Jews in Germany Today,* pp. 19–31.

20. The response was widespread. Some interesting reactions by Jewish intellectuals were gathered in Peter Märthesheimer and Ivo Frenzel, eds., *Im Kreuzfeuer: Der Fernsehfilm "Holocaust"* (Frankfurt am Main, 1979).

21. Stuttgart, 1978.

22. Reinbek bei Hamburg, 1979.

23. See Henryk M. Broder, "Gegen meinen Willen in die Geschichte verknotet," *Konkret* (April 1981), p. 56.

24. Frankfurt am Main, 1979.

25. Hamburg, 1980.

26. Munich, 1979.

27. Cf. Peter Gay, *Freud, Jews, and Other Germans* (New York, 1978).

28. *Fremd im eigenen Land,* pp. 23–24.

29. Stuttgart, 1982.

30. There are numerous books in this series published by the Leo Baeck Institute in London and New York and J. C. B. Mohr in Tübingen.

31. See *The Jew as Pariah* (New York, 1978).

32. The contributors to the anthology are Heinz Abosch, Reiner Bernstein, Léon E. Bieber, Erik Blumenfeld, Eva Bornemann, Leon Brandt, Artur Brauner, Henryk M. Broder, Emil Carlebach, Heinz Elsberg, Peter Finkelgruen, Ossip K. Flechtheim, Lea Fleischmann, Bruno Frei, Eva, Peter, and Silvia Gingold, Ralph Giordano, Jakob Goldberg, Werner

Goldberg, Arie Goral, Sarah Haffner, Gloria Kraft-Sullivan, Georg Kreisler, Micha Labbé, Jürgen Landeck, Jeanett Lander, Michel R. Lang, Herbert S. Levine, Emmi Löwenthal, Konrad Merz, Alfred Moos, Peggy Parnass, Ilse Rewald, Curt Riess, Hazel Rosenstrauch, Thomas Rotschild, Alphons Silbermann, Michael Stone.

33. *Fremd im eigenen Land,* p. 29.

34. Ibid., p. 205.

35. Ibid., pp. 90–91.

36. Ibid., p. 74.

37. *Dies ist nicht mein Land,* p. 249.

38. See *Dankeschön. Bis hierhier und nicht weiter* (Cologne 1980); "Gegen meinen Willen in die Geschichte verknotet," *Konkret* (April 1981), pp. 55–57; "Für Juden gibt es hier keine Normalität," interview in *Der Spiegel* 17 (1981), pp. 39–55; "Alice Schwarzer und der Antisemitismus," *Profil* 51/52 (1982), pp. 62–69.

39. "Für Juden gibt es hier keine Normalität," p. 55.

40. "Leben im Land der Mörder," p. 10.

3

IN THE HOUSE OF THE HANGMAN

Detlev Claussen

In the house of the hangman you don't
mention the noose. It stirs up resentment.
—Theodor W. Adorno

Entanglements

"Maybe you thought it, or maybe you even wrote it—I don't know what you wrote then—but isn't it irrelevant since the New Left was anti-Semitic from the very beginning?" This was the question put to me in 1982 by an outside observer, who justly held a certain position about this matter.

Our discussion was sparked by letters to the editor reacting to the reports about Lebanon by *TAZ (Tageszeitung)*, a leftist daily newspaper. The letters revealed an unabashedly aggressive mentality completely untouched by a sense of history. Rather than simply criticize the Israeli carpet bombing of Beirut for what it was, systematic, extensive terror for the purpose of dispersing and demoralizing the Palestinian people, they drew forced parallels. Most of the writers compared the Israeli army with the Nazis, as if crimes committed in war could not attain a conscious level without this false equation. Long after the letters appeared in *TAZ*, critics continued to ask: Was the New Left in Germany always anti-Semitic? And was it just the New Left?

Am I an exception? No, I was there. But wasn't I there with the wish

50

not to be there, at least, not to be the son of my parents? Did I want the outside observer to grant me absolution? What was my role in preparing the ground for anti-Semitism of the Left? And there is anti-Semitism. One need only look at the facts and actions—the letters to the editor, the teach-ins, the posters, the slogans, and the demonstrations about the events in Lebanon that have anti-Semitic overtones. The European climate permits one assassination attempt after another against Jewish persons and institutions. Those who somehow prepare the ground for this can only say: "We didn't intend for that to happen." Yet, whoever has a memory and whoever can listen ought to know better. A feeling of powerlessness toward one's own history manifests itself. The guilt of the Nazi generation has caught up with their children. Yet, the outside observer in my discussion did not want to hear about any of this. Instead he asked: "How is it that someone like you, who grew up in an anti-Semitic environment, cannot simply accept being an anti-Semite?"

Of course, I could have answered him politically. I could have documented my history as a leftist. I could have gone down into my cellar and looked for old leaflets from 1967 and onward. But that would have been taking the false course of personal self-righteousness. The desire to overcome the web of guilt in German history is understandable, but how quickly does it get distorted? In the beginning there was the guilt for being the offspring of the Nazi generation. Why wasn't such an effort successful, the effort to develop this sense of guilt into a collective, critical consciousness that kept faith with the victims? Sweat gathers on my brow. I don't know the answer.

The road to truth appears to be blocked. The fighting around Beirut brings out those anti-Semitic sentiments that have been wallowing beneath the surface for a long time. I can't bear to watch the news on TV and I feel uncomfortable at the demonstration. The bold tone of the demonstrators has a hollow ring to it (not only in Germany) when Israel is at issue. The false parallels multiply. Begin compares Arafat in West Beirut to Hitler in his *Führer* bunker. Posters plastered on walls read "The Palestinians are the Jews' Jews." After Arafat escaped from Beirut, he tried to trap the antifascist Italian president in Rome with the toast: "As you did in those days, I am fighting fascism today." No, neither Israel nor Palestine is a long way off. On the contrary, we Germans are also the subject of discussion. In this situation one can't remain passive, and one begins to resort to the weapons of an intellectual—speaking and writing, the weapons of criticism. In order to be able to speak and write truthfully, no limitations can be imposed upon reflection, let alone self-reflection. The points where self-reflection can get a foothold are the cracks in the facade of normality. Rationalistic evasions as well as individual psychological explorations are barred.

In the summer of 1982 the rift between rational politics and personal unease grew unbearably. Uri Avneri's visit with Arafat in besieged Beirut, the mass demonstrations in Israel against the war, the different tone of many of the Palestinian contributions to discussions and speeches at meetings—all these were encouraging signs that the life-and-death confrontation between Israelis and Palestinians was not the whole truth. The irrationality of mutual threats of annihilation can be broken only if those forces are strengthened that acknowledge reality, not the status quo. Compulsive reinterpreting of reality leads to those dreadful tendencies to make the horrors of reality larger than they are, at least on an unconscious level, merely to prove a point. To be freed from the entanglements of reality, the anticipatory power of consciousness is needed, the criticism of unconscious tendencies—here in West Germany and in the Middle East. This is the task for those indirectly involved, which is the case for Germans in the Palestinian conflict.

Unsuccessful Escape Attempt

Something so straightforward can also be so deceptive. June 2, 1967. In front of the famous Paulskirche in Frankfurt we set up the public-address system for our demonstration against the Shah. A number of us, members of SDS, wanted to go to Berlin that evening. While waiting for the march to arrive at the church I talked with the deputy national chairman of my organization. His book on Vietnam qualified him as an astute critic of international relations. So I asked him: "What's the situation with Israel? The Arabs want to drive them into the sea. Shouldn't we demonstrate again this week? Not just against the Shah?" Pause. "Well, you know, comrade," he answered, "Israel is an imperialist country." The procession of demonstrators turned the corner. That evening a student demonstrator, Benno Ohnesorg, was shot to death in Berlin by a policeman. Saturday we demonstrated once again—against the murder of Benno Ohnesorg. On the sidewalk some Jewish friends of mine were distributing leaflets against the threat to Israel. They were protesting against the Springer newspaper chain, accusing it of inciting a pogrom. The same Springer newspaper appeared on Monday: "VICTORY! Dayan—Israel's Rommel."

Nightmare—reality interfered with us. The Six-Day War did not fit into our image of the world. In *The Interpretation of Dreams*, Freud made the following critical remark about morality: "It remains instructive in each case to discover the turbulent ground from which our virtues spring up and assume their haughty superiority. The complexity of a human being's moral make-up, agitated dynamically in every direction, very rarely submits itself to a resolution by a simple alternative."

The highly turbulent German ground was supposed to submit itself to a resolution by a simple alternative. The highly ethical, leftist children wanted to separate themselves from the guilt of their rightist fathers. From 1967 on we pursued the dialectics of abstract morality. It reached its logical conclusion in the uncritical solidarity with the Palestinians. Designating the events in Lebanon a "holocaust" fit this tendency exactly—new perpetrators, new victims, new innocence. The mass annihilation of the Jews that occurred in the Third Reich reentered the sphere of historical everyday occurrence. Morality has long since been sacrificed on behalf of simple black and white equation: evil = imperialism, good = anti-imperialism. In postfascist Germany the origin of the New Left cannot be separated from the burden of the National Socialist legacy. The liberation of Germans from fascism was due to an international constellation. There was no self-liberation; the sin of omission, of the nonexistent liberation, implicates the German Left. The moral impetus of the New Left cannot be reconciled with the ideology of the "zero hour," the notion of the clean slate that prevailed in both German states at the end of World War II. The legacy of that postwar era determined the eventual founding of the New Left, and it affected the very core of the established democratic milieu because it demonstrated that West German democracy was not the product of greater insight, but of the Cold War. The dynamics of APO (the "extraparliamentary opposition") had its motor in the nonexistent self-liberation. Its impulse, however, came from outside. The New Left in Germany is a product of postfascist democracy imposed from without, a product of "reeducation." Despite current anti-American sentiment, it must be admitted that this was a good thing.

Yet, Western allies, particularly the United States, halted a radical democratization of West Germany, economic deconcentration, and military disarmament in the interests of the Cold War in order to erect an anticommunist bastion. The more the United States became entangled in Vietnam, the more transparent it made repression in advanced capitalist democracy. During the 1960s, a historical opportunity fell into the lap of the New Left in Germany, an opportunity it did not seize. The possibility of making authentic history under conditions not of one's own choosing can only be realized when one's motives translate into critical consciousness. Such simple slogans as "capitalism leads to fascism, capitalism must go," did not allow the anti-Nazi motive to reach full development. On the contrary, they obscured it. Germans did not become consciously aware that anti-Semitism was a genuine relapse into barbarism. Rather it was downplayed as a mere element of Nazi ideology. Here the New Left succumbed to the need to have no history, a need that results from a longing for historical innocence. If social psychology has a justification, then it is where too little is done to satisfy a need for a political and theoretical understanding of problems. The New Left itself pushed aside the slogan "Auschwitz Never Again," and abandoned the guilt of anti-Semitism to the mechanisms of psychology, that is, to the fatal dialectics of the sense of guilt. Here lies the root of that endless evil which wishes that the victims should no longer be victims, but victimizers instead. From the sense of guilt comes false consciousness. The predilection for anti-Americanism and the emergence of the question of nationalism among the Greens in the 1970s and 1980s correlate with the abstract anti-imperialism that appeared so unhistorically on the political scene during the armed conflicts in Lebanon.

The self-designation "New Left," taken from the American movement, reflects one element in the reality of advanced capitalism. We realized that it was not the practical coming to consciousness of the working class that had defeated Nazism or that had created the social conditions which made a return to fascism impossible once and for all. So we developed a receptive ear to what was presented to us as the mediated experience of the traditional Left in the form of "Critical Theory" that returned from America. In *Education after Auschwitz,* Adorno formulated the political task to which Horkheimer, Marcuse, and others had dedicated themselves. "I would like to stress emphatically that whether fascism recurs is not essentially a psychological, but a social, question. I talk so much about the psychological, solely because the other, more essential elements are to a large extent removed from education, if not from the grasp of the individual altogether." The contradiction between insight into the social conditions that made Auschwitz possible and social impotence to abolish these conditions produced the ambivalent aspect of the extraparliamentary voluntarism of the 1960s. This voluntarism proved productive insofar as it attacked the continued existence of the fascist legacy in an advanced capitalist society. West German society, torpid in anticommunism and economic compensation, reacted as if the power of the state itself were at stake. The New Left allowed the logic of this power struggle to be forced upon itself. Grotesque distortions of reality were revealed in the sectarian extremes of the 1970s—the Maoist groups, the orthodox Marxist-Leninist organizations, and the Red Army Faction (RAF), which became terrorist.

In the Cellar of the Left

The motives behind the evolution of the Left, the postulate "Auschwitz Never Again," had been all but forgotten by the middle of the 1970s. The cost of denying reality is the erosion of the substance of a leftist movement. The independence of theory has long since been sacrificed to the principle of effectiveness for social change. Since the very beginnings of the New Left, anti-intellectualism has been available at cut-rate prices, particularly among leftist intellectuals. Following on the heels of students dressed up as proletarians of the 1920s, are those equally dull-witted types who truly see the belly as the focal point of the world. Animosity toward intellectuality and critical thought is, however, a common inheritance of fascist praxis. Over the roundabout route of leftist sectarianism it enters unnoticed into the ranks of those who consider themselves the social alternative.

The New Left's attachment to traditional Marxism is connected to a hereditary guilt of the old Left. The traditional Left comprehended anti-Semitism in a functionalist and rationalist way—as an instrument of the ruling class for the purpose of diverting the oppressed away from their true tasks. Anti-Semitism was not viewed as the consequence of changed social conditions which resulted from rendering the individual powerless in capitalist industrial society, and which possesses in these powerless individuals a real substratum. In the new as well as the old German Left, this rationalism led to reducing National Socialism to a notion of fascism that has as its sole content the continuity of class domination without bourgeois democracy. The insane designs of the RAF, through direct actions to lure fascism out of advanced capitalism in order to generate revolutionary consciousness among the masses, carry the denial of Auschwitz to the extreme. Fortunately, the defensive program for the preservation of postfascist democracy, as has been and is advanced by the old Left, proved itself more realistic and more effective among the masses.

The New Left sought to break out of the house of the hangman in which it had grown up in order to take refuge in the house of revolution. And so it began to take up residence in the visitors' gallery in the house of revolution—and avoided a glancing into the cellar. The denial of present-day elements of the National Socialist past is without a doubt the socio-psychological corollary of the Cold War. However, the anticommunism that picked up neatly where the racist antibolshevism of the Nazis left off cannot be eliminated by a simple alternative. The self-deprecation of socialism was to be replaced by true communism, the actual anti-imperialist revolution by the ideal one. In the attempt to ward off the ruling ideology of the West that blatantly resurrected National Socialist aspects in its hatred for the East, the New Left began apologizing for socialism. The repressive side of the social developments associated with the October Revolution were increasingly downplayed so as to arrive at a completely distorted interpretation of revolution in the present. Since their enemies were also our enemies, their revolutions should also be ours. The nationalist side of anti-imperialist revolution, which determined its content and limitations to a decisive extent, was completely ignored. A socialist ideal of society was projected as existing in fact, which can at best lead to a rude awakening about the postrevolutionary circumstances. These distortions of consciousness end in a distorted perception of reality—uncritical identification with the enemies of our enemies, hatred toward the friends of our enemy. In this simplistic view, the world reality is degraded to a puppet theater under the direction of the United States president. Thus, whatever might hamper this direction is welcomed. On the basis of this most abstruse common denominator everyone gathers together once or twice a year in Bonn.

Distorted Internationalism

The need for social change has grown since 1960 in the Federal Republic, yet the postulate "Auschwitz Never Again" has been pushed aside. The *ne plus ultra* of social criticism in Germany was formulated by Adorno in the essay cited above, *Education after Auschwitz*. "One speaks of the threat of a relapse into barbarism. But it's not just a threat, Auschwitz was *it*. Barbarism will continue to exist as long as the conditions which prompted that relapse endure in essence."

The sense of powerlessness to change these conditions all at once strengthens the need for simple alternatives. The suspicion that a revolution is necessary to bring about such a radical change was to become a certainty in the real revolutions of the Third World. Identification with them entailed renunciation of German National Socialism, a pertinent element of criticism, and simultaneously a false international expectation that these revolutions would possess precisely that power required to destroy the conditions of a capitalist class society that we assailed in vain. At the time that this contradiction began to tear apart the New Left with full force, the Palestinians were discovered as a new cause. The reality of the Palestinian conflict became intertwined with the myth of anti-imperialist revolution, a process appearing to lead to an unacceptable alternative—either anti-Semitism out of international solidarity or the withholding of solidarity from the Palestinian victims of Israeli colonialism.

The truth content of direct experience in the anti-Semite is distorted into an aggressively organized, false consciousness, "so that he cannot gain any experience at all" (Adorno, *What Does "Working Through the Past" Mean?*). Leftist self-consciousness, especially in Germany, is not compatible with open anti-Semitism, but the leftist individual is no more immune from learning nothing whatsoever from experience than any other individual in advanced capitalism. In order to maintain simple alternatives for itself, consciousness has to seal itself off from experience. Our roundabout paths for approaching the problem of anti-Semitism in the German Left demonstrate the increasing emptiness of socially critical categories of experienced reality. The categories socialism, internationalism, and revolution, which were directed against the one-dimensionalism of the Nazi legacy in the present, are becoming merely lofty platforms that exhaust themselves in a vague ideality. With the discovery of the Palestinians a new magic word entered this nominalist purgatory—anti-Zionism. The fact that the public sphere disallows any differentiation between anti-Semitism and anti-Zionism seems consistent only in the sense of Mao's old dictum, "When the enemy is fighting us, that's good and not bad." The fact that the false sense of certainty in one's position is not shaken, even when the enemy doesn't fight him at all anymore, indicates the indifference toward the revolution with which he vehemently declares himself in solidarity. If it comes to negotiations, one group declares the matter resolved, and the other smells a betrayal. All too many self-proclaimed friends of the Palestinian people spoke out in the summer of 1982 demanding that the battle in West Beirut be fought to the last bullet. Victims and victimizers would then be firmly established once and for all in the sense of the simple alternative. This maximalist anti-imperialism can only make itself felt in verbally radical cruelty.

An anti-Zionist self-conception is no protection against anti-Semitic stupidity. Since the term anti-Zionism stems from the leftist tradition, it is ostensibly historically untainted. Ever since the nationalist regression of the October Revolution into "socialism in one country," anti-Zionism belongs to the stockpile of manipulative devices of Marxist-Leninist ideology. In the "anti-Zionist campaign" after World War II it proved itself eminently useful in reconciling Stalinist brutality against former emigrants to the West with the traditional anti-Semitism of Eastern and Central European countries. Just as with socialism, internationalism, and revolution, the term anti-Zionism can only be dissociated from the delusory Marxist-Leninist context if it designates an experiential emancipatory content. The interesting thing about the reality of the Palestinian conflict is not principally the collision of Jewish with Palestinian nationalism, but rather the unmediated appearance of a Manichaean world, as Fanon characterized colonial conflict—with the macabre twist that the direct victims of our history appear as victimizers and the Palestinians as the new victims of the former ones. There is a correspondence between the need for innocence of the New Left and their successors, who call themselves in a political Mickey Mouse language "anti-impi's" and "antifa's," and the political rationalism of the simple anti-Zionist alternative. And the more

Zionism seems to be the sole alternative for the Israeli-Jewish people and for Jews in the diaspora, the more reality is taken as confirmation of the Manichaean world view of good and evil. If one can purge history of the results of the victimizer-victim relationship of the Palestinian conflict, then one can also do away with his or her own history. Entrance into the logic of annihilation has succeeded: either Israel is destroyed, to which the victims have a right, or the victims become heroic victims ("struggle for Beirut to the last bullet").

The Highly Turbulent Ground of Palestine

To take a detour by way of the highly turbulent ground of Palestine does not have to preclude renewing the historical, moral postulate "Auschwitz Never Again." Even if a solution to the Palestinian conflict is improbable, more desperate efforts are nevertheless required to bring it about. Even if the powerlessness of critical consciousness in light of the last fifteen years provides cause for despair, there are nonetheless signs in reality that could lead to correcting false consciousness—the mass demonstrations in Israel against the Lebanon invasion and the politically more realistic behavior of the Palestine Liberation Organization leadership during the siege of Beirut. The actors in the conflict are themselves beginning to push open the door leading out of the Manichaean world. For Germans, the indirect participants in the conflict, these factors compel us to do everything possible to bring about an end to violence because this violence without end in Palestine is the result of the National Socialist logic of annihilation. Here, indeed, there is a special responsibility, and not only for leftist Germans.

To place Israel's right of existence into question is to deny the National Socialist violence whether one likes it or not. It was the Zionist structure that at least secured the survival of a part of Europe's Jews threatened with annihilation. Whoever escapes from the house of the hangman as a potential victim is not concerned, in his mortal terror, if he runs over someone in the street. He can only come to his senses when the fear of death is gone. There are signs that this has become possible in Israel today, though there is no guarantee of it.

In their struggle for survival the Palestinians are beginning to emancipate themselves from the need for revenge resulting from the wrongs they have suffered. A fundamental difference exists between the chauvinist tirades of a Shukeiri, who in 1967 wanted to drive the Jews into the sea, and Arafat's offers to negotiate and compromise in the summer of 1982. With the establishment of a separate Palestinian state the conflict would not yet be resolved, but it would regain its social dimension. Neighbors can acknowledge each other and develop relations. One can and must turn to the arrangement and alteration of one's own house. How is that to happen in a life-and-death struggle in which one side barricades itself in a fortress while the other is locked out, trying to keep its head above water? We haven't said a thing about the fate of the Palestinian Arabs in Israel and of the Palestinians in the occupied areas, but their chance to live must also be considered. What would they have won, if the fight in Beirut had been waged to the last bullet? Nothing, absolutely nothing.

The opening in the Palestinian conflict for the logic of recognition also makes it possible to loosen the entanglements in the house of the hangman. The distortion of the critical postulate "Auschwitz Never Again" into a knot in the anti-Semitic noose is not inevitable, but it does possess an inherent fatal feature, for it denies the preconditions of reality. Not only are the adventures of false consciousness in the Federal Republic alarming, so are the entanglements in real horrors. It began with an attack on a Jewish old age home in 1970 and reached its dreadful peak in Entebbe in 1976, when two Germans with guns in hand separated Jewish from non-Jewish hostages. That was and is barbarian.

The nonconceptual and unhistorical relationship to violence is one of the consequences of barbarism in the present. Due to the uncomprehended experience of Auschwitz one comes to believe erroneously that terror can only be fought with counter-terror. The inherent historical meaning of the concentration camp universe consists in the obliteration of any human alternative linked to changing and improving life. Violence without end, a permanent threat of the Palestinian conflict, follows directly from this "domination of the present's past through the past." Terrorism only has the illusion of autonomous action over against state-organized terror. In this point the false consciousness of the RAF coincided with the terrorist mistakes of Palestinian nationalism.

Consciousness of Guilt and Recognition

The power of the past in the present cannot be broken with a magic wand. The indirect participant has no excuse to drop the weapon of criticism when the life-and-death struggle seems to sabotage every reasonable solution. However, in order to criticize the false consciousness of the actors when they degrade the National Socialist legacy into cheap propaganda gadgets, one has to develop a critical self-consciousness about living in the house of the hangman, where there is still talk of the noose. The appeal to the unbroken power of the past must be considered part of the unenlightened side of the Palestinian conflict, when Begin speaks of Hitler and means Arafat, and when Arafat speaks of fascism and means Israel. If that were indeed the case, then there could be no solution to the Palestinian conflict, but at most a postponement of the barbarian catastrophe of annihilation.

Here, I believe, the point of departure has been found for criticizing German postfascist reality which is of international significance. For in both parts of Germany different types of compromises with the National Socialist legacy have been adopted, and more light must be shed on them. According to the state's official position in East Germany, National Socialism has ostensibly been eliminated through the simple alternative of socialism, although a conscious emancipation has not occurred at all and has never been ventured by the SED party either. Beneath the surface of a fragile Marxist-Leninist ideology, an unmasked and unclarified resentment smolders, in which anticommunism and prejudice against Poles and Russians have formed their unholy alliance. Danziger has broached this sensitive theme in his book, *Die Partei hat immer Recht* (The Party Is Always Right); those witnesses bought free from GDR (German Democratic Republic) prisons attest to this thesis in frightening fashion.

Official anti-Zionism as well as the criticisms of the events in Poland try to collude with the smoldering bitter feelings of the masses. In 1968, the SED leadership did not hesitate to have East German soldiers march into Czechoslovakia. Since August, the threat of invasion has been raised against their Polish neighbors. It is worth recalling the grotesque lies and loathsomeness of East German propaganda: There was allegedly a "Zionist conspiracy" that lay behind the Prague Spring. On August 25, 1968, there were a series of articles in the official press, *Neues Deutschland,* and in the *Berliner Zeitung* that sought to defame important proponents of the reform process as "militant Zionists" and "agents of Israel." GDR propagandists did not hesitate to distribute an inflammatory publication in the Czech language with the name "Zpravy," and to transmit a radio program on the Vltava broadcasting station. The campaign was commented upon by Czech radio on August 26 with utmost clarity. "They didn't say Jews directly, they said international Zionism." It is not far-fetched to contend that the indifference with which the entire West German alternative scene and the peace movement in particular put up with the anti-Semitic defamation of the Polish opposition sheds a bad light on the repression of anti-Semitism as a social reality.

On the political surface, interest in peace in Europe seems to be pushing aside interest in the international interweaving of emancipatory processes, if it does not fit into the global picture of simple alternatives. The repression of international connections, or their distorted perception based on animosity toward the leaderships of the respective blocs, aids the resurrection of militant nationalism which ought to have found its just end in the forceful destruction of National Socialism. The uncritical rejuvenation of such terms as "homeland," "nature," "country life," these unrelinquishable components of "blood and soil" ideology, has been pushed through mainly by the leftist alternative scene. So depressing may have been the destruction of nature through the construction of the west runway at the airport in Frankfurt, that the colloquialism "ecological holocaust" is more than a linguistic lapse. It is on the same plane with pacifist propaganda that warns of the dangers of an atomic war, compared to which "Auschwitz and Treblinka were child's play" (these were the words of an eminent pacifist author who was persuaded by his editors to drop this formulation). What is intended to be critical stirs up attention at the cost of trivializing. The oft-repeated phrase that the foreign workers are the Jews of today or tomorrow hinders the insight into the indirect connection between the National Socialist legacy and the racist present for the sake of a propaganda effect.

Anti-Semitism remains an integral component of advanced capitalism; even as anti-Semitism without Jews, it is directed against Jews. Modern anti-Semitism signifies more than xenophobia. Both stem from the same root, but the special thing about anti-Semitism rests in its limitlessness and boundlessness. Anti-Semitism needs the Jews, and precisely imaginary Jews, who cannot be substituted by blacks, Russians, gypsies, or Turks. The anti-Semite of today denies the annihilation of European Jewry; he fights the "Auschwitz lie" in order to be able to repeat Auschwitz. The fewer real Jews he actually meets, the easier they become the victims of his global imagination. And yet, he needs reference points in uncomprehended reality. Israel, the Jewish lobby in the United States, and the relationship of Jewish intellectuals to socialism and communism, to radical social criticism in general, are and remain his inexhaustible sources. Mere hatred for foreigners leaves him unsatisfied.

The resurrection of this kind of anti-Semitism seemed hardly conceivable in Germany twenty years ago. In the dominant ideology of philo-Semitism a limited anti-Semitism found expression, according to the motto: "They're great, the Jews, when they're in Israel." The real Jews who did not correspond to the philo-Semitic fantasies are bothersome because the philo-Semites are concerned neither with the victims nor with the Jews, but with themselves, their sense of guilt. The spectrum stretches from moral self-righteousness ("I, as an Aryan, am not so bad at all") to masochistic complacency ("Each of us has a little Hitler in him"). The predominant consciousness as well has discovered the power of psychology in the meantime. Well-intended beginnings, such as Margarethe and Alexander Mitscherlich's criticism of the "inability to mourn" have long since been integrated into the official canon of solemn adjuration—and unfortunately it must be said that their works are far from immune to that sort of thing. The deed, technically and highly organized mass murder, is removed from reality in psychology. "Remember, repeat, work through"—with what ease is that put on paper! Repeat fascism— even if only in the imagination? The repeated reality strikes back without mercy. Even the possibility for the victimizers and their children to mourn remains inadequate to offset the deed, to compensate the victims. It reverts to self-pity, which only with difficulty can restrain aggression against the victims and their children.

The philo-Semitic period during which time the Federal Republic wanted to let anti-Semitism be forgotten is drawing to a close. The swaggering and contemptuous tones of a puppet-man such as Mollemann, state secretary of the Ministry of Foreign Affairs, are aimed at the ability to form a consensus among oil opportunists, in whose interests Israel would be dropped if necessary. The transformation of historic guilt into debts, whereby the Federal Republic wanted to buy itself free, always carried with it the qualification that eventually the outstanding balance would be canceled. That may be very true in business, but it is an immoral demand in history. Support for Israel, halfhearted in any event, has from the start been attached to a curious demand for reconciliation. The victimizers and their successors demand it of the victims and their children like payment in cash. The forgiveness demanded is, however, a historical, moral impossibility. Simon Wiesenthal, who is personally confronted with this demand constantly, related the following story during a televised interview on December 7, 1982:

"A dying SS man who had participated in the massacre of Jews pleaded with me for forgiveness. Without a word I turned away. I told the story to a young rabbi in the concentration camp. 'God has just preserved you from a grave sin. When one day the dead awaken, they would have asked you: Who gave you the right to forgive in our name? Who gave you authority?'"

One correct aspect of the solidarity with the Palestinian people, whose existence nobody wanted to know anything about fifteen years ago, is that they must be helped by recognizing their rights. Only through criticism of Israel's policies has this been and is this possible. But the consistently realistic view of the Palestinian conflict in the Federal Republic requires increasing normalization of the relationship between Germans and Jews.

The pen resists when the subject is normality between Germans and Jews, for the German normality toward the Jews is anti-Semitic. Guilt, which—never accepted—concealed itself behind the mask of conscientious philo-Semitism, breaks out in new anti-Semitic tendencies. Consciousness of guilt genuinely concerned about loyalty to the victims cannot expect a verdict of not guilty. Its work begins where psychology ends. Born part of the anti-Semitic world, in which one always becomes guilty over and over again, one has to try to transform it with all available means into a world of recognition. Only recognition of historical guilt enables cognition of the present. The house of the hangman can only be cozy when reality is denied.

What transpires outside the official political framework must no longer be taken lightly. When I left the Frankfurt soccer stadium with a Jewish friend in 1979, a Gladbach fan said to us: "Well, they won again, your Jewish club." Drunk and with tears in his eyes. Did the remark have any significance? The remark seemed to us so abstruse that we simply moved on. In *Der Spiegel* I read the following report: "In the Frankfurt soccer stadium youths don't drone 'pig' or 'damned faggot' when one of their heroes has been fouled, but instead, with arm upraised in the Hitler salute: 'Jew, Jew, Jew!'" And in a chant fans shout for the Dortmund goalie, Immel, to be shipped "off to Auschwitz!" (November 29, 1982)

Social psychology can explain the physical violence authoritarian social concepts engender in the heads of youthful dropouts (cf. in the same issue of *Der Spiegel:* "Wir sind die Geilsten" ["We are the horniest"], Peter Seewald on the Hamburg soccer fan club, "The Lions"), but it cannot be overcome by psychological means—most definitely not by fetishizing spontaneous violence. Behavior aimed at shocking the middle classes has nothing emancipatory about it, either in its right-wing, or in any other averred radical form. Yet, sensitivity to neo-Nazism does not correspond at all with becoming sensitive to the survival of National Socialism in its suit-and-tie variety. No matter how subtly it may be phrased in the manner of Chancellor Helmut Kohl, the demand to speak no more of the noose in the hangman's house cannot be overlooked in the affirmation of tradition and the demand for continuity. Isn't the Left really worried about the wrong thing when it expresses the view that the parliamentary system can integrate everything? Isn't it true instead that, in the center of parliamentarianism, forces remain poised to assimilate antidemocratic forces from outside parliament?

The demand for a break with the tradition that produced Auschwitz is not formulated by official policy. Federal Chancellor Kohl stated before the successors to the German *Wehrmacht* in December 1982: "Each of us knows that, after the Second World War, we in the Federal Republic set out to learn from history. But learning from history must not mean that we drop out of history. Obviously, to history belongs the affirmation of the continuity of history."

Before, during, and after Auschwitz.

Translated by Merle Kruger

Jewish Responses

4

MY JEWISHNESS
Manès Sperber

I write these lines in the city whose name I murmured in prayer every day as a small child, even before I knew the name of my family or the place of my birth. Jeruschalahim—these five syllables and their intriguing sound were to stay with me through years to come. They were like those solemn vows that are frequently more binding on us than their actual realization. Thus, I knew like all my kind that Jerusalem was the city to which we would all return: "Next Year!" was the oft-repeated wish which simultaneously expressed the messianic hope.

I learned to translate the Prophets, primarily Isaiah, whose message still concerns me today though I'm an unbeliever, and Jeremiah, whose sufferings with his own people gave me insight into the fact that love can be an inexhaustible source of unhappiness. Jeremiah, whose speeches first introduced me to great rhetorical poetry, lamented: "They say: three peaces, then peace, but there is no peace!" During the sixty-five years that have transpired since my first encounter with the Prophets, this lament has accompanied me like an insistent refrain of a song that has remained a useless admonition for centuries.

This essay first appeared in *Mein Judentum*, ed. Hans Jürgen Schultz (Stuttgart, 1978) and can also be found in Manès Sperber, *Churban oder Die unfassbare Gewissheit* (Vienna, 1979). It is reprinted here in translation with permission of the author.

God sent those Prophets to alternately threaten his chosen people with punishment and misery and to promise them the fortune of an ever more bountiful life. Wrathful or merciful, He always promised them immortality and the land of Canaan, the eternal homeland, which they first had to conquer but then lose over and over again.

Jerusalem is a very old city, but it is Jeruschalahim, which was destroyed by Nebuchadnezzer. Moreover, it is not the city of the Second Temple nor of the Heroditian Temple, which was captured by Titus in the year 70 and demolished in the second century after the final victory of the Romans over the rebellious people of God. Aelius Hadrianus had the earth of this city's steep hills and narrow valleys plowed under in order to build Aelia Capitolina named after himself, but its memory has only survived as a name printed in small letters in a few history books.

Since then, this city has been rebuilt and destroyed repeatedly, not infrequently in the name of the same God, the God of my forefathers. In the two millenia of our present calendar, the promised land and its capital city have suffered the remarkable fate of being violently coveted and celebrated by its conquerors but never being loved by them. If one reads the reports of earnest travelers of former times, such as that of Chateaubriand, one will discover how the city of holy places was allowed to deteriorate and to what extent the country was barbarically devastated by its conquerors. All this is indeed true. This stony, sandy, and destitute earth had to be made fertile over and over again. The ground had to become drunk with water so that it would forget to be ungrateful. But this can only be accomplished by someone whose love for this land is like the loving care given to a child suffering from an incurable disease. Only the young Jews of the last eighty years have done that, no one else. They were no longer satisfied with the constant dangers to the land which was always preserved, despite everything. They wanted their people finally to establish their presence not only in constantly changing times but in their own inalienable space.

Now as I look at the walls that surround this conflict-ridden city, I search slowly and with equanimity to discover the nature of my Jewishness, to attain a sense of what it means to me here and now—that Jewishness to which I belong not only by birth, but over and beyond this because I always desired it even under the worst of conditions. And that happened from the very beginning not on account of, but despite being God's chosen people. Whether this can be considered an unavoidable blessing or an intolerable burden is a question that bothered me only during my youth. I learned early enough that we carry our blessings like the hunchback carries his hump. It is no easier to rid oneself of the latter than it is to dissociate oneself from a blessing, the most oppressive encumbrance of all.

It was also because I was unable to forget the threatening nature of such a blessing, it became impossible for me to explain the singular fate of the Jewish people with rational arguments. And even less than before would I be able to say today why it has been precisely we who have managed to outlast everything and survive everyone. For a long time it has seemed to me that the price was too high to pay for our longevity and the undesired ubiquitousness and homelessness. Although this fate constitutes a historical and philosophically inextricable problem which raises more questions than we can ever hope to answer, my Jewishness is as natural to me as, say, the certainty of a Tyrolean peasant, who knows that he belongs nowhere else but in his native village. Thus, self-understanding needs no explanations in my daily interaction with Jews and Gentiles alike, or in my attitude toward the fortune and misfortune of being a Jew—in the year 70 A.D. or the year 135 or 1,000 years later during the Crusades or ultimately after the emancipation of the bourgeoisie when there was an epidemic of conversions by German and French Jews, who frantically and unsuccessfully sought to escape their identity.

As an active contemporary in the twentieth century, I have followed my forefathers along their myriad journeys, and I have witnessed all the outrages whose chosen victims they became as well as the miracles that finally saved them from total extermination.

It might seem, therefore, all the more surprising that the west wall of the temple, the so-called Wailing Wall, which is the goal of so many pilgrimages, does not mean that much to me. In fact, it means less to me than the Acropolis at Athens, for example. To be more precise and clearer, the loss of the temple along with the abolition of the priesthood has persistently, indeed decisively, promoted not only the perseverance of the Jewish people, but has as well helped preserve its faith and every tradition that could be of value to it. Judaism was preserved because it was no longer dependent on any place or any institution. There was nothing left that could still be lost.

Consider the Acropolis: it does not force its admirers to believe in Zeus or Athena or any of the other dwellers of Olympus. Human creativity is extolled in its temples. The gods are there only in works formed in the image of humankind, and it is our eye which gives them a measure of life.

It was not until God lost his temple and became as homeless as His people that he triumphed over the heathen gods and the attraction of false idols to which the progeny of Jacob in Canaan were so often the victim. Not until the Diaspora was this temptation diminished, and it finally disappeared when Christianity was transformed into a church and became heathen with the cult of Mary and the idolization of parochial protective saints.

Not only because I am an unbeliever, but because I belong to Jewry, do I suspect in all heathen practices the cowardly self-humiliation of mankind before animals, monsters, and fellow humans made into idols. And, in this regard, I am undoubtedly stricter than many orthodox Jews, who in their thirst for faith take unto themselves many of the superstitions of their host nations.

If there were a God, he would in my opinion be the Jewish God. Even though I stopped believing in God when I was thirteen, my heretical development was from the very beginning influenced by my strong resistance to every kind of idolatry. For that reason I became, like so many of my fellow Jews, an irreconcilable foe of Stalin, who for his part became an enemy of the Jews by demanding with wide-open violence that he be worshipped as perfect.

To conclude these introductory remarks, I want to recall the fact that Judaism is predicated on a direct link between God and humankind. This relationship was obscured by the priest caste and repeatedly disrupted; it was not the priests, but the prophets who put their lives on the line to proclaim the truth of Judaism. Thanks to the hope the prophets gave the Jews, they have always remained unsubdued even though they have continually been beaten. The prophets demanded far more than they promised and cast upon the Jews the burden of human existence as if that were a blessing which one could earn or had to earn by practicing human compassion.

Never does a host culture ever sufficiently understand the nature or the determining factors of the "otherness" of a minority present in its midst but which always leads a marginal existence. For its part, the minority must constantly and correctly assess its own motives in order to avoid doing anything that might cause the displeasure of the majority. The latter takes it for granted that only its manner of being and doing, its value system, is the natural one, the one that is the most moral and protective of the best interests of the greatest number. Even when coexistence has become the custom, there is still a final problem that apparently can quite suddenly and unexpectedly threaten to damage this peaceful harmony between unequal partners.

This happens when the natives suspect that the others have designs which threaten the supremacy of the majority and thereupon would call into question the validity of all the established prerogatives associated with that supremacy. One need only think how incompatible Catholic infallibility can be with the heretical challenge of a Lutheran minority. Or, one can think of the "shamed synagogue" statue carved in stone on the south wall of the Strasbourg Cathedral—she wears a blindfold and thereby makes herself blind by refusing to see the light of pure truth. Next to her is the statue "Modest Ecclesia"—innocence in triumphant pursuit.

To become one of the majority and to lose one's own identity is either the fear or the desire of many who belong to a minority as long as the latter is not the ruling elite. But whether enslaved, demeaned, disenfranchised, or persecuted, the Jews have remained free from that fear and that desire, for it was always taken for granted that they had to remain true to their God and thereby to themselves. Later, in the fourth century of their exile, this faith became a curse that followed them like their own shadow wherever they went in the Christian world. At that point the Christian hope for a Second Coming, for a return of the savior, which had been predominant until then, evaporated. According to one account, this was a hope without which "it became impossible to believe in the first coming since not all of its prophecies have been fulfilled. . . . For this reason the Jews are loathe to believe that it was the Messiah who had already come."

A contemporary of the writer of this passage, written sixteen hundred years ago, the church father and saint John Chrysostom (345–407) known as "the golden-tongued speaker," preached therefore a merciless war against the Jews in order to rescue, through their extermination, the legitimacy of the Christian belief in salvation. The Jews were supposed to finally recognize Jesus as the Messiah or be eliminated if they chose to persist in their anti-Christian stubbornness. This particular church leader, who struggled just as relentlessly but equally unsuccessfully against the paganization of the church, was the most important initiator of organized anti-Semitism that would soon evolve from a functional antagonism into total hatred. Whoever harbors such sentiments finds it possible to completely disdain the object of his hatred while at the same time overestimating him, as if he possessed some secret and therefore dangerous power.

Ever since my childhood I have known that "in every generation there have been those who hate us in order to destroy us"—from the Amalekites to the slanderers of the French-Jewish officer Dreyfus up to those primarily theological anti-Semites, who still testified in ritual-murder trials at the beginning of this century as experts of anti-Semitism and initiated pogroms. I was taught quite early to recognize open and concealed hatred, and it was impressed on me at the same time not to allow myself to be carried away by hate. In one of my novels[1] I have a holy rabbi say that we, we alone, have remained unconquerable despite all our defeats because we have always prevented ourselves from becoming like our enemy in the fight. We were allowed to abhor Haman, Titus, or the Czar, but not the Persian, Roman, or Russian people. In an essay about hate I did in fact analyze the hostility to Jews as a psychologically revealing example, however, not from a Jewish standpoint but rather in view of the fact that nobody can continually hate without dehumanizing the hated one and distorting his image to a point past recognition. One does that in order to find the absolute affirmation of one's value in the total negation of the other and thus to silence any doubt one may have about one's value.

More than the belief in the chosen people, then it was martyrdom which forced the Jews into a Judaeocentric orientation. Without ever forgetting this history of suffering, I resolutely keep myself from thinking in a Judaeocentric way. As in the case of many of my fellow Jews, I have unhesitatingly participated in activities that had absolutely nothing to do with being a Jew. Since my early childhood I have felt myself affected, challenged, even personally touched by the events of our times, by the hopes and sufferings throughout the world to no less a degree than my non-Jewish friends.

Anti-Semites have for ages accused the Jews of participating too avidly in all emancipatory movements. It is indeed true that their participation in liberation movements of our own times has been relatively larger than that of other intellectuals. This can be explained by the fact that the intelligentsia of practically every religious or national minority feels drawn to those who are dissatisfied insofar as these intellectuals defend the disenfranchised and take a stand against any form of discrimination. The biblical training of the Jew, moreover, makes it imperative to struggle for equality and justice for all.

The general bourgeois emancipation guaranteeing equality to all minorities awakened inclinations toward assimilation in those Jews, who no longer felt bound to the Jewish faith. This occurred precisely to the degree that modern society disengaged itself from the tyranny of institutionalized belief and secularized relationships. The Jews, with few exceptions city folk, secularized themselves more rapidly than their Christian neighbors and believed that complete integration was possible since the difference of faith no longer separated them from the Christians.

In the effort to irrevocably dissolve once and for all all ties to the past, many of those desiring assimilation had themselves baptized. The case of Heine is still exemplary as well as that of the convert Karl Marx. In contrast to the poet Heine, who neither denied nor denigrated his Jewishness despite his baptism, Karl Marx was a rabid, indeed an extreme anti-Semite, who fanatically attempted to eradicate his undesirable Jewish heritage by hatefully ridiculing his people and their God in everything he said and wrote.

In fact, complete assimilation was successful only for those who were descendants from mixed marriages of ancestors two, three, or four generations earlier. The secularized anti-Semites for their part effortlessly replaced the traditional religious basis of their hatred by a racial, nationalist, or social ideology. "The causes of hatred are inexhaustible; deeds inspired by hatred and their unavoidable consequences multiply these causes almost daily. The person who is hated, is powerless against collective hatred. It is not even certain that this hatred would disappear if its victim were to destroy himself."[2] These lines from my essay on hatred conceived twenty-five years ago were not written as a result of the organized destruction of the Jews. As a psychologist examining the psychic prerequisites of such extreme hatred, I came to the conclusion that the perpetrator of hatred, this untiring pursuer and persecutor, is himself pursued by an anxiety that would not cease to frighten him even if he were able to dance on the mass grave of his victims.

As for my existence as a Jew and my everyday mortal life, hatred has little significance—perhaps precisely because from early on I was able to perceive the hatred of the Jews as an extremely aggressive paranoia, as a completely false and therefore constantly unsuccessful overcompensation of a spirit and attitude of tyrannical allophobia, a fear of others run amok, but which the persecutor attempts to hide from his own consciousness. In his monomaniac enmity he convinces himself that he is superior to the object of his hatred whom he must not only despise but also fear, because of the latter's demonic cunning.

The oft-cited and more frequently misinterpreted self-hatred of Jews that accompanies their constant struggle to escape their identity—as often the latter's cause as it is its consequence—this self-hatred is in no way specifically Jewish, inasmuch as it governs anyone who identifies himself with those who despise him in the belief that, if he can not disarm them, he can in that way use them to his own advantage. People who separate their own judgment of themselves from that which others, namely their enemies, pass on them, act in this manner. Driven by a kind of basic insecurity, they constantly reflect on what their opponents might be thinking of them; most of all they fear displeasing those whom they sense as enemies or who, they feel, dislike them. Out of anxiety of being subjugated, they subjugate themselves; they despise themselves and become contemptible in the hope of escaping contempt. They pawn their honor to the enemy and disavow the basis of their existence.

The self-esteem of Jews like me is in no way affected by this anti-Semitic propensity toward self-deprecation and humiliation: we perceive the motives of those who despise us, and we despise them. It is easy for me, for example, to disregard Dostoyevsky's anti-Semitism and at the same time admire his work and pity the unfortunate man that he was. I turn away from a person at the moment that person feels ashamed, but I find myself looking him in the face when he attempts to shame me. I do not brag about the exemplary, truly inimitable religiosity of my forebears—I have only inherited it, not earned it. Yet, every anti-Semitic slur reminds me that I am their progeny, while those who spurn me are with few exceptions descendants of those who over the course of time have frequently and opportunistically switched their beliefs. They have destroyed that which they earlier worshipped and have worshipped what they had previously destroyed.

On the whole, the Jews are not more intelligent, more clever than their neighbors: they are no better, they are no worse; no more greedy; although frequently more helpful, no more generous; no more arrogant, no more modest. But over the centuries they have above all remained true to their teachers, and to the Prophets, by whom they have consistently been strictly and severely judged. Certainly, I can never forget how often my forefathers had to stoop even lower in order to save their bare skin. But they remained always the race of tough-skinned people of whom the Bible speaks. And, if it were not somewhat perverse to be proud of something that one did not actually accomplish oneself, but had only preserved, I would sing the praises of this tough skin. It may be—I say this half in jest—our only reward for the demanding blessing of being the chosen people.

As I indicated at the beginning, the lack of understanding for the peculiarities of its assimilated minorities which the host nation exhibits in its interaction with them corresponds more or less to an inadequate reaction, a specific lack of understanding, with which the minority views its hosts. The following misinterpretations are particularly in evidence: The religious or ethnic minority is inclined to overestimate its own importance and thereby fails to recognize the fact that the majority always makes its decisions in view of its own interests, that it does not seek to provide itself with most of the advantages at the expense of others. Every majority is egotistical, every minority becomes egotistical as soon as it becomes the majority or assimilates itself into a majority. The immigrant of long ago may forget that he is not a native, but the natives never forget.

Everywhere (except in Israel) the Jews constitute not only an ethnic, but also a religious minority which exercises its vested right to remain faithful to its traditions. Yet, they sense hostility whenever their special status is pointed out in discussions of nationality. As stated earlier, many Jews attempt to escape this apparent contradiction by breaking with tradition and in some instances by conversion. Now I am just such an irreligious

Jew. Not one of the numerous rituals that govern the daily lives and the holidays of the faithful has any significance for me. And yet, I have never felt inclined to deny my Jewishness nor to dissociate myself from it. If I am not religious and not an Israeli—what kind of Jew am I then? This question only permits a very personal reply, is pertinent therefore only for the individual, in this case me, and not for other Jews, whose situation might be similar to mine.

I am a Jew because I am the product of an early upbringing that was completely and pervasively Jewish. I was taught to view, understand, and interpret everything in relation to God's commandments: Even before I was of school age I was reading the Bible in the original plus a little German—for example, Grimm's fairy tales and the Viennese newspapers. I was thoroughly instructed in the rules of life based on the biblical ethic, the most peremptory of which has remained for me unchanged: to strive for the unison between belief and action, between theory and practice, and to live accordingly. I won't dare to claim that I always followed this commandment, but I have never stopped using certain standards to determine whether at any time my life was meaningful or whether I was in danger of frittering it away senselessly: to act as though one's behavior could be a model for others; never to forget that one is not only responsible for one's own actions, but for all the evil that one could prevent or at least lessen, to act always according to the advice that Rabbi Hillel bequeathed to us: "Don't do unto others what you would not have them do unto you!" And finally, to acknowledge that which one believes to be the truth—even if one has to stand alone with it, although one should not stand alone if at all possible, but rather opt for solidarity.

When several years later I came across Dostoyevsky's ruefully challenging statement—"We are guilty of everything!"—it seemed to me at first glance exaggerated and perversely megalomanic. But then I recognized and felt that the writer was indeed correct. In the end it was as if he were repeating a message that I had already received during my childhood. For that has been my Jewishness from the very beginning: solidarity with the Jews, clear and unquestionable identification with them—how should it be otherwise after all that has happened to them during this century?

And this, too, is my Jewishness: solidarity with those who are victims of injustice. That has been my socialism from the very beginning; it has remained my socialism despite the numerous unsuccessful and impatient efforts to bring about a world in which theory and practice would be united and would remain so forever. I feel in no way obliged to say "yes" to everything that my people do. On the contrary, I feel justified in being more critical than usual of that which is unjust, unworthy, too pretentious, or opportunistic and therefore inauthentic in their actions. I myself have experienced such strictures and made them unhesitatingly my own. But since then there have been years when being Jewish has signified inescapable suffering and unending compassion. What remained was not stricture but a minimal residue of confidence accompanied by a will to resist, though there was hardly any real possibility for resistance.

For decades hardly a day has gone by when I don't think of that period in which my people were humiliated, dehumanized, and exterminated by the ruling murderers in the heart of Europe. Hardly a day goes by that I don't remember the indifference with which the world allowed this to happen for years on end. Extreme loneliness resides in the likes of me now. The sun's warmth is interrupted by a cold shiver. What has transpired impinges on the present as if it were not a memory but rather an unceasingly repeated act of violence.

The events to which I refer here have not changed my Jewish nature, but they have—in the biblical sense—toughened my skin to the point of petrifying it. The enormous confidence with which I anticipated a future in which all peoples and nations would be reconciled and united—this confident sense of expectation I still have, but frequently I find it accompanied by my own irony or severe impatience. My memory has not grown weak. It still recalls the ships with Jewish refugees, crossing the oceans back and forth, ultimately to no avail since there was no one, no port and no country, neither the mightiest nor the smallest, which wanted to guarantee them even temporary asylum. I cannot but think back to those in the Warsaw Ghetto who provoked the ultimate enemy—like in some lunar landscape devoid of human habitation. They hoped for nothing since despair itself was no longer possible. They perished in a void. Yet, we live—helpless, innocently guilty of their demise, of everything.

The belated reply to these young victims could not come from Poland, nor from Europe, but only from Jewish Palestine, which won its statehood and national independence in struggles that had appeared hopeless. Secretly but effectively supported by the British, the Arabic armies attacked the country. The victory achieved by the Jews was gained not only through weapons. It was also the success of all those who had transformed a barren land into a habitable region, into a homeland. Without this rebirth of a young nation from ancient soil, Jewry would never have managed spiritually and psychologically to survive the catastrophe organized by the Germans, supported by other nations, and observed by the rest of the world with indifference. Jewry's misfortune would have turned into an incurable malady which could have destroyed the nation's vitality and, with it, the will to live. This fact was again made obvious to all contemporaries, Jews and non-Jews, in 1967, in those few weeks preceding the Six-Day War, when Nasser and all the other leaders of the Arab states announced ahead of time that their united armies would destroy Israel, the nation and the people, that they would annihilate them once and for all. In those weeks, the Western powers seemed strangely paralyzed. They prepared themselves to witness Israel's demise without doing anything and were ready to show deep sorrow about the forthcoming catastrophe. During those weeks in May and the first days of June, the Jews, even the most assimilated and even those who followed the anti-Zionist line of Moscow's foreign policy, grasped the fact that Israel's end would endanger their own existence. Even if they were indifferent toward Israel, her imminent destruction threatened their equilibrium. They suspected that they could escape the extermination only for a provisional period of time.

There is a kind of humiliation which neither an individual nor a people can survive without existence itself becoming questionable and identity becoming inadmissible and yet crystal clear. The rebels of the Warsaw Ghetto uprising had not fought for their own lives, but for the dignity of their people. In like manner Israel's men and women helped their people recover from its deepest humiliation and reconstituted their reason for existence, which had almost been totally destroyed.

I have never been an anti-Zionist and am today a declared opponent of anti-Zionists whether they are oriented ideologically to Moscow or to the pseudorevolutionary terrorists of both Europe and the Arab world. But I am also not a Zionist because I never believed nor do I believe now that the existence of a Jewish state can solve the Jewish question of the Diaspora. Nonetheless, I do give considerable credit to the post-1933 Zionist movement insofar as it saved so many human lives from extermination in Europe at a time when it was easier to let a thousand Jews die than to save a single one from the murderers.

Yet, another reason makes me defend that truly democratic nation created under the aegis of Zionism: it was here that the kibbutz could develop, the only communal form in this century of pseudocommunist despotism that has combined the concept of socialism with the practical aspects of communal life. The kibbutz is proof that without believing in God or in a Messiah sent by him, it is possible, according to the basic commandments as prophesied by Judaism, to align oneself with a permanent group in which no one is the object of the other, but always remains a companion. Even though such organization does not in any way presume Jewish lineage for its members, the success of the kibbutz can nevertheless be explained on the basis of that kind of education to which I, too, was exposed. This socialist community has up to now remained a Jewish, an

Israeli phenomenon whereas so many similar attempts, particularly during the first half of the nineteenth century, ended rather quickly in failure, ruined by ideological and personal conflicts.

These remarks about my being a Jew are intended primarily for German readers—thirty-three years after the end of the tyrannical reign of Hitler and his innumerable accomplices, whom millions more served as cohorts. To be sure, it would not be unreasonable to turn from the past completely and follow the old adage, "Let the dead bury the dead." But my nature and particularly my kind of Jewishness does not accommodate this kind of amnesia. I have to be faithful to my godless religion "of a clear conscience." That means neither bitterness nor revenge, but rather a conscious experience of life and living, so to speak, against the grain. The essence of what I've tried to articulate about my position with regard to the Jewish question is contained in the following excerpt from a letter to a gentile colleague of mine:

> Yes, the philo-Semitism inherent in what you wrote worries me, and humiliates me as would a compliment based upon an absurd misunderstanding—a compliment that one would rather not have deserved.
>
> You dangerously overestimate us Jews, you insist on loving our entire people. I do not ask, I decidedly do not wish, that we be loved in this fashion (we, for that matter any other people). . . . The pitiless battle against anti-Semitism is your concern. For if this hatred is sometimes a mortal danger to us, for you it is a disease, a cancer, that you carry within yourselves. It has made us suffer horribly but we continue to overcome it, each day. The proof of this? We are free of all hatred towards you, and we feel ourselves fraternally linked with you in the defense of all those values which justify the presence of man here on earth.
>
> *"The world is yours, and your world is filled with murder—why? God is just: He makes us the victims, but He makes you the executioners."*
>
> You reproach me for these words which I put into the mouth of a young Jewish boy, dying at the hands of his Christian brothers-in-arms. You recall the terrible deeds of which my ancestors were guilty long ago in the land of Canaan. This is unnecessary, for I have not forgotten. That is why I do not imagine for one instant that my people are any less capable of practicing total hatred. But we have never pretended to be 'new men,' quite the contrary, for we have never ceased to affirm that the Messiah has not come.[3]

No sacrificial death, no redeemer's grace brings the longed-for transformation, for the coming of the Messiah depends on us ourselves, on all of us, on the deeds of every one of us.

I have never found an idea that so overwhelmed me or guided me so forcefully as the idea that this world cannot remain as it is, that it can be different, that it will be different. Ever since I can remember, this single challenging certitude has determined my being a Jew and an active individual of our times.

Translated by Robert A. Jones

NOTES

1. The novel referred to is the trilogy *Eine Trañe im Ozean* (Europa Verlag, 1961). More specifically this incident takes place in the third part, *Die verlorene Bucht.—Ed. Note*

2. See "On Hatred" in *The Achilles Heel* (New York, 1960), pp. 111–134.—*Ed. Note*

3. *The Achilles Heel*, pp. 133–134.—*Ed. Note*

5

ON THE NECESSITY AND
IMPOSSIBILITY OF BEING A JEW
Jean Améry

Not seldom, when in conversation my partner draws me into a plural—
that is, as soon as he includes my person in whatever connection and says
to me: "We Jews . . ."—I feel a not exactly tormenting, but nonetheless
deep-seated discomfort. I have long tried to get to the bottom of this
disconcerting psychic state, and it has not been very easy for me. Can it be,
is it thinkable that I, the former Auschwitz inmate, who truly has not
lacked occasion to recognize what he is and what he must be, still did not
want to be a Jew, as decades ago, when I wore white half socks and leather
breeches and nervously eyed myself in the mirror, hoping it would show
me an impressive German youth? Naturally not. The foolishness of my
masquerading in Austrian dress—although it was, after all, part of my
heritage—belongs to the distant past. It is all right with me that I was not
a German youth and am not a German man. No matter how the disguise
may have looked on me, it now lies in the attic. If today discomfort arises
in me when a Jew takes it for granted, legitimately, that I am part of his
community, then it is not because I don't want to be a Jew, but only
because I cannot be one. And yet must be one. And I do not merely

    This essay is a translation of Améry's "Zwang und Unmöglichkeit, Jude zu sein," which
appeared in *Jenseits von Schuld und Sühne* (Stuttgart, 1976). This book was published by
Indiana University Press in 1980 as *At the Mind's Limits: Contemplations by a Survivor on
Auschwitz and Its Realities,* and the essay is printed here with permission of the publisher.

submit to this necessity, but expressly claim it as part of my person. The necessity and impossibility of being a Jew, that is what causes me indistinct pain. It is with this necessity, this impossibility, this oppression, this inability that I must deal here, and in doing so I can only hope, without certainty, that my individual story is exemplary enough also to reach those who neither are nor have to be Jews.

First of all, concerning this impossibility. If being a Jew means sharing a religious creed with other Jews, participating in Jewish cultural and family tradition, cultivating a Jewish national ideal, then I find myself in a hopeless situation. I don't believe in the God of Israel. I know very little about Jewish culture. I see myself as a boy at Christmas, plodding through a snow-covered village to midnight mass; I don't see myself in a synagogue. I hear my mother appealing to Jesus, Mary, and Joseph when a minor household misfortune occurred; I hear no adjuration of the Lord in Hebrew. The picture of my father—whom I hardly knew, since he remained where his Kaiser had sent him and his fatherland deemed him to be in the safest care—did not show me a bearded Jewish sage, but rather a Tyrolean Imperial Rifleman in the uniform of the First World War. I was nineteen years old when I heard of the existence of a Yiddish language, although on the other hand I knew full well that my religiously and ethnically very mixed family was regarded by the neighbors as Jewish, and that no one in my home thought of denying or hiding what was uncon-cealable anyhow. I was a Jew, just as one of my schoolmates was the son of a bankrupt innkeeper: when the boy was alone the financial ruin of his family may have meant next to nothing to him; when he joined us others he retreated, as we did, into resentful embarrassment.

If being a Jew implies having a cultural heritage or religious ties, then I was not one and can never become one. Certainly, it could be argued that a heritage can be acquired, ties established, and that therefore to be a Jew could be a matter of voluntary decision. Who would possibly prevent me from learning the Hebrew language, from reading Jewish history and tales, and from participating—even without belief—in Jewish ritual, which is both religious and national? Well supplied with all the requisite knowledge of Jewish culture from the prophets to Martin Buber, I could emigrate to Israel and call myself Yochanan. I have the freedom to choose to be a Jew, and this freedom is my very personal and universally human privilege. That is what I am assured of.

But do I really have it? I don't believe so. Would Yochanan, the proud bearer of a new self-acquired identity, be made immune on the 24th of December by his supposedly thorough knowledge of chassidism against thoughts of a Christmas tree with gilded nuts? Would the upright Israeli, conversing fluently in Hebrew, be able so completely to obliterate the white-stockinged youth who once took such pains to speak a local dialect? In modern literature the switch of identity is quite a stimulating game, but in my case it is a challenge that one meets with no certainty of success, in one's human totality, without the chance of an interim solution, and would—it seems to me—be wholly predestined to fail. One can reestablish the link with a tradition that one has lost, but one cannot freely invent it for oneself, that is the problem. Since I was not a Jew, I am not one; and since I am not one, I won't be able to become one. A Yochanan on Mt. Carmel, haunted and spirited home by memories of Alpine valleys and folk rituals, would be even more inauthentic than was once the youth with his knee socks. To be who one is by becoming the person one should be and wants to be: for me this dialectical process of self-realization is obstructed. Because being Something, not as metaphysical essence, but as the simple summation of early experience, absolutely has priority. Everyone must be who he was in the first years of his life, even if later these were buried under. No one can become what he cannot find in his memories.

Thus I am not permitted to be a Jew. But since all the same I must be one and since this compulsion excludes the possibilities that might allow me to be something other than a Jew, can I not find myself at all? Must I acquiesce, without a past, as a shadow of the universal-abstract (which does not exist) and take refuge in the empty phrase that I am simply a human being? But patience, we haven't reached that point yet. Since the necessity exists—and how compelling it is!—perhaps the impossibility can be resolved. After all, one wants to live without hiding, as I did when I was in the underground, and without dissolving into the abstract. A human being? Certainly, who would not want to be one? But you are a human being only if you are a German, a Frenchman, a Christian, a member of whatever identifiable social group. I must be a Jew and will be one, with or without religion, within or outside a tradition, whether as Jean, Hans, or Yochanan. Why I must be one is what will be told here.

It didn't begin when schoolmates said to the boy: You're Jews anyway. Nor with the fight on the ramp of the university, during which, long before Hitler's ascent to power, a Nazi fist knocked out one of my teeth. Yes, we are Jews, and what of it? I answered my schoolmate. Today my tooth, tomorrow yours, and the devil take you, I thought to myself after the beating, and bore the gap proudly like an interesting duelling scar.

It didn't begin until 1935, when I was sitting over a newspaper in a Vienna coffeehouse and was studying the Nuremberg Laws, which had just been enacted across the border in Germany. I needed only to skim them and already I could perceive that they applied to me. Society, concretized in the National Socialist German state, which the world recognized absolutely as the legitimate representative of the German people, had just made me formally and beyond any question a Jew, or rather it had given a new dimension to what I had already known earlier, but which at the time was of no great consequence to me, namely, that I was a Jew.

What sort of new dimension? Not one that was immediately fathomable. After I had read the Nuremberg Laws I was no more Jewish than a half hour before. My features had not become more Mediterranean-Semitic, my frame of reference had not suddenly been filled by magic power with Hebrew allusions, the Christmas tree had not wondrously transformed itself into the seven-armed candelabrum. If the sentence that society has passed on me had a tangible meaning, it could only be that henceforth I was a quarry of Death. Well, sooner or later it claims all of us. But the Jew—and I now was one by decree of law and society—was more firmly promised to death, already in the midst of life. His days were a period of false grace that could be revoked at any second. I do not believe that I am inadmissibly projecting Auschwitz and the Final Solution back to 1935 when I advance these thoughts today. Rather, I am certain that in that year, at that moment when I read the Laws, I did indeed already hear the death threat—better, the death sentence—and certainly no special sensitivity toward history was required for that. Had I not already heard a hundred times the appeal to fate—coupled with the call for Germany's awakening—that the Jew should perish? "Jude verrecke!"—that was something completely different from the almost cheerful "L'aristocrat, à la lanterne!" Even if one did not consider or did not know that historically it linked up with countless pogroms of the past, it was not a revolutionary clamor, but rather the carefully considered demand of a people, compressed into a slogan, a war cry! Also in those same days I had once seen in a German magazine the photo of a Winter Relief event in a Rhenish town, and in the foreground, in front of the tree gleaming with electric lights, there was proudly displayed a banner with the text: "No one shall go hungry, no one shall freeze, but the Jews shall die like dogs." And only three years later, on the day of Austria's incorporation into the *Grossdeutsches Reich*, I heard Joseph Goebbels screaming on the radio that one really ought not to make such a fuss about the fact that in Vienna a few Jews were now committing suicide.

To be a Jew, that meant for me, from this moment on, to be a dead man on leave, someone to be murdered, who only by chance was not yet where he properly belonged; and so it has remained, in many variations, in various degrees of intensity, until today. The death threat, which I felt for the first time with complete clarity while reading the Nuremberg Laws, included what is commonly referred to as the methodic "degradation" of the Jews by the Nazis. Formulated differently: The denial of human dignity sounded the death threat. Daily, for years on end, we could read and hear that we were lazy, evil, ugly, capable only of misdeed, clever only to the extent that we pulled one over on others. We were incapable of founding a state, but also by no means suited to assimilate with our host nations. By their very presence, our bodies—hairy, fat, and bowlegged—befouled public swimming pools, yes, even park benches. Our hideous faces, depraved and spoilt by protruding ears and hanging noses, were disgusting to our fellow men, fellow citizens of yesterday. We were not worthy of love and thus also not of life. Our sole right, our sole duty was to disappear from the face of the earth.

The degradation of the Jews was, I am convinced, identical with the death threat long before Auschwitz. In this regard Jean-Paul Sartre, already in 1946 in his book *Anti-Semite and Jew,* offered a few perceptions that are still valid today. There is no "Jewish Problem," he said, only a problem of anti-Semitism; the anti-Semite forced the Jew into a situation in which he permitted his enemy to stamp him with a self-image. Both points appear to me to be unassailable. But in his short phenomenological sketch Sartre could not describe the total, crushing force of anti-Semitism, a force that had brought the Jew to that point, quite aside from the fact that the great author himself probably did not comprehend in its entire overwhelming might. The Jew—and Sartre speaks here, without making a value judgment, of the "inauthentic" Jew, that is, the Jew who has fallen victim to the myth of the "universal man"—subjugates himself, in his flight from the Jewish fate, to the power of his oppressor. But one must say in his favor that in the years of the Third Reich the Jew stood with his back to the wall, and it too was hostile. There was no way out. Because it was not only radical Nazis, officially certified by the party, who denied that we were worthy of being loved and thereby worthy of life. All of Germany—but what am I saying!—the whole world nodded its head in approval of the undertaking, even if here and there with a certain superficial regret.

One must remember: when after World War II streams of refugees poured out of the various Communist-ruled lands into the West, the countries of the proclaimed free world outdid one another in their willingness to grant asylum and aid, although among all the emigrants there was only a handful whose lives would have been directly threatened in their homeland. But even when it long since should have been clear to any discerning person what awaited us in the German Reich, no one wanted to have us. Thus, it necessarily had to reach the point where the Jews, whether authentic or not, whether secure in the illusion of a God and a national hope, or assimilated, found within themselves no powers of resistance when their enemy burned the image from Streicher's *Stürmer* into their skin. It should be noted that this weakness had only little to do with the classical Jewish self-hatred of those German Jews of the time before the outbreak of Nazism who were not only willing but craving to assimilate. The self-haters had believed that they were unable to be what they so much wanted to be: Germans, and therefore they rejected themselves. They had not wanted to accept their existence as non-Germans, but no one had forced them to reject themselves as Jews. When, on the other hand, between 1933 and 1945 precisely the brightest and most upright Jewish minds, authentic or inauthentic, capitulated to Streicher, that was a wholly different act of resignation, no longer moral, but rather social and philosophic in nature. This, so they must have told themselves, is how the world sees us, as lazy, ugly, useless, and evil; in view of such universal agreement what sense does it still make to object and say that we *are* not that way! The surrender of the Jews to the *Stürmer* image of themselves was nothing other than the acknowledgment of a social reality. To oppose it with a self-evaluation based on other standards at times had to appear ridiculous or mad.

In order to discuss it, however, one must have experienced it. When I think about the social reality of the wall of rejection that arose before us everywhere, my stay in Auschwitz-Monowitz comes to mind. In the camp itself, but also among the so-called free workers at the worksite, there was a strict ethnic hierarchy, imposed by the Nazis on all of us. A German from the Reich was regarded more highly than a German from an Eastern country. A Flemish Belgian was worth more than a Walloon. A Ukrainian from occupied Poland ranked higher than his Polish compatriot. A forced laborer from Eastern Europe was more poorly regarded than an Italian. Far down on the bottom rungs of the ladder were the concentration camp inmates, and among them, in turn, the Jews had the lowest rank. There was not a single non-Jewish professional criminal, no matter how degenerate he may have been, who did not stand high above us. The Poles, whether they were genuine freedom fighters who had been thrown into the camp after the ill-fated Warsaw insurrection, or merely small-time pickpockets, despised us unanimously. So did half-illiterate White Russian workers. But also Frenchmen. I still hear a free French worker conversing with a Jewish-French concentration camp inmate: "I'm French," the inmate said. "Français, toi? Mais, tu es juif, mon ami," his countryman retorted objectively and without hostility; for in a mixture of fear and indifference he had absorbed the teachings of Europe's German masters. I repeat: the world approved of the place to which the Germans had assigned us, the small world of the camp and the wide world outside, which but rarely, in individual heroic instances, arose in protest when we were taken at night from our homes in Vienna or Berlin, in Amsterdam, Paris, or Brussels.

The degradation proceedings directed against us Jews, which began with the proclamation of the Nuremberg Laws and as a direct result led all the way to Treblinka, met on our, on my, side with an equivalent proceeding aimed at the reattainment of dignity. For me, until today, this case is not closed. Let my endeavor to gain clarity concerning its stages and its preliminary result be recorded here, and permit me to request that the reader accompany me awhile along this path. It is short, but difficult to tread, and full of obstacles and traps. For what, after all, actually is the nature of the dignity that was first denied me in 1935, officially withheld from me until 1945, and that perhaps even today one does not want to grant me, and that I must therefore attain through my own effort? What is dignity, really?

One can try to answer by inverting the above-formulated identification of degradation and death threat. If I was correct that the deprivation of dignity was nothing other than the potential deprivation of life, then dignity would have to be the right to live. If it was also correct when I said that the granting and depriving of dignity are acts of social agreement, sentences against which there is no appeal on the grounds of one's "self-understanding," so that it would be senseless to argue against the social body that deprives us of our dignity with the claim that we do indeed "feel" worthy—if all of this were valid, then every effort to regain our dignity would have been of no value, and it would still be so today. Degradation, that is, living under the threat of death, would be an inescapable fate. But luckily, things are not entirely the way this logic claims. It is certainly true that dignity can be bestowed only by society, whether it be the dignity of some office, a professional or, very generally speaking, civil dignity, and the merely individual, subjective claim ("I am a human being and as such I have my dignity, no matter what you may do or say!") is an empty academic game, or madness. Still, the degraded person, threatened with death, is able—and here we break through the logic of the final sentencing—to convince society of his dignity by taking his fate upon himself and at the same time rising in revolt against it.

The first step must be the unqualified recognition that the verdict of the social group is a given reality. When I read the Nuremberg Laws in 1935 and realized not only that they applied to me but also that they were the expression, concentrated in legal-textual form, of the verdict "Death to the Jews!" which already earlier had been pronounced by German society, I could have taken intellectual flight, turned on the defense mechanisms, and thereby have lost my case for rehabilitation. Then I would have told myself: Well, well, so this is the will of the National Socialist state, of the German *pays légal;* but it has nothing to do with the real Germany, the *pays réel,* which has not thought whatever of ostracizing me. Or I could have argued that it was only Germany, a land unfortunately sinking into a bloody madness, that was so absurdly stamping me as subhuman (in the literal sense of the word), whereas to my good fortune the great wide world outside, in which there are Englishmen, Frenchmen, Americans, and Russians, is immune to the collective paranoia scourging Germany. Or finally, even if I had abandoned the illusion both of a German *pays réel* and of a world immune against the German mental disorder, I could have comforted myself with the thought: No matter what they say about me, it isn't true. I am true only as I see and understand myself deep within; I am what I am for myself and in myself, and nothing else.

I am not saying that now and then I did not succumb to such temptation. I can only testify that finally I learned to resist it and that already at that time, in 1935, I vaguely felt the necessity to convince the world of my dignity, the world that by no means indignantly and unanimously broke off all relations with the Third Reich. I understood, even if unclearly, that while I had to accept the verdict as such, I could force the world to revise it. I accepted the judgment of the world, with the decision to overcome it through revolt.

Revolt, well, of course, that is another one of those high-sounding words. It could lead the reader to believe that I was a hero or that I falsely want to present myself as one. I certainly was no hero. When the little gray Volkswagen with the POL license plate crossed my path, first in Vienna, then in Brussels, I was so afraid that I couldn't breathe. When the Kapo drew back his arm to strike me, I didn't stand firm like a cliff, but ducked. And still, I tried to initiate proceedings to regain my dignity, and beyond physical survival that provided me with just the slightest chance to survive the nightmare morally also. There is not much that I can present in my favor, but let it be noted anyhow. I took it upon myself to be a Jew, even though there would have been possibilities for a compromise settlement. I joined a resistance movement whose prospects for success were very dim. Also, I finally relearned what I and my kind often had forgotten and what was more crucial than the moral power to resist: to hit back.

Before me I see the prisoners' foreman Juszek, a Polish professional criminal of horrifying vigor. In Auschwitz he once hit me in the face because of a trifle; that is how he was used to dealing with all the Jews under his command. At this moment—I felt it with piercing clarity—it was up to me to go a step further in my prolonged appeals case against society. In open revolt I struck Juszek in the face in turn. My human dignity lay in this punch to his jaw—and that it was in the end I, the physically much weaker man, who succumbed and was woefully thrashed, meant nothing to me. Painfully beaten, I was satisfied with myself. But not, as one might think, for reasons of courage and honor, but only because I had grasped well that there are situations in life in which our body is our entire self and our entire fate. I was my body and nothing else: in hunger, in the blow that I suffered, in the blow that I dealt. My body, debilitated and crusted with filth, was my calamity. My body, when it tensed to strike, was my physical and metaphysical dignity. In situations like mine, physical violence is the sole means for restoring a disjointed personality. In the punch, I was myself—for myself and for my opponent. What I later read in Frantz Fanon's *Les damnés de la terre*, in a theoretical analysis of the behavior of colonized peoples, I anticipated back then when I gave concrete social form to my dignity by punching a human face. To be a Jew meant the acceptance of the death sentence imposed by the world as a world verdict. To flee before it by withdrawing into one's self would have been nothing but a disgrace, whereas acceptance was simultaneously the physical revolt against it. I became a person not by subjectively appealing to my abstract humanity but by discovering myself within the given social reality as a rebelling Jew and by realizing myself as one.

The proceedings, I said, went on and still go on. At present, I have neither won nor lost the case. After the collapse of the National Socialist Reich there was a brief global hour in which I was able to believe that from the bottom up everything was transformed. For a short time in those days I was able to foster the illusion that my dignity was totally restored, through my own, no matter how modest, activity in the resistance movement, through the heroic uprising in the Warsaw Ghetto, but above all through the contempt that the world showed toward those who had stripped me of my dignity. I could believe that the deprivation of dignity that we had experienced had been a historical error, an aberration, a collective sickness of the world, from which the latter had recovered at the moment when in Reims German generals signed the declaration of surrender in the presence of Eisenhower. Soon I learned worse. In Poland and in the Ukraine, while they were still discovering Jewish mass graves, there were anti-Semitic disturbances. In France the ever sickly petty bourgeoisie had allowed itself to be infected by the occupiers. When survivors and refugees returned and demanded their old dwellings, it happened that simple housewives, in a peculiar mixture of satisfaction and chagrin, said: "Tiens, ils reviennent, on ne les a tout de même pas tué." Even in countries that previously had hardly known any anti-Semitism, as in Holland, there suddenly existed as a relic of the German propaganda a "Jewish Problem," though scarcely any more Jews. England barred its Mandate of Palestine to those Jews who had escaped from the camps and jails and who tried to immigrate. In a very short time I was forced to recognize that little had changed, that I was still the man condemned to be murdered in due time, even though the potential executioner now cautiously restrained himself or, at best, even loudly protested his disapproval of what had happened.

I understood reality. But should this perhaps have occasioned me to come to grips with the problem of anti-Semitism? Not at all. Anti-Semitism and the Jewish Question, as historical, socially determined conceptual phenomena, were not and are not any concern of mine. They are entirely a matter for the anti-Semites, their disgrace or their sickness. The anti-Semites have something to overcome, not I. I would play into their unclean hands if I began investigating what share religious, economic, or other factors have in the persecution of the Jews. If I were to engage in such investigations I would only be falling for the intellectual dupery of so-called historical objectivity, according to which the murdered are as guilty as the murderers, if not even more guilty. A wound was inflicted on me. I must disinfect and bind it, not contemplate why the ruffian raised his club, and, through the inferred "That's Why," in the end partly absolve him.

It was not the anti-Semites who concerned me, it was only with my own existence that I had to cope. That was hard enough. Certain possibilities, which had emerged for me in the war years, no longer existed. From 1945 to 1947 I could not very well sew on a yellow star without appearing foolish or eccentric to myself. There also was no longer any opportunity to punch the enemy in his face, for he was not so easy to recognize anymore. The reattainment of dignity, just as urgent as in the previous years of war and National Socialism, but now—in a climate of deceptive peace— infinitely more difficult, remained a compulsion and desire. Except that I had to recognize even more clearly than in the days when physical revolt was at least possible that I was confronted with necessity and impossibility.

At this point I must stop for a moment and separate myself from all those Jews who do not speak from the realm of my own experience. In his book *La condition réflexive de l'homme juif* the French philosopher Robert Misrahi said: "The Nazi Holocaust is henceforth the absolute and radical reference point for the existence of every Jew." That is not to be doubted, yet I am convinced that not every Jew is capable of thinking out this relationship. Only those who have lived through a fate like mine, and no one else, can refer their lives to the years 1933–45. By no means do I say this with pride. It would be ridiculous enough to boast of something that one did not do but only underwent. Rather it is with a certain shame that I assert my sad privilege and suggest that while the Holocaust is truly the existential reference point for all Jews, only we, the sacrificed, are able to spiritually relive the catastrophic event as it was or fully picture it as it could be again. Let others not be prevented from empathizing. Let them contemplate a fate that yesterday could have been and tomorrow can be theirs. Their intellectual efforts will meet with our respect, but it will be a sceptical one, and in conversation with them we will soon grow silent and say to ourselves: Go ahead, good people, trouble your heads as much as you want; you still sound like a blind man talking about color.

The parentheses are now closed. I am once again alone with myself and a few good comrades. I find myself in the postwar years, which no longer permit any of us to react with violence to something that refused to reveal itself clearly to us. Again I see myself confronted with necessity and impossibility.

That this impossibility does not apply to all is obvious. Among the Jews of this time, whether they be workers in Kiev, storekeepers in Brooklyn, or farmers in Negev, there are enough men and women for whom being a Jew was and always remained a positive fact. They speak Yiddish or Hebrew. They celebrate the sabbath. They explicate the Talmud or stand at attention as young soldiers under the blue-and-white banner with the Star of David. Whether religiously or nationally or merely in personal reverence before the picture of their grandfather with his sidelocks, they are *Jews* as members of a community. One could briefly digress perhaps and, together with the sociologist Georges Friedmann, ask the secondary question of whether their progeny will still be Jews and whether the end of the Jewish people may not be imminent in that Mediterranean country where the Israeli is already displacing the Jew, as well as in the Diaspora, where perhaps the total assimilation of the Jews—not so much to their host peoples, who for their part are losing their national character, but to the larger unity of the technical-industrial world—could take place.

I'll not pursue this question further. The existence or the disappearance of the Jewish people as an ethnic-religious community does not excite me. In my deliberation I am unable to consider Jews who are Jews because they are sheltered by tradition. I can speak solely for myself—and, even if with caution, for contemporaries, probably numbering into the millions, whose being Jewish burst upon them with elemental force, and who must stand this test without God, without history, without messianic-national hope. For them, for me, being a Jew means feeling the tragedy of yesterday as an inner oppression. On my left forearm I bear the Auschwitz number; it reads more briefly than the Pentateuch or the Talmud and yet provides more thorough information. It is also more binding than basic formulas of Jewish existence. If to myself and the world, including the religious and nationally minded Jews, who do not regard me as one of their own, I say: I am a Jew, then I mean by that those realities and possibilities that are summed up in the Auschwitz number.

In the two decades that have passed since my liberation I have gradually come to realize that it does not matter whether an existence can be positively defined. Sartre had already said once that a Jew is a person who is regarded by others as a Jew, and later Max Frisch dramatically portrayed this in *Andorra*. This view does not need to be corrected, but perhaps one may amplify it. For even if the others do not decide that I am a Jew, as they did with the poor devil in *Andorra*, who would have liked to become a carpenter and whom they permitted only to be a merchant, I am still a Jew by the mere fact that the world around me does not expressly designate me as a non-Jew. To be something can mean that one is *not* something else. As a Non-non-Jew, I am a Jew; I must be one and must want to be one. I must accept this and affirm it in my daily existence, whether—showing my colors—I butt into a conversation when stupid things are said about Jews at the greengrocery, whether I address an unknown audience on the radio, or whether I write for a magazine.

But since being a Jew not only means that I bear within me a catastrophe that occurred yesterday and cannot be ruled out for tomorrow, it is—beyond being a duty—also *fear*. Every morning when I get up I can read the Auschwitz number on my forearm, something that touches the deepest and most closely intertwined roots of my existence; indeed I am not even sure if this is not my entire existence. Then I feel approximately as I did back then when I got a taste of the first blow from a policeman's fist. Every day anew I lose my trust in the world. The Jew without positive determinants, the Catastrophe Jew, as we will unhesitatingly call him, must get along without trust in the world. My neighbor greets me in a friendly fashion, *Bonjour, Monsieur;* I doff my hat, *Bonjour, Madame.* But Madame and Monsieur are separated by interstellar distances; for yesterday a Madame looked away when they led off a Monsieur, and through the barred windows of the departing car a Monsieur viewed a Madame as if she were a stone angel from a bright and stern heaven, which is forever closed for the Jew. I read an official announcement in which "la population" is called upon to do something or other, told that the trash cans are to be put out on time or that the flag is to be displayed on a national holiday. *La population.* Still another one of those unearthly realms that I can enter as little as I can Kafka's castle; for yesterday "la population" had great fear of hiding me, and whether tomorrow it would have more courage if I knocked at the door, unfortunately is not certain.

Twenty years have passed since the Holocaust. Glorious years for such as us. Nobel prize winners in abundance. There were French presidents named René Mayer and Pierre Mendès-France; an American UN delegate by the name of Goldberg practices a most dignified anticommunist American patriotism. I don't trust this peace. Declarations of human rights, democratic constitutions, the free world and the free press, nothing can again lull me into the slumber of security from which I awoke in 1935. As a Jew I go through life like a sick man with one of those ailments that cause no great hardships but are certain to end fatally. He didn't always suffer from that sickness. When he attempts, like Peer Gynt, to peel his self out of the onion, he doesn't discover the malady. His first walk to school, his first love, his first verses had nothing to do with it. But now he is a sick man, first and foremost and more deeply than he is a tailor, a bookkeeper, or a poet. Thus, I too am precisely what I am not, because I did not exist until I became it, above all else: a Jew. Death, from which the sick man will be unable to escape, is what threatens me. *Bonjour, Madame, Bonjour, Monsieur,* they greet each other. But she cannot and will not relieve her sick neighbor of his mortal illness at the cost of suffering to death from it herself. And so they remain strangers to one another.

Without trust in the world I face my surroundings as a Jew who is alien and alone, and all that I can manage is to get along within my foreignness. I must accept being foreign as an essential element of my personality, insist upon it as if upon an inalienable possession. Still and each day anew I find myself alone. I was unable to force yesterday's murderers and tomorrow's potential aggressors to recognize the moral truth of their crimes, because the world, in its totality, did not help me to do it. Thus I am alone, as I was when they tortured me. Those around me do not appear to me as anti-humans, as did my former torturers; they are my cohumans, not affected by me and the danger prowling at my side. I pass them with a greeting and without hostility. I cannot rely on them, only on a Jewish identity that is without positive determinants, my burden and my support.

Where there is a common bond between me and the world, whose still unrevoked death sentence I acknowledge as a social reality, it dissolves in polemics. You don't want to listen? Listen anyhow. You don't want to know to where your indifference can again lead you and me at any time? I'll tell you. What happened is no concern of yours because you didn't know, or were too young, or not even born yet? You should have seen, and your youth gives you no special privilege, and break with your father.

Once again I must ask myself the question that I already raised fleetingly in my essay "Resentments": Am I perhaps mentally ill and am I not suffering from an incurable ailment, from hysteria? The question is merely rhetorical. I have long since provided myself with a fully conclusive answer. I know that what oppresses me is no neurosis, but rather precisely reflected reality. Those were no hysteric hallucinations when I heard the Germans call for the Jews to "die like a dog!" and, in passing, heard how people said that there really must be something suspicious about the Jews, because otherwise they would hardly be treated so severely. "They were being arrested, so they must have done something," said a proper social-democratic worker's wife in Vienna. "How horrible, what they are doing with the Jews, *mais enfin . . .* ," speculated a humane and patriotic-minded man in Brussels. I am thus forced to conclude that I am not deranged and was not deranged, but rather that the neurosis is on the part of the historical occurrence. The others are the madmen, and I am left standing around helplessly among them, a fully sane person who joined a tour through a psychiatric clinic and suddenly lost sight of the doctors and orderlies. But since the sentence passed on me by the madmen can, after all, be carried out at any moment, it is totally binding, and my own mental lucidity is entirely irrelevant.

These reflections are nearing their end. Now that I have explained how I manage in this world, it is time to testify how I relate to my kinsmen, the Jews. But are they really related to me after all? Whatever an ethnologist may determine—for example, that my external appearance presents one or another Jewish characteristic—may be relevant if I land in a screaming mob that is hounding Jews. It loses all significance when I am alone or among Jews. Do I have a Jewish nose? That could become a calamity if a pogrom breaks out again. But that does not align me with a single other Jewish nose anywhere. The Jewish appearance that I may or may not have—I don't know if I do—is a matter for the others and becomes my concern only in the objective relationship they establish toward me. If I were to look as if I had stepped out of Johann von Leer's book *Juden sehen euch an,* it would have no subjective reality for me; it would, to be sure, establish a community of fate, but no positive community between me and my fellow Jews. Thus there remains only the intellectual—more correctly, the consciously perceived—relationship of Jews, Judaism, and myself.

That is a nonrelationship I have already stated at the outset. With Jews as Jews I share practically nothing: no language, no cultural tradition, no childhood memories. In the Austrian region of Vorarlberg there was an innkeeper and butcher of whom I was told that he spoke fluent Hebrew. He was my great-grandfather. I never saw him and it must be nearly a hundred years since he died. Before the Holocaust my interest in Jewish things and Jews was so slight that with the best of intentions I could not say today which of my acquaintances at that time was a Jew and which was not. However I might try to find in Jewish history my own past, in Jewish culture my own heritage, in Jewish folklore my personal recollections, the result would be nil. The environment in which I had lived in the years when one acquires one's self was not Jewish, and that cannot be reversed. But the fruitlessness of the search for my Jewish self by no means stands as a barrier between me and my solidarity with every threatened Jew in this world.

I read in the paper that in Moscow they discovered an illegally operating bakery for unleavened Jewish Passover bread and arrested the bakers. As a means of nourishment the ritual *matzoth* of the Jews interests me somewhat less than rye crisps. Nevertheless, the action of the Soviet authorities fills me with uneasiness, indeed with indignation. Some American country club, so I hear, does not accept Jews as members. Not for the world would I wish to belong to this obviously dismal middle-class association, but the cause of the Jews who demand permission to join becomes mine. That some Arab statesman calls for Israel to be wiped off the map cuts me to the quick, even though I have never visited the state of Israel and do not feel the slightest inclination to live there. My solidarity with every Jew whose freedom, equal rights, or perhaps even physical existence is threatened is *also*, but *not only*, a reaction to anti-Semitism, which, according to Sartre, is not an opinion but the predisposition and readiness to commit the crime of genocide. This solidarity is part of my person and a weapon in the battle to regain my dignity. Without being a Jew in the sense of a positive identification, it is not until I am a Jew in the recognition and acknowledgment of the world verdict on the Jews and not until I finally participate in the historical appeals process that I may speak of freedom.

Solidarity in the face of threat is all that links me with my Jewish contemporaries, the believers as well as the nonbelievers, the national-minded as well as those ready to assimilate. For them that is perhaps little or nothing at all. For me and my continued existence it means much, more probably than my appreciation of Proust's books or my affection for the stories of Schnitzler or my joy in seeing the Flemish landscape. Without Proust and Schnitzler and the wind-bent poplars at the North Sea I would be poorer than I am, but I would still be human. Without the feeling of belonging to the threatened I would be a self-surrendering fugitive from reality.

I say reality, with emphasis, because in the end that is what matters to me. Anti-Semitism, which made a Jew of me, may be a form of madness; that is not what is in question here. Whether it is a madness or not, it is in any event a historical and social fact. I was, after all, really in Auschwitz and not in Himmler's imagination. And anti-Semitism is still a reality; only someone with complete social and historical blindness could deny it. It is a reality in its core countries, Austria and Germany, where Nazi war criminals either are not convicted or receive ridiculously mild prison sentences, of which for the most part they serve hardly a third. It is a reality in England and the United States, where one tolerates the Jews, but would not be unhappy to be rid of them. It is a reality, and with what dire consequences, in the spiritual global domain of the Catholic Church. The complexity and confusion of the Vatican Council's consultations on the so-called Declaration on the Jews were, despite the honorable effort of so many a prelate, grievously shameful.

It may well be—but in view of the given circumstances one can by no means count on it—that in the Nazi death factories the final act was played in the vast historical drama of Jewish persecution. I believe that the dramaturgy of anti-Semitism continues to exist. A new mass extermination of Jews cannot be ruled out as a possibility. What would happen if in a war against the small land of Israel the Arab countries, today supported by arms shipments from East and West, were to gain a total victory? What would an America that had come under the sway of fascism mean not only for the Negroes but also for the Jews? What would the fate of the Jews have been in France, the European country with their greatest number, if at the beginning of the 1960s not de Gaulle had triumphed, but the OAS?[1]

With some reluctance I read in the study of a very young Dutch Jew the following definition of the Jew: "A Jew can be described as someone who has more fear, mistrust, and vexation than his fellow citizens who were never persecuted." The apparently correct definition is rendered false by the absence of an indispensable extension, which would have to read: ". . . for with good reason he awaits a new catastrophe at any moment." The awareness of the last cataclysm and the legitimate fear of a new one is what it all amounts to. I, who bear both within me—and the latter with double weight, since it was only by chance that I escaped the former—am not "traumatized," but rather my spiritual and psychic condition corresponds completely to reality. The consciousness of my being a Holocaust Jew is not an ideology. It may be compared to the class consciousness that Marx tried to reveal to the proletarians of the nineteenth century. I experienced in my existence and exemplify through it a historical reality of my epoch, and since I experienced it more deeply than most other Jews, I can also shed more light on it. That is not to my credit and not because I am so wise, but only because of the chance of fate.

Everything could be borne more easily if my bond with other Jews were not limited to the solidarity of revolt, if the necessity did not constantly run up against the impossibility. I know it only too well: I was sitting next to a Jewish friend at a performance of Arnold Schönberg's "A Survivor from Warsaw" when, accompanied by the sounds of trumpets, the chorus intoned the words "Sh'ma Israel"; my friend turned as white as chalk and beads of perspiration appeared on his brow. My heart did not beat faster, yet I felt myself to be more wanting than my comrade, whom the Jewish prayer, sung to the blasts of trumpets, had powerfully affected. To be a deeply stirred Jew, I thought to myself afterwards, is not possible for me, I can be a Jew only in fear and anger, when—in order to attain dignity—fear transforms itself into anger. "Hear, O Israel" is not my concern. Only a "hear, O world" wants angrily to break out from within me. The six-digit number on my forearm demands it. That is what the awareness of catastrophe, the dominant force of my existence, requires.

Often I have asked myself whether one can live humanly in the tension between fear and anger. Those who have followed these deliberations may well see their author as a monster, if not of vengeance, then at least of bitterness. There may be a trace of truth in such a judgment, but only a trace. Whoever attempts to be a Jew in my way and under the conditions imposed on me, whoever hopes, by clarifying his own Holocaust-determined existence, to draw together and shape within himself the reality of the so-called Jewish Question, is wholly void of naïveté. Honey-sweet humane pronouncements do not flow from his lips. He is not good at gestures of magnanimity. But this does not mean that fear and anger condemn him to be less righteous than his ethically inspired contemporaries are. He is able to have friends and he has them, even among members of just those nations who hung him forever on the torture hook between fear and anger. He can also read books and listen to music as do the uninjured, and with no less feeling than they. If moral questions are involved, he will probably prove to be more sensitive to injustice of every kind than his fellow man. He will certainly react more excitably to a photo of club-swinging South African policemen or American sheriffs who sick howling dogs on black civil rights protesters. Because it became hard for me to be a human being does not mean that I have become a monster.

In the end, nothing else differentiates me from the people among whom I pass my days than a vague, sometimes more, sometimes less perceptible restiveness. But it is a *social* unrest, not a metaphysical one. It is not Being that oppresses me, or Nothingness, or God, or the Absence of God, only society. For it and only it caused the disturbance in my existential balance, which I am trying to oppose with an upright gait. It and only it robbed me of my trust in the world. Metaphysical distress is a fashionable concern of the highest standing. Let it remain a matter for those who have always known who and what they are, why they are that way, and that they are permitted to remain so. I must leave it to them—and it is not for that reason that I feel needy in their presence.

In my incessant effort to explore the basic condition of being a victim, in conflict with the necessity to be a Jew and the impossibility of being one, I believe to have recognized that the most extreme expectations and demands directed at us are of a physical and social nature. That such knowledge has made me unfit for profound and lofty speculation, I know. It is my hope that it has better equipped me to recognize reality.

Translated by Sidney and Stella Rosenfeld

NOTE

1. As of 1980 France had the largest European Jewish community, with 535,000 Jews, followed by Britain with 390,000.

The OAS (Secret Army Organization) was composed of anti-Semitic former military officers who conducted a terror campaign against the withdrawal of France from Algeria in the early 1960s. Ed.

6

DREAMS OF A BETTER LIFE
INTERVIEW WITH TONI OELSNER

Greffrath: Do you regard yourself as an American today?

Oelsner: It's hard to say. I feel almost totally out of touch with reality. Sometimes I have more hate for the things that I've experienced here. There's so much more deception and lying in this country. Vietnam and Cambodia were disastrous, nearly as bad as the gas chambers.

Greffrath: So you're still living in emigration after almost forty years?

Oelsner: As someone who wasn't born with a silver spoon in her mouth, I feel the social pressures and barriers which are difficult to overcome. Even before Hitler I had a hard time in my youth. My mother died when I was fifteen, and this resulted in personal grief. Her death broke the family ties. It was during the period of inflation, and my family took me out of school before I had finished high school. Without a diploma I couldn't pursue anything decent. I began working in jobs for which I wasn't very well suited. Most involved household work, taking care of children and teenagers, working with kindergarten teachers. I was in Kolberg on the Baltic Sea and in Berlin where I went to the museums and the theater, including

This interview was originally printed in *Die Zerstörung einer Zukunft. Gespräche mit emigrierten Sozialwissenschaftlern,* ed. Mathias Greffrath (Reinbek bei Hamburg, 1979). Anson Rabinbach, and Wieland Schulz-Keil continued and expanded the interview in 1979/80. The present English version is printed with the permission of Toni Oelsner.

Irwin Piscator's Volksbühne. In Berlin I could attend modern art exhibitions as well as exhibitions by Georg Grosz and Käthe Kollwitz. I had good friends there, but otherwise it was hard for me. I wasn't very well suited for these kinds of jobs, and I wasn't satisfied with being pushed by my family to serve an apprenticeship in a publishing firm. Finally I began studying in Frankfurt as a special student *(kleiner Matrikel)* and hoped to acquire the *Begabtenabitur.*

Greffrath: Weren't you from a traditional, but not orthodox, Jewish family?

Oelsner: Yes. We observed the Jewish holidays, but we were culturally assimilated. My mother and I read Goethe, Schiller, Heine, Thomas Mann, and many poems together. We had a conventional library, and my father, a businessman, had the three volumes by Graetz, entitled *The Popular History of the Jews.*

Greffrath: I think it was Max Horkheimer who once said that he believed for a long time that the Germans were the least anti-Semitic people. What were the conditions like when you were going to school?

Oelsner: One time we had a very ugly anti-Semitic incident. It was just before a Christmas celebration. A tall, pretty Jewish girl was supposed to play the angel in a play. The others said that a Jewish girl shouldn't be the angel. My girlfriend was furious about it and made a big stink. I think she played the angel in the end, but it was really ugly in those days. We had Jewish prefects, and I was one. Of course, I never experienced any anti-Semitism from the teachers. I also had Christian girlfriends. One of them was very friendly, but because she was such a religious Protestant—and for children that's often important—there was always a barrier between us. Sometimes my brother experienced anti-Semitism in school. It was in a suburb, in Bockenheim. They wrote in the school paper: "Garlic is the food of the Oelsners." In Wilhelm Busch the sentence reads: "Garlic is the food of the Jews."

Greffrath: Had you already begun to study at the university when the Republic began to fall apart?

Oelsner: It was in 1931, in the very last years of a period when the Frankfurt University was exceptionally good. It was when Max Horkheimer, Karl Mannheim, Paul Tillich, Theodor Wiesengrund Adorno, and Max Wertheimer were there. The atmosphere was outstanding. Everyone went from one seminar to the next carrying ideas from one seminar into the next. Horkheimer lectured on Bodin and Hobbes. Tillich held lectures on Hegel; he said that Hegel had become reality in a part of the world today. Unfortunately it sounds a little stilted today. Tillich's seminar was outright political. The entire atmosphere was permeated by discussions of a new society and how to realize it. In one of Horkheimer's last seminars we read Freud's *Civilization and Its Discontents*. It was a great opportunity to deal with socially critical issues.

Greffrath: What were the students like who attended the seminars?

Oelsner: A few serious National Socialist students came to the seminars. They weren't the hoodlums, but rather the ones who believed in the National Socialist ideology. We tried to explain to them that believing in nationalism alone couldn't eliminate the contradictions in capitalism, and that the evils of our times were a result of the economic crisis. Actually, there were hardly any thugs at the university, anyway, not in the circles in which I moved. I don't know what it was like in other departments, but in ours, there were no difficulties.

Greffrath: Weren't the Left-liberal and socialist students and instructors in the minority?

Oelsner: Oh, no. The Left students were very active, and sometimes antifascist demonstrations were organized in which the Zionist students participated as well. We often worked on a broad popular front basis. There were "red student groups," there were also Trotskyites, and we felt a lot of pride that CP people were working together with left-wing social democrats. The Left was much less a minority at the universities than is the case today. Of course, we never engaged in violence. We distributed leaflets for the most part. In the beginning of 1933 we had an "LLL celebration" in commemoration of Lenin's death and the murders of Liebknecht and Luxemburg. I was selling tickets at the time, and a few people to whom I sold some appeared a few weeks later in their Nazi uniforms. Unfortunately everything we did was to no avail. When Prussia succumbed in 1932, we were terribly unhappy with how Severing just let himself be led out of his office. Yet, we still demonstrated and retained our hope until the very end. We continued to demonstrate until the Nazis took over. Up until the burning of the Reichstag and the ensuing emergency decree there were mass gatherings in the huge auditoriums in Frankfurt. The last time I participated in a demonstration it was broken up by the police, and I ended up alone on a side street, thankful that nobody had been arrested.

Rabinbach/Schulz-Keil: To what extent did Horkheimer discuss Jewish history or problems of Jewish identity in his seminar when you were there? Where else were these questions discussed?

Oelsner: They were not among the topics of his seminar, or not regarded as such. Nobody realized or wanted to realize that they would soon become the most burning issue and within a decade mark one of the most catastrophic events, not only in Jewish, but in human history. Most people were not aware of the problem yet. Günther Anders (Stern) organized a seminar about Hitler's *Mein Kampf* in Berlin, and he had great difficulties recruiting participants. Privately, Horkheimer told me that he was in contact with the director of the Frankfurt Jewish community about the acute problems of anti-Semitism. I should explain at this point that in Germany we did not have individual private congregations, but that the Jewish community in each city or town was a "publicly constituted corporation," empowered to levy taxes. These corporations administered religious as well as cultural, educational, health, and welfare services.[1] Horkheimer's contact with the director remained merely private. The problem of anti-Semitism was never discussed in any of the seminars or lecture courses. No one imagined that it would soon become bitter reality. Horkheimer did not believe that anti-Semitism would succeed so soon in Germany. On the contrary, he believed that Germany was less anti-Semitic than other European countries. This was true. We had students from Eastern Europe, Hungary and Poland, where they really experienced anti-Semitism, for example, in quota systems and such things. This is my point: people hardly realized that Jewish emancipation was actually only of a short duration in Germany. It is common to speak of the era of Jewish emancipation and assimilation beginning with the Enlightenment. As I have shown in my book *Three Jewish Families,* emancipation in Germany was an unequal and long-drawn-out process.

Rabinbach/Schulz-Keil: Adorno once remarked that "anti-Semitism has nothing essential to do with the Jews." By this he meant that it was a projection of hostile and negative images on an outsider group by a class or group that felt threatened economically or socially in terms of status. To what extent can anti-Semitism be discussed in this way?

Oelsner: Well, the first part of your question is actually the gist of Adorno's generalizations in his concluding chapter of *The Authoritarian Personality,* which was published in 1950, and which was not very much concerned with social structure. Here he speaks of the "functional character of anti-Semitism" and "its relative independence of the object." He sees "anti-Semitism as a device for effortless 'orientation' in a cold, alienated, largely ununderstandable world." Adorno admitted, however, the risk of drawing conclusions from one political setting to another. In the mechanism of stereotypes the Jew becomes the "chosen foe" to whom excessive and sinister power is attributed. Insofar as Part I of the book was based on questionnaires in which common anti-Semitic stereotypes were used, one wonders to what extent they brought about their recurrence in the selected interviews of Part II, or the deduced exaggeration. I am always sceptical of this kind of attitude research. At any rate, such concepts as the Jew's "alienness" as "the handiest formula for dealing with the alienation of society" do not explain anti-Semitism. The form that was still prevalent in the 1940s in this country had roots similar to those in Europe, and particularly Germany, where by the mid-nineteenth century the Rothschilds had become the epitome of so-called Jewish financial power. The Jew became the source of all the evils of modern finance capitalism, of uprooting from pastoral rural life.

If in the history of modern anti-Semitism certain historical, political, and economic circumstances can be identified in which the involvement of a small segment of Jews was either distorted, magnified, or the respective role of others ignored and a huge body of anti-Semitic propaganda built on it, the savagery of the Final Solution (which even impeded the war effort) was rarely adumbrated in previous anti-Semitism, and it exposed the utter destructiveness of German fascism which reached a pinnacle in the war.

For the Nazis the previous images of the Jew no longer fit. Jews were declared to be subhumans to be exterminated from all over occupied Europe. Still, the initial methods were mainly shootings by special SS units asked by Himmler to commit "superhuman acts of inhumanity."[2] Such abandonment of any human feelings and the reversal of moral duty may, of course, be explained as the characteristic of a schizoid, compulsive-obsessive personality like Himmler's, who, with the sanction of the super-ego Hitler, gained the support of his followers. Perhaps for this final, totally destructive stage psychological explanations are called for. But it should never be forgotten that all the willing followers of "superhuman acts of inhumanity" had been trained for many years in the old slogans of anti-Semitism and racism. The first stages of Aryanization of Jewish firms, of academic and civil service dismissals as well as of Jewish (even converts) corporate board members had long been accomplished. Now the program was extermination on an unprecedented mass scale.

But to come back to Adorno and Horkheimer, they do of course discuss anti-Semitism in *Dialectic of Enlightenment*, but the history of the Jews is dealt with in only one and a half pages. There are some things, for example, that Adorno writes about Kierkegaard and religious criticism which are just brilliant and excellent. But when he writes about the three-thousand-year course of Jewish history in one and a half pages, it makes your hair stand on end. There he repeats all the clichés: The Jews were the trailblazers in trade from the Roman empire, or pioneers in finance and urban living; there were tolerated or protected Jews; the peasants and the artisans were always their enemies; the Jews made capitalism. Of course this is what my Roscher article[3] deals with—and what I did in the article that appeared in the YIVO annual.

Greffrath: Do you still remember January 30, 1933?

Oelsner: Yes, of course. On that evening I sent my application for the

Begabtenabitur to Berlin. I had recommendations from Horkheimer, Tillich, and Wertheimer. In addition, my personal history contained information that I had worked in a Jewish home and had graduated from a Jewish home economics school. The rejection came two weeks later. It was pretty clear by the middle of February, 1933, that I had been rejected because I had recommendations from left-wing Jewish professors, and because I myself was Jewish. Horkheimer had left by then. In June of 1933 a decree was released that forbade all Jews from acquiring the "extreme Abitur."

Greffrath: You continued to take part in smaller oppositional activities. What kind of groups were involved?

Oelsner: I knew a few workers who distributed illegal literature—very small booklets, so small that you could take them in the palm of your hand. On the cover there was usually a title like Gottfried Keller's *Der grüne Heinrich,* and inside you could read: "Germany, once the land of poets and philosophers, now the land of judges and executioners," or "What is an Aryan? Hair and eyes like Hitler, and first name like Goebbels and a last name like the author of the *Mythos des 20. Jahrhunderts.*" It was an attempt to actively resist, but unfortunately all the people who published such things were arrested, and after a while it stopped.

Greffrath: How were these leaflets distributed?

Oelsner: They were given to people who could be trusted, but some of them said that they didn't want to distribute on a regular basis any longer. Sometimes they were just left on a park bench after dark. When I think about it, I'm really astounded even now at how much information was still disseminated during the Nazi period, even among people who weren't directly affiliated with a politically illegal organization. I had an older cousin in Bockenheim, where the University of Frankfurt is located. She knew everything, for instance, that there was a strike at Opel in Greisheim, or that the Nazis wanted to deport Jews to Madagascar. I'm just telling this in order to demonstrate the extent to which information was spread and known. My cousin was deported either to Auschwitz or to another death camp in 1942.

Greffrath: These groups that you just referred to, were they just workers or were there leftist students among them?

Oelsner: At the time we were in small groups of four, at the most five people. They were all workers and CP members. I had met two of them in a soup kitchen as a student. We could get lunch for ten pfennig at the kitchen—noodles with dried fruit, rice with sugar and cinnamon, pea soup and lentil soup.

Greffrath: Were you a member of the party?

Oelsner: It took a long time until I decided to join. Actually it wasn't until it was illegal, and as a result, I was never officially a member. Only a few comrades could be seen together at that time. Once it became illegal it was very important that only a few people meet each other at one time. We would take walks together, but eventually that ceased as well. Once in a while I would go up to an artists' kitchen that was founded by Heinrich Simon of the *Frankfurter Zeitung*. Art students received free lunches there, and left-wing people would meet there. I came into contact with some of them just as the artists' kitchen was closed by the Nazis. There wasn't much more you could do, but it was still important to get together with others who were opposed to the Nazis. That in itself was very important. There was a small bookstore near the University that served as a place for an exchange of information. That's where you heard when someone was arrested again. I had a few friends, and we still tried to form Marxist reading groups in apartments. Of course it was very difficult. There was a physicist among us who was taken prisoner by the Nazis at the end of the war. He was shipped out to the Baltic Sea, and the ship was sunk with all the political prisoners on board. We were always terribly afraid that somehow we . . . But I had contacts up until the end, also among students, even though we couldn't accomplish very much. There had to be hundreds of such groups, and sometimes there were even connections which transcended party affiliation.

Greffrath: How was it in everyday life as far as fellow citizens and neighbors were concerned? Did you detect aggressive anti-Semitism?

Oelsner: No, absolutely nothing. Only on the days of the pogroms. After the burning of the synagogues I rode my bike through Frankfurt. There was the orthodox synagogue in the Friedberger Anlage, it was once fabulous, and now it stood in ruins. The people stood there and looked at each other in shock. I overheard members of a family talking among themselves: "This used to be called arson," they said. On that same day I visited an elderly woman, not a religious woman, and she told me that she had been on the streets and had asked a few hoodlums: "What did the synagogue ever do to you?" It shows that even non-religious people were furious. There were other terrible incidents. As I was watching a Jewish man being led away by the SA [Storm Troopers], I saw two people in the house across the street laughing maliciously. And once in a grocery store when a young woman came in with her daughter (she was the mother of one of my pupils), I heard the salesman comment: "Not that again." Such things really bothered me, but I never personally suffered in the entire anti-Semitic time, with the exception of being restricted to Jewish houses the last time I looked for an apartment.

Greffrath: Then how do you explain the public impact of the Nazi's anti-Semitic propaganda?

Oelsner: You could say that anti-Semitism, the barbarism of the Nazis, was nothing more than sustained atavism. I'll give you an example of how it functioned. About two dozen children in my house amused themselves for a time by teasing me. I don't know why they chose me—maybe because I was lost in thought most of the time. I didn't look like a grandmother type. One child just started and the others followed. That was a small example of how it functions. The human being has an enormous capacity for both destruction and social improvement. The direction it takes depends entirely on socialization and the social order. In Germany the depression was the trigger. Mass unemployment intensified mass misery. One should not forget that from October 1931, after twenty-one weeks of unemployment, the individual was reduced to a welfare recipient and no longer counted in the statistics. The young members of the SA were, for the most part, unemployed, and they received pea soup and uniforms from the Nazis. Wasn't that generous of them? Maybe even a little bacon. Well, going hungry isn't very pleasant. Have you ever gone hungry? No? It's not pleasant—it hurts. The war also uprooted many people from the upper class. The stab-in-the-back legend and other such tales were easily combined with anti-Semitism.

Anti-Semitism always appears in times of economic crisis. That was the case even in the Middle Ages. The most terrible persecutions and burnings took place during the Black Death. The Jews were accused of poisoning the wells. People were desperate. They were dying, and they couldn't explain it except to say that it was the fault of the Jews. Likewise during the Crusades they said: "Let's kill the Jews first before we go to the Holy Land." Economic historians say that the persecutions during the first Crusades weren't carried out by the bourgeoisie or the merchants. It was the poor farmers from France who participated in the first Crusades because they had had a bad harvest and were starving. When people maintain today that it was the Catholic Church, then this is good insofar as the Church is put to test, but the Church wasn't the actual cause of the persecutions. They occurred in times of economic or political crises, or during natural disasters like the plague.

Greffrath: In regard to the National Socialists, wasn't their anti-Semitism a kind of harmless anti-capitalism for the capitalists?

Oelsner: Yes, you could say that, to be sure. Yet, I don't know if the capitalists themselves pulled the strings. I can't say that since there were originally many Jews in large factories who continued to work in high places. I don't know if the capitalists actually instigated anti-Semitism or not. This is an issue that still hasn't been fully clarified even today. However, one thing is clear, they wanted Hitler because they didn't want Communism.

Greffrath: You weren't allowed to obtain the *Abitur* in Germany, but you continued to study "unofficially." Was it still possible for Jewish students to attend the university at this time?
Oelsner: Yes. I still attended visiting lectures. I was in Kurt Riegler's lecture in 1933 when the SA men appeared and announced that he was a Jew. He was married to the painter Max Liebermann's daughter, who was very charming. They maintained that Tillich had brought him to the university. It caused a terrible scene, and of course, his classes were canceled after that. Later they stood at the entrance to the university and asked for Jews to identify themselves and then proceeded to confiscate their student identification cards. Jewish students received a red one in exchange, and the records were changed so that they were no longer members of the student body. The more advanced and regular students were allowed to go to their professors, but most of them left immediately.
Greffrath: Did you stay?
Oelsner: I couldn't leave. My situation was very difficult. Officially I had studied only one semester, had no money, and was often sick.
Greffrath: So you continued your studies in the years between 1933 and 1939, but you weren't an official student, is that right?
Oelsner: Yes, I could use the library until 1938. I was just learning to develop a scholarly research method when the Nazis came into power. Hans Gerth was a colleague of mine. We often met and talked either in the student cafeteria or in a café. We still learned a lot from other students. Occasionally I would go to the student cafeteria and discuss literature with other students.
Greffrath: You worked at the same time with a Jewish study group at the *Freien Jüdischen Lehrhaus*. What kind of an institute was it?
Oelsner: It was founded in the early 1920s by the philosopher Franz Rosenzweig, who unfortunately died of a terrible illness in 1929. It started to fade out during his illness, but was understandably revived in 1933. Dr. Joseph Soudek, the financial editor for the *Frankfurter Zeitung*, gave a seminar on Jewish economic history. I knew who Soudek was because he had helped lead Mannheim's interdisciplinary seminar on liberalism. He conducted a very interesting seminar with good presentations. At that time I was working on a long paper about the place of the Jews in the economic life of Eastern Europe. I showed that Jews worked in factories and had unions, and so on, and as a result, Soudek became very interested in my work and gave me tremendously intelligent and friendly advice. I told him that I had boxes full of family letters—Jews were interested in family research at the time—and he advised me to use the letters and write something from a sociohistorical perspective. He stayed in Frankfurt until 1936, and I showed him each chapter. This work, *Die Geschichte dreier*

jüdischer Familien in Deutschland von der Voremanzipation bis zur Vorkriegszeit, appeared in the American journal *Jewish Social Studies* in 1942 under the title *Three Jewish Families in Modern Germany: Studies of the Process of Emancipation.* I gave a presentation for the Jüdischen Frauen-bund in 1936 in Frankfurt entitled "How Family Research Leads to Historical Research," which appeared in two editions of their journal and again in shorter form in the journal *Jüdische Familienforschung.* I tried to pursue this project further, but there was too much agitation. The situation got worse, as you know, and the people became increasingly agitated. I still worked on it, but I was poor and sick, probably due to malnutrition. I wasn't able to complete the work in Germany.

Rabinbach/Schulz-Keil: When you studied in Frankfurt were there any seminars or courses dealing with Jewish theology or Jewish history at the University? Was there any relationship between the *Lehrhaus* or the Franz Rosenzweig circle and the University?

Oelsner: As I mentioned, Rosenzweig died in 1929 and the *Lehrhaus* was reduced to a mere skeleton—a weekly Bible course held by Eduard Strauss, a biochemist by profession, and a yearly Rosenzweig memorial lecture. But Jewish history, whether regional history dealing with the special status, expulsions, readmissions, economic and community life, and so forth, or with philosophical developments, was not a subject of university courses. The *Lehrhaus* never had a university connection. Buber held lectures on Jewish theology from 1923 to 1931 within the department of philosophy, which was something quite unique at the time, and he was succeeded then by Nahum Glatzer until 1933. I recall that Buber attended a lecture by Tillich at the "Kant Society" on the meaning of history in the Old Testament, namely the projection in the future. Buber contributed to the discussion. You must remember that it is quite recent, only in the years after World War II, that in this country most universities established a department of Jewish studies. Prior to that such a thing was exceptional. This was precisely the complaint of the Jewish organizations, that the university had a theological faculty (since European universities developed from scholastic studies, and theology was one of the early mainstays) but the Jewish organizations were not allowed to have a chair of Jewish theology and therefore no Jewish history.

Greffrath: How did you support yourself?

Oelsner: I gave English lessons to emigrants, I typed, and so forth. After my article was published, I received a scholarship for the year 1937–1938. This was the result of a recommendation from Martin Buber. I even learned English stenography in 1938, but we literally forgot everything we learned during that time. What was happening was so shocking—the men between sixteen and sixty were being taken away, and nobody knew if the women would be next. I had always planned to emigrate, but I wanted to finish my work first. In the spring of 1939 I was desperate because my American visa hadn't come through yet. I sent my article to Dr. Cecil Roth in London. He wrote me a friendly response: If it were possible to pass through England on my way to America, he would see if he could do something for me. Subsequently, I went to the English Consulate in Frankfurt and got a visa for England. People who saw me pass through so quickly were envious. They were all waiting desperately for a resident visa.

I got the visa which made it possible to leave Germany for London just eight days before the outbreak of the war of nerves on August 18. Time was short, and several friends helped me. Lists had to be made, and every handkerchief had to be counted. You could take only ten German marks out of the country. I was able to obtain my books through my uncle, although I lost almost all of them later in one of my moves. I had all the classics, Schiller, Goethe, Lessing, Heine, and also several historical works. They were all lost except for a few of Max Weber's works. I only wanted to spend a week in England, just enough time to go to Oxford and visit Roth. On the way back, as we were ready to take off from Southampton, we heard that the German steamship had been called back to Hamburg. It was exactly at the time of the signing of the German-Soviet Pact which caused so much controversy. At that time we thought it must be the dialectic at work.

Greffrath: You don't believe that anymore?

Oelsner: Why? I don't really know whether it was so bad. As far as I know, it gave Stalin a better chance to prepare for war. I wasn't totally enlightened about Stalin until 1956. Unfortunately he killed a lot of Communists and other acquaintances of mine. At any rate, in comparison with Hitler and Himmler, at least his main goal wasn't extermination and annihilation. I will always have a greater dread of Hitler. People in Europe were probably better informed after the war than we were in the United States. Up until Khrushchev's speech I thought that it was all just propaganda. It still takes me a while to believe all the details of what is happening in the Soviet Union now. But above all I am furious at the chaos that exists here in American society. Just walk down the street one block, you'll find entire residential sections in New York that have been devastated and are in a state of ruins. There are a number of such things that dissidents who are attacking all sorts of things in Russia don't know about here. In addition, there are authors in the Soviet Union who write critical novels and aren't attacked as a result. I'm convinced that Solzhenitsyn could have stayed there as well if he hadn't been so rigid. It infuriates me that hardly a day passes without reading something in the papers about Sakharov [this was in 1977]. If Sakharov would put his energies toward fighting with Western physicists against nuclear armaments, then he would be making a worthwhile contribution. Instead he complains about restrictions being placed on certain religious sects like groups that fight against equal rights for women and government-funded abortions in this country. Solzhenitsyn even wrote an article for the *New York Times* stating that the removal of American troops from Vietnam was a crime against freedom. That was in 1975. If they only knew what life is really like here.

Greffrath: Could we get back to your history?

Oelsner: Well, the steamship returned to Hamburg, and I realized for the first time how lucky I was to be in England because, after the war started, only people who could finance the trip themselves were allowed to leave. The *Hilfsverein der deutschen Juden* had paid for my trip. It would have been a terrible situation. I went back to London, where we had to register ourselves the following Monday as enemy aliens. I lived in a suburb of London with relatives, where Karl Mannheim also happened to be living. He didn't have British citizenship yet, and he and his wife were standing just ahead of me in line. I spent a couple of hours with him one afternoon, and he became very interested in my work. As a result he wrote some people at the New School that he knew me from the University of Frankfurt and had the impression that I'd made very favorable progress and was especially talented in the area of sociological research. In addition, he said that I had struggled heroically for my intellectual existence in Germany—I was imprisoned in the fall of 1933.

Greffrath: How did that come about?

Oelsner: A student had asked me to keep some materials for her, and someone must have reported it. I spent four weeks in prison. When they took me in to the Gestapo, they showed me photographs and mentioned names, but I didn't know anybody and was released. My father even came down to Gestapo, which was a very brave thing to do. Most people were immediately taken away after such an incident.

Greffrath: What was your situation like when you arrived in New York?

Oelsner: I arrived practically broke. The Quakers had given me twenty dollars in London, which at least allowed me to use the subway and buses at first. I had Mannheim's recommendation, but it wasn't much good. Soudek helped me a lot; he gave me the address of the journal *Jewish Social Studies,* which eventually accepted my article. With some difficulty I received a scholarship for the New School in 1940, and one month after the beginning of the semester I got another small scholarship which helped me live. I say with some difficulty because I didn't have my *Abitur,* but just a transcript of one semester at the university. Consequently I was accepted only on a provisional basis at first, even though I was able to submit work that I had completed in the meantime. Everything went wrong at the New School. I had developed a method of work that involved the selection of a single topic and thorough elaboration. I was thirty-three years old already, and I didn't want to study *per se*. Rather I wanted to get involved in research work. At the time there were several people doing research in the adjustment of emigrants. I spent a lot of time developing something in that area and also began work on a topic dealing with Max Weber's thought. I had no idea that in America you had to prepare a written presentation for each course, and as a result, they didn't continue my scholarship. It was a terrible time, but eventually I received my M.A. in 1942 with a thesis on three Jewish families. When it was published in 1942, I made the big mistake of not sending enough offprints to professional people and institutes. I received fifty free ones, was very short of money, and didn't know that it was so important to send them away. If I had I probably would have found a job sooner. At least I received some extremely appreciative letters.

Greffrath: What was the political attitude of the German emigrants at the New School?

Oelsner: There were general seminars every week, and of course, everything was connected to a victory over the Nazis. There were also a few refugees from Italy and Spain, and, as far as that goes, there was some kind of mutual understanding between us, although I'm sure a few of them had the feeling that I might be too left-wing. Mannheim's words, "she struggled heroically for her intellectual existence," displeased many of them, I'm sure. They were afraid that, since I wasn't a prominent person when the Nazis came to power, I must have been too left-wing. It was too much for me. I was often seriously ill, which was looked upon as a crime. I'm convinced that most of my illness was caused by malnutrition. If I had been the wife of an important man, then he could have managed to get support from an organization, but, when you want to achieve something independently, you don't dare mention that you're not healthy. A friend of mine in Germany always told me never to mention it or else you would be dumped like garbage. I had nobody here who could help me. At least in Frankfurt there was always somebody who helped.

Greffrath: Didn't you know anybody from Germany well enough that he could have helped you?

Oelsner: No. Most of the German refugees were only employed on a temporary basis themselves, earned small salaries and lived in cramped quarters, and so forth. In my opinion they were far too insecure themselves to be able to help. That is the best explanation I have for it. I made the mistake of telling the people at the refugee organization how unpleasant they were. Actually, they were more than just unpleasant, but a refugee doesn't have the right to complain. They were of the opinion that when you're a refugee you should be grateful to have any work at all. They couldn't conceive that there were limits to what one could do—well, perhaps there were a few who did.

Greffrath: Weren't there any student friends or groups, who had been here longer and could have helped you out?

Oelsner: The New School was a night school. Most of the students worked during the day. We didn't meet each other in the cafeteria like in Germany, and, as a result, there wasn't much interaction among students. I was busy myself doing all kinds of jobs such as secretarial and household work.

Greffrath: That means that you were isolated for the entire year?

Oelsner: I knew absolutely nobody from the New School. At first I went to different meetings and events, but then I lost interest. Eventually I wrote articles for the emigrant newspaper *Der Aufbau*. At the time there was the *Tribune für freie deutsche Literatur und Kunst* with performances of Brecht and readings by Anna Seghers and Oskar Graf. Ernst Bloch gave a lecture about dreams of a better life. I wrote articles about these events for *Der Aufbau* and the *New Yorker Staatszeitung*. Eventually I made connections with the YIVO Institute and became involved in a circle of historians, Raphael Mahler among them, where I gave a presentation on Wilhelm Roscher's "Theories of the Economical and Social Position of the Jews in the Middle Ages," which wasn't published until 1958.

When the war was over, I went to the employment office and was given a job with the military government in Germany. My duties included medical examinations, finger printing, and so forth, and then suddenly the word came down that the position had been discontinued. There had been investigations, and it was reported that I was a leftist and had studied philosophy at the University of Frankfurt. Soudek, my former advisor, said that I was not a Communist. At any rate, the whole thing was drawn out until the position was eventually abolished. The employment agency at the New World Club advised me at that point to apply for a position as a translator for the Nuremberg trials. My application was, however, neglected until Robert Kempner came to New York, found it, and asked me to come see him. He wanted to hire me to research documents, but it was already 1947, and there was an age limit against hiring women over thirty-five in Germany. I was already forty years old. In addition they said it would be too difficult for people who had just become American citizens. I had a good recommendation from Kempner, but it was to no avail. It would have been a well-paid position, and I could have used it.

For years afterward I applied for positions at colleges, but I didn't have a Ph.D. I'm not even sure of the reasons. . . . All my work was on Jews, and maybe that played a role in not being accepted for college positions. Right upon my arrival Hans Gerth had written: "You have no idea how much anti-Semitism exists here, especially in the Midwest." Then the McCarthy era began, and anybody suspected for ever having been a leftist was mistrusted.

Greffrath: Although you were never able to get a permanent position after the war, you continued with your academic work.

Oelsner: Yes, I didn't want to give it up because I never lost hope that I might establish connections. I also had several small scholarships over the years, for which I submitted proposals. However, due to bad living conditions and illnesses, I could never devote all my energies to my projects. I often ran around like a peddler, but in most people's eyes I was just a person with no Ph.D. In 1943 another publication resulted in a scholarship from the Emergency Committee in Aid of Displaced Foreign Scholars, a committee which was supported by all the important people like Tillich, Thomas Mann, and Buber. At the time I was writing a paper on the Frankfurt ghetto and an essay on Roscher's theory of economics. I gathered a lot of material, but the money ran out, and I didn't complete it until 1957 when I received reparation money from Germany.

Greffrath: How much was it?

Oelsner: It came to about one thousand dollars, out of which I had to pay for an operation so that the money was soon gone. After that I received another scholarship from a reparation fund and worked as a collaborator on the *Germania Judaica,* a large work in which information concerning the history of the Jews (in the Middle Ages) in Germany was compiled. I'd gathered an enormous amount of material through the years and with the assistance of the American Philosophical Society I was able to get microfilms of the registration collections from various archives in Germany— from city archives, from Württemberg, from the national archives in Munich. I used all this material in writing a work on the economic condition of Jews in southern and western Germany in the thirteenth and fourteenth centuries.

I was able to obtain only minimal assistance in grants for the completion of this work, even though the American Philosophical Society's consultant had written that it was an extremely important work and the materials alone (many original documents) would be indispensable for future work on the history of Jews in the Middle Ages. He emphatically recommended its printing; however, nobody was interested in sufficiently funding the project, not even the Leo Baeck Institute. They didn't even want to read it. A job working in an archive would have made the tiresome work a little easier, but instead I wrote a series of articles for the *Encyclopedia Judaica.* The pay was bad, and I never succeeded in getting research assistance.

Greffrath: Do you think that you were raked over the coals because your opinions were challenging to academia?

Oelsner: That, too, of course. The Leo Baeck Institute tended to celebrate the upper middle class *(Grossbourgeoisie)*. They just published another volume entitled *German Jews under Wilhelm II from 1890 to 1914*. Both Rathenaus are in it, and Gay wrote the article on culture, but it only pertains to the upper class. It's not the case that all Jews were rich. There were many unimportant and poor Jews in the villages and the cities. A Jew from Breisach in Baden just paid me a visit; his father was a cattle dealer, and he worked a few acres with his farmhand. They certainly weren't wealthy people, but the Leo Baeck Institute is interested in nothing but prominent people. They only deal with baptized Jews, who were prominent in politics, and the like.

On top of that I'd written an article for the Leo Baeck Institute's yearbook entitled "The Jews in Economic History from the Point of View of German Scholars." Although I was somewhat unaware of it at the time, the entire article went against the traditional approach to history. According to conventional Jewish history, Jews were the primary traders in the early Middle Ages, were then squeezed into banking, and for this reason people began to hate them. However, a close evaluation of the sources shows that, on the contrary, a large number of Jews owned and worked agricultural lands. Conventional history also mistakenly assumes that Jews weren't allowed to own feudal land, which is in contradiction to the information in the sources I used in my article. In 1965, two issues after my article appeared, they printed an article on Max Weber that contained all the suppositions that I had just proven to be false. I was furious.

Greffrath: Did you direct your work toward disproving this theory?

Oelsner: For me, the historian is on a voyage of discovery. You can never know what will be discovered, and we've paid far too little attention to original sources in the writing of Jewish history. When you're on such a voyage, you can make fantastic discoveries that will destroy all the old clichés. One of the most interesting documents I found on a microfilm from Stuttgart contained the following information. The small town of Wildberg in the Black Forest, which formerly belonged to Graf Hohenburg in the fourteenth century and was sold to the Pfalzgraf am Rhein, came into Jewish ownership. A Jew, Jakob, was able to make the transaction by mortgaging his own person for a loan to Graf Ruprecht von der Pfalz in return for this land. That was in 1388, but in 1392 Graf Ruprecht banished all Jews from his land, and, as a result, a royal page acquired all of Jacob's gardens, fields, and vineyards. The incident is extremely unfortunate—the banishment of all Jews and expropriation of their property. A very unfortunate incident; yet, the historian is happy to find such evidence. We learn from these sources that a Jewish family in southern Germany indeed owned gardens and fields, that Jews were in fact farmers and vintagers. That is what is important. Everybody maintains that Jews were moneylenders. However, there is other information lying hidden in archives somewhere. I believe the Jews lived as farmers and artisans in many of the small cities and villages, but we have too little proof. I have other evidence, for example, that a Jew from Stuttgart, Leo, owned a vineyard and vegetable garden, and, based on a collection of names, we can postulate that other Jews were landowners as well. The view that Jews were *only* moneylenders will collapse when we have more such evidence. It's just as unreasonable to believe that only Jews were moneylenders. There is abundant evidence that loans to princes came from burghers as well. I feel that it's an unspeakable loss for the development of scholarly research that I haven't been able to counteract outmoded ideas by publishing this work. It's quite an expensive and voluminous research project, and I hope to complete the work, perhaps with the help of a secretary. It would be so important because the theory of Jews as moneylenders continues to perpetuate itself from generation to generation and from dissertation to dissertation. Just last month I gave a lecture at a university in New York on the persecution of Jews during the Black Death subtitled "The Accused of the Past and Contemporary Explanations." A young historian, a doctoral candidate at Harvard, who has worked in the archives in Freiburg, gave a paper just before I did. He presented information on Strassburg Jews, who lent money to princes, a total perpetuation of the traditional thesis that all Jews were moneylenders. Information to the contrary is not available, and it's really sad that articles in the *Germania Judaica* maintain that Jews were predominantly involved in business. I would have to go from one university to another today to counter this thesis. I still have hopes that I will get it done.

Greffrath: How do you explain the continuity of these money-lending theories?

Oelsner: I don't maintain that people like Roscher, Stobbe, and Sombart were anti-Semitic, but they did perpetuate extremely old prejudices. It's been that way since the Apostle Paul: the Jews lost the truth. There was in fact a usury prohibition for Christians in the Middle Ages, but they found loopholes for all kinds of tricks.[4] People like Sombart simply singled out highly visible groups and phenomena and recorded it. But it was not the case, as Roscher stated, that the barbaric persecutions of Jews in the Middle Ages were due to a credit crisis (today referred to as a social revolution) with the sole purpose of obtaining promissory notes. This occurred in only a few cities. And besides, it just contributed once again to the notion that all Jews were moneylenders. Textual criticism is a relatively recent discipline. I mean the fact that scholars took the time and effort to study and date the various manuscripts. For instance, chronicles that contained the cancellation of debts written in 1410, almost sixty years after the persecutions, were referred to as contemporary with the outbreak of the Black Death. As a result it's been maintained that money caused the murder and burning of Jews during the Black Death. And even today, despite several articles that I have written to the contrary, the standard notion of Jews as predominantly financial merchants of the early Middle Ages is still prevalent. This view has been reiterated time and time again, from Roscher to Sombart and from one dissertation to the next. No one takes the time to criticize it or confirm it. It also fits very well with the notion of the suffering Jewry. Isn't it cruel that Zionism and anti-Semitism so often coincide? For both Zionism and Israeli ideology, the entire Diaspora has been negative.

There is another reason for the blossoming of this theory. When Sombart wrote his book *Die Juden und das Wirtschaftsleben*, it was at a time when Jews had participated in the economic rise of Germany. In Berlin a considerable segment of the textile industry belonged to Jews: there were Tietz and Wertheim. The whole thing was a capitalist mixed marriage. It was an optical illusion. One simply used a perspective that looked at the visible. The department stores of Tietz, the manufacturing of textiles— these things were obviously visible. In every little town there was a small Jewish business. No one ever thought of the small Jewish cattle merchant or the traveling salesperson.

Greffrath: With your sources and documents you wanted . . .

Oelsner: Yes, of course, everything was aimed at the demolition of racial theories. The Nazis were quite inconsistent. On the one hand, they talked about Jewish Bolshevism, and on the other, about Jewish capitalism, although they primarily talked about Jewish capitalism.

Greffrath: And you attempted to show with your documents and the many articles you have collected that for long periods of history Jews were engaged in professions that were not different from those of others: merchants, owners of vineyards, moneylenders, farmers, and that Jews were not the only ones subjected to pogroms.

Oelsner: That, too. Heretics have always been persecuted, and then there were the witch-hunts. Princes also received credit from burghers. So little is known; yet, the interesting thing that has been written in memoirs about the persecutions is that so many Jews lived in small villages. Here again I am of the opinion that it is impossible to assume that their only livelihood should have consisted in trade with aristocrats.

Greffrath: Does this mean that you have always considered it your task to go against this mainstream of research?

Oelsner: No, it is not the mainstream. I am not the only one who is against it, but I try not to romanticize. I just want to emphasize what has been neglected. Perhaps you're not aware of it, but there are Jewish Marxist historians. For instance, Raphael Mahler, a former Pole who left New York after the war to go to Israel and now teaches at the University of Tel Aviv. He wrote an excellent book about modern Jewish history, in which he states that it was always the elite in the villages who dominated the poor Jews. There *are* Jewish Marxist historians. However, Jewish historical research has always been done as a sideline. It has mostly been written by rabbis. I don't mean to speak against rabbis. There were some good historians among them, but it was mainly a sideline and never dealt with as a historical priority itself. All the history that has been written about Jews has to be taken out of isolation and understood as part of the general economic and social history. It is also wrong to say that only Jews have been persecuted. In the Middle Ages there were witch and heretic hunts as well.

Greffrath: So, you have been engaged since 1933 in the tedious business of correcting errors through a kind of detective work in history.

Oelsner: Yes, the historian is a kind of detective, and sometimes one is successful. Through correspondence with a Freiburg city official, for instance, and in an article in the New York newspaper *Aufbau* in 1967, I was successful in helping secure the removal of the relics of two children from the altar of the church in Endingen, near Freiburg. They had been venerated because they were thought to be the victims of a ritual murder that had been attributed to the Jews of Endingen. In 1470 a number of Jews were burned at the stake in Endingen after alleged confessions. Jews had been frequently accused of using the blood of Christian children for ritualistic purposes, even though in 1235 Frederic II had rejected such accusations. I helped bring about the removal of these relics in 1967, and I am proud of my participation in this project, which in itself constituted a kind of withdrawal of accusations. Unfortunately, the accusations had been maintained for five hundred years.

Greffrath: For forty years now you have been working without a steady position, on your own initiative, and without the backing of any institution.

Oelsner: Well, I had my research obligations and was hoping for employment. However, my life seemed utterly incomprehensible to many people, and they blocked my chances. Of course, one must always accept responsibility for one's actions. Just like Job. Three friends came to him and said: "When all your cattle have been lost, and you are suffering the way you do, then you must have committed a sin." I have been behind ever since the beginning, but it almost was impossible to make up for it. Today nobody knows anymore the confusion that existed in the refugee organization. Accidents, coincidence, you name it, we depended on them. In January

1933 I was working on two articles, one about C. G. Jung for the Horkheimer seminar, and another one for T. Wiesengrund Adorno. Maybe both would have remembered me better here if I could have finished them. But even that cannot be said for sure. Horkheimer once told me: "The whole world is clinging to me." Most of the people had family who helped out. But my brother, everybody, kept telling me in their letters that I should go to work in a factory. It has always been used against me. I also made the mistake of never belonging to a Zionist organization, not even to the central association (Zentralverein). This became impossible once I began to orient myself politically. This put me at a large disadvantage. The naive opinion still prevailed that among Jews who had suffered under the persecutions of the Nazis, there must be a certain degree of solidarity. For Goethe had once said: "Be wealthy and the law is on your side. And in gratitude the crowd will reward you." One had to be prosperous already, or have a wealthy father, perhaps. There were, of course, people who showed a lot of stamina and succeeded at working any job and still pursued their academic work. For several years I was completely severed from any kind of academic work when I worked as a free-lance interpreter and a private tutor for foreign languages. But even that is risky for an independent person because commissions come in irregularly, and the telephone has to be used, and so on. People do not know how it feels to be so completely alone. Nobody can imagine it.

Greffrath: Are political differences the reason for your isolation?

Oelsner: I could not join leftist groups during the McCarthy era. I am convinced that the Leo Baeck Institute is dominated primarily by people who previously had been active in Zionist or assimilatory organizations in Germany or were social democrats. As soon as one stood to the left of the social democrats, they became sceptical. But, of course, it also is due to the fact that there was someone who dared to stubbornly resist. I grew up in a social order where the father was expected to pay the school tuition. My teacher insisted that I go on to the upper division of a technical high school *(Oberrealschule)*. He contacted my mother, and, when she came to see him, she said: "We cannot afford it. Toni may complete only the lower division." He probably thought that we were wealthy when my mother put on the little fur that my father kept in his shop. The teacher's wife could not afford one. Teachers were paid very little. Many others whose fathers were not officials could not afford it either. I am sure he must have thought that my mother was close-minded. Once when we stayed for the summer school (Landheim) in the country, he called me into his office. On that occasion I dutifully told him that my father was too old. It had never occurred to him, and I myself never thought of it when applying. But the problem also lies in a societal order in which the family is everything and where nobody bothers to care about it. The school had to be paid, and a merchant family would never have understood the purpose of a scholarship.

Greffrath: In 1934 you began work on problems of Jewish history. After what happened in Germany did you ever feel obliged or sentenced to pursue these histories in the course of your life?

Oelsner: I still find it most interesting and, as I have said, research into history is an adventure. Do you know Marc Bloch? "You never know where you are going to end up." It is like taking a walk a little ways outside the city; you never quite know where you will end up. All of a sudden you read a document, and something entirely different is written in it than what you found in the summary. No, I have never felt obliged. I am still fascinated by it.

Greffrath: Finally I have one more question, which leads us back to the beginning. Do you still have contacts with Frankfurt after all this time?

Oelsner: No. It is because, well, I had thought at the time . . . Well, the last years have been almost lost for me. I have always dreamed of receiving an honorary degree from Germany because of my work. I always thought it might be possible to meet people then. No, I have contacts with no one.

Greffrath: Would you like to go back to Germany one more time, if only to see it again?

Oelsner: I'm feeling too old. Maybe I'll feel better tomorrow, but today I'm just feeling too old.

Translated by Mary Rhiel and Andreas Lixl

NOTES

1. For a convenient summary see Marion A. Kaplan, "Women's Strategies in the Jewish Community in Germany," *New German Critique* 14 (Spring 1978), 110ff, n. 4.

2. Peter Loewenberg, "The Unsuccessful Adolescence of Heinrich Himmler," *American Historical Review* 36 (June 1971), 616–618; 638, ff.

3. Cf. my "Wilhelm Roscher's Theory of the Economic and Social Position of the Jews in the Middle Ages: A Critical Examination," *YIVO Annual of Jewish Social Science* (1958–1959), 176–195.

4. On the usury prohibition and the usual subterfuges, cf. Gerald A. Hodgett, *A Social and Economic History of Medieval Europe* (London, 1972), pp. 64–66. It should be noted that

the Lateran Council of 1215 enacted a law stipulating that Jews were only to charge moderate rates of interest and laid down sanctions which included "boycott," namely, if borrowers complained about "immoderate" interest rates charged by Jews. Actually, in many loan contracts Jews followed the principle of Thomas Aquinas: *Damnum Emergens* (in German *Schadennehmen*). This meant that whereas the Christian lender demanded a fee for "late payment," the Jewish lender would ask a specific interest charge, usually 0.86% per week, after the due date. In my ms. I have verified this in numerous cases, and I consider this one of the major clarifications. It is just on this score that most historians of Jewish history have been so careless by stating the annual rate of 43.33% without indicating that payment was due only after a specified period of time. As there was no unified practice, it could range from several months to more than one year, or even two years. Hence the real per annum rate was reduced in proportion to the interest-free period. On Christian money-lending practices cited by Hodgett, cf. my "The Place of the Jews in Economic History," *Yearbook of the Leo Baeck Institute* (1962), 202–204.

7

FRAGMENTS OF AN UNCOMPLETED JOURNEY

ON JEWISH SOCIALIZATION AND POLITICAL IDENTITY IN WEST GERMANY

Dan Diner

Even before the fascist mass annihilation, the notions and expectations that were associated with the image of "Germany" had a particular significance for Jews. Of course, the image was quite different from the one we have today, virtually its opposite. Isaac Deutscher, the Polish-Jewish Marxist and biographer of Trotsky, was once told by his father long before the catastrophe that the cultivated cosmopolitan world began "to the west of Auschwitz," that is, west of the Polish-German language frontier. Germany was imagined as a promised land of the Western tradition, a land of universal enlightenment. This image was largely an expression of the

---

This essay was originally written for a published volume about Jews in Germany. However, it was turned down by the editors for undisclosed reasons. Its origins can be traced to a discussion initiated by the Sigmund Freud Institute and held in a lecture hall at the University of Frankfurt following the telecast of the TV film "Holocaust." Many of my friends and comrades tried to empathize with the situation of the Jews during the Holocaust period; their openness as well as helplessness eased my attempts to record some personally important aspects of my political identity which I had previously withheld. Yet, this is not intended as a biographical text, as could be mistakenly assumed. It is, rather, an attempt to present a view of "Germany," of a German development, which is of course bound to my person. Thus, my concern is with a practically experienced reality of the Federal Republic.

The text is not formulated as a coherent whole, although it presupposes a coherent context. To stress its tentative nature, I have focused only on several aspects that are based on general experience and could be elaborated. That is why, in my judgment, the succession of images and reflections are an appropriate form for this purpose, particularly since reflection can be a constituent part of experience.

admiration felt for the classical German writers. In an unimaginably terrible and fatal reversal, Auschwitz did assert itself as a cultural frontier. Instead of culture and civilization, instead of sublimation and assimilatory resolution, there was atrocious barbarism.

For the Jews living in postwar Germany the past remains repressed. The physical and psychological closeness to "Germany"—that negatively laden source of identity—leads to a reinforced denial of what happened then. In the house of the victim the corpse is just as seldom discussed as the noose in the house of the hangman. This phenomenon is intensified inasmuch as the present carries the past with it everywhere in everyday life and in a banal form that is hard to grasp. Yet, in order to prevent the past from dictating the present, it is imperative to overcome it by working it through in an active manner. Such a "working through" can then express itself in the form of a practical generalization of experience.

For conscious Jewish individuals who seek to work through that history associated with their ancestry, life in Germany cannot remain private individual history. The suffering experienced collectively, and hence also individually, thus becomes crystallized in political intention. The personal encounter mobilizes political energy; the sensory perception becomes an occasion for reflection that can generate change.

The willingness to generalize—one that is rooted in, and yet detaches itself from, the active and individual Jewish experience of suffering—can lead to a political morality. This process involves an extremely difficult and painful separation from Judaism, or, from the Jewish people as a particular context of organization and identification. The result is a Jewish identity which in its practice anticipates universality. The elements of various historically nonsynchronic levels that blend in such an identity were grouped by Isaac Deutscher in his notion of the "non-Jewish Jew." However, such a separation from ancestral attributes does not mean a renewed assimilation to an Other that already exists, such as another nation or culture. The only way open for such an identity is constant preparation of the future. The *Here-and-Now* has the character of being underway, of something constantly incomplete.

For a Jewish identity that conceives of itself in such a way, there can be no full and self-identical life in Germany. What remains is a life *through* Germany—along the course of that history and its consequences with which the historical phenomenon Germany is saturated. Jewish nonidentification with the psychological and physical *Here-and-Now* means to confront those elements essential to the Jewish identity of a non-Jewish Jew as filtered through the traumatizing experience of the mass annihilation—that is, through Zionism, communism, and fascism. Reflection, thus, becomes an aspect of lived identity and is not split off from it.

Reflection about the past gives particular weight to history. When one orients action in the present with reference to historical contents of identification and counteridentification and demands of oneself to act "better" than the persons of the emotionally charged past had done, one either runs the danger of emptying oneself as a concrete person and treating oneself as an abstraction, or of emphasizing the experience of fear so excessively that it becomes the only collective interpretation of the world and guiding principle of individual action.

This impulse, which, in terms of its origins, is virtually absolutely Jewish, must therefore be relativized as a part of a new life—an important part, but, nevertheless only a part of a new and politically informed identity. In this perspective the particular historical realm, experienced directly or indirectly as one of great suffering, can shrink from a position of total significance, if mourning is to be really effective. The result can be what Ernst Bloch sought to bind together with the symbol "ubi Lenin, ibi Jerusalem"—separated from its particular and personal reference, of course.

The point of departure for the new development of my identity was Eastern Europe. I neither knew prewar Eastern Europe directly, nor does it exist today in the same form. As a result, roots of identity, passed down more unconsciously than explicitly in my parents' home, had no ground; they had to prepare the ground by themselves.

The Jews of Eastern Europe stood in a process of intercultural exchange with the other ethnic groups living there. They were a vital component of those peoples, who themselves cannot be understood without their Jewish element. The many facets and richness of social life in the secularized Jewish domain led to the emergence of the first organized socialist workers' movement of Eastern Europe, among other things. The Nazi machinery of destruction extinguished its existence in a direct material sense; its leaders were liquidated by Stalin, and its historical memory was obfuscated for the most part by the Zionistic monopoly on the interpretation of Jewish history.

The leveled debris of old Eastern Europe left behind a void that nothing can ever replenish. The irretrievably lost social context of Jewish life is not due solely to the physical extermination of human beings. An entire culture was extinguished so that the survivors lack the possibility of any continuity of identity. They are not survivors in the sense that they lost relatives—they are the leftovers. Although fragments and splinters still have their hidden effect, they are felt more than they are known. It's no wonder that Zionism was able to plunge into this void and could satisfy and direct the individual as well as collective need for a historical explanation of the catastrophe by propagating the necessity to fall back on one's particularity. The Israeli identity which is thus created can only cover up that void. In the way, it is like a filling—a particularly appropriate image conceived by the psychoanalyst Paul Parin.

At age eight, nine years after the war's end, my Israeli-Levantine childhood was abruptly interrupted so that it could continue on a historically opposite terrain—in Germany. The cultural circumstances were different, and yet they were historically complementary to those of Israel. To be sure, the Orient continues to affect me in the form of non-European identity traits and infiltrated feelings as well as perceptions. However, the experiences I had in Germany were those that really left their imprint on me. This occurred also because a previous, perhaps even prechildhood memory of old Europe was brought to life through the new environment. I was still able to find traces of this old Europe: the cobblestones, wet with rain upon our dreary arrival; the houses perceived as particularly high and dark, with dirty gray facades pockmarked by the scars left by peeled-off stucco; the rows of houses interrupted by lots filled with ruins—all of which appeared to me like shattered dentures. But this very image of Europe, whose clammy dampness replaced the glistening Oriental sun, was presented to me differently a few years later when I made my first visit back to Israel as a fifteen-year-old. It was expressed in a Sibylline way by an old Jewish bagel vendor in the port of Haifa. He asked me where I came from, and in response to my shamed reply—"I come from Germany"—the bent old man with the broad-rimmed cap and squinting eyes nodded understandingly. Then he made a pronouncement in Yiddish that astonished me and which I couldn't understand at that time: In Israel the sun would also burn out that which Auschwitz had spared.

Everything is saturated with the past. Israel, though not actually in Europe, is of Europe. The two worlds, separated only geographically from each other, thrust themselves upon each other within consciousness and thus interweave. My early connection to Israel was reinforced by Germany, simply through the experienced chronological and spatial proximity to those past events. In the closet of a schoolmate's father the black SS uniform could still be found hanging among the garments of everyday life as a matter of fact. Today many hidden attributes of the past are revealed by the articles taken from attics and basements and sold at the flea market. In this way, the objective character of the commodity induces to make itself known a history that otherwise would have remained repressed.

I came to Germany nine years after the end of fascist rule and the mass extermination of the Jews. Nine years is truly a short span of time. (It has already been twelve years since the central event of my generation—the student movement.) This temporal proximity was heightened by the fact that in West Germany there was no break, neither politically nor culturally, with the past. One way this proximity was expressed, for example, was in the emphatic distinction made between the Wehrmacht and the SS, a distinction that reinforced the legitimacy of an ideology of domination. Perspective, however, is a function of participation: from the standpoint of the victim, Wehrmacht and SS were not divided by very deep trenches; the mass graves were their common denominator. To be sure, officially decreed policy in the newly formed Federal Republic of Germany expressed abhorrence toward the millionfold murder of Jews. However, the crusade mentality against the supposedly Communist-Bolshevik enemy in the East persisted. Small wonder, then, that—in everyday life, schools, streets, families, and local bars—standard behavior continued to consist of justification rather than criticism, legitimization rather than opposition. A superficial anti-Nazism was superimposed by school curricula and further watered down in the form of antitotalitarianism. It remained a very thin veneer that cracked when, for example, the teacher, an aging philologist and a former occupation officer in France, mourned nostalgically in the classroom for the many sweet fruits of the occupation he was prevented from fully reaping; or when a younger teacher could no longer conceal his primary educational goal and quickly supplemented the curriculum in order to convey his admiration for the spirit of camaraderie during World War II among antiaircraft personnel and night-fighter pilots. In the face of such open/hidden nostalgia the best I could do was to duck behind the protecting back of the person in front of my desk.

The everyday anti-Semitism of classmates led to fistfights that occurred during the breaks in the schoolyard and especially outside its perimeters. The violence was liberating: Fists make everyone equal, even if this equality is offset by physical inequality and does not result in any externally visible success. The subtle, intellectually refined racism and anti-Semitism of teachers was much worse. For example, my parents were obtrusively badgered to consider business as the prospective future career for their son. In a lecture on genetics the biology teacher could not resist transposing social phenomena into the animal world in a Darwinistic fashion. The consequences of such oblique references were only too clear to me. Besides—as I remember—it was then that the search for the Nazi Dr. Mengele had begun, who for the betterment of science tormented people to death in Auschwitz.

One case is particularly clear in my memory. Some time after my classmates had informed a teacher about a physical fight between myself and the strongest pupil in the class, the robust class bully, because of anti-Semitic taunting, the teacher called on me—I was fourteen at the time—to pay me due recognition for having kept silent about the incident. As far as

I can remember, there was talk about my upholding the spirit of cam-
eraderie, that collective ritual of secrecy laced with a dash of the mystical
Nibelungen faithfulness which had always been promoted in our school
years. The other pupils who, at the time of the incident, had expressed
their solidarity against me with laughter, knew nothing, according to the
teacher, about the great and grand significance of the Jews in Germany.
He began with the usual philo-Semitic talk about Jewish Nobel prize
recipients, even of a Jewish pediatrician, who, following the well-known
pattern, had saved his life when he had been a baby. I already had dark
forebodings. Glancing at my classmates, children of refugee and resettled
parents of the 1950s, he concluded by asserting that many were themselves
just half-Poles and Czechs. Racism as anti-anti-Semitism! This incident
taught me an important lesson about the indivisibility of morality, which
cannot be sufficiently realized by human concern and experience alone,
but which also demands appropriate generalizations and therefore, a
necessary degree of abstraction. To this extent, everyone has his Jew; even
the Jews have theirs. In particular, the Jewish people in Israel will have to
pay a high and bitter price for having identified with their European
aggressors. It is to be hoped that this price will take only a material and
political toll and not involve a blood bath. There is something fatal about
the reproduction of European history in the Orient. It is painful to admit,
but in a superordinate sense, the question is one of German fascism's
victory over the Jews. It is not coincidental that, as a projection, Israel's
feat of arms in 1967 was celebrated in West Germany. But just as Israel can
be used advantageously as the West's bridgehead in the Levant at one
point, it can also be abandoned at an opportune moment.

The variant of Jewish identity described here not only resulted from the
open encounter with anti-Semitism and racism, but was also subtly influenced by a cultural symbolism which I experienced as something strange.
National cultures cannot be picked up at will. They not only assume a
particular form, but that form is also filled with historically rooted contents. In spite of the validity of such a generalization there are differences
in each respective case. France, for example, is—in spite of the racism
existing these, which should not be underestimated—a land more open to
assimilation than Germany where, as a result of the folkish-agrarian elements in the entire culture, anti-Semitism was able to become a component part of the national self-understanding.

In the Federal Republic, individual and collective consciousness underwent substantial alterations because of the protest movement of the 1960s
which cannot be simply reversed. Consequently, there is a significant and
substantial increase in the possibilities for identification compared to the

1950s, when I was confronted with Germany on the level of mundane everyday life. Merely my relatively dark appearance required constant justification and explanation of my ancestry. But this also elicited self-definition and counteridentification.

The manner in which I was compelled to perceive symbols and learn contents in schoolbooks as a youngster, and the way I had to appropriate an alien alphabet and language as my own, reinforced a growing sense of my difference which was supposed to be counteracted by an even greater effort to adapt. The words spread out in rows of clumsy letters failed to awaken familiar tones, and the illustrations loomed at me almost threateningly. For example, Christmas scenes were always portrayed with national folkish and quasi-religious symbols; families always depicted as light blond, playing music at home; the allegories were dominantly agrarian and coupled with the eternal sower. I encountered an atmosphere that Franz Degenhardt, the political folksinger, presents in his song about the "little German town." Moreover, I had to join in prayers every morning at school, sing church chorals in music class, obey the round shaved heads of authoritarian teachers, and, as a break from religion, learn the somewhat national-folkish traditional songs of the Wandervogel and German Youth Movement.

In German class I acquired a deep and passive dislike for Adalbert Stifter, which puzzled me then. I felt excluded from his "Well in Front of the Gate." I found myself unable to take part in the trivial "Struggle for Rome" of Felix Dahn and inwardly preferred ancient Roman imperialism to the Germanic opponents, thus moving history forward several millenia. Having grown cautious I sensed how politics and current events were already implicit and being made in a class on ancient history. To defend myself I needed to counteridentify.

I was also skeptical about the classical German writers. After all, they had been easily transferred and integrated into fascism. Aside from that I sensed something deceptive and humanistically nonbinding in the sort of abstractions expressed in the figures of the Enlightenment. And, as a Jew, I immediately had to correspond to the image of "Nathan the Wise" in order to be accepted. A Jew who wore "payess," long earlocks, would have been enjoyed by being scrupulously ignored. Moses Mendelsohn, the figure who was commemorated by Lessing as "Nathan the Wise," is still considered philo-Semitically as something like the first Jewish Nobel prize recipient antedating Alfred Nobel. Max Frisch's *Andorra* dealt with the problem of prejudice and xenophobia in the land of the gnomes of Zurich. Its rationalistic approach could not grasp the anti-Semitic German cultural component. This is why it was easy for a pupil to argue that Andrei, the protagonist, was not a Jew in any way, and his point was valid.

Since my petit-bourgeois Jewish background endowed me with a typically pronounced "catastrophe-consciousness," which makes only that which is useful worth learning, it was impossible for me to develop an alternative, bourgeois cosmopolitan identity based upon universal Western cultural contents. The experience of the emerging counterculture of rock 'n' roll was therefore all the more important for me: It drowned out the stifling racist-laden music genres exemplified by the "schönen Westerwald" with a mighty, violent explosion. About the same time, that dreary Occidental consciousness of mission cloaked in the uniform of the Foreign Legion suffered its final military defeat at Dien-Bien-Phu at the hands of a colonial people which had previously been humbled and was now victorious.

Images, symbols, and language are cultural contents that cannot be abstracted from one's identity. They brandmark the psyche, cause heavily scarred wounds, and heal only conditionally in a process of confrontation as the means to forming a new identity. The helpless confrontation of a child with other cultural contents experienced as alien, inimical, or delimiting leads to profound injuries. Franz Fanon mentions in *Black Skin, White Masks*—a book which, not untypically, has yet to be translated into German—an example of a small black girl from the Antilles where, as in every other French district, the centralized cultural and educational policies demand usage of the same (white) schoolbooks. The black girl—just like a white child in Paris—writes an essay in class about how her cheeks turn red with glee in expectation of the approaching school vacation. This is a grotesque consequence of colonial alienation and shows how identity is destroyed in the process of adapting by necessity to an alien ruling culture and its values. In West Germany today Turkish children and other immigrant youngsters are losing their language without ever being able to be sure of German.

A Jewish child is not faced with the unambiguous rejection and segregation of colonial situations. Identification and participation appear to be open to the Jew by means of social integration through the aesthetics of social class learned in school. This is why I attempted, using the figure of Mann's "Tonio Kröger" as my example, to gain bourgeois acceptance. This endeavor ultimately failed when the offer to give the graduation speech at school was withdrawn upon the faculty's intervention. The old hallowed monastery hall of the small-town school would probably not have been able to bear this blasphemy. As far as I was concerned then, they could keep their "Nathan the Wise"—the promised land waved.

One teacher is said to have played a prominent role in bringing about this rejection. A few years earlier, a pupil had thrown a brick through the window of that same teacher at night while shouting, "You Nazi!" The student was dismissed from the school. Later he became editor of the Frankfurt student magazine *Diskus*. That brick was a symbol for me and anticipated the later action of the student movement.

The dominant form of dealing with Jews in the Federal Republic of Germany is philo-Semitic. Philo-Semitism in the form of pro-Zionism is a subtle and integral component of the particular historical legitimacy of this state. In its function as producer of ideology, this means of legitimization resembles that dogma which distorts history, according to which, the radical Left was just as responsible for the collapse of Weimar as the reactionary Right. Consequently, victim and hangman were equally guilty.

The Jews play a contradictory role for the general legitimation of the Federal Republic. On one hand the anti-Semitism of the Nazis, which was realized in such a horrible way, was presented in the supposed coming to terms with the past, as the only distinguishing factor of that barbarism. Thus, the continuity of those economic and political conditions, which were ultimately decisive for the actual fascist takeover, and which, even in terms of individuals, extended into the Federal Republic, was veiled. On the other hand, there was a clandestine philo-Semitic acceptance of the expulsion of the Jews from Germany, if not of their annihilation, as a constituting element of what became "home" in the Federal Republic. The noted historian Golo Mann admitted this with the confessor's gesture of openness and honesty, to magnates of heavy industry in the trusted circle of the Rhine-Ruhr Club. It is worthwhile to take note of the ambiguous unambiguity of his statement: "(The Weimar Republic) was seen by millions of German citizens actually as a Jew-Republic, as un-German and as a foreign matter. If the Federal Republic today is more fortunate, if this framework, in spite of its fragmentary character, is considered by a majority of Germans as their own home more than the Weimar Republic ever was, then it is doubtlessly due to a large extent to the fact that there are practically no more Jews in the Federal Republic. What I am saying here sounds cynical, and is, in fact, an extremely dangerous, delicate observation. But it must be made. The astonishing success of the Bonn Republic in the eyes of its own people and thus in the eyes of the outside world, the relative composure that characterizes public life in Germany today, has something to do with the fact that the German Jews have fled or were murdered" (Golo Mann, *Der Antisemitismus*, Munich, 1960, p. 29). A reconciliation is suggested, if not with the virtual murder of the Jews then at least with the consequences of their extermination. In fact, there appears to be a positive side to the annihilation of the Jews in that it has led to the stabilization of the system.

Here is the point where all the hidden and explicit correspondences unite to form the foundation of the structurally anti-Semitic philo-Semitism that must by necessity be pro-Zionist: The Zionist quest for a homeland maintains implicitly and explicitly that anti-Semitism will persist forever, just as anti-Semitism speaks of the caricature of the "eternal Jew." Beyond this, the image of the Jew used by many Zionist theoreticians depends heavily upon anti-Semitic distortion. Examples can be seen in the journalistic work of Max Nordau or Theodor Herzl, who wrote about the fictive Jew "Mauschel." The dominant trend of philo-Semitism can reassuringly point to the intention of Zionism; after all, the goal of Jewish nationalism had always been the migration of the Jews to Palestine. Thus, it becomes important to represent this movement as thoroughly genuine and not to play it down, for example, by pointing to it as a mere reaction to anti-Semitism. Thus, the weeding out of Jews from Europe becomes despicable only in its form, but not in its essence. It is easy to join in singing about how all Jewish suffering will find its end in a Zionist Israel. With the best philo-Semitic intentions, allowance is thus made for a Middle East "Götterdämmerung" for the Jews in the Jewish State if only as a result of the stubborn refusal to recognize the colonial conditions of the conflict in Palestine.

In the Federal Republic of Germany, a Zionist historical interpretation of the catastrophe has the effect of freeing public consciousness from assuming historical responsibility for the occurrences in Palestine inasmuch as it suggests that the particular way Jews came to live in Israel resulted from a self-made decision on the part of the victims to leave Europe. Those responsible are provided with a comfortable, easy way out when the surviving victims of Nazi barbarism interpret their fate as inevitable and even necessary in terms of such an understanding of history. It is easier for the victims to bear their fate by attributing such a meaning to it than it would be to withstand the feelings of shame, injury, and helplessness involved in seeing themselves as the driftwood of world history, cast upon the Levantine coast. Yet, that latter insight would contribute to a development in which much ideological ballast could be cast off in Israel. This, in turn, would make a non-Zionist integration of the Israeli Jews into the Arab Orient easier. Nevertheless, a distinction must be made: The conception of the Jews takes on the character—even if only alleged—of a survival, or it functions in a historically apologetic, guilt-alleviating manner in view of the prevailing German consciousness regarding the past.

It was the New Left that helped to reveal how the prevailing philo-Semitism in the Federal Republic served to conceal and repress the past. This assessment remains valid even if the way in which this "unmasking" was performed hurt the feelings of those Jewish victims who were directly concerned. The official philo-Semitic treatment of the Jews made one particularly sensitive to the fact that this obsequious civility had something more basic to conceal. There were sufficient indications that this was the case. How, for example, could one take West Germany's reparations seriously as an expression of an intention to make amends when the legal commentator of the Nuremberg race laws—Hans Globke—was tolerated and promoted as one of the highest civil servants in the Federal Republic? Moreover, it gradually became evident historically that exterminatory anti-Semitism was essentially able to become materially realized in such a catastrophic manner only because of the interest powerful social groups had in Nazi terror. As National Socialism rightly began to be compre-hended in postwar Germany as a composition of interest groups and not as some kind of natural catastrophe that broke over Germany, it became clear that those same interest groups supportive of the Nazis had been able to save themselves and survive unscathed in the Federal Republic. Conse-quently, the anti-philo-Semitism which arose on the Left had to lead to a critique of capitalism. Yet, at the same time, this critique fostered a specific form of historical and psychic repression. Although the critique of cap-italism could explain the social conditions of the fascist takeover as well as the function of anti-Semitism, a consideration of the form and substance of Jew-hating as a latent force of German history that had erupted under fascism was neglected. It was not taken seriously—and perhaps one even preferred not to do so.

However, this substantial social criticism that glossed over the phenom-enon of anti-Semitism resulted in a turnabout. If the prevailing state ideology considered anti-Semitism and the annihilation of the Jews as the decisive criterion of the National Socialist rule by force (*na-tionalsozialistische Gewaltherrschaft*), as it was euphemistically called, to conceal the continuity of the social conditions and to obfuscate the per-sonal responsibility of also those now in power, the recourse to a general critique of capitalism on the Left necessitated by such official ideology negated the subjective point of departure. I am referring to one's own personal history of antifascist politicization and the historical specificity of anti-Semitism which can indeed be explained materialistically. The turn-about involved appropriating Horkheimer's correct thesis ("whoever speaks of fascism cannot be silent about capitalism") in an unmediated and, hence, false manner. It led to a distancing from one's own particular history as well as from the concrete history of suffering experienced by the victims. Consequently, the subjective side of leftist identity was undermined by means of generalization and abstraction. Because the German leftist no longer wanted to be a German in light of the preexisting collective history, the Jew was also to be relieved of his particular history and identity.

This equality claimed on the basis of inequality made it difficult for me to identify with the radical movement. In particular, when the Palestinian question became an important political subject, I became alienated, and this led me to concern myself with Zionism for an important period of my history. The groundwork for such a turn toward left Zionism had been laid emotionally in my early childhood, and because of its complex and ambivalent nature, it has been particularly difficult for me to break from it.

The Nazis were the first to make Zionism into a Jewish mass movement. Who could subjectively blame the survivors from camps and forests if they not only wanted to get away from Europe physically, but also psychologically sought to reach Palestine in expectation of salvation? The material force that Zionism used against the Arabs of Palestine to bring about a Jewish state appeared to the European victims like a legitimate extension of that counterforce which had been their defense against their mortal enemies in Europe. One did not perceive the innocence of the helpless Palestinian Arabs, who were not to blame for the Jewish tragedy, and who in May, 1948, were made to pay the price, colonially, for the failure of a German revolution almost exactly one hundred years earlier. This made it possible for the same individual, who had been honored with Soviet citations as an antifascist partisan in the Eastern European forests, to become a colonial oppressor of Palestinian Arabs in the Oriental karst with the intention of founding and maintaining a Jewish state. But the experience of persecution is no justification for new persecution. What was it that Colonel Mathieu said in the film *Battle of Algiers* when accused of using fascist torture techniques? "How can we, who were tormented in Dachau and Buchenwald, be fascists?" The biographical self-perception of the victim—displaced in space and time—can become a noose for new victims.

Myths have a long life. As a four-year-old in Israel I experienced the first of May in a curiously compelling way. On this international workers' holiday my mother and I stood together with a playmate from kindergarten and his mother along the main street in Petah-Tikva and observed the demonstrators passing by: groups from factories, youth clubs, and party organizations. The entire city was drenched in the red of the flags which was only occasionally interrupted by the blue and white of the national flag. People were crowded together on the flat roofs to watch. Our excitement grew as that group from the youth organization approached which was to be led by my friend's older brother, who had been permitted to carry the group's red flag as an honor. I was never certain why I became disappointed when we saw him carrying the blue and white flag and not the red. I believe it was the spontaneous reaction of a child identifying closely with my friend which caused me to join in crying with him.

Right after this I experienced something in addition that left deep marks on me. In fact, I even assume that the entire memory of what happened was preserved by means of this event. All around us a solemn silence set in; then the national anthem flowed together in my memory into one, and from that point on I felt them to be an insoluble unity for a long time.

Later in Germany this event acquired greater psychological significance as I believed that I had to identify with Israel and the Soviet Union to protect myself against an alien surrounding. Among the symbolically effective images of my counteridentity which was evolving from my experience in Germany were the picture of the Red Army soldier atop the shell-pitted Brandenburg gate as well as the documentary film showing victory scenes on the Red Square in which the captured Nazi flags were thrust into dirt with one swift gesture by a formation of Soviet armed forces. The liberation of the surviving Nazi victims from the concentration camps by the Red Army, the Warsaw Ghetto revolt, the partisan battles, became all the more strongly interwoven with an Israel that had grown into a myth, the more the confrontation with the anti-Semitic culture of my German surroundings grew, and the more this confrontation became generalized in everyday racism. This mythic image was reinforced by the racist components in West German anticommunism and attitudes toward the peoples of Eastern Europe.

My identification with the Soviet Union triumphing over Nazism led me to assume an emotionally and morally grounded defensive posture in regard to the USSR. Initially I was unwilling to change this posture even in light of the political mock trials in Eastern Europe, the suppression of the Hungarian people's uprising, or even oppression of various nationalities, including the Jewish. During my childhood and early youth, my consciousness of the realities in the USSR was blocked by the awareness of the practical military antifascism of the Red Army and the 20 million Soviet lives lost. I virtually gave the Soviet Union unlimited political and moral credit because of its contribution to the defeat of Nazism. Only through painful struggle and effort was I able to come to terms with that past which made itself felt in the present.

My temporary separation from the New Left began in the wake of the June 1967 War in the Middle East. It was incomprehensible to me at the time that the Left in West Germany did not perceive the link between their history and that of those people who, as victims of Nazism, had been catapulted to Palestine and sought to realize their national identity in the State of Israel. I was certain then that this national statehood was the "solution" to the Jewish question and represented a consistent and evident consequence of the previous course of European history. The problems of the Palestinians I believed to be solvable within the framework of an Arab national state founded alongside Israel. In turn, Zionism itself seemed to me to be merely an ideological form of justification of the Jewish state, not, however, a material form of domination. Only later did I begin to understand that the establishment and maintenance of an exclusively Jewish state in Palestine was only possible through the employment of discriminatory measures and the continued use of colonial force. As a soldier patrolling the occupied West Bank, I experienced directly what had originally been an intellectual insight. In light of my history in Germany I, too, was humiliated by the humiliation of the Palestinian Arabs.

My separation from Zionism was a long and bitter process. It was additionally protracted by the fact that the prevailing notion of Zionism among parts of the Left was and is without historical foundation and tended to demonize it. Only too often was the Left conception of Zionism linked to that East European anti-Semitic tradition, which shamelessly introduced the word "Zionism" in the factional struggles of the ruling Communist parties against comrades of Jewish descent in order to slander them, paradoxically because of their internationalism, as "alien to the people," "cosmopolitan," and "unpatriotic." Insofar as Zionism was considered virtually identical with Jews, the Left accomplished precisely that which was the aim of Zionism and thereby justified it. This false "anti-Zionism" performed a disservice to that political anti-Zionism, which directs itself, because of discrimination and oppression, against the maintenance of an exclusively national Jewish state in Palestine and strives toward a common perspective for Arabs and Jews together. To paraphrase August Bebel's dictum on anti-Semitism, this type of false anti-Zionism can be termed with historical accuracy as "the anti-imperialism of fools."

Germany and Israel, or Palestine, mark the two poles of my identity, and I exist in the tension between the two. When I was younger, I considered a decision between the two unavoidable so that I could consciously and actively participate in history. Now I believe I know that I cannot make a decision of this sort. On the contrary, a decision for the one component against the other would be a decision against my history. Perhaps it might be best to convert this tension practically through internationalism. By this I mean to work for socialism in Germany and for a socialist Middle East. Both areas are interwoven with one another through real history and personal history. This link has to be recognized.

One final point. There is a particular danger for Jews living in Germany that they might become prisoners of earlier experiences particularly because the past is so close to them. For that reason there is a constant need to politically work through "Jewish anxiety" (Wolf Biermann), which repeatedly threatens to assert itself. This must be done, however, without denying the role of the past as a historically driving force. Only in this way is it possible to bear the tension between a personal history grounded in the past and a general political intentional desire for change, and to bring both of them together in a new identity. This means concretely to strive for the human being and therein to accept the significance of the Jew.

Translated by Gary Smith and Moishe Postone

8

GROWING UP IN GERMANY
AFTER THE WAR—AFTER HITLER—
"AFTERWARDS"
Yudit Yago-Jung

After what? This question has had a key influence on my childhood and the process of my becoming an adult. My identity represents a patchwork of shocking experiences as a child. It is the product of a slow and tedious gathering of information about the mysterious behavior of the adults around me and also a product of the endless attempts to find a rational, political or social explanation for that behavior.

I was born in Bonn in 1946 and grew up as the youngest of six children in a typical small town in central Germany. (It was so typical that in 1954 Renate Mayntz carried out a sociological study of this German "Middletown.") Four of my brothers and sisters were born between the years 1929 and 1938, the fifth, a sister closest to me in age, in 1941. The first thing that she used to blame me for whenever we had our little fights was that she had not gotten to know my father well until she was five years old. Why did she blame me for this, and what did I have to do with it? From the beginning my parents used to call me the "peace child." I was born exactly nine months after their first reunion following the war and the time of the concentration camps *(Lagerzeit)*. But why did my sister blame me for these things, anyway? What war were they talking about and what was the meaning of this strange word *"Lagerzeit"*? These were questions and mysteries that were there from my earliest childhood; they started with sibling rivalry and became even more encompassing as I began to explore the problem in greater depth. And there certainly was a lot to discover, for

135

starting with my earliest memories my family and I were somehow "different."

My father was a contractor. For the first fourteen years we lived in a barrackslike building next to his old office. The large building that housed the business was surrounded by a wall and had a huge entrance gate for the trucks; the gate was locked at night. My father had bars put in front of the windows, curliqued and very elegant, but bars nevertheless. What for? Other children didn't have to grow up in a fortress. My mother told me that years earlier, the Gestapo had kept watch on the house and had overheard conversations between my parents. But how were bars on the windows to protect against that?

My father also had the blinds lowered on all the windows after five o'clock, and locked all the doors. Our family never permitted unannounced visits. My parents had a small group of friends with whom they sat and talked together Sunday mornings: adult conversations—about Hitler, about the Nazis, the Gestapo, and about the *Lagerzeit*. We children had to leave the room, for it often happened that one or another of the grown-ups would begin to cry. I was the only one who was ever allowed to stay in the room once in awhile. After all, I was very small, two or three years old, "the peace child." What I understood, of course, was the fear on the faces of the adults and the merciless silence toward me. My brothers and sisters, with the exception of my youngest sister, were all away at boarding school. I was alone in this huge world, in this adult postwar Germany—alone with the fear-infusing behavior of the adults around me and alone with my strange dreams that I had been having since earliest childhood—dreams about burning houses strewn with corpses, my parents among them; horrible dreams about dismemberings, the tortures of women, murdered children, and the like. When I woke up screaming night after night, my father would take me in his arms and comfort me: "Go to sleep, sweetheart, everything is over, don't dream about such terrible things. It's never going to happen again. Peace is here now." During the day my dreams were quietly ignored (overly sensitive child, too much imagination, and so on). If in the sunlight, in the daytime, in front of the open gate, or outside in the courtyard or on the street in front of the house I were to ask questions such as what is peace, who are the Nazis or the Gestapo, who is Hitler, then my mother would answer me speaking for all the adults in my world: "Little girl, you can't understand such things. Hitler was the devil, evil itself, and the Nazis were his helpers, they murdered millions of people. But such awful things are not for children to hear." And as a child one is reluctant to look into matters of the devil anyhow. What's more, he was constantly creeping around in my dreams at night anyway. That there really was a devil was proved to me day after day by my father. His hands would always begin to tremble whenever anyone started talking about Hitler, the Nazis, or the Gestapo. Besides that, he always left the room, sometimes with tears in his eyes, if I began to ask concrete questions.

And so I tried to be a good, loving little girl in order that nothing bad would happen to me as had happened to my parents or the friends of my parents. But there were all these questions, these inconsistencies in the behavior of my parents, these terribly abstract, incomprehensible answers. My mother was my only source of enlightenment. And she supplied me— and still supplies me today—with her unpolitical "political" answers. Hitler and the Nazis were simply "evil incarnate" sweeping across the world.

My mother is Catholic and comes from a very poor peasant family in the Rhineland. My father converted to Catholicism for her sake when they got married. His grandparents, clerks who had emigrated from France, were living in a small village near Frankfurt. According to my father, they were Jews. Whether that was one or two generations back made little difference to my mother's family or to the Nazis. For them my father was of Jewish descent. My father was a self-taught man who in the 1920s had managed to finish engineering school in Frankfurt and wanted to found his own construction business. As a stranger and new arrival to the town, Catholicism appeared to him quite logically a necessary ticket of admission to the local bourgeoisie. In spite of this, he never did succeed in being socially accepted, not even after the marriage to my mother in 1926. At that time he began building his business, which was soon a success. It was on the basis of his economic position that he was able to maintain himself without having to join the Nazi Party.

Half a year before the *Kristallnacht* (1938) my father was asked as chief construction manager to provide engineering specifications for the local branch of the Tietz Department Store chain whose building he and his Jewish business partner had built. The store was to be "Aryanized"— National Socialist terminology for the official expropriation of Jewish businesses, under the pretext that it was dilapidated and would have to be evacuated. My father refused, whereupon the Gestapo began to look into his family background and examine his political views. It was soon discovered that no one in his business was in the Party and, in addition, that most of the workers were old Social Democrats. The Gestapo issued him a warning and placed an SS man as foreman in the factory. From that point on things took their course. Between 1938 and 1943, according to the official reasons given at his arrest, he was guilty of "seditious activities"— he had actively taken up contact with other resisters and, as he himself said, "made himself useful where he could" in giving work to "Non-

Aryan" foreign workers *(Fremdarbeiter)*, in helping concentration-camp prisoners escape, and similar kinds of activities. For my father this was perfectly natural—he never saw himself as a hero or as a political resister, and maybe he did not do much against the inferno around him, but he simply could not accept a world where there was no respect for law and humanity, even if he knew that in so doing he would endanger the life of his family. In 1943 the unavoidable occurred—the Gestapo arrested him and confiscated his family possessions. Since he was destined for transport to Sachsenhausen, my mother took my brothers and sisters and hid in the town of his birth. After a year and a half in transitory labor camps, my father managed a daring escape and remained hidden in the woods until the arrival of the Americans in 1945. After the end of the war, physically and mentally exhausted from the torturing and suffering of the *Lagerzeit,* my father gathered his family around him and with his status as "politically persecuted" began to rebuild his business. Now it was time for peace, for forgetting, for concentrating on economic survival: I was born into and was a product of this forced unproblematic politics of forgetting. My parents were already forty-six at the time of my birth. What for them was subjective forgetting became for me an objective covering-up. Even as a young child I was quite aware that on all sides a massive concealment was going on. At one end of the scale were my parents, who cut themselves off inexplicably, who had no contact with their families, and who surrounded themselves with friends and neighbors, all of whom had gone through "the worst" and whose behavior, even today, was and is marked by fear and total distrust toward their immediate environment. The climate of fear only relaxed when friends of my father from the *Lagerzeit* came to visit, or if distant Jewish relatives from abroad were there. Then I cheered up too, seeing how the fear disappeared from my father's face and in a mood of laughing and warmth how they praised me as "the peace child."

On the the other side there were the neighbors' children, the people living on our street, the teachers in the Volkschule, the outer world of Germany. Out there, on the street, I was "different." Even my physical appearance separated me from the other children. My dark hair and bony little body had nothing to do with the blond, full-cheeked image of the other kids in our neighborhood. Upon venturing out of my territory away from the family business to play marbles with the kids on the outside, I would sometimes end up crying. Either out of disappointment or jealousy they would often yell at me, "You Juddekind, go back where you came from." Horrified, I would run to my mother and ask her what "Judde-kind" meant. She would get pale suddenly and mumble something about it being a terrible word and that Jews were good people and that maybe I shouldn't play with children who would yell such things. Once again an explanation that was no explanation.

By the time I started school I had managed to put together my own explanation for the spoken and unspoken mysteries of my world. To be a Jew had to be something pretty awful if the neighborhood children could scream it out with such hate. And yet, the only Jews I knew, an aunt of mine and a neighbor who had been in Theresienstadt, were among the few friends whom my parents had in the postwar period; indeed, they were the only people with whom my father relaxed and could be spontaneous and funny. They were the ones whom I wanted to belong to and not to the neighbors' children, for whom I was so "different." Anyway, people in the neighborhood whispered that my father, "ol' Albert," had become very different since his *Lagerzeit* and that even the children, especially the youngest, were a little weird. They could think that I was "different" for all I cared—because I was! With a kind of spiteful determination, I began to explore things with my schooling and compare the inconsistencies between my family and our environment. Why was my father at home and all the other fathers of my schoolmates either missing or killed in the war? Why did my mother do most of her shopping at stores owned by people who had not been Nazis? Why did my parents know so many people in Belgium, England, America, and the other children's parents did not? Why did I know my father's family only by hearsay and others had even their grandparents still living near them? Why did my elementary school teacher write such strange things into my poetry collection like "Be proud of the courage that your parents showed in the face of tyranny. Your parents fought for their convictions." That was not the kind of thing that one could show around in second grade. I would have been a lot happier if he had written something like "roses are red, violets are blue, . . . and I love you too." And again and again the concrete questions: What are Nazis? Who was Hitler? What happened before the war?

I never got any answers. For my parents, memories of the past were simply traumatic, and for years I didn't dare to stir them up, especially with my father, by trying to find out what I had to know. My teachers avoided the subject because they themselves were too directly implicated in the events. For them, history books ended in 1933. In history class we would spend half a year treating the Weimar Republic in detail only to end up racing through the "modern" history from 1933 to 1945 with a kind of vague nostalgia in the last class before the summer vacation. After the vacation it was Konrad Adenauer and the postwar miracle. No explanations from this section either. All I had left were books. Other kids on the street didn't know anything, since their parents were as silent as mine were. Just as with me, their parents hadn't told them anything either. The past experiences and present motivations might have been quite different, but the results were the same: When it came to questions about the past, the postwar generation, Jews and non-Jews alike groped helplessly in darkness despite the dawning of the Adenauer reconstruction period. By remaining silent about everything, my parents hoped to be able to survive psychically and also to protect me, their youngest, from reality. Yet, by not giving me concrete answers to the questions I asked, they managed to reproduce in me the very fears and the very distrust toward the immediate environment from which they wanted to shelter me. In the social and historical vacuum in which I grew up, I came to experience my "being different" as threatening, which in turn led me to transform my distrust toward the world around me into an obsession to find out everything humanly possible about the Third Reich, about anti-Semitism, about my parents' past and the past of all the parents of my schoolmates and those around me.

By hushing things up, the parents of my German friends tried to conceal their own cooperation with or, at best, their passive tolerance of horrors in the Third Reich. They, too, rarely gave concrete answers. For the most part they gave none. They, too, reproduced fear—the fear of having their own past discovered and the fear of being morally judged by their own children, my generation. And my friends dared not ask the crucial questions at home. They, too, feared living with the knowledge that their fathers might have been members in the SS (Storm Troopers) and their mothers in the BDM (League of German Girls). But the older we became, the more we were able to obtain information. During the early 1960s we reached puberty and could no longer be pacified with evasive answers. The puzzle was pieced together, and we were enraged at what we saw—enraged at how our parents could have permitted such a thing. The fears emanating from our childhood turned into outrage toward our parents, our teachers, the university system, and the authoritarian mentality still prevalent in Germany, and we rebelled against the generation of our parents who let things come to pass and who had prostituted themselves morally and humanely.

Yet, where could my generation find a moral starting point? At first we looked to America for direction, to John F. Kennedy, but our faith in the American democracy was soon to be undermined by the immorality of the Vietnam War. Intellectually it was the critical theory of the Frankfurt School (Adorno, Horkheimer, Marcuse, Habermas, and the rest) that provided a political alternative, since socialism, with its premise of humanitarian and individual liberation, appeared as a possible choice in a West Germany mired in authoritarianism. In addition, the liberation movements of the Third World fed the romantic yearnings of my generation. And, it appeared that even the Nazi past of one's own family history could be amended by rediscovering the old Communist party. Identification with an antifascist proletarian movement, which up to then had been officially repressed, now served as a bridge over the past of one's own parents.

So much for the growing up of my classmates. My personal maturation took a different course. Protected and cut off from my friends on the street and in the classroom, locked within the cotton walls of parental silence, I retreated to my books. I read anything I could get my hands on—ancient legends from the Catholic municipal library, my brothers' old Karl May novels, and especially the old schoolbooks that had survived the war in the air-raid shelter of our house. And here, once again, I encountered the dreaded past, for the anti-Semitism of the Third Reich sprang from the pages and was something even a child could see.

I was concerned and struck by what I read. I began to sense something: Perhaps I was Jewish, too—and perhaps that's why we were "different." But how come my parents still lived in Germany? Why did it take such an effort to raise me as a nice German girl, if I had been born into peacetime anyway? Why didn't they just give me answers? My sisters and brothers were not especially helpful as sources of information. They only knew that they all had difficulties in school because of my parents, that my father had been picked up in 1943 by the Gestapo, that my mother sent them to a private school run by nuns who had also helped Konrad Adenauer against the Nazis, and that it was best not to upset our parents with questions about the past.

So I made my discoveries through books. When I was twelve years old, a girlfriend whose parents had a connection to the Kreisauer Circle happened to give me the book by Gross, *Das Brandopfer* (The Burnt Offering), to read. Somehow I had the feeling that the same thing must have taken place in our city, on our street, between my parents and their neighbors. The butcher store on our street had also sold kosher meat—my mother mentioned this often when I was a child—to Jewish families (perhaps even to my mother??) and our neighbors also had hidden a Jewish family—I learned about this, too—and smuggled food and false passports. And where did my parents stand? My questions became more concrete and relentless. And, besides, the child reads too much. She ought to get out of the house and play with children her own age, she ought to learn to cook and sing and behave properly. Otherwise she'll become weird, and nobody will marry her. So off to private school at age twelve.

This prep school was different from the one my brothers and sisters had attended. It was in Bad Godesberg where the teachers were supposedly more enlightened and liberal, where the education was better and more refined. In the meantime the sensitive child with an overflowing imagination had developed into a rebellious young girl—"obstinate to the nth degree," as the teachers used to describe me. The private school was supposed to help me overcome the fear of my surroundings, transform my distrust into cheerful cooperation through total control in the group, quench my thirst for information about the past with Christian stories and Catholic spiritual literature, lower my rage against adults, and break my stubbornness in any way possible. In response to my incessant questioning about how the nuns could allow thousands of orphans and mentally disturbed children who were entrusted to them to be killed in Hitler's euthanasia program, came a veritable torrent of temporary groundings which prevented me from leaving the premises. I was also assigned additional prayers—for pedagogical reasons, of course. Thus burdened with groundings and prayers, I began to concern myself with Zionism. In the process, I came to realize that I would convert to Judaism whether my ancestors were Jewish or not. Furthermore, I had no intention whatsoever of remaining in Germany. I was now old enough to understand and to want to plan. So I planned my spiritual and physical emigration.

After six years of private school I began to study sociology, the only one out of a class of twelve girls to enter the university. Ten of the others chose to become elementary school teachers. My decision to study the social sciences was easily understood by my classmates and teachers. Such an unfeminine and intellectual girl like Fräulein Jung could be expected to do something shocking like studying sociology. And what's more, she had already managed to bring about the elimination of compulsory religious drills, and it was clear that Fräulein Jung was quite different from the rest, but this time she was rebelliously "different."

My studies at last gave me the freedom that I had wanted so long. A new language, new insights and information, contact with people who thought differently, participation in an investigation about the results of Adorno's *Authoritarian Personality,* critical examinations of the West German reality in the seminars of Habermas and Dahrendorf. In addition, there were friends rebelling in ways similar to mine—against the banal German conformity in our homes, against rigid structure in the public sphere, against prescribed role expectations in the private sphere.

But in spite of all the newly acquired freedom of thought and action, it was still only partial freedom. There was something—in fact, a great deal—that was wrong with my new rebellious way of life. Not only did I want to know everything about Germany, fascism, and sociology, but I also wanted to contribute my views. I wanted to be actively involved in change—intellectually, politically, and personally. Well, fortunately at that time females who wanted to be active were accepted in the seminars at the University of Constance where I studied. To be sure, it was at first difficult to gain equal rights as a co-discussant *vis-à-vis* male students, but when a woman allowed her intelligence to shine publicly, she was accepted by the others. And even in my personal life it seemed possible to create a synthesis between work and pleasure, one that men appeared to achieve so effortlessly. Besides, it was extremely flattering to be regarded as a "super-woman" by the SDS (Sozialistischer Deutscher Studentenbund) "men," a woman who not only discussed in grand abstractions but who could also cook Chinese food and had classy long legs. Yet, by the end of my studies, the hierarchies had established themselves within the seminars, and some-how my Chinese cooking and long legs became more important for my comrades than did my opinions. Even as a leftist woman, I discovered, I was prevented from voicing my views. Though they used other pretenses than their conservative brothers, who felt that women have only straw in their heads and are meant just for rearing children and listening to male problems, it still amounted to the same thing when my comrades explained to me that political thinking and perseverance were unfeminine qualities that would make me unpopular. A feminist, Yuck!

But it was too late for a second "Andorra" phase in my life. Ever since the Six-Day War (1967) I had spent my vacations in Israel and worked enthusiastically for Zionist socialism in the Jewish Student League. Another society, warmth, openness, humor, apparent equality between men and women at work—all this seemed to be realized in everyday life. In Israel, I felt for the first time in my life that I could be at home, sheltered and freed from the fear of omnipresent fascism. But I still had to finish my studies in Germany and complete my doctoral dissertation on the national question in the Jewish working-class movement before I could settle in Israel. So every time I returned from Israel and crossed the German cultural and legal borders, I felt an increasing estrangement. In addition, SDS—I mean those groups left over when SDS fell apart at the end of the 1960s—had switched their position on Palestine. For a long time Israel was discussed in the anti-imperialism study groups, and proletarian Zionism had seemingly revealed itself to be "false socialism." The national liberation movement of the Palestinians, on the other hand, offered far greater possibilities for identification because it was more unacceptable, more immediate, and, above all, more brutal.

Suddenly, as a leftist, I encountered ghettos very similar to those of my childhood. I was not accepted by men because I expressed my personal fury at all forms of oppression using the academic language of their university world, and moreover, I did not play the role of the soft, lovely female. I was no longer accepted by my German comrades because I was

Jewish, which implied maintaining a right to be different in Germany and to live out my life in Israel. I was thought to be too emancipated in the personal realm, too assertive in the academic realm, too old-fashioned in the religious realm, and moreover, still a Zionist. However, for me nothing much had changed in Germany. Whether it was a new generation or not, the rejection of different ways of thinking and acting seemed (and seems) to be subjectively just as strong in Germany today as in my childhood, in my father's childhood, and in the childhood of previous generations. It took my father thirty-three years to find the courage to show me his restitution file and to tell me about the torture he experienced and the psychic disturbances that resulted from his imprisonment. I am a product of those scars, which fascism left on this more or less "proper German" family. But the vicious aspect of this is that it was not just fascism alone, but especially the period thereafter, the "lovely" silence of all those people who produced the economic miracle, that transformed the wounds into permanent scars. My experiences with my own generation were similar to my experiences with the generation of my parents. In my childhood my family did not conform to the notions held by the community, and it was dangerous to be different. In my adult years I did not conform to the notions of feminity and the socialist, non-Jewish culture of the new German generation.

This tragic situation put me into a different double bind as woman and mother, and I solved the conflict only through emigration. As a woman I could not, through an aggressively intellectual obsession with work and a successful career, simply channel and forget my fear and outrage about what had happened in the past. As a mother in Germany I would constantly have to produce new explanations for my two Jewish sons, explanations that I myself don't have about National Socialism, about earlier anti-Semitism, and about the bias against Jews that still prevails. Furthermore, I would have to explain why I needed thirty-three years before I myself could demand answers from those responsible for the past in my home city—answers which I eventually received. But I could never explain to my sons the causes lying at the root of everything, namely, how the fear of authority and order that had helped bring about National Socialism in the 1930s repeated itself in Germany of the 1950s as fear of discovering the past and in Germany of the 1970s as fear of different ways of thinking, foreigners, and terrorists.

Thirty-three years are a long time to tear down the psychological barriers built up by fascism. I began this process only recently, after experiences with my young family in another country enabled me to develop the courage of an independent adult. But it seems that others of my generation in Germany have been undergoing a similar process and have come to similar conclusions. One of these people is Lea Fleischmann. Her book *Dies ist nicht mein Land—Eine Judin verlässt die Bundesrepublik* fascinated me and brought me to the verge of tears, not so much because I identified with her in many situations but more because she recognized the underlying reasons for my fear during my youth in Germany—the worship of anonymous and constraining authority, the flight from the past, and the rejection of everything that is different, spontaneous, humane, and therefore, potentially chaotic.

I happened to read her book while I was on my way to visit Germany from the United States. My plane had been delayed by the time I had reached Luxembourg, and since train connections to my hometown were scant, I was forced to take the airport bus to Cologne so that I could possibly catch a train from there to my parents' house. After approximately two hours in the bus, I saw familiar villages glide by my window and realized that I was only twenty kilometers away from home. Therefore, it occurred to me that I might ask the bus driver if he could make an unscheduled "restroom stop" so that I might disembark. However, how could I have forgotten that I was traveling in the land of orderliness? "You could have gone to the bathroom in Luxembourg (= regulate your needs) and anyway, rules are rules. Otherwise anyone could come to me with just about any request (= anticipation of a chaotic future). We don't do things like that here, not us (= the firm, the government, the society). After all we're not a private taxi company." That was enough for me again. I sat down in outrage, resigned and silent. Suddenly the back tire blew out, and the huge vehicle rolled onto the sidewalk in the middle of Blankenheim, twenty kilometers from my home. I told the driver that next time he had better let me out immediately and such things wouldn't happen. I took my suitcase and within one hour I was home.

Will it ever be different in Germany, thirty-four years afterward?

Translated by David Bathrick and Jack Zipes

9

GERMANS, JOURNALS, AND JEWS/ MADISON, MEN, MARXISM, AND MOSSE

A TALE OF JEWISH-LEFTIST IDENTITY CONFUSION IN AMERICA

Paul Breines

In August, 1979, *New German Critique, Social Text,* and the kindred German journal, *Ästhetik und Kommunikation,* held a small conference to discuss some of their shared theoretical and practical concerns. The gathering took place on the campus of the University of Wisconsin in Madison, where a number of associates of the two American journals reside. In the opening session some of the editors outlined their publications' problems and perspectives. For good measure they sketched their intellectual roots. This last matter, that of roots or heritage, did not occupy the conference as a whole. But it led me to the personal reflections that follow.[1]

When David Bathrick, Jack Zipes, John Brenkman, and Stanley Aronowitz referred to the young Lukács, Gramsci, Benjamin, Adorno, Marcuse, and Habermas, this list of forerunners seemed to most of us unexceptional, almost obligatory. The *Social Text* editors spoke in addition of some contemporary Parisian influences, which caused a ripple of mutters among us Germanophiles present. But even this seemed a matter of prescribed roles and assumptions; Frankfurters versus French Fries, as one participant commented. To German ears our approach to the business of forerunners and influences evidently had a different ring. Peter Hohendahl thus opened the discussion with a disarmingly obvious question:

What of the *American* sources of these journals' work; the native well-springs of their thinking? Could it be that we American radicals draw no sustenance from indigenous traditions and currents? Presumably we do, but the interesting thing is that none was mentioned, and that none of us thought this odd.

Nor was the question really addressed. The discussion moved instead to a more pressing matter of historical-political identity: the role of women in the two journals and the larger problem of tensions between Marxist and Feminist theory. And I cannot answer it properly here, at least not in connection with *New German Critique* and *Social Text*. I know them only as a friendly outsider. But as soon as Peter Hohendahl posed his question, my thoughts began to scurry down a trail of memories and associations centering on questions I had fumbled with before, and in the same place, Madison. I had been an undergraduate student there from 1959 to 1963, and then a graduate student between 1966 and 1968. Those were for-mative years, personally and for the New Left movement generally. When-ever I return to Madison, I get submerged in nostalgia, and this time was no different, except that circumstances prompted me to try to see it through. At the conference, then, the thought occurred to me that of course Madison itself is in some sense the American root of the two journals, as it had earlier been the home of *Studies on the Left, Radical America*, and a host of other expressions of the New Left's intellectual culture in this country. One need look no farther than the very place in which we were gathered.

Yet just as quickly, the picture blurred in my mind's eye. For the Madison Left experience, at least in the early and mid-1960s, was never simply an American experience. It was more jumbled, at least more composite—like America itself? In my own not untypical case, Madison helped turn me into an American leftist, but at no point in the process was I really drawn to American models of Leftism. They were available in relative abundance, but so were others—western, central, and eastern European models—which I found more compelling. Why, for example, was I drawn more deeply into the European cultural history course taught by the nonleftist German-Jewish émigré, George Mosse, than to the course on American foreign policy offered by the very American socialist historian, William Appleman Williams? Was this because of the differing styles of academic charisma of the two teachers, both of whose courses were vital experiences for so many students? Or was my leaning toward Europe an expression of some budding estrangement from things Amer-ican; a sophomoric but critical sense that genuine *Geist* could be found anywhere but here?

Or does the answer involve a yearning for something Jewish, a little bit

Jewish in any case? After all, I was what some might call an A.W.O.L. Jew, while Mosse's initial impact was primarily that of a cosmopolitan German, rather than a Jewish, intellectual. Or all of the above? And these led to further queries like what really is a political heritage? Why and how do you make it your own? What is the relation between being influenced by and constituting the things that influence you? And what is the relation in all this between private fantasies and objective factors? How do you share a heritage, and can you have more than one? The only clear element was the fact that I was on *this* merry-go-round again and, no surprise, in Madison.

Three Representative Careers

There are, then, two magic rings to reach for here. One is Madison, the University of Wisconsin, as a specific center of New Left intellectual culture in this country.[2] The other is the Jewish part of that story as I experienced it. Since I approach these matters from the standpoint of historical materialism, the proper starting point is with the occupant of the chair next to mine at the conference, Stanley Aronowitz. He enters the picture not because he happens to be a Jew or because he has any special relation to Madison, which he has only visited. I refer to him because the main outlines of his career indicate some of the social backdrop of these notes. At the close of his initial remarks, Stanley Aronowitz reiterated the great dream of so many leftist journals today. *Social Text,* he announced, was dedicated to reaching an audience beyond academic circles. The fact that he could say this in 1979 in Madison was in my mind laden with symptoms of our shared historical situation.

I first met Stanley Aronowitz in New York City in 1963, when he had been recruited onto the editorial board of *Studies on the Left,* which had been launched in Madison in 1959, moving to New York some two and a half years later. I was then one of *Studies'* undergraduate friends and hangers-on. The journal itself was the main periodical publication of the germinal New Left in this country. Part of the reason for its move from Madison to New York City was to be located more suitably for building ties to leftist activity beyond campus confines. The recruitment of Stanley Aronowitz, at the time an organizer for the Oil, Chemical, and Atomic Workers' Union, was to further this aim. Through him, *Studies,* which from the start had a less academic cast than most comparable journals today, was not only reaching into the working class, but bringing the working class into the journal. Now, with some water under the bridge, Stanley Aronowitz, one of the three editors of *Social Text,* is a tenured professor. He is seeking among other things exactly what *Studies on the Left* had found in him in the first place.

Then there is the case of Paul Buhle. He is not a Jew, nor was he present at the conference, although he should have been. In 1965–1966, while a student at the University of Connecticut, he founded *Radical America*, a journal of American socialist and labor history. Paul Buhle, his wife, Mari Jo Buhle, the feminist historian, and *Radical America* moved to Madison in 1966–1967. At roughly that time, *Studies on the Left*, long resettled in New York, ceased publication. I had just returned to Madison following two years at Cornell. While there, Sam Weber and Shierry Weber introduced me (and my wife—the story of couples on the Left awaits its chronicler) to the ideas of the Frankfurt School. That opened the way for what we soon considered *the* book, Marcuse's *One-Dimensional Man*, which appeared in 1964. Paul Buhle's arrival in Madison, then, coincided with the little efflorescence of Marcusean ideas in Madison in which I, along with a group of old and new friends, was involved. Buhle, a sort of new-syndicalist, was initially interested in labor history. But through his attention to questions of working-class culture, he began building nice if often polemical links to those of us who were buried in Marcuse, Adorno, Horkheimer, and the Frankfurt School's critique of the culture industry. Making a longer story short, the polemics centered around Paul Buhle's opposition to what he saw as our elitist scorn for popular culture; our blindness to its oppositional elements.

When I left Madison for Germany early in 1968, I corresponded with Paul Buhle on some of these problems. One theme our exchange of letters took up was whether the distance we Frankfurt School disciples felt from popular culture was a Jewish distance; a case of estrangement between cosmopolite Jews and the American grain. As I recall, Paul Buhle and I at least agreed that this was, in some important sense, the case, even if the little circle of *Frankfurterkinder* did not consist of Jews alone. While he never warmed to what he deemed our aloof cosmopolitanism, nor we to what we considered his populism, Paul Buhle and the rest of us were together intrigued by these issues. In the meantime, he was opening the pages of *Radical America* to writings of a neo-Frankfurt School variety. And today, while the journal he founded is in other hands, Paul Buhle is an expert on Yiddish socialist culture in America. He is fluent in the language, filled with knowledge of Yiddish working-class theater, poetry, and press, and more conversant in numerous Jewish matters than are many of his Jewish friends from the Madison Left. What is one to say of such an evolution: only in America? or only in Madison?

The third career is Ralph Leavitt's. In accord with one strand of experience that I had in 1959 brought with me to Madison from the prosperous

New York suburb of Scarsdale, I joined a fraternity, Pi Lambda Phi. Lonely and apprehensive as an incoming freshman, my first social contacts were with some boys who were fraternity bound and I went along. I looked over some Gentile houses—the dividing lines were clear enough— and finally chose "Pi Lamb." It was a Jewish fraternity whose members tended not to look especially Jewish and generally paid special attention to parties with Gentile sororities. Characteristically, I avoided the one or two houses that were more obviously Jewish, less sports-minded and more religiously oriented. My own impulses to deny my Jewishness, to be a Gentile, fit well with the Pi Lambda Phi ambience.

Anyone entering a fraternity went through a trial period as a pledge, each of whom was assigned to a pledge father. Mine was one Ralph Leavitt. Brilliant and troubled, Ralph Leavitt held the informal title of house animal, meaning he was a master of all sorts of vulgar stunts, some funny, others sadistic. When as a pledge I naively proposed that our fraternity contribute money to the movement of black students then engaged (1959–1960) in sit-ins in the South, Ralph Leavitt denounced me as a nigger-lover. Not long afterward, I quit Pi Lambda Phi. And as a small sign of those times, when my class graduated in 1963, only three or four of the twenty boys who had entered Pi Lambda Phi in 1959 were still in the fraternity. Eventually Ralph Leavitt, too, departed from the pre-scribed path. He found his way to Israel, became a Zionist, then re-nounced Zionism and emerged a well-known figure in the Trotskyist movement. As a graduate student in Soviet Studies at the University of Indiana in the mid-1960s, he was one of the politically persecuted "Bloomington Three." In 1968 or thereabout, my ex–pledge father was running for political office in the state of New York on a slate of candidates put forward by the Socialist Workers' Party.

Pi Lambda Phi suggests a fourth career, about which more will be said below: that of Professor George Mosse. For several years prior to my own arrival in Madison, George Mosse had been the fraternity's faculty advisor. Normally this is a perfunctory role, but he managed to get himself expelled from it. When in 1958 a handful of Pi Lambda Phi members tried by a sort of coup d'etat to reform the Hazing Week, the disgusting and in several instances lethal initiation rites, their plot was exposed and the perpetrators were sent packing. With them went their active supporter, Professor George Mosse—a small harbinger of the student activism to come and of his ties to it.

The History Department

George Mosse is of course not known primarily as a former advisor to a Jewish fraternity. In the late 1950s and early 1960s he was merely one outstanding member of an exceptional history department in an unusual university in a politically interesting state. For some, the state of Wisconsin is notable as the homeland of Senator Joseph McCarthy, the infamous witch-hunter of the early Cold War years. But it has other credentials, including such Progressives as Senator Robert LaFollette and William Evjhue, founding editor of the once muckraking paper, *The Capitol Times;* a strong socialist movement in the early decades of this century, especially around Victor Berger in Milwaukee; later, a durable branch of the Communist Party, and so forth.

That the University of Wisconsin, too, should have a certain heritage of academic radicalism is thus not surprising. This reaches back at least to the turn of the century when John R. Commons founded the country's first school of labor history; to Alexander Micheljohn, iconoclastic and experimental university president in the 1930s; and to such beleaguered leftist faculty in the 1940s as the Marxist, Alban Winspear, author of *The Genesis of Plato's Thought* and one of the teachers with whom Norman O. Brown studied classics. In the post–World War Two years, the history department in particular collected a handful of independent-minded (and at the time leftist) scholars, among them the Americanists, Fred Harvey Harrington, Merrill Jensen, Howard Beal, and William Best Hesseltine, who created a certain space for critical reappraisals of the national past. This would then be expanded further by two graduate students who in the 1950s and 1960s were to return to the university to teach—the socialists William Appleman Williams and Harvey Goldberg. While the history department was emerging as the main vessel bearing, altering, and enhancing older radical traditions, the university also counted among its faculty the sociologist Hans Gerth, who had in 1942 approved a doctoral study of American pragmatism by another talented Madison graduate student, C. Wright Mills.

These are but some highlight personalities of a story that awaits its interpreter, although much of the story *is* one of the coming together of teachers and students, the ties and tensions among them being central to the transmission of ideas. In the absence of that larger story, three summary observations will serve as a momentary substitute. The first is that the University of Wisconsin crystallized some of the state's rich political dynamics and in doing so provided the historical terrain for the fusion of oppositional activism *and thought* which was to flourish in the 1960s. The second point concerns the vital place in this picture of the history department, a few of whose members managed to create, often quite without intent, a politically and morally charged milieu which, in the rapidly shifting climate of the late 1950s and early 1960s, helped give birth to the New Left in Madison. And the last point is that the state's and the university's radical tradition, while hardly dominant, nevertheless served as a magnet attracting students from among the children of leftist Jews from New York.

These strands came together in the group of graduate students around William Appleman Williams who in 1959 constituted *Studies on the Left*. I know I am not the only younger student for whom contact with the journal and its milieu was a turning point. In trying to reconstruct some aspects of its impact, several personal details may help. My parents are second-generation Americans from east-European Jewish families. My grandfathers were skilled craftsmen who worked themselves to death before I was born. My father is an architect. In their early years and during my childhood, my parents were part of the fellow-traveling Left. They are both intellectuals. Born and reared in New York City, they became thoroughly modern in relation to their cultural pasts. Our home was areligious, our ties to Jewish custom, thin. Neither my brother nor I was bar mitzvah. Yiddish, which my parents spoke fluently, was heard in our home only at the occasional gatherings of the larger family.

I knew we were Jewish but had little notion of what this meant. Nor did I ever ask. Not when, at around ten years of age, I told my best friend's devoutly Catholic grandmother, as she sat in her darkened little room surrounded by crucifixes and statuettes of the Holy Mother, working her Rosary beads, that, yes, I had gone to Mass that morning. Nor several years later when, with awe, I beheld my father lead a family Passover Seder, reading the Hebrew text with ease and authority. Nor when he noted that he knew someone was a Jew because, well, such things you just know. None of this troubled me, perhaps in part because as far as I can remember, I never experienced anti-Semitism. Nor did my parents instill in me the idea that I was especially lucky in this respect. Being Jewish, then, was a private and very obscure part of my youth. I became adept at keeping it that way.

In the early 1950s we were part of the exodus from the city to the suburbs. I had no difficulties integrating myself fully and happily into the upper-middle-class life of Scarsdale, where I initiated our family's regular celebration of Christmas. My parents tolerated this, drawing the line only on the occasion when I proposed we place a little Nativity scene beneath the tree. If my conscious ties to things Jewish had been loosened from the start, I was likewise only dimly aware that I was a kind of closet leftist. Unlike other "red diaper babies" (children of leftist parents) I would later meet in Madison, I was largely oblivious to politics, and never felt myself at odds with neighbors or classmates. On the other hand, I knew my parents were leftists, a fact I admired more than I understood. With the same admiration and a bit more understanding, I knew they lived according to more bohemian and less commercial values than did the parents of my friends. That they did not quite fit into the Scarsdale ambience sometimes made me uneasy, yet among my circle of friends my parents were highly regarded, were considered something like the cultural hero and heroine of the neighborhood. I read and loved the novels of Howard Fast, then a Communist, and noticed such material as *I. F. Stone's Weekly, Monthly Review,* and *The Nation* on my parents' reading table, though I do not recall reading them. Had anyone scratched my surfaces, they would have found a socialist. But no one did, least of all me.

While I loved many of my high school teachers, I never thought of myself as an intellectual. Instead, I pursued sports and a social life among the popular crowd in my class, which graduated in 1959. Scarsdale, whose Jewish population was growing at that time, was above many things but it was not above racism or anti-Semitism—the two black students in the high school were children of live-in domestics. Now and then word would circulate that a local realtor had refused to sell to a Jewish family; a Jewish boy would be turned away from a debutante cotillion at one of the WASP country clubs. My high school girlfriend came from a German-Jewish family that belonged to an exclusively German-Jewish country club, closed to Americanized *Ost-Juden.* All of this was kept under the rug of harmony, and I kept it under my personal rug.

I did not know, yet I knew, what was an *Ost-Jude.* Virtually all my relatives came from this stock, but for me my father's mother and aunt were its palpable representatives. I feared that some of my friends might confront them and, witnessing their noisiness, accents, funny eating habits, their Jewishness, would discover who I was. But I was also drawn to their Jewishness which, in some small cranny of my Scarsdale soul, meant very precise things: little black whiskers on their chins; the smells of their, by then, dumpy bodies; the foods they made; my grandmother's bitterness and my great-aunt's cackly laughter and wit. Of Hanukkah or the Holocaust I knew next to nothing.

In a sense, I was an all-around latent person: latent Jew, latent leftist, latent intellectual. The one mode of otherness I chose was both impossible and tame. It amounted to a mild version of Norman Mailer's White Negro, and consisted of a passion for black basketball, rock n' roll and gospel music, fumbling efforts to talk in black city dialect, empathy and admiration for black people, and outrage at how America treated them. For blacks I would have fought; for Jews, perhaps not immediately. In any case, at age eighteen I recognized I would probably not go on to become a black person, but was sure of little else. Originally planning to attend a small New England liberal arts college, I switched at the last minute to the University of Wisconsin when a Scarsdale teacher I liked spoke highly of his summer-school experience there. My parents, familiar with the university's tradition, endorsed the idea.

It may make sense, then, when I report that after the brief transition through the fraternity, my discovery of the group of students who had just launched *Studies on the Left*, who composed the little University Socialist Club, and who were mostly Jewish intellectuals from New York City— that all this struck me as something like a return to the home I never realized I had been looking for. In fact, I did not really discover this new milieu, but was introduced to it by the woman I would later marry, Wini Jacoby. In I rushed to that world of ideas, young bohemian intellectuals, books, journals, folk music and Danny Kalb's blues guitar, intense debates, a shared attempt to live by humanistic values, a will to end class society. As I began the process of shedding my reluctance to embrace the fact that I am a Jew, I donned a cloak of guilt at having come from Scarsdale. But these seemed small and private concerns admidst the nascent Civil Rights movement and on the enthusiastic fringes of the Cuban Revolution.

The history of *Studies on the Left* should soon be written. The journal drew on the work of Williams and C. Wright Mills, and was encouraged by Hans Gerth. It was inspired by the sense that its efforts were part of a broader, if embryonic, national and international New Left. *Studies* accomplished several important things. It advanced the idea of a post-Stalinist, humanistic Marxism (many of the editors were former members of the youth section of the Communist Party), stressing its relevance to contemporary American life. It insisted on the centrality of historical thought and criticism, highlighting in particular William Appleman Williams's insights into the "corporate capitalist" character of American society. And, against the backdrop of the conformity of 1950s academia, the *Studies* group represented a new and alternative community of intellectuals. They were not alone in this. It hardly needs saying that Marcuse, Mills, Paul Goodman, Harold Cruse, and others were at work along roughly kindred lines. But *Studies,* as a milieu of a younger generation, was vital. Between the prevailing Cold War liberalism and the small orthodox Marxist groups, it carved out the terrain—not only in Madison—on which many of us now stand.

One aspect of *Studies* is especially notable in view of the seemingly inevitable tendency toward departmentalization on the part of so many Left intellectual journals today. Its editorial group, both in Madison and later in New York, included historians, economists, political scientists, Germanists, sociologists, a novelist and poet, a literary critic, a couple of academic dropout intellectuals, and Stanley Aronowitz. It included several women, though the journal was certainly male-dominated. *Studies* was also imperfect, that is, it mirrored the dominant order, insofar as only one or two black people stood among its associates. On the other hand, some of the most important articles it published were those by Harold Cruse, a black, reinterpreting black historical experience in America. Nonetheless, in the range of credentials among its associates and in the coherent breadth of the articles in its pages, *Studies on the Left* set standards that any Left journal today could be proud to match.

In this brief homage to the journal, I want to mention one other flaw, both because there were efforts to overcome it and because it bears indirectly on the Jewish theme to which I will return. *Studies* had a definite tendency toward a kind of American provincialism; a generally latent but now and then manifest hostility toward European Left theorizing. This is neither the time nor place for sectarian squabbles. Yet, I still think it notable that, although the journal died in 1966 and one might thus say there was not enough time, it never did reckon with Marcuse's *One-Dimensional Man*—which was not merely European theorizing—and all it represented. On the other side of this coin, in its final year, *Studies* did publish an important article by Marcuse's student, Ron Aronson ("The Movement and its Critics"), who had also become an editor. More generally, thanks to the background encouragement of Hans Gerth and the work of editors Ellie Hakim and Lee Baxandall, political and cultural Leftism from Europe was not absent. In fact, the journal carried the first English translation of Walter Benjamin's "The Work of Art in the Age of Mechanical Reproduction." It also ran translations of early essays by Karl Mannheim, dealing with themes in Lukács's work, and the first significant appropriation of Antonio Gramsci in this country, written by Eugene Genovese.

In their Madison days, most of the *Studies* editors were also involved in the University Socialist Club, a band of some two or three dozen members and friends. It was primarily a discussion circle and forum. We heard Herbert Aptheker of the Communist Party denounce William Appleman Williams's revisionist historiography; listened to the humbly charismatic presentations of Martin Sklar, the gray eminence of a good deal of Madison Leftism in the early 1960s; and plunged into debate on whether or not to condemn bomb testing in the People's Republic of China. But the Socialist Club, sometimes in tandem with the even smaller crew of pacifists, was also the vehicle for what leftist action there was on the campus: support for the sit-ins in the South, for the Cuban Revolution, for disarmament and related causes. Its beleaguered demonstrations invariably met with catcalls of Go Back to Russia, or Go Back to Brooklyn. Now and then there were real threats of violence. There was as yet no such thing as a mass mobilization.

The particular call from the hecklers to Go Back to Brooklyn gets me back to the Jewish theme. Had someone yelled, Go Back to Scarsdale, I might really have been perplexed. But the Brooklyn advice was in its way helpful. I could see and affirm myself through the hecklers' eyes: we were Jews, not merely Commies. Of course, not all of us were Jews. And I do not know just what any of us who were not Jews thought about all this, since we never really discussed it. Nor, for the same reason, do I know if other Jews in our circle were as ambivalent as I about being a Jew. But this is what I believe: by becoming a leftist and an intellectual, I was beginning to become a Jew. And in their own ways, those in the Madison Left who were not Jews had already found or were beginning to find a Jew within each of themselves.

These were subterranean, one could even say repressed, themes at the time—at least in Madison. Only later in the 1960s did they even begin to come somewhat to the fore. But I do not think I am merely reading later concerns into the earlier situation; they were there all along. The chief reason for the silence is that, both early in the 1960s and later, we considered ourselves first of all and all together leftists. This was a matter of real, that is, felt, priorities, not mere rationalization. But it was a little bit of rationalization. No doubt we were all reluctant to amplify the fact, obvious to all, that the Left in Madison was composed largely of Jews. Moreover, as antiracists and, as far as we believed, rationalists, none of us relished admitting that cultural/racial myths, fantasies, and stereotypes played roles in our lives. Typical of the situation and sensibility involved was the appearance in our midst in 1962 of one Doug Korty. A freshman from Ohio, ruggedly handsome, blond, blue-eyed, and a socialist, Doug Korty was happily dubbed our token Goy, although he was only the most Aryan specimen among the bunch of non-Jews. The good cheer in this case was mutual. So, as far as I remember, was the impulse to leave it unexamined.[3]

Some of the peculiarities of the Madison scene and my experiences with the question of Jewish identity are crystallized in the following story. At the end of the school year, 1961, I decided to take part in the freedom rides in Mississippi. This was the Civil Rights movement's main project at that time. The freedom rides aimed at forcing the integration of Mississippi's bus terminals by having integrated groups of riders enter the segregated terminals. Before my departure, my friends held a small send-off party. Among the well-wishers was Martin Sklar, the brilliant and nurturant *Studies* editor to whom I and a number of peers looked as an idol and model. He took me aside to offer a piece of advice: Rather than go on the Mississippi project and spend time in jail, I should consider remaining at my desk in Madison to do theoretical work. The danger, as Sklar saw things, was that theory would get lost in a shuffle of action. Perhaps no one but Marty Sklar could have made such a proposal. Yet the episode is in its way characteristic of the Madison situation, its preoccupation with ideas and intellectuals. Far from considering the advice bizarre, I was deeply honored to have been deemed capable by the likes of Sklar of even doing theoretical work. But I did reject his advice, and went South.

Once there, several things relevant to these notes happened. Arrested for disturbing the peace (violating racist codes), the group I was with found ourselves in the Jackson, Mississippi, city jail. From there we would be transported to the State Penitentiary at Parchman Farm. It happened that I had a book with me, John Hersey's *The Wall,* a novel about life in the Nazi camps, which someone had given me during the training session in Nashville prior to the action. I was able to read bits and pieces of it in the cell. At one point I was awakened by a warden who was shouting: "All o'youse get your shoes on and get ready to line up out here!" I was certain, semi-awake, that he had yelled: "All Jews."

After several days we were transferred to the Parchman Farm Penitentiary. Freedom ride prisoners were kept apart from the rest, and among us, black males, white males, white females, and black females were kept in separate dormitorylike cells. The only direct contact we had with things outside came in the form of periodic visits from a priest, a minister, and a rabbi, all from Jackson. My initial impulse was to meet with the priest or minister. In flight from Jewishness as a stigma? Or in a gesture toward the universalism that had brought us all together on the freedom rides in the first place? Or both? But I went to the rabbi. This decision, so small in the scheme of the Civil Rights movement and amidst the problems of being in jail, remains large in my memory. But it remains large because of the ambivalences attached to it, not because it involved any sense of homecoming or positive identity. In fact, as an atheist I was discontent that we could connect only to clergymen, although making the visit took courage on their parts, especially on the part of the rabbi.

The other episode revolves around several prisoners who were members of the Catholic Worker movement. At one point during our confinement they approached a few of us who were Jews—we were a handful out of some thirty-five white males in the cell—with an unusual question. They wanted to know how they themselves could become Jews. What would they need to do, they wondered, so that we would recognize them as Jews? Would conversion suffice, or obeying Kosher dietary laws, or learning Hebrew or Yiddish, adopting Jewish names, or simply declaring themselves Jews? They explained that they saw becoming Jews as the most truly Christian decision they could make—this while in prison as Catholic Workers and participants in the Civil Rights movement, which was guided by a Christian liberation theology. Blacks they could not be, but becoming

Jewish somehow seemed within reach. By getting there, they said, they would be among the oppressed because of what they *were,* not merely because of what, as Catholic Workers, they did. In the event, they were asking the wrong Jews. Or were we the right ones? In good and bad faith, we were not even clear what made *us* Jews. Our Catholic comrades found our situation as strange as we found theirs.

When I subsequently returned to Madison in the fall of 1961, these matters remained in the background, where they had been all along. Yet there was at least one form in which the issue of Jew and non-Jew on the Left was addressed. It is connected to the question Peter Hohendahl posed regarding relations between Leftism and America in the thinking of particular American leftists. And it involves at least part of the problem of what is a leftist heritage—or leftist mythology? In Madison in the early 1960s this issue took shape as a counterpoint between several key faculty personalities. William Appleman Williams stood on one side, George Mosse and Harvey Goldberg on the other. It is important to stress that they were friends and far from intending to represent polar currents. Yet among their students on the Left there was a certain awareness of cultural differences. These were expressed more in jokes and anecdotes than in analytic discussions—which is not to say that the matter was insignificant.

Consider Williams. In appearance, style, quirks, and background (born in Iowa, athlete, decorated naval captain, and so on), as well as in the patriotic impulse of his socialism, he was robustly American. He always noted his intellectual debts to European social theory—I believe he learned some things from Hans Gerth—but it was hard to miss the homespun character of his radicalism. In his lectures and writings he consistently sought to uncover forerunners, including thoughtful, independently minded conservatives, in the American past. This last dimension of his work had substantial if complex influence on some of the associates of *Studies on the Left* (and discloses parallels between his own perspectives and those developed by Raymond Williams in *Culture and Society*).

Now as far as I know, the first generation of Williams's graduate students, among them John McCormack, Walter Lefeber, and Lloyd Gardner, all of whom had left Madison before I arrived, was not preponderantly Jewish. And I do not know if the numerical picture shifted in the early 1960s. Yet by that time, the most visible of his students were for the most part New York Jews, primarily those around *Studies on the Left*. His most dedicated and able publicist among undergraduates, for example, was Fred Ciporen, a veritable archetype of *Yiddishkeit*. My dear friend and for two years my roommate, Fred Ciporen influenced me deeply. He did so in part by introducing me to both Williams's work and one of its sources, Karl Mannheim's *Ideology and Utopia*. As Williams himself had been some years earlier, so now in the early 1960s, Fred Ciporen was enthusiastically in contact with Hans Gerth. Thanks to my friend, I began to see everything under the sun in terms of its socially formed theoretical context.

But he exerted a sharper impact on me and perhaps on others not only through what he said, but because of what he was: *Ost-jude* as New Left intellectual. Fred Ciporen did go back to Brooklyn often because his family lived there. Yiddish was his native language. He consumed large amounts of garlic, smoked pipes and cigars, and had a kind of rumpled Jewish academic appearance. To me this was nectar. If you asked me right now what is Jewish, I would say it is the smell of Fred Ciporen in the early 1960s in Madison. His Jewishness was spontaneous. It was helping to bring mine out. And his immersion in ideas, even for their own sake, was shaping my sense of becoming an intellectual. In and about the Socialist Club, Fred Ciporen was renowned among other things as the transmitter of the theory that when you're in love, the whole world is Jewish. He himself was perfectly capable of being in love. And among his loves at that time was the most *goyische kopf* around: William A. Williams.

I do not know what Williams himself thought about his notable (if not entirely) Jewish audience in the Madison Left. We, though, Jews and non-Jews, took up the matter now and then. I, of all people, in a flash of super-Jew intuition, once proposed to none less than Freddy Ciporen and several others, the following thesis: Their enthusiasm for Williams involved the attempt to submerge their Jewishness in a highly Americanized socialism, even a socialist Americanism. In response, some people considered this a moronic subterfuge. They insisted that what mattered was the critical content of Williams's thought and its applicability to our political present. Others argued that both his historiography and his deeply ethical socialism amounted to a kind of realization of historical Jewish socialism in the American context. I distinctly remember the brevity of our debates.

The Jewish dimension per se was not the only one that concerned us. For these issues also revolved around relations between American and *European* socialism and social thought. This is where the two European historians, George Mosse and Harvey Goldberg, enter the picture. Yet they happened to be Jews. For some of us, Jews and not, they rather than Williams, to whom we also felt attached, were the decisive figures. In my own case, I was at first only dimly conscious of the Jewish element. The real magnets were what lay behind the doors of European, mainly German, culture that George Mosse opened, and European and world socialist history that Harvey Goldberg opened. My interest in their courses and writings, moreover, entailed a rejection of America. Through them I took off, in the company of friends, into a historical (fantasy?) world of European, partly Jewish, leftist intellectual culture. This choice has marked some of us with a sense of being displaced persons within American radicalism. It is some solace that I know Jews on the Left who do not have the same feeling and non-Jews who do.

It bears repeating: None of this was the aim of the teachers. Take Harvey Goldberg. His brilliant lectures on the Sans Culottes, comparative revolutions, and French social history often flowed into chanted messages of redemption. They reminded me of the great performances by cantors and rabbis I had never heard or seen. Yet Harvey Goldberg was the representative figure of socialist internationalism in our midst. He was preoccupied with Jean Jaures, whose biography he was completing, rather than with Jewish matters.

Nor was George Mosse, to whom I felt closest, actively Jewish. He simply, or not so simply, seemed to embody cosmopolitan German-Jewish learning. Neither was he really a leftist. Critical of Marxism, communism, and the totalitarian potential of social revolutions, George Mosse *could* have been the voice of liberal anti-Leftism in Madison. That was, after all, the path taken by so many Jewish intellectuals, American-born and German émigré, since the 1950s. But he avoided it. One reason for this belongs to the Madison situation. Mosse's friendships with Williams and Goldberg, neither of whom was an orthodox Marxist let alone a Stalinist, made many Cold War clichés superfluous. The other reason belongs to George Mosse himself. He has always been hostile to what he has spent most of his career as a historian studying: ideology and ideologues. Yet he has always had a deep empathy, even a taste, for the utopian impulse. More than that, he has always had a kind of affinity with a certain type of leftist. In his lectures in 1960 and in his book, *The Culture of Modern Europe,* he referred to this type as the "Marxist of the heart" (a phrase adopted by C. Wright Mills in his *The Marxists*).

When he encountered some echoes of this type among his students in the early 1960s, he responded as a supportively critical friend. His lectures on European cultural history were often addressed to the handful of leftist students among the three hundred or more in attendance. And it was there that some of us were first introduced to the early Marx, Lukács, Gramsci, Sartre, Koestler, Orwell, Malraux, Caudwell, and others. Beyond that, George Mosse also placed at the center of his course the whole question of intellectuals in revolutionary movements (Left and Right), their post-Christian quests for absolutes, their peculiar susceptibility to both disillusionment and betrayal of humane values. In doing so, he provided us with a set of historical images and reference points that enabled us to begin reflecting on our own situation. Often, after a lecture, he retired for further discussion to the terrace of the Memorial Union. There he would challenge our Marxism with his insistence on the role of the irrational and mythical in history. Or he would counter our idealism with reminders of the dimension of power and organization in revolutions. We sometimes debated if he was for us or against us. We knew he was with us. In time, George Mosse's own utopia became clearer. It is the utopia of humanistic skepticism, with its hope for a tolerant world, whatever its economic foundations. In this sense he has been a real liberal and a real friend of the student Left. Much has happened since that would seem to dwarf the significance of the exchanges with George Mosse in the early and mid-1960s. Yet memory of them remains vivid enough.

Some of my friends would say the same not only of Harvey Goldberg, but of the late Hans Gerth as well. He not only introduced European social thought; he *was* it. Neither a leftist nor a Jew, Hans Gerth was nevertheless not so well assimilated into American society as Harvey Goldberg, who was born here, or George Mosse, who attended college and graduate school in this country. Gerth remained an outsider, an *Einsamer,* scorned and mistreated by the sociology department, which saw him as an academic scofflaw. If the scope of his impact on students was relatively low, its quality was high. His most dedicated students in the 1960s were on the Left.

A sub-theme in George Mosse's lectures was the role of *Männerbünde* in European, particularly German, culture. These were circles of males, generally youngish, gathered in an intellectual and emotionally highly charged atmosphere around an older dominant figure, the *Grossmeister.* The prototype was the group around the poet, Stefan George, the George-*Kreis* (in which the reciprocal love-hate relations between Germans and Jews played a significant role). Often, after our own heated discussions with Mosse, some of us joked about the *männerbundische* aspects of the experiences. Such talk was both on and off target. These were but pale shadows of their Germanic forerunners. But the little gatherings were infused with a cultural and political enthusiasm heightened by the fact that Mosse himself had raised the idea of the *Männerbund.* He was the central figure, and the get-togethers with him plainly contained repressed homoerotic dimensions. Women were present only in a subsidiary way, if at all. Similar occasions took place, if less often, around Williams, Goldberg, and Gerth. Yet, while all these men could have been gurus, none chose to be. They neither wanted nor needed acolytes. As I mentioned, when we gathered around Mosse, we did so to argue with him, often angrily. He encouraged this.

At that time I had in my mind a kind of upside-down *Männerbund*. In it there was not a master and a group of disciples, but one disciple, me, and three masters. Our gatherings took place more often and with more effect than any of us was aware. Some of Mosse's gestures became my own. In private moments I imitated the authoritative tone of his lectures, anglicized Prussian accent and all. I bought a pen and cheap yellow writing paper of the sort Sklar used, and planned to produce, like him, the endless Marxist manuscript pages I now and then had a chance to eye on his desk. My patterns of thinking became Ciporenesque. They began to proceed backward toward the subject of a thought-sentence by way of long strings of dependent clauses and qualifiers. Friends sometimes noted that they could not figure out what I was saying. I considered this proof of the great depth of my reflections. My once rounder Scarsdale diction began to give way to a New York accent.[4]

The Mid-1960s

Equipped with pen and accent I left Madison in 1963 for what turned out to be two years of graduate work in history at Cornell University. I went there more or less on the coattails of a large grant won by my wife-to-be for study in city planning. The emotional impact of Madison was not and could not have been duplicated in Ithaca. But the two years were not dull. Kennedy was assassinated; the Free Speech movement blossomed in Berkeley; the Civil Rights movement took its first turns toward Black Power; Lyndon Johnson ordered the bombing of North Vietnamese harbors, and the antiwar movement emerged in response. Amidst these developments, John Laffey, then a graduate student, now a professor at Concordia University in Canada, plied me with stories of life in some of the back alleys of Trotskyism and ex-Trotskyism in America and Europe. Then one day, wandering through the library stacks, I came on an unoccupied carrel with some intriguing books on its shelves. I was struggling with German and could recognize mostly authors' names. Among them were Hegel, Goethe, Kleist, Lukács, Bloch, Benjamin, and others related. I soon met the books' owner, Sam Weber, who, with Shierry Weber, opened my and Wini's eyes to the Frankfurt School.

We left Cornell in 1965 to see parts of Europe and because I was by then desperate to learn German. Our first stop was Frankfurt, where Sam and Shierry Weber had already gone to study with Adorno. They were immersed in an intense little group of budding American critical theorists.

Among them was Jeremy Shapiro, the one genuinely prophetic figure I have known, and with whom I would later become close friends. The group was too intense for us, and we moved on, finally stopping in Vienna. Our stay there was then interrupted by word from the U.S. Selective Service that married men without student deferments would be inducted into the armed forces. The question of where and how to go back to school was solved when George Mosse passed through Vienna, met with us, encouraged me to return to Madison, with Wini now able to anticipate work in city planning. He also suggested that I begin investigating Gustav Landauer's career.

We returned in 1966 to a Madison and Madison Left in flux. The big developments I leave aside: the unfolding and radicalization of the student revolt and antiwar movement; the rise of Black Power; the expansion of the counterculture, and so on. As to the other matters: Mosse, Goldberg, Williams, and Gerth remained. A number of new faculty more or less friendly to the Left had arrived. One of them, the late Georges Haupt, was only a visitor. But this Rumanian Jew, survivor of Auschwitz, ex-Communist, and *déraciné* Left intellectual par excellence, was for some of us a vital visitor. Most of the old *Studies on the Left* group had departed, although a few remained and were joined by several new members of the "Madison Associates." The Socialist Club was all but defunct. Its place had been taken by an energetic and chaotic S.D.S. chapter.

Paul Buhle and *Radical America* had arrived. So had an expanding bevy of student radicals including Evan Stark, with his ingenious mind and voice, and Bob and Vicki Gabriner, who launched one of the decade's first underground papers, *Connections*. Some old-timers and newcomers constituted the little Marcuse community (Russell Jacoby, Lowell Bergman, David Gross, Bill Netzer, Liz Ewen, Stuart Ewen, Elton Eisenstadt, Evan Stark, Jeff Herf, and Jessica Benjamin along with many others). And I had changed, at least in the sense that now I was part of the Madison Left's upper crust, that is, its graduate student segment. While I was still impressionable, I was more formed, not least by the early 1960s in Madison. Politically less volatile than what was coming by mid-decade, the 1959–1963 years are for me nevertheless vivid.

But between 1966 and 1968, when I left Madison for good, the Jewish theme continued to percolate in the Left. One part of the story is that what had been a small milieu was becoming a movement. And as the student Left grew and became action-oriented, it also got less exclusively Jewish. There is a nice irony to this. By 1968 the Wisconsin State Legislature initiated measures to restrict the number of out-of-state students able to attend the University of Wisconsin. Official discussions of the proposal included a lot of anticommunist and openly anti-Semitic talk. Clearly, the aim was to cut the supposed flow of New York Jewish revolutionaries into Wisconsin's placid middle-American pool of WASP respectability and good works. But this all coincided with the turn of events (nationally, not only in Madison) in which a generation of middle-American students was opting for disrespect and bad works.

Another part of the story is that, within the Left, the Jewish issue momentarily boiled over in response to the 1967 Six-Day War in the Middle East. Several impassioned teach-ins were held at the campus Hillel, although most of the participants were Jewish students and faculty along with non-Jewish sympathizers with the Israeli cause—not, for the most part, leftists or Jewish leftists. Among the latter, there were a few fist fights between pro- and anti-Zionists. Some of my Jewish friends shared in the feeling of pride that, at last, our people had a real army. I myself had no deep feeling for Israel and could not readily warm to its military prowess. Among the participants in the Hillel teach-ins was George Mosse, who since his visit to Israel in 1962 had been drawing closer to Zionism. Characteristically, he never sought to bring me or other of his Jewish students along. Overall, within the Madison Left the reverberations of the Six-Day War were less substantial than one might have expected. We continued to be preoccupied, along with theoretical questions of Marxism, with the Vietnam War and the impending race crisis in America.

But for some of us, Jewish preoccupations, apart from Zionist ones, continued apace amidst the undercurrents. So did the earlier Madison concern with relations between American and European leftist heritages. This was the time, for example, of the lively contacts and debates among Paul Buhle and some of the Marcuseans. And it was a time when my own Marcusean perspectives were being filtered through the early-twentieth-century neo-Romantic German anarchist, Gustav Landauer, in whose writings and career I was joyously immersed. The secular religiosity and emotionalism of his thinking appealed to me; it clarified the possibility of warmth and affection in social theory and action. These are present in Frankfurt School thought, especially in Marcuse and Benjamin—they are its very basis—but present only negatively, only as the unstated hope of unrelenting critique. For me, Landauer let them out. I wonder now: Was I attracted to Landauer along with the Frankfurt School because he was a more Jewish Jew than they? Or because his whole program was a more closely attuned forerunner of the New Left? Or because, while even more Germanic than Frankfurt theory, Landauer's millenarianism and communitarianism nevertheless struck specifically American chords? Or because he was a more feminine thinker? Or, once again, all the above?

The Jewish dimension in Landauer was unquestionably of special interest to me. I was not about to be troubled by the fact that the Frankfurt

School intellectuals had fairly consistently muted their own Jewishness. But as a model in this respect they were no longer sufficient. Landauer offered more. For roughly the first thirty-five years of his life (he was born in 1870), he had been a minimal Jew. Neither the Dreyfus Affair nor the spread of political anti-Semitism across western and eastern Europe at the turn of the century forced any immediate changes in his views. In fact, in the first years of the 1900s, the anarchist paper he edited reprinted, over the objections of some Jewish readers, articles by Eugen Dühring, the socialist and anti-Semite. Even when, around 1910, he spoke out on behalf of Mendel Beiliss, on trial in Russia for the alleged ritual murder of a Christian child, he did so primarily as a libertarian lover of justice. If anti-Semitism eventually pushed Landauer in new directions as a Jew, there were stronger if closely related sources behind his change of heart. One of these consisted of the lower-class *Ost-Juden* who were flowing into Germany in flight from pogroms in the east. In their plight and flagrant Jewishness, as well as in their artisan-craft traditions, they provided Landauer with a new image of the Jew, with a positive alternative to that offered by the assimilated bourgeois Jews.

More important still was Landauer's friendship with Martin Buber, which blossomed in the several years before World War One. About their fascinating exchange of thoughts, it is enough to say here that the influences were reciprocal. Landauer did much—unfortunately not enough—to shape Martin Buber's social thought. Buber was vital in drawing out the Jew in Landauer. Yet, unlike his friend, Landauer kept his distance from a univocally Jewish identity. Along with an identity as a Jew, he insisted, he had German and South German identities, European identity, identity as a member of the human species, anarchist identity, literary identity. In a letter to Buber in December, 1914, Landauer said that his family would not have a Christmas tree that year. But this was not because he had become a more affirmatively conscious Jew, which he had. It was because Europe was at war.

In Landauer's experiences, then, there were two stories with which I closely identified. One was the story of his *becoming* a Jew, the other was his refusal to be *only* a Jew. At the time, though, my thoughts were in a bit of a whirl. Thanks to George Mosse, for example, I had the opportunity in 1967 to interview Gershom Scholem. The great scholar of Judaism, who was visiting Madison for a lecture, had met Landauer in 1913. Scholem began by describing the meeting, which had taken place at a colloquy of young Berlin Zionists. On that occasion, Landauer and Buber were discussing no less a question than what is involved when a Jew recognizes another Jew on sight. Several hours in Scholem's captivating presence sent my brain into an orbit of Jewish mysticism, anarcho-Leftism, and related forms of esoteric belief. When, shortly afterward, our daughter was born within hours of Landauer's birthday, I was sure messages were being sent by my racial-political ancestors.

At this time, too, I read an unusual book: *Die Juden als Rasse und Kulturvolk* (1921), by a leftist German Jew, Fritz Kahn. His thesis is that, from Moses and Christ through Marx and Landauer, revolutionism flows in Jewish blood. I knew this was a popular theme among anti-Semites. But never before had I found it expressed, and with such enthusiasm, by a Jew. I was persuaded. It was clear, of course, that both in Madison and history roughly 98 percent of the Jews had long since lost whatever revolutionary corpuscles they might have had, while some non-Jews seemed to have had some pretty revolutionary blood of their own. As a statement of fact, Fritz Kahn's claim may be fantastic. As prescription, it may be something else again. In my own case, it seeped quickly into inner conviction: Activity in the radical movement is the best way to be a Jew. If my blood is Jewish, my people are leftists.

These latter thoughts were encouraged by another writing I came across soon afterward: Isaac Deutscher's beautiful, semiautobiographical essay, "The Non-Jewish Jew." Unlike Kahn, Deutscher does not deal in racial concepts. Nonetheless, in his view, from Spinoza through Heine and Marx to Freud, Trotsky, and Rosa Luxemburg, there is a lineage of critically minded Jews who had transcended Jewry toward a cosmopolitan and radical intellectual culture. As Jews, they already stood at the crossroads of several cultures. Through the power of their wills and imaginations, they managed to lift themselves above the peculiarly uprooted roots of their original community. As "non-Jewish Jews" they had become free, then, to generate revolutionary insights. In Deutscher's view, the Jew who had transcended Jewry belongs to a Jewish tradition. But it is a tradition of speaking and acting on behalf of universal human emancipation.

Since I found this personally so full of meaning, I want to add to it two small thoughts. In his essay, Deutscher was in part interpreting and enriching his own development. From a youth spent in an orthodox community of Polish Jews, he had moved into the Communist and then the Trotskyist opposition movements, finally establishing himself in London exiled as an independent neo-Trotskyist intellectual. I do not mean to compare myself to Deutscher except to say that my own development and that of others in my generation followed something of a reverse course. My *parents* had become non-Jewish Jews in Deutscher's sense. I was born one; my youth was spent outside Jewry, assimilated, Americanized. To *become* a non-Jewish Jew in anything resembling Deutscher's sense, I had first to find Jewry. The other thought here is that, if there is such a figure as the non-Jewish Jew, there is also the figure of the Jewish non-Jew. It is not just that this type, too, tries to transcend (while preserving!) the particularity of his or her own origins. It is also that, in getting beyond those origins, the Jewish non-Jew has taken a special interest in the question: What, when all is said and done, is a Jew?

After Madison

Guided by this jumble of thoughts, I went ahead not with Jewish but with leftist matters. Throughout the 1966–1968 period, the number of students attending the Mosse, Goldberg, and Williams lectures kept increasing. So did the number of those demonstrating against university complicity with the war and job recruiting on campus by the Dow Chemical Corporation. Tear gas made its first appearance, as did dope. It was not easy to leave Madison, but in the winter of 1968 we did. We went to West Berlin, where I began work on a dissertation examining the genesis of the Marxist ideas presented in the early 1920s by Georg Lukács and Karl Korsch.[5] West Berlin provided us with some continuity with the movement we had left behind. Sam Weber, our Cornell friend, was there. Through him, we came in contact with the group of American antiwar activists known as the *"Berliner Kampagne."* We also began spending as much time as we could with David Bathrick and Fina Bathrick. In the spring of 1968, Rudi Dutschke was shot. Mass demonstrations followed and were further energized by the bigger events in Paris. Herbert Marcuse made his memorable appearance at the *Freie Universität. Kommune I* and *Kommune II* were scandalizing the citizenry. In the several movement bookstores, the shelves were packed with inexpensive pirated editions of Lukács, Korsch, Pannekoek, Horkheimer, Reich, Benjamin, and more. For the moment, the city seemed to vibrate with New Leftism.

Near the end of the summer, 1968, we returned to the States in time to join friends and listen to radio reports of the Soviet invasion of Prague. We soon moved to the Boston area and have been there since. I cannot recall any sustained preoccupation on my part with Jewish themes between 1968 and roughly the mid-1970s. Periodic discussions and occasional thoughts, but little more. Along with most of my friends, I was caught up in the reverberations of the Nixon-Kissinger butchery in Indochina and at Jackson State and Kent State as well, the New Left movement's suicide by both cults of violence and Stalinism, and the emergence from the ashes of two new movements—Women's and Gay liberation.[6] I was also at work on Lukács and Korsch, and in 1969–1970 I joined the editorial group of *Telos*. Regarding the issues at hand, I would describe it as the work of an Italian-Jewish male clique into whose shifting ranks

WASPs, women, and others have entered, often at their own risk—the journal owes much to their courage. I mean to say only that it has not been a Jewish affair, unless you take the view of some *Telos* associates that all Italians are really Jews and vice versa.

But since sometime in the late 1970s my Jewish interests have returned. Without plan or structure, I find myself reading and thinking more about Jews. One specific reason for this is that since 1975 I have been teaching at Boston College, a Catholic, largely Irish-Catholic, school. Its generally ethnic ambience, including clear streaks of anti-Semitism (and more than streaks of antiblack racism), has made me particularly aware of being a Jew—not beleaguered or threatened, just Jewish. As an example, not until very recently had I read a line of Isaac Bashevis Singer's fiction. One of my Catholic students gave me a copy of his *Shosha*, saying she thought I would find it most interesting. She was right. I had introduced her to some currents of Catholic leftism; she introduced me to Singer. In this way, it is a funny place, Boston College. Conceivably, were I at Boston University or Brandeis, with their larger Jewish populations, I might have been inclined to flee a kind of Jewish overload. As it is, I have gotten into my own little Jewish groove.

There are probably other reasons for it as well. In a recent letter, Paul Buhle touched on some. "All of us," he writes, "are thinking a little autobiographically now. Is it our age? The end of the 70s?" Or, one could also ask, is it part of the widespread American preoccupation with "self" and identity? Or the rise of a religious mood on a national scale, a mood that, beneath the commercial hype, is bound up with feelings of doom and horror? Then again, in connection with New Left experience in particular, this would not be the first time in history that the dissolution of a universalistic social movement pushed its disoriented participants toward religious-ethnic consciousness; and toward a kind of privatization in the wake of the collapse of a more public, shared movement life.

If these are among the social sources of my recent concern with things Jewish, what of the content? As far as I can fathom it, the crux is something like this: I have not finally found my long-lost Jewish identity. Nor have I any new interest in shared expressions of Jewishness through study groups, participation in religious ritual, Jewish training for our children, and so on. But I *have* come to a new phase in the *mess* of my Jewish identity. And this is connected to other messes as well. That is, I wonder more about what a Jew is because I have to wonder more about what a leftist is and what an intellectual is. As identities, these have never been what you would call crystal clear, at least not in the modern Western world. But the last ten years or so, in flagrant disregard for our feelings, have thrown the terms Jew, leftist, and intellectual into radical doubt. If I could be more certain about what a leftist intellectual is in America in 1980, I personally would know better what sort of Jew I am. The problem is that, thanks to Madison, Marxism, and Mosse, I cannot imagine having one of these identities without the other two. And neither separately nor together do they have anything approaching firm foundations.

As to the Jewish part of the picture, the anti-Semites can be counted on to lend it some clarity.[7] Beyond that, obviously there is a range of choices, of degrees and types of Jewish identity. Mine consists first of going into the kitchen, rubbing garlic on a piece of stale dark bread, covering it with chicken fat, eating it slowly, and feeling Jewish. Often, this will make me think of Freddy Ciporen, Marty Sklar, George Mosse, my father, and others. Then I go on thinking about what is a Jew; what is a leftist; what are our prospects for hope within despair? Outside, now and then someone asks what I do in the way of imparting to my children the meaning of being Jewish. I have always answered, sometimes hesitantly: Nothing. From now on, should our children themselves ask, I will try to tell them as much of this story as they have the patience to hear. It is about a way of being a Jew in the contemporary world. Like most of the other ways, it is not so new.

NOTES

1. Wini Breines shared in much of what is recounted here. Since we do not see eye to eye on all of it, I especially appreciate her tolerance of my views. Without particular reference to Madison, she has studied the New Left more closely and more fully in her *Community and Organization in the New Left, 1962–1968: The Great Refusal* (South Hadley, Mass., 1982).

2. Madison as a center of revolt in the streets has been more visible, most recently in the film, *The War at Home,* and I say little here about the activist political movement. I recognize that such a distinction is problematic, but so is the failure to make it. In any case, I focus not only on ideas and intellectual experiences, but on the early to mid-1960s, which preceded the big actions and mobilizations.

3. I recall no discussion of the Jewish business in the Socialist Club. In *Studies* the one pertinent article appeared in 1965, written by one of the newer New York editors, Norman Fruchter: "Arendt's Eichmann and Jewish Identity," a fine and provocative essay.

4. On the subject of role models and internalizing them, it is bracing to realize that the University of Wisconsin's sizable history department included not a single woman faculty member. Other liberal arts departments had not many more. This created special problems for women among the Left student milieu, in fact, for any women seeking an intellectual

vocation. The issue was not discussed in the early 1960s, except perhaps among the women themselves. We touched on the Jewish question hesitantly, on the woman question not at all.

5. A couple of years later, I briefly saw Gershom Scholem again and told him I had moved from Landauer to Lukács. He said: "Yes, well, philosophically you are advancing; morally you are regressing."

6. Clearly these developments, especially Women's and Gay liberation, have a great deal to do with questions of personal identity within the New Left and beyond it, just not with questions of specifically Jewish identity. While it was quite different, even the phenomenon of Weatherman involved matters of identity more than political matters in any customary sense. Weatherman confronted the New Left with strategic alternatives, but these were in many ways secondary. Most incessantly, Weatherman was asking: As white middle-class young people at this historical stage, who are we, really, and for what are we prepared to die?

7. The anti-Semites are no joke. But I am sorry to say neither are Gush Emunim or some of today's Israeli terrorist groups. How should I put it . . . as they clear out more Palestinians, it does not exactly clear up my Jewish identity. Nor do the anticommunist, racist, antifeminist, antigay Jewish currents in this country as well as in Israel. There is much in the Middle East situation I do not understand; nor is this the best place for my naïve musings regarding it. But I do wonder which is more tragic, Jewish statelessness or the Jewish State?

10

QUESTIONS OF JEWISH IDENTITY
A LETTER FROM NEW YORK
Atina Grossmann

This article was published in *Die Tageszeitung (TAZ)*, the leftist German daily, on May 5, 1981. I had left Berlin—finally, after three years, more or less—in January of 1980 and the piece was written in New York, in anger and relief. Relief at having "escaped" homeward, relief at the end of my excursion into Germanness; anger at how little I had protected myself against the bitterness and *Angst* I would experience, how little I had been understood, and how little I had been able to explain. I had left very abruptly; this was both my good-bye letter and my statement of return to New York. It was my counterpart to Henryk Broder's angry and polemical farewell to Germany in *Die Zeit* on Feb. 27, 1981, "You Remain the Children of Your Parents."

Broder's outburst ("I am at the end of this story, at the end of my rage and also at an end with you, my leftist friends, I no longer want to suffer from your dull stupidity, no longer want to tell you what your parents were silent about, I don't want to criticize you and I don't want to enlighten you, I no longer want to be your antifascist professional Jew—I no longer want to have anything to do with you.") was the catalyst for mine. It wasn't true, of course: Broder continues to exist between Israel and Germany, continues to write in the German press, to be outraged by and provoke outrage among the leftist Germans he bid farewell to; I too continue to return, to be fascinated and embittered and fascinated again,

171

even as three years later and ensconced in the United States I feel distanced from the urgency of my statement.

But at the time, the two letters and other testimonies from Jews living in Germany (*Fremd im eigenen Land, Juden in der Bundesrepublik*, edited by Broder and Michel Lang, 1979, and especially Lea Fleischmann in her witty, wrathful *Dies ist nicht mein Land*, 1980) represented a kind of coming out for a postwar generation of Jews. They signaled a beginning confrontation for Germans with the fact that there were indeed Jews still living in Germany and that some of them had even been their teachers and comrades. The time was ripe for such a discussion: Jewish veterans of the student movement in Germany were finally ready to reflect critically—like many of their non-Jewish comrades—on 1968 and its aftermath; the 1979 television broadcast of *Holocaust* generated discussion not only about the intensity of public response but also about the intensity with which the historical Holocaust had been forgotten and denied; and finally the pressure of events in the Middle East meant that any Jew living in Germany and identifying in any way with the Left was daily forced to confront her/ his Jewish identity, relationship to the state of Israel, and idea of Zionism, and thereby also sense of separateness from other German leftists.

Henryk Broder, the muckraking Cologne journalist, was born in Poland in 1946 to concentration-camp survivors, came to Germany in 1958, and moved to Jerusalem in 1981. He has made a career out of driving Germans crazy, especially those, in particular leftists and feminists, who might be tempted to see themselves as his antifascist allies. It is an important function and he fulfills it exceedingly well, even as he earns himself general animosity from those who think "he goes too far." Perhaps he does, but his vision is sharp. I was both intrigued and repelled by his attack on the German Left as well as his search for "normality" in the resolution to live in Israel where he would presumably no longer be "special" or "exotic," precisely those qualities that made him such an effective critic and troublemaker in Germany. I was drawn to his piece in part because I sensed how different our lives were, because he saw his refuge as Israel, despite everything, and because I could go home to New York; because he had grown up and gone to school in Germany and I on the Upper West Side of Manhattan; because he was in a sense leaving "his country" while I was leaving a country that had once been the country of my parents; because I was a woman and a feminist and he a man who enjoyed needling feminists; because he was writing out of a lifetime of experiences and I out of three years. But nevertheless I responded to his piece because of how much it resonated, how much of it made sense to me even as my options and choices were quite different.

And interestingly, despite my situation as "outsider writing a 'letter from New York,'" the *TAZ* article (later reprinted in the journal *Die Alternative*) generated an enormous response: from those who felt that the piece was too "pro-American" or too rooted in a very particular experience of the comfortable Upper West Side "ghetto," but also from Jews my age who had left Germany and shared the curious experience of feeling safer—in some existential sense—on a New York subway in the middle of the night than in a German office or classroom in broad daylight, as well as from Jews in Germany who recognized their own experiences in mine even as they pointed out that I after all had someplace to go home to and they—for better or worse—had to create that home in Germany or find a new one. An intense set of discussions and interchanges began, which still continue. Indeed, much of what I tried to formulate about my rage and unease has been further developed as part of the current discourse between Germans and Jews. And it is because of the necessity to continue those discussions—still and again—that I reprint the article in English now, even though it has been somewhat overtaken by the events and debates of the past four years.

Much has happened since the piece was published. The war in Lebanon brought the confrontation of Germans and Jews in leftist circles to new problems, recognitions, and differences (much of it played out in the lively pages of the *TAZ*) and that in turn brought another wave of self-analysis and misunderstandings, some of which are documented in this volume. Finally, Left-identified Jews in the German-speaking countries of Central Europe—West Germany, Austria, and Switzerland, even a few from the German Democratic Republic—have begun to meet regularly and self-consciously as "Die jüdische Gruppe." They have begun to talk not only about relations with the Left in their respective countries, about the continuing existence of rightist extremism and attacks on non-European minorities as well as Jews, about the conflicts in the Middle East, but also and increasingly about their daily lives: about non-Jewish lovers and spouses, about how to rear Jewish children in the "land of the murderers," especially if one parent is not Jewish, if one is not particularly religious, and there is no "bagels and lox" popular Jewish culture to painlessly transmit identity. Those are questions that concern us as American Jews with deep ties to Germany (and perhaps as any kind of "leftist American Jews") as well. Yet we can approach them from a more privileged but also perhaps less urgent and therefore less acute place. It seems to me that we have much to learn from one another and that the trans-Atlantic dialogue on commonalities and differences between those Jews whose parents crossed the ocean and those whose parents did not must continue—not least because Jews living in Germany and looking to Israel rather than New York as a potential (and highly problematic) refuge have been forced to confront issues of Zionism and Jewish identity in ways that we have been careful to protect ourselves from. At the same time, the very sense of distance that living in the United States provides also allows us to intervene in the polemics between Germans and Jewish-Germans (as in the *Ästhetik und Kommunikation* debate, continued in *New German Critique 31*) with persistent outrage but also a kind of astonishment that we as the second generation are so compelled to address the history of our parents and to remain connected to the worlds that they were forced to leave (and lucky enough to manage to leave). How that history continues to live and work within us, in our personal, political, and academic lives, is a question that—despite all our discussions—still needs more conversation, reflection, and trans-Atlantic connections.

DEAR HENRYK,

What you write (in *Die Zeit* and *Der Spiegel*) fascinates, angers, and concerns me. Despite our differences, it speaks to me. The child of parents who had managed to escape Berlin and emigrate to the United States—after many adventurous detours and the loss of families whom I know only from old photographs and deportation lists supplied by the International Red Cross—I "returned" to Germany for a few years to search for the traces of old stories, nostalgias, and nightmares. I could not let go of Germany because my parents could not let go of Germany. At home on the Upper West Side of Manhattan, all my parents' friends were émigrés and only German was spoken, the *Aufbau* (German-Jewish newspaper) came punctually every week. The pediatrician, dentist, shoe salesman, butcher were all German Jews; an entire neighborhood in Washington Heights was ironically titled "The Fourth Reich"—for years, the rabbi read his sermons in German. My father was a restitution lawyer, refugees were his business and his life; his *Stammtisch* was in the Cafe Éclair on West 72nd Street, where the *Gugelhupf* was especially good.

Nevertheless, I was the "American child," not as you describe yourself, the "Jewish child" in the land of the tormentors. When I entered kindergarten speaking German and very little English, the ethnically and racially mixed New York City school system matter-of-factly placed me in the "non-English-speaking" class where I played at learning Puerto Rican Spanish. My parents' determination to hang onto their language and traditions was not so different from that of generations of other immigrants, though my mother and father, like many other German-Jewish refugees, were perhaps a bit more arrogant toward their new home. For Berliners of the 1920s the rest of the Western world appeared hopelessly Philistine. Not one of my playmates or friends was a "real" American. At least their grandparents if not their parents had been born elsewhere; all could speak a little Yiddish, Spanish, Italian, or German. And yet we understood precisely that phenomenon as "American." We took it for granted that one could be a hyphenated American—black-American, Italian-American, Irish-, Hispanic-, Jewish-American. We lived in a world marked by racism but lacking *Volksgemeinschaft* (folk community).

The Other Perspective

The continued existence of this *Volksgemeinschaft*—healthy and relatively unquestioned—was the biggest shock of my three-year stay in Germany. You must have experienced this fact of life every day. I had to travel to Berlin—the former metropolis of Weimar German-Jewish culture—to discover what an incredible luxury it had been to grow up and live as a Jew in New York City. For the first time I learned to value the "normality" that you yearn for (and seek in Israel), my straightforward nonexotic position as a Jewish woman, which had not however developed in an embattled "Jewish state" but in a very particular part of the Diaspora. I was surrounded not only by Jews (as you know, more than in Israel) but also by many other minorities who were all attempting to comprehend and experience their heterogeneous identities as an enrichment and not as a burden. That was my good luck. Your situation was quite different, but more about that later.

Three years in Germany help me to understand and empathize with what you say, as well as to understand where we differ decisively. I too understood that I could not live in Germany—not only because I am a foreigner there—but because I am a Jew. Even though German is my "mother tongue," even though I research and teach German history, even though I live with a German man, and even though I have friends and even relatives in Germany, I felt as if Germany threatened to destroy me, drive me crazy. I too could not escape from the *Volksgemeinschaft* and its relentless need to draw rigid boundaries and demolish all that which was different—not even in the bars, cafés, and meetings of the Berlin scene, perhaps especially there because it was there that I sought and wanted to expect something different. But unlike you I could leave, not for a foreign country with a foreign language—Israel—but home, to New York.

The Germans and the Other—I

After Auschwitz there can be no "normality" for Germans in Germany, let alone for Turks, Italians, Yugoslavians, and all the rest. I sensed that pretty quickly, for example, in the embittered rigidity of confrontations between the generations and the sexes; in the silences of my friends and acquaintances who, themselves historians, had no sense of their own history and knew or wanted to know little about their parents' lives; in the exaggerated intensity—brutality, even, or its mirror opposite, a forced softness—with which personal or political conflicts were enacted. I was often criticized as a "pragmatic American opportunist" who was unable to withstand conflicts, when it seemed to me that I was simply human and capable of compromise. People in the "scene" (or "scenes," since Berlin produces such a multitude of political and intellectual circles that it is now no longer fashionable to be simply "Left") claimed to have broken with the recent German past because they only saw their families during Christmas and lived in collective apartments *(Wohngemeinschaften)* instead of "fascistic" nuclear families.

Such a stubborn lack of historical consciousness, such a massive denial of their own socialization—by parents who had grown up in the Third Reich—terrified me. But on the other hand, what else could I have expected? There were not many people like you who might force Germans of my generation to such uncomfortable considerations. And for a long time you too rejected that role, you wanted to be "normal" and integrated. It is after all finally the triumph of National Socialism that the most obvious and disturbing minority in Germany—the Jews—were forced into exile or exterminated. The *Volksgemeinschaft* has indeed been purified; Germany, or at least the Germans (foreign residents—*Mitbürger* but not *Bürger* are after all foreign, and thankfully look that way), remain Aryan. If here and there a few German Jews survived underground or returned, or east-European Jewish survivors came out of the DP camps to settle in Germany, then they should at least act as inconspicuous and untroublesome as possible. They should celebrate their mysterious rituals in their communities if they must and appear at official antifascist memorials; otherwise they should split for Israel where they belong and would feel better anyway. But what is not said is that it is the *Germans* who would feel much better, anxious as they are to rid themselves of the last remnants of this irritation, this memory of an uncomfortable past.

And besides, there were so many more important and urgent things to do: There were the student movement, Vietnam, and Chile. And there was the academic debate about fascism where, with all the discussions about the role of capitalism and the working class in National Socialism, no one ever mentioned the Holocaust, racism, anti-Semitism, or the position of women. My own sense of justice and injustice has its roots, like yours, in Auschwitz and Buchenwald, but it never felt separated from Vietnam or the Civil Rights movement. Even as a child I assumed that racism, fascism, and imperialism could touch me, and that it was therefore in my self-interest to be politically engaged and to identify with the Left.

These fluid connections characterized my politicization, without denying the particular nature of the persecution of Jews in Europe, and also not without conflicts, including of course those about Israel. In Germany, however, the protests against American imperialism and against Israeli policies appeared all too often as an attempt to escape a conscious confrontation with the German past, indeed as a kind of consolation for German history. Such protests seemed to say, "Look, others—even and especially the Jews—act the same way," as if that could explain anything or "make it good" again *(wiedergutmachen)*. The automatic identification in such statements with "the Germans" who had done that which could now be made comparable with other atrocities terrified me. Germans are perversely grateful when others are monstrous.

This "non-normal," or, even more frighteningly, "normal" life of Germans in Germany would have been reason enough for me to leave. But strangely, the full realization that there can be no "normality" for Jews in Germany after Auschwitz required a longer and more complicated process.

Paranoia

I finally knew that I had to get out of Germany when once again I went to the police station to register a new address and the uniformed man behind the counter as usual asked me if I hadn't forgotten to list my religion on the form. As an American (I thought) who wasn't accustomed to such questions I had always refused to offer the information, but this time, during my third year in Germany, I suddenly said "Jewish" (and thought, oh, well, at least I'll spare myself the mailings from Catholic and Protestant congregations who asked in their friendly way why I was not a church member). The police clerk wrote my answer down without a word; everything was in order, I was now properly registered. But then I suddenly realized that I had just declared myself a Jew to the German police, exposed myself to German files and data processing. My identity would be fed into all the computers, there could be no escape, no passing, no hiding—this was pure suicide! Of course my panic was unrealistic and paranoid, but I sensed how deeply anchored the fear and mistrust were. I too wanted to flee, as my parents had done, even though there was really nothing from which to flee. No thanks, I thought as I left the police station, I don't have to do this to myself: I'll go home to imperialist America where there are muggings and Ronald Reagan, but no residency registration office, no national identity cards, and no official papers that ask about my religion.

That moment in the police station represented a kind of "last straw," but this attack of "paranoia" had been preceded by other "real" events which I could only fully identify and understand later, back in New York. There was for example an evening in April of 1978 in Berlin's Lesbian Action Center (LAZ) when Charlotte Wolff, the lesbian psychoanalyst who had emigrated from Berlin to London, came to speak about female homosexuality. It was an unforgettable evening for me because in that room full of Berlin movement women—of all places—I was able to sense, really for the first time, how it had been possible for so many Germans, including intellectuals and the politically conscious, to hate Jews and sanction anti-Semitism. The eighty-year-old Charlotte Wolff, with her short cropped hair, sharp facial features, beautiful long nose (yes), and commanding, even arrogant air, was the quintessence of the intellectual Jewish woman of the twenties. No German woman looks like that. After many long years and much painful hesitation she had returned to Berlin at the repeated invitation of the lesbian movement. Now her research into women's bisexuality as well as her relaxed pleasure at and acceptance of her own lesbianism was provoking resentment, anger, mistrust. The women in the audience demanded to know how she could so lightly maintain that she had never had conflicts about her sexual identity. Wolff responded in her self-confident way that she had always felt comfortable in the gay sub-culture of Weimar Berlin and that furthermore she had grown up in a warm, open Jewish family that never failed to support her in everything she did.

There was a dissatisfied rumbling in the room and I became nervous. It was clear to me as it had never been clear before that these German women absolutely could not deal with Charlotte Wolff's specifically Jewish style. They felt personally threatened and attacked by her sharp and lively self-confidence. I felt very much alone, and thought anxiously, this is what it must have been like back then, this rage at Jews who act as if the world belongs to them and who seem to think that they know everything better—something is going to happen tonight. And it did, just as I had imagined. A woman stood up and reviled Wolff in an openly anti-Semitic manner: How could a woman say something so positive about the Jewish family when everyone knew that Judaism was an especially patriarchal religion and that *the* Jewish community in the United States stood at the forefront of the antihomosexual movement. And in a grotesque twist of history, the Berlin woman announced that Israeli gays received a special stamp in their passports when in fact it had been the Jews in Nazi Germany whose passports had been marked with a "J."

No one said anything, nobody protested. Somehow the outburst fit into the atmosphere, it was not a disturbance. After the meeting, still a little shaky, I confronted the woman with her lies. Then came the worst moment. She looked at me and coolly said, "You must be a Jew, because otherwise you wouldn't be so upset." And of course she was right about that. As far as I knew, nobody else had been upset. As so often happened to you, Henryk, I too with my "hypersensitivity" had been forced into the position of carrying the antifascist flag—because it was my problem and not anyone else's. Again I felt the identification of Germans with their own Nazi tradition. And not even the frequently facile connection between the persecution of Jews and of homosexuals in the Third Reich could help me that night in the LAZ.

Then there was the horror that overcame me when my mother visited me in Berlin and wanted to gaily march along in a women's Take Back the Night demonstration. The situation itself was remarkable enough. My mother, born in Berlin and living in New York, visits her daughter who was born in New York and lives in Berlin, and meets the daughter's German friends and lover. But that was nothing compared to the in- credulous shock on my mother's face as she suddenly saw a long torchlight procession before her. No one had even fleetingly considered the pos- sibility that older Jews or antifascists might want to join in, and the kind of associations and memories a *torchlight* parade would stir up. That repre- sents what I mean by the scary lack of history displayed by the "new, other" Germans. Clearly the Nazis did not discover torchlight parades; it's a good old German tradition. But much too little attention has been paid to the necessity of breaking with the symbolism of that tradition and its continuities, of acknowledging the use of such traditions by the National Socialists. No one really wants to accept that it is necessary after Auschwitz to requestion an entire history and culture, including its most cherished symbols and rituals. It's too much of a strain, too threatening, too close. Thought taboos persist. Hence my cynical mistrust of those who say they've broken with the ideas of their parents and grandparents.

The Germans and the Other—II

Those are just two dramatic examples. There are countless others: little things, unconscious attitudes and remarks continually piercing into me. It just got to be too frustrating, too tiring to deal with them, to always feel that I had to answer back, to explain, to enlighten. I can well understand that you want to be rid of this role; after only three years I too felt exhausted from a constant feeling of responsibility and defensive alertness. Almost every day there were things that upset me. I made a game of testing people's reactions when they found out that I was an American and then wondered why I spoke such good German. They guessed everything and anything, that my father was a diplomat or a soldier in the United States "Occupation Army," that I had a special gift for languages—but never the historical reality that my parents were German-Jewish refugees. Not even when I helped them by saying that my parents were from Berlin: "When did they leave?" people wanted to know. "1935? Why?" Questions so ignorant were hard to take. And then always the moment of embarrassed silence when the real story was revealed. "Oh, well, what of it, Jews in Germany today are just people like everybody else. You shouldn't make such a big deal of it, what's past is past." But no, not so. And then my wanting after all to make a big thing of it—to acknowledge my identity and my ties to history—left me open to the reproach, "Stop being so oversensitive; why do you Jews always have to be something special, always insist on exposing such an unpleasant past?"

German anger then is directed not against themselves but against the victims or their representatives. The anti-Semitism of today's neo-Nazi youth seems grounded in that anger—but it is not only theirs. It is not so easy to project anti-Semitism onto real Jews when one hardly knows any. The Jew therefore becomes simply a symbol for a history with which they want to have nothing to do. Jews remind younger Germans of platitudes of guilt and remorse, voiced in a knee-jerk, hypocritical fashion by teachers and other authority figures who cannot be taken seriously. The rebellion turns outward against the unknown Jew instead of only against teachers and parents who speak so inadequately or not at all—thus the identification with the Nazi, the anti-Semite. Furthermore, I suspect that many Germans of our generation, in the Left and in the women's movement, don't want to confront the subject of "the past" because they are simply afraid of their own reactions. They are afraid of themselves, suffer from an unspoken and unexamined terror at an unconscious anti-Semitism derived from their own families and history. They are afraid of what they might find in themselves, and so they are relieved that Israel too has committed atrocities that they can condemn.

What Is Jewish Identity?—I

I too—as you are continually—was troublesome when I affirmed my Jewish identity. I insisted that it was not only religious or gastronomic (bagels and lox and matzoh balls), but precisely this hypersensitivity to anything that rang of anti-Semitism, racism, intolerance, fascism. I don't want to relinquish that sensibility. With my overdeveloped antennae, I can react quickly, ferret out dogmatism; in fact, that's what makes it possible and necessary for me to think and work politically.

Therefore, Henryk, my tremendous uneasiness with your understanding of Jewish identity. Up to this point I have tried to substantiate your experiences from my own perspective. But once we are past our common anger with Germany and come to the complicated question of positive Jewish identity, we part company. I use my "luxury identity" as a New York Jew to reject your statement, "Sometimes I just want to be part of the mass."

It seems to me that just this position of outsider, this view from the "enclave of negation" (Horkheimer) is the most creative, stimulating, positive aspect of Jewish identity. Your desire to be of the "mass"—normal—like everybody else, liquidates this identity, the particularity which is the essence of Jewish life in the Diaspora. It does not have to be a crippling exoticism, but can be an affirmation of the variety of a society, a challenge to every national community *(Volksgemeinschaft)*; a provocation against monotony or homogeneity, along with other ethnic groups—to use Marcuse—"a hindrance to the one-dimensional society." That means, among other things, that if "Israel is the only country where we don't notice that we are Jews," then that is reason enough for me not to want to live there.

I find it unspeakably sad that when *Der Spiegel* asked you "You have no more desire to be a Jew," you could answer "Yes," even as I think I understand what you mean. I conclude from that remark that life in Germany has deformed not only the generation of your parents but you too. Your life as a Jew in Germany seemed so impossible that you could only conceive of your Jewishness as burden that you would shed as quickly as possible. With such a sentence you negate an essential part of yourself.

What Is Jewish Identity?—II

To say, "We are the first Jews who have stood up and said no and refuse to kowtow" is an incredibly arrogant falsification of history. I hear that as Israeli Sabra mythology, which wants to tell us that a completely new ahistorical race has sprung up in Israel that wants to cut itself off from the supposedly bowed, passive (that is, not militarist?) European ghetto Jews. You thereby wipe out thousands of years of tough survival and resistance (assuming that resistance does not always involve the use of arms). Do you really mean to suggest that macho Israeli men with big Stars of David on hairy chests and guns on their shoulders are the only Jews who stand straight? You see your parents as humbled, broken people, and you even label them with the psychological term "bonding with the aggressor"— whatever that means. It can't be that simple, that clear. After all, some of your sense of injustice, your drive for active engagement, even your complicated family ties, are a legacy from your parents. I too experienced my parents as crippled in certain ways. They had not themselves been in concentration camps; they "only" experienced the fear, persecutions, and humiliations before 1938. They still live with the guilt of not having succeeded in saving other members of their families. They never managed to make peace with the destruction of their old way of life. But their crippling is very different from that of my German cousins, who grew up near Frankfurt as Catholic half-Aryans, and who thought their father was fighting at the front when actually he was in Auschwitz. Even today they don't really know who they are—and that twisted fate pales in comparison to that of German acquaintances whose fathers are former SS men, and who don't even want to know how crippled they really are. At least we never had to doubt the essential humanity of our parents. I hope, Henryk, that you'll change your own standards for strength and weakness the farther away from Germany you get.

And I hope that in Israel—a land that is very far away for me, although I have many relatives there—things go well for you, that you can do important political work there. When my friends and I read Lea Fleischmann's book here in New York, it was only half a joke to say that we could hardly wait for her next book from Israel, "This is not my country either." I know that that's easy for us to say, that we don't have to worry about American immigration regulations, that for us as leftist Jewish Americans, the existence of a Jewish state where every Jew can go at any time without a visa does not seem so crucial, that we don't feel ourselves as a minority in New York. But I cannot see your emigration to Israel as your triumph. Rather, your strong and angry "no" is a sad sign of the failure of the new "Model Germany" as a humane (tolerant) society that can tolerate and value heterogeneity. Then a state of Israel might not be necessary. For, to once again borrow from the Frankfurt School, I qualify my criticisms of Israel and my rejection of the equation Jewish = Zionist by insisting that any German who wants to talk with me about Zionism must also be ready to talk seriously and honestly about anti-Semitism in its contemporary and historical contexts. And with you, Henryk, I don't want to discuss anti-Semitism and the effects of persecution without simultaneously reflecting on the meaning of Jewish identity today.

Translated by Miriam Frank and Atina Grossmann

"Holocaust"

11

THE HOLOCAUST, WEST GERMANY, AND STRATEGIES OF OBLIVION, 1947–1979

Jean-Paul Bier

The "denazification" and "reeducation" undertaken by the Allies in 1945 had both a punitive character and an educational objective. The desire to punish those responsible for war crimes led to an absurd system of classification according to the degree of guilt. The grotesque mechanism of individual statements, the questionnaires that Ernst von Salomon was to parody in 1951, gave birth to a crafty system of fakes, truncated biographies, and exchanges of mutually accommodating testimony. For method's sake, the victors dealt first with the least complex cases. There-fore, those who were least guilty received a heavier punishment dispropor-tionate to that of criminals whose sentences were meted out later with the Cold War or European integration in mind. It should also be noted that "reeducation" to democracy by pedagogic methods, which were not al-ways democratic, and by victors, who in no way upheld the values they claimed to embody, could not produce the expected results.

The horror of the crimes perpetrated against humanity in concentration camps, reproduced in pictures and on film, constituted one of the essential means in the Allies' psychological undertaking. In 1946, the celebrated

This essay was originally published as Chapter 1, "Auschwitz, les Juifs, le Troisième Reich: points de sensibilisation (1945–1977)" in Jean-Paul Bier's *Auschwitz et les nouvelles littératures allemandes,* Brussels, 1979. It has been revised, expanded, and printed by permission of the author.

Nuremberg trials had a punitive and educational function. But the particular circumstances surrounding the trials and judgment of the defeated by the victors were from the outset an obstacle to the desired objectives of moral purification and the raising of intellectual consciousness. After the first emotional effects took their toll, the German people became concerned more with survival in their country's ruins and were not ready for the moral indignation and the feeling of collective guilt that these trials were supposed to provoke in them. Quite the contrary, by condemning Nazism mainly on grounds of genocide and industrial homicide, the victors elicited resentment from numerous strata of the population— people who themselves had been drastically affected by the catastrophe and recognized little of their daily life during twelve years under Hitler in apocalyptic images of genocide and murder.

Beyond these contestable plans, the first attempt at an objective and scientific study of the concentration camp phenomenon as revelatory of the totalitarian system was made after December 1945 by the sociologist Eugen Kogon in *Der SS-Staat*. A militant Protestant and cofounder of the journal *Frankfurter Hefte,* Kogon had written a doctoral thesis on fascist corporatism in 1927 and had himself lived through the hell of Buchenwald for six years. In the introduction to his inventory of systematized horrors, the author attempted to justify his work: The truth should have a therapeutic value and free us from a collective guilt which was not simply limited to Germans, and it should be brought to those who had ignored everything. He knew that he would be the object of much criticism and could only hope that the truth he defended would be put to the service of good. Kogon was the first to advance a systematic theory in his introductory chapter, included in the 1948 edition as *Der Terror als Herrschaftssystem* (Terror as a System of Domination), which pointed to the total failure of eighteenth-century progressive rationalism.[1]

Another survivor, the novelist Viktor Klemperer, who had received the "privilege" of working in a factory and of observing daily German life from the inside because of his non-Jewish wife, published his personal diary of those years of anguish and humiliation in 1946. *LTI Die unbewältige Sprache* (Dresden, 1946) was without irony the work of a philologist who, with the infinite patience of the etymologist, uncovered the deleterious role language played in the systematic destruction of the German people's moral and political conscience under Nazism. This incrimination of language as a privileged manipulative and alienating instrument was developed at the same time by critics and linguists such as Dolf Sternberger, Gerhard Storz, and W. E. Süskind in a series of articles found in the journal *Die Wandlung*. While these writers shed light on the semantic terrorism of Nazi totalitarianism, they paradoxically revived the mental conceptions of Leo Weisgerber's linguistic school which had been in favor during the Third Reich. The moral principle that founded the undertaking of reeducation through language was based on the notion that the destruction of language underlay man's destruction and that words were never innocent; semantic analysis became henceforth part of any attempt to explain the Nazi phenomenon.[2]

The new sovereign state of the Federal Republic of Germany, which took Bonn as its provisional capital in 1949, and which was identified for twenty years with the Christian Democrat Parties (CDU/CSU), never attempted politically to avoid its responsibility for the crimes of the past; the idea of historical continuity was an essential constitutive element in the establishment of its political institutions because of the Cold War. In the East, on the other hand, the German Democratic Republic postulated historical and political discontinuity and believed it possible to establish a completely new national reality with no ties to the Nazi past.

The political circumstances that prevailed during the Konrad Adenauer regime explain why democratic restoration in the Federal Republic occurred by means of a moral, somewhat religious acknowledgment of a past whose consequences had to be assumed—at least politically—at all costs. It is for this reason that Chancellor Adenauer signed a treaty with the young state of Israel in 1952 which established the principle of financial reparation to the survivors of genocide. But 1952 also marked a time of a certain negligence in the pursuit and condemnation of Nazi criminals, as if giving money to the victims was in some way the final page of the Auschwitz trauma.

During the first years of West Germany's formal existence as the second German Republic, a new theme, the resistance movement against Hitler, contributed to providing a moral foundation to the new social elite. The July 20, 1944, attempt on Hitler's life was consequently rediscovered along with the symbolic figure of a young Prussian officer, Klaus von Stauffenberg, heir to a certain national and military ethic, disappointed by the madness, adventurism, and vulgarity of the new political class of National Socialism.

Beginning in 1946, the author Ricarda Huch, who had a bone to pick with the Gestapo, had proposed the creation of a center for the research and documentation of the multiple heroic and unknown forms of resistance to totalitarianism in a well-known appeal in the new German press. Eugen Kogon, working in the *Frankfurter Hefte* for a political renewal founded upon a universal morality of religious inspiration, published numerous accounts, like that of Inge Scholl in 1952, concerning her brother and sister, Hans and Sophie Scholl, decapitated in 1942 for having distributed leaflets against the regime in university hallways, and their Munich movement "Die Weisse Rose."

In order to fight against the evident political exploitation of such accounts and examples of resistance, the writer Günther Weisenborn, himself imprisoned in 1942 for illegal activities, published in 1953 a detailed listing of the different groups that had actively resisted the regime. In this work, which is relatively unknown, though it was published in a paperback edition under the title *Der lautlose Aufstand* (The Silent Rebellion), it became evident that more than a million Germans had been incarcerated for political reasons before 1939, that the clandestine opposition had been both religious and ideological, that it had been based in all milieux and all social classes, and that a group of Jewish resistance fighters called "Gruppe Baum"[3] had even existed in Berlin during 1942.

In his introduction, Weisenborn held the Allies responsible for the German population's ignorance of these multiple acts of courageous and desperate opposition: The Allies had pilfered all the related archives and had systematically refused to take the German resistance into consideration because this would have further complicated their task of dealing with a conquered Germany. In passing, the author, a former member of the *Rote Kapelle* (Red Orchestra) group, regretted the fact that the religious and political oppositions, which had been in solidarity at one time, formed opposing camps immediately after the war, but he argued that publicizing the history of the one and of the other would contribute to the destruction of the fiction of collective guilt.

The very crucial viewpoint of Weisenborn, whose cultural and political ties with the GDR were well known, was already part of the framework of the ideological struggle of the Cold War. Objectivity requires that we distinguish in the Allies' attitude between a somewhat arbitrary cultural policy which varied according to sector[4] and an extremely generous attitude toward academics and scientific researchers. It is in this manner that the historian Hans Rothfels, who had voluntarily resigned from the University of Königsberg under the Nazis, was able to consecrate his research efforts to Hitler's opposition thanks to American support.[5]

At the beginning of the 1950s, the problems posed by the multiple attitudes possible in regard to the Nazi past began gradually to stray away from difficult questions like anti-Semitism, genocide, concentration camps, and extermination. It was obviously a question of taboos which the new German society was trying to forget at all costs. This situation was turned upside down by the publication in Germany of the *Diary of Anne Frank*. The murder statistics took on a child's face in such a way that, ten years after the end of the war, genocide became a key factor in the conflictual relationships between generations.

A second emotional and moral blow was the large Ulm trial in 1958 of crimes committed by a special task force *(Einsatzkommando)* in Lithuania. It appeared more and more clearly that genocide was no longer conceivable in terms of individual crimes, but as the logical result of an enormous, efficient machine of systematic extermination, conceived in the manner of a highly rationalized industrial enterprise. The horror shifted as well. From the demonization of a few sick or perverted individuals, public opinion moved to the diabolization of a very elaborate method, representative of an advanced and therefore universal stage of civilization. However, the protests concerning the sluggishness of the German judicial system when dealing with Nazi criminals provoked by this trial obliged the judiciary authorities to create a centralizing tribunal in 1958 at Bad Harzburg to which the federal government could not be an obstacle in the pursuit and judgment of these crimes.[6] But an increasingly large segment of public opinion was questioning the sense of such trials after so many years, during which the defendants seemed for the most part to be peaceful, settled pensioners, while witnesses animated by a spirit of vengeance and with questionable memories came for the most part from Israel or from socialist-bloc countries.

This new sensitivity to genocide in the particular conditions of a Cold War which centered on the Berlin question and the first signs of a resurgent extreme Right in the Federal Republic doubtlessly explain the profanation of Jewish cemeteries in December, 1959, and the epidemic of anonymous anti-Semitic graffiti in the first months of 1960. The emotions which seized German public opinion because of what proved to be only acts of vandalism by young hoodlums compelled Adenauer to make a declaration over the radio. Addressing himself to the Federal Republic's Jewish population, to its "jüdische Mitbürger," whose security he guaranteed, the Chancellor minimized the scandal by reducing it to the dimensions of imbecile provocations without political signification, implicitly recognizing that anti-Semitism, Jews, and the Holocaust belonged to many of the taboo subjects for the German society's new democratic conformism. German sociologists from the Frankfurt School, disciples of Max Horkheimer and Theodor Adorno, who were particularly sensitive to such problems because they were neo-Marxists and Jewish "re-immigrants," attempted to describe the diverse possible attitudes regarding these scandals.[7] The study confirmed the school's theses: 16 percent of those asked were openly anti-Semitic and expressed an excessive inclination for authority and for the death penalty. This group, somewhat marginal in comparison with the 41 percent of those evasively indifferent, belonged principally to the petty bourgeoisie and poorly hid its satisfaction in finding its opinions that were ostracized in the new German press confirmed by graffiti, and they eventually adopted a rather conciliatory demeanor that shifted the blame to the press and the media, which were "stirring up the public with child's games."

The new Jewish religious communities started during these years were very sensitive to this anti-Semitic revival. As part of the inauguration of a new Cologne synagogue in Roonstrasse at the end of 1959, a new rabbi with a Hebrew name invited the writers Heinrich Böll and Paul Schallück to a public debate on the meaning and legitimacy of Jewish presence in Germany. Since 1945, diverse religiously inspired organizations like the numerous "Societies for Christian-Jewish Cooperation" began combatting prejudice against Jews and trying to emphasize the latters' contribution to German culture. It was principally a matter for theologians, some of whom, like Hans Joachim Schoeps, professor at the University of Erlangen and an eminent religious historian, had always devoted their work to this subject.[8] The Tübingen Institute of Judaism played an essential role in the dissemination of more accurate knowledge of Jewish cultural and religious specificities.[9] The "Germania Judaica" section of the Cologne Library, founded in 1958, which was later to organize the most remarkable "Monuments of Judaica" exposition in 1963–1964, tried to emphasize the extraordinary cultural symbiosis which more than ten centuries of Jewish life in Germany had produced. But such acts were most often acts of piety; the organizers themselves were those most concerned and interested, and they addressed only a limited number of people.

But beyond this archaeological prospecting of religious dimensions, the first balance sheet of the Jewish contribution to German culture proper since the eighteenth century consisted of acts of intellectual mortification whose implicit moral objective was to show what Germany had lost in murdering and driving out "its Jews." The considerable work of the historian Hans Günther Adler is exemplary in this respect. In 1960 he simultaneously published a history of the Jews in Germany which produced its own school of thought. *Die Juden in Deutschland. Von der Aufklärung bis zum Nationalsozialismus* and an immense work on *Theresienstadt 1941–1945. Das Antlitz einer Zwangsgemeinschaft. Geschichte, Soziologie, Psychologie.*

Mass media, particularly television, played an essential role in the enhancement of two events that rendered the Holocaust a painful actuality: the Eichmann trial in Jerusalem (1961) and the Auschwitz trial at Frankfurt which lasted from December 1963 to August 1965. Without being able to say that there was a veritable silent conspiracy in popular literature, one must recognize that until the beginning of the 1960s, literature directly touching upon Nazi crimes was not at all abundant. If a few articles and documents in specialized reviews,[10] autobiographies treating a few extreme cases,[11] and some startling accounts,[12] are left aside, only Walter Hofer's collection of documents remains—*Der Nationalsozialismus. Dokumente 1933–1945,* which openly treats the politics of genocide. Hofer's small work, which has been published in paperback almost every year since 1957 and was reedited four times in 1960 alone, includes a chapter on "Jewish Persecution and Jewish Extermination" with revealing official Nazi texts along with the authenticated account of a civilian, Hermann Friedrich Gräbe, who had accidentally witnessed the mass execution of several thousand Ukrainian Jews. For sadly evident reasons, the systematic massacre of Jewish populations and the memories of concentration camp martyrdom were always associated with Eastern Europe[13] so that it only took a little for all the polemic's about Germany's notorious past to be classified as political intrigues inspired by the Soviets. This was quite apparent in the 1966 discovery that the president of the Federal Republic at that time, Heinrich Lübke, had taken part as an architect in the construction of concentration camp barracks.

However, the maturation in the early 1970s of the postwar generation, disappointed by the lack of an existential ideal in a consumer society, marked the beginning of a shameless exploitation of the Nazi past in books and films. This "Hitler-Wave" along with the vogue of cruel jokes about Jews undoubtedly had and has little or no political meaning, though the anonymous accounts collected by Walter Kempowski in his book *Haben Sie Hitler gesehen?* (1973) reveal some unreserved nostalgia. Elsewhere, in opposition to the 1960 Erwin Leiser film *Mein Kampf,* which denounced the crimes of Nazism, the 1975 film biography *Hitler, Eine Biographie* by Joachim Fest, which had considerable success, plays very ambiguously with the meaning of the spectacle and the enthusiasm of the masses and hardly mentions the persecution and the murder of the Jews.

It appears that the masses of the German Federal Republic, which has now become a considerable economic power, feel nostalgic about the large collective festivals that had been offered by the Hitler regime. Compared to Stalinist gulags and napalm bombings in Vietnam, the disgrace heaped on a period of their national history appears illegitimate to them. Since the large Springer Press has consistently taken an un-nuanced philo-Semitic position, which consists not only of taking a unilateral pro-Israeli position but also of vaunting authors and artists of the past in a partial and obsequious manner simply because of their Jewish origin, it is understandable that the new generation's young intellectuals, whose irreducible enemy since 1968 has been this reactionary press, have mitigated feelings toward philo-Semitism of any sort.

The Springer Press, which pleases small pensioners and the older generation, the majority of its readers, has been propagating a veritable civil war atmosphere against defenseless minorities since the end of the 1960s by suggesting, as did the Nazis with the Jews, that these minorities are extremely powerful and dangerous. Some of the younger generation have been duped by this and have ended up hunted like wild game believing that they and their bombs were actually close to overthrowing the prosperous and powerful state they so dislike.[14] It is undoubtedly not by chance that "leftist" intellectual anti-Semitism in Germany is an insidious anti-Semitism, found where one would least expect it. Due to their ignorance of Jews, these intellectuals interpret the virtues and the grandeur of all that the Jews have done or are doing, when printed in large-circulation Springer newspapers, as a thinly veiled call to murder. The attitude of the young generation, aware of social issues, thus constitutes a paradox: These same people who insist that the older generation assume responsibility for fascist Germany's crimes and who, in their opposition to the latter as to the heirs of this same post-1945 fascism, want Auschwitz and genocide to remain morally and politically revelatory, are also the ones who are most predisposed to criticize the idealization of Jews and philo-Semitism. In fact, this response explains the extremely rapid moral erosion of the Auschwitz theme in cultural and political life.

The majority of the Jewish intellectuals who had helped engender the literary and artistic golden age of the Weimar Republic and the Jewish-German bourgeoisie, who had contributed so much to the establishment of Germany as a nation since the nineteenth century and were then murdered or deported, now exist only as vague memories. For this reason young generations now have only a deformed image of the Jewish phenomenon. Confronted with the myopic prism of guilt or of nostalgia for the older generations and with the new character of the political conflict in the Middle East, the only point of comparison they have in daily life between these two poles is a Jewish population whose sociological and psychological characteristics do not fit the Jewish image in literature.

A 1961 study, not very susceptible to political prejudices,[15] categorized the Federal Republic's twenty-five thousand Jews in 1959 into three quite distinct groups: survivors of the Third Reich, refugees from Central Europe, "re-immigrants."

(1) Nearly fifteen thousand people who had converted or had been married to a spouse, who did not fall within the provisions of the race laws, along with numerous Jews illegally hidden by friends until 1945,

reappeared after the catastrophe and consequently took part in the country's reconstruction even though the persecutions had often awakened a feeling of socioreligious belonging to Judaism within them.[16]

(2) The displaced persons from Central Europe, the majority of whom had escaped from concentration camps, who, after some hesitation, had decided to stay in the country of their former persecutors now humiliated in defeat, were in no way ready to take part in the reconstruction. Amassing fortunes quickly through the black market and because of other advantages related to their unfortunate circumstances, these people, perverted by their harsh experience in the camps, sometimes behaved as if in conquered territory. The old antagonism between German Jews and Eastern European Jews was rekindled in this atmosphere; these groups, whose mentality bordered on the criminal,[17] seemed to stir up *a posteriori* anti-Semitism which most mortified Germans were trying to overcome.

(3) The third category, consisting of "re-immigrants," is subdivided into subgroups according to return dates and motivations in such a way that distinctions are made between those who took part from the beginning in Germany's political and cultural reconstruction, those who returned in 1956 following the passage of a law giving immediate aid to "re-immigrants," and those who were drawn back by the benefits of new German economic prosperity.[18]

In general, the re-immigrants of German origin were not in the labor force; they were for the most part older persons, pensioners, widows, without a profession and living almost completely from reparations called *Wiedergutmachung*. In these "cemetery communities" a class of "professional Jews" originated, specialists in German bureaucracy, who were for the most part the authority in those communities which singularly lacked religious leaders.[19] Until the end of the 1960s the exterior image of these Jewish re-immigrant communities had more the character of a political pressure group for economic gain than of a religious or cultural community. The good political and economic relations between the Federal Republic and Israel slowly transformed the shape of the Jewish population in Germany, largely dominated by nationals of other countries.[20] Accordingly, these "Jews in Germany," who can no longer be called "German Jews," form a somewhat heterogeneous and rather cosmopolitan group which contrasts strikingly with the slightly idealized image of the Jewish-German bourgeoisie of the Weimar Republic.

One of the important tasks that the Federal Republic's liberal political scientists and sociologists imposed upon themselves was to examine the causes and the conditions that led to the Nazi catastrophe. Without passing through the eyepiece of the murderous system, they attempted to safeguard the second democratic and parliamentary republic of West Ger-

many by analyzing the roots of the failure of political and cultural pluralism in the Weimar Republic. While the nostalgia for the lost minority
perpetuated itself in the works that vaunted the brilliant Jewish contribution to the Weimar spirit,[21] these first "politilogical" studies revealed the
eminently secondary role of anti-Semitism in the Right's antidemocratic
thought.[22] Little by little the idea was established that to consider totalitarianism from the angle of anti-Semitism and to comprehend the sociological or cultural "Jewish" reality in collective terms would mean
falling into the trap of archaic thinking habits revitalized by the Nazis.

An official 1966 document is evidence of this evolution and reveals a
characteristic ambiguity: the collective work *Auswärtige Kultur-
beziehungen* (Foreign Cultural Relations) edited by Berthold Martin under
the aegis of the appropriate governmental ministry,[23] contains an essay
several pages long on the Jewish contribution to the German culture's
international character which is a veritable list of national origins; however, the author, Hellmut Diwald, simultaneously insists that, in each case,
it is a question of individuals and of individual contributions, and that it
would be arbitrary and false to bring them all together under the concept
"Jewish-German."[24] In so doing, the entire essay loses all legitimacy.

Accordingly, the rediscovery of the flourishing Weimar culture, whose
effervescence and miraculous pluralism were politically translated into
chaos and anarchy by the rather uneducated masses, also constituted the
rediscovery of numerous authors, artists, and forgotten personalities who
had been persecuted under Nazism. In discovering their works and texts,
the public of the 1970s had the feeling of confronting a gap which had to
be filled and certain accumulated needs which had to be presently satisfied.
It was, therefore, no longer a question of examining this cultural inheritance from the angle of piety or mortification. The fact that men as
different as Kurt Tucholsky, Joseph Roth, or Carl Zuckmayer were effectively of Jewish origin did not transform them *a posteriori* into representatives of a murdered or misunderstood collectivity. At the time that
Auschwitz was no longer anything but a moral or literary quotation, the
Jewish origin of this or that famous person of the Weimar Republic, finally
rediscovered with pleasure, was nothing more than a small secondary or
exotic route.

These paradoxes in the evolution of thought habits form only the tip of
the iceberg of public opinion in the Federal Republic that no demoscopic
test would be able to completely comprehend. At most could one establish
the distinction between two problems in the political arena. In the case of
the Jews, the federal government attempted without a single doubt to win
over international opinion by a policy of considerable reparations which
were assuredly slow in coming, but which today are only contested by a

small fringe of nostalgic demagogues, and a nuanced but coherent pro-Israeli policy abundantly diffused by a well-read press. As if by compensation, the German judicial system showed reserve in judging and condemning murderers, and treated foreign criticism, quite scattered as it was, in a blunt fashion.

As for the National Socialist past, the government had attempted to set up judicial and political institutions in 1949 which would preclude any return to a situation comparable to that which had permitted the advent of totalitarianism. Nonetheless, in the domain of foreign policy, Adenauer as well as his successors Erhard and Kiesinger refused to recognize the new historical reality as irreversible and continued to cling to the utopian belief that the lost territories, presently Polish or Russian, would be returned to Germany. The year 1969 marked a turning point in this doubly moral and political problem when the liberal-socialist coalition, which dominated after the national elections, took as its leader Willy Brandt, a former émigré, who had fought in the Norwegian resistance against his own country. This new government broke with the CDU/CSU illusions concerning the Oder/Neisse frontier. Brandt kneeling in front of the Warsaw Ghetto monument in honor of dead Jews was a moral event without precedent that illustrates the link between the problem of responsibility for crimes against the Jews and the attitude concerning the Nazi past in general. Beginning in 1969 the new president of the Federal Republic, Gustav Heinemann, played the role of a bad conscience and never stopped returning to the theme of Auschwitz and the bad past during his term.

This normalization of political and cultural relations with Eastern Europe, the displacement outside of Europe of the problems raised by conflict between the two blocs, and also the distance in time and moral evolution removed the tragic poignancy from the memories of Germans: having lost all political function in Germany, a moral and religious summons in the name of Auschwitz lost all credibility. Likewise, the Central Council of Jews in Germany, embodied by its Berlin spokesman Heinz Galinski, gradually stopped being a respectable and quasi-sacred group and is no longer anything more than a phantasmal lobby group in the service of the large Springer press.

In fact, by associating the German people's collective guilt since 1945 concerning Auschwitz with the political necessities of "denazification," the path toward all types of manipulation was opened. The moral questioning of the Nazi regime in the name of politics gave the Germans, in the long run, the right to judge this same policy in the name of morality, to subordinate all morality to the laws of politics or, in the worst of cases, to refuse any association between the two terms. The Adenauer regime perpetuated this confusion by its attempt to legitimize its policies with an air of morality that gave high priority to the memory of Auschwitz, while the critics of this Adenauerian "restoration" questioned the inanity and the dangerous character of the concept of collective guilt.

It was in the name of ethics once again, but for manifestly political reasons, that in the early 1960s this concept of collective guilt came back into vogue. Cooperation with Israel and the financial reparations depleted the moral trauma of Auschwitz, leaving it without political impact, so that after the Eichmann trial of 1961, the politicization of the collective guilt concept by the Left and the Right's reaction against any such political exploitation provoked a perceptible erosion in the moral dimension of the problem.

With the memoirs of Albert Speer, released from prison in 1966, in which a man of superior intelligence put himself on trial and attempted to explain his fascination for Hitler, a veritable avalanche of books in the same vein began to descend on the public.[25] In 1965, the historian Percy Ernst Schramm had proclaimed that the study of Hitler's personality ought to be the most urgent and foremost task of modern historians. From that moment on, nobody was afraid to publish the dictator's writings or speeches in Germany.[26] The press spread the conflicts between Allied historians concerning the responsibility for the catastrophe that seemed to justify certain German scruples.[27] Thus each year saw biographies of the cursed personality appear, each bringing new and authentic documents, particular perspectives, and definitive affirmations. This abundant literature culminated in 1973 with the success of the scandalous movie taken from Joachim Fest's book, *Hitler: eine Biographie*, which was the absolute bestseller of the year.[28]

The experts of the famous Wiener Library in London have established that nearly eight thousand books treating Judaism and its tragedy in Germany were published between 1945 and 1968. An important bibliography with regard to this can be found in two remarkable books that give an overall view of this literature. They are W. E. Mosse and A. Paucker, eds., *Entscheidungsjahr 1932. Zur Judenfrage in der Endphase der Weimarer Republik*, (Tübingen, 1965) and *Deutsches Judentum in Krieg und Revolution 1916–1923*, (Tübingen, 1971). The majority of these works were published after 1960 and show evidence of a remarkable objectivity which did not fear saying things that went against accepted notions. Despite its slightly bothersome title which brings to mind a certain Nazi vocabulary, H. J. Gamm's manual *Judentumskunde* (1962) was a clear and exact introduction to Jewish history from Genesis to the state of Israel. In the same year, Edmund Silberner published *Sozialisten zur Judenfrage. Ein Beitrag zur Geschichte des Sozialismus vom Anfang des 19. Jahrhunderts bis 1914*, which showed that German socialism and social democracy had in no way been exempt from anti-Semitism despite Bebel's celebrated saying on anti-Semitism.

In 1964 the German translation of Cecil Roth's entire work, *Geschichte der Juden,* was published and was truly a best-seller. More arduous were the attempts to touch upon anti-Semitism; this subject was painfully reemphasized by the long Auschwitz trial of 1963–1965. In 1965, H. Andies' book *Der ewige Jude* presented this hatred of the Jews as ineluctable and without any reference to sociopolitical conditions. In 1966, P. J. Pulzer in *Die Entstehung des politischen Antisemitismus in Deutschland und Österreich* insisted on the Austrian roots of this modern tragedy, while, in 1972, W. Mohrmann in *Antisemitismus. Ideologie und Geschichte im Kaiserreich und in der Weimarer Republik* interpreted the anti-Semite phenomenon in orthodox Marxist terms as a capitalist maneuver to exploit the masses.

Although most of these books were addressed to somewhat specialized intellectuals, Gerhart Binder's and Jarmut Wasser's excellent 1974 work, *Deutschland, deine Legenden,* was intended for a larger public. The two authors had taken as a starting point lies, prejudices, and errors concerning German history from Bismarck to Willy Brandt and attempted, using documents and quotations, to shed some light upon the inanity of certain legends that delighted the majority of Germans. An important point in this respect was the idea that genocide was only the malevolent invention and the fruit of a systematic propaganda hostile to Germany. Having shown the absence of cogency and the utter immorality of those who, while not denying the extermination, attempted to diminish the number of victims, profiting from the difficulty that historians have had over the last twenty years in procuring all the required documentation, the authors completely disproved the theory which maintained that the Germans had known nothing about Auschwitz and that they were consequently innocent by reason of ignorance. Even if they had not been aware of the size of the crimes, it was evident that almost the entire German people had been at the mercy of the racist and anti-Semitic madness developed by the regime. It was false, for example, that Jews constituted a demographic danger to the nation, since the figures showed that their integration as well as their assimilation had noticeably diminished. Indeed, it was true that the number of Jews who played an eminent role in cultural life was quite considerable, and that they constituted the wealth and grandeur of the Republic. By ridding itself of them, Germany was reduced overnight to the level of a cultural province. Binder and Wasser showed that the criticism leveled against this Jewish intelligentsia, or at least Germans of Jewish origin, that they subverted and destroyed traditional values, was quite absurd when doctors such as Paul Ehrlich, philosophers such as

Ernst Cassirer, or physicists such as Albert Einstein were placed in the same group. It was undoubtedly true that critics such as Karl Kraus, Kurt Tucholsky, or Alfred Kerr had a corrosive spirit and a satirical verve that could be quite disconcerting, but why weren't the anti-Semites overly bothered by non-Jews such as Carl von Ossietzky or Erich Kästner?

After treating the subject of the "Jewish Republic," Binder and Wasser systematically refuted the legend of the international Jewish conspiracy and of the Jewish inclination for revolutionary subversion. They turned to Norman Cohn's book, *Die Protokolle der Weisen von Zion. Der Mythos der jüdischen Weltverschwörung*, which had been published in Germany in 1969. Other nations' attitudes toward those Jews driven out by Hitler after 1933 showed the insanity of the international conspiracy legend, and the authors demonstrated that, even if the number of Jews in revolutionary movements had been particularly large, this characterized in no way the majority of German Jews, who were rather middle of the road. In any case, most socialist or communist groups in Germany did not back down from a certain anti-Semitic, demagogic overbidding in attacking Jewish capitalism.

For the most part, Binder and Wasser sought to destroy the myth about Germans who knew nothing about Jewish extermination and versions which attempted to exonerate Hitler by putting the blame on his accomplices or on certain factions of the party. It was an incontestable fact that the desire to exterminate the Jews had originated above all in the sick mind of the Führer, who never swerved from this course, since his 1945 will was nothing more than a warning against racial impurity caused by the Jews. Genocide had not been prepared in secret, and public opinion was well aware of the Nazis' intentions from the beginning even if many Germans had not taken them seriously. The gradual elimination of Jews from public life, the successive racial laws, and the organization of pogroms in 1938 could count on the tolerance of this public opinion, even before the public was subjected to continuous terrorism. The physical liquidation of the Jews, the *Endlösung*, was written in black and white on all newsstands in the March 21, 1941, edition of *Völkischer Beobachter*, even if the methods of its execution, finalized on January 20, 1942, at the Wansee Konferenz, had effectively been decided in utmost secret. But, the bureaucratic mechanism and the extent of the undertaking were such that the number of people participating, directly or indirectly, must have been considerable. This is also true of those notorious falsifiers who continued in 1974 to deny the evidence after all that had been said and written about these crimes. But these falsifications of a phantom "National Opposition," which had crystallized in 1966 around the neo-Nazi NPD, gradually lost their credibility with a German public opinion much more open to the world and better informed, particularly because of an admirable television network little troubled by Byzantinism.

For the new generations, the "unburdened generations," the Nazi history has lost its traumatizing character. Of course, it has been impossible to deal with everything in this domain despite the remarkable activity of the Munich Institut für Zeitgeschichte, founded in 1950 under the name of the "Deutsches Institut für Geschichte der nationalsozialistischen Zeit." Twenty-five years of research has regularly been published in the *Vierteljarhszeitschrift für Zeitgeschichte* under the direction of Hans Rothfels, Theodor Eschenburg, and Helmut Krausnick, and since 1977 of Karl Dietrich Bracher and Hans Peter Schwarz. Despite the work of Martin Broszat and Thilo Vogelsang, there is no complete biobibliography of National Socialism. This institute certainly played a considerable role in the events of the various trials of Nazi criminals, during which its archives were used a great deal. However, it must be acknowledged that the institute did not play the expected pedagogic role in public opinion. Therefore, the public was at the mercy of commercial practices of publishers who saw in recent history a subject likely to attract a clientele of readers who have found it more and more difficult to read fiction and are more inclined to read documentaries, biographies, and nonfiction. This undoubtedly explains the unprecedented success of Joachim Fest's book on Hitler in 1973.

The film, based on the book by Fest, a noted historian and editor of the very serious and very conservative *Frankfurter Allgemeine,* was an unprecedented success in 1977, proving that Hitler and Nazism were no longer taboo subjects in Germany, thirty-two years after their defeat. The main objection made to the new image propagated by Fest was that he attached all the historical facts to the single charismatic personality of the Führer without attempting to explain or to "disengage" the socioeconomic, financial, or ideological forces which had permitted this average individual, tormented by a single obsession, to torment an entire people. Hitler was no longer a demonic madman or a power-hungry psychopath, but a crafty tactician who sincerely considered himself the savior of the world and of the nation. The historian had undoubtedly restricted himself to facts and to cinematic documents of the period—singularly forgetting the horrible images of genocide—but the producer Christian Herrendorfer had arranged the image and the text in such a way that it was less the critical and sometimes sarcastic commentary which remained in the spectator's mind than the overwhelming image of Nazi propaganda, showing the sincere and delirious enthusiasm of the crowds which this man had succeeded in arousing. He had given national dignity back to the Germans, had solved the unemployment problem, and had reestablished in the hearts of millions of Germans a feeling of law and order. Germany had not been raped by the Führer but, like two partners, they had searched for each other and had found each other in a fabulous orgasm.

Joachim Fest's film was in no way a rehabilitation of the character, but the filming of facts acquired by scholarly research in an enclosed environment which contrasted with the image of the criminal usurper in the service of big industry. It occasioned demoscopic studies, reflections, and surveys in the popular press and on television whose object was less historical truth than the manner in which public opinion conceived it in 1977, and what young people knew of it. Paralleling the film, a young professor published the results of a survey in schools of what children in the Federal Republic of Germany knew about Hitler and the Third Reich. This collection by Dieter Bossmann, *Was ich über Adolf Hitler gehört habe? Auszüge aus 3042 Aufsätzen von Schülern und Schülerinnen aller Schularten der Bundesrepublik Deutschland*,[29] revealed such an unbelievable ignorance that it was possible to ask oneself rightly if the work was not a joke. The magazine *Der Spiegel*, which published some examples of the responses, reported that even the author had sometimes asked himself the question.

Rudolf Augstein, the respected editor-in-chief of *Der Spiegel*, borrowing a celebrated statement by Karl Kraus, "I can think of nothing to say about Hitler," did not draw any pessimistic conclusions from these aberrations. Hitler and Nazism were no longer subjects of our time, and not a single political or social fact on this planet could be explained or resolved by a reference to this German past. In 1977, thought Augstein, the Hitler phenomenon no longer constituted a danger, and he was even less dangerous if he was unknown, as with these children naively questioned by a young teacher born after the war.

At the dawn of this last quarter of the twentieth century, one can thus conclude that German public opinion has been delivered from its demons. If a National Socialism without Hitler and with Auschwitz can be conceived, the genocide long prepared by an anti-Semitic tradition was in no way a necessity in German history. The superb ignorance of children who will be in their twenties in the year 2000 readily shows that the Führer was no longer considered as a typical phenomenon, but as a particular and atypical case which in no way determines the future and the history of political consciousness in Germany. According to this ignorance, Hitler was nothing more than a brilliant, demagogic politician who had made the mistake of making war against the world and of wanting to exterminate the Jews. Even in his crimes, wrote Rudolf Augstein, the character had nothing more to say.

But, if it is true that the concern of German historians for objectivity and the book industry contributed to a certain serenity in public opinion so that Hitler and the Third Reich stopped being taboo, this same attitude is not true concerning Jews past and present. The international situation, and the new peaceful coexistence which pushed the Federal Republic's government to a certain political realism and to sign contracts with the East and with the other German state in 1969, recognized *de jure* and *de facto*, necessarily led to the acknowledgment of Nazi crimes in these countries. However, it is almost as if this political change had liberated Germany from its trauma in such a way that the nostalgia for the past which struck most western countries could here take on strange forms. The most obvious result was a general feeling of extreme indifference. But in the case of the Holocaust, such a casual attitude does not seem possible.

This is what quite manifestly occurred at the end of the 1970s, at a time when the Federal Republic of Germany, the largest economic and financial power of Western Europe, seemed particularly disquieted by its world image. In fact, the absurd policy of professional proscription *(Berufsverbot)* and the somewhat hysterical repression of urban terrorism along with the suspicious suicides of the RAF (Rote Armee Fraktion) leaders in the Stammheim prison in October 1978 cast some doubt upon the democratic reputation of this second German republic. The scandalous revelation of Hans Filbinger's past as a criminal judge under the Nazi regime, the repeated lies told by this president of the state of Baden-Württemberg, whom the CDU/CSU opposition had considered a candidate for the Federal Republic's presidency, and the sluggishness in the process that would eliminate him from politics as well as the government's refusal to extradite the former SS officer Kappler, who had escaped to Germany while dying in an Italian prison, gave credence to the idea in a certain international press that NATO's German partner was slowly leaving the terrain of pluralist democracy.[30]

The possibility of a statute of limitations on Nazi crimes, which the Bundestag would have to debate for the fourth time since 1949 and which could have gone into effect December 31, 1979, was superimposed upon the fact that 1978 was also the fortieth anniversary of the 1938 Kristellnacht pogrom. The SPD/FDP government attempted to disentangle the political and judicial errors it had committed while fighting terrorism and its "sympathizers." Thus, it believed it necessary to stress the fight against far-rightist groups against whom a publicity campaign was waged inversely proportionate to their importance and to the dangers they constituted.[31] Accordingly, the minister of Youth and Family took the risk of intervening in order to put an end to the propagation of Nazi literature and publications, craftily presented as historical documents. International uneasiness was confirmed at the end of April 1978 by the European protest movement against Nazi renewal in the Federal Republic which brought together more than fifteen thousand people from all parts of the globe in Cologne, while the TV movie "Holocaust" was shown in the USA, Great Britain, and Israel with reactions which are already known. At the same time, Sebastian Haffner's remarkable book *Anmerkungen zu Hitler*,[32] which showed that the Führer's pathological personality and the genocide of Jews were essential factors in the complete comprehension of the National Socialist past, became a stunning best-seller.

The combined effects of all this made the decision by certain people in the West German mass media not to telecast Gerald Green's American TV film for "aesthetic and moral reasons" scandalously incomprehensible. It seemed inconvenient to present a dramatic, "simulated" version of Auschwitz to the German public,[33] when, at the end of 1978, there were two interminable and contested Nazi criminal trials still in court which were both apparently going to end in acquittal due to lack of evidence and despite the judges' inner convictions to the contrary.[34] Likewise, the parliamentary debate over the statute of limitations, during which all party discipline broke down, and which finally concluded with the abolition of the statute of limitations for crimes against humanity, was all the more delicate because of the revelation about Brazil's refusal to extradite the "Sobibor butcher," Gustav Franz Wagner. Most other countries did not worry about such nuances in their statutes of limitations.

Therefore, it is evident that there is a connection between the telecast of the TV film "Holocaust" and this widely publicized debate. After a long period of psychological preparation for the spectator, the film appeared on television on January 22, 23, 25, and 26 and was regularly followed by a television debate so that nearly four consecutive evenings were consecrated to what had been until then a taboo in German daily life. More than any documentary or any personal account, this fiction film, though of mediocre quality, provoked a truly emotional outburst: After the first telecast on Monday, January 22, 1979, the ARD staff received more than five thousand frenzied, passionate telephone calls, which constituted a veritable event in the history of the relationship between German television and its public. For more than five days, the only topic of discussion in homes, offices, and schools was the genocide. Newspapers received hundreds of letters daily from readers who bore witness to the failure of general education and historians with regard to Auschwitz; indeed, the majority of the problems and questions raised had been touched upon by specialists, but never had it been more evident that public opinion had not benefited from scientific progress.[35]

More than in other countries, "Holocaust" was an important event in the Federal Republic of Germany. Having destroyed a taboo and created a climate favorable to discussing in the family, at school, or at work, what, until now, had been repressed, it has seemingly permitted the realization that it is less a question of assuming the past than of preventing a future through recollection of the past. The matter has not disappeared.

From now on German has been enriched by a new American word "Holocaust," which simultaneously covers the Jewish genocide, the TV movie and its personalized tragedy, and the emotional and political reactions it provoked. These five days of collective emotion seem to have permitted the younger generation to perceive the Auschwitz trauma and the Jews from a totally new perspective, which could be called "the pedagogy of the Holocaust."

Translated by Michael Allinder

NOTES

1. The book's first sentence is, in this respect, symptomatic after 1948: "The age of Enlightenment, that is, of optimistic faith in unlimited progress through reason, has for all intents and purposes failed in Europe outside of science." It should be noted that this edition enlarges the totalitarian system to include the "Bolshevik" regime.

2. These articles were assembled in 1957 and published under the title *Aus dem Wörterbuch des Unmenschen*. In the 1967 edition of this book, which was reedited several times in paperback, the authors explicitly declared: "Words are not innocent. They can't be. Rather, the guilt of the speaker attaches itself to the language itself and becomes part and parcel of the speech at the same time" (Munich, 1967), p. 10.

3. The "Gruppe Baum," from the twenty-nine-year-old leader's name, Herbert Baum, was decimated in the autumn of 1942 after a successful act of sabotage because of the treachery of one of its members who was a Gestapo agent. Günther Weisenborn, *Der lautlose Aufstand* (Hamburg, 1962), p. 150f.

4. The intolerance of some American officers is well known; they eventually censored and banned Alfred Andersch's and Hans Werner Richter's journal *Der Ruf,* which brought about the birth of the Gruppe 47, whose role in German literature after the war has been of utmost significance.

5. See Hans Rothfels, *The German Opposition to Hitler: An Appraisal* (Hillsdale, Illinois, 1948); *Die deutsche Opposition gegen Hitler. Eine Würdigung,* (Krefeld, 1948). Rothfels's principal work on this subject appeared in 1958.

6. From 1959 to 1963 this institution brought about 110 trials.

7. Cf. Peter Schönbach, "Reaktionen auf die antisemitische Welle im Winter, 1959/1960," *Frankfurter Beiträge zur Soziologie* (Frankfurt am Main, 1961).

8. One of the first such texts was Schoeps' book *Israel und die Christenheit,* published in 1937 in one of its rare authorized versions, intended only for Jews. The new edition of this study of the relationship between Jews and Christians in the 19th century was published by Mohn in Tübingen in 1949, but, after 1960, it found a publisher who specializes in this area, Ner-Tamid-Verlag (Munich/Frankfurt am Main). The rediscovery of this problem characterized the 1950s and was consistent with the religious and moral approach to the Jewish problem in Germany at that time. Schoeps, *Theologie und Geschichte des Judenchristentums,* (Tübingen, 1949); Karl Thieme, *Kirche und Synagogue, Die ersten nachbiblischen Zeugnisse ihres Gegensatzes im Offenbarungsverständnis,* (Olten, 1945); Wilhelm Maurer, *Kirche und Synagogue, Motive und Formen der Auseinandersetzung der Kirche mit dem Judentum im Laufe der Geschiche,* (Stuttgart, 1953), etc. In the early 1960s, these specialized studies were popularized in paperback editions: an example is Karl Thieme, *Judenfeindschaft. Darstellungen und Analysen,* (Frankfurt am Main, 1963).

9. In 1962 Reinhold Mayer published passages and commentaries of the Babylonian Talmud in a cheap paperback book in the collection Goldmanns Gelbe Taschenbücher.

10. Here are some noteworthy examples: Hans Lamm, *Über die Entwicklung des deutschen Judentums im Dritten Reich,* doctoral dissertation (Erlangen, 1951); Kurt Gerstein, "Niederschrift vom 4. Mai 1945 über Massenvergasung am 18. August 1942," *Vierteljahreshefte für Zeitgeschichte,* 2 (1953); Gerald Reitlinger, *The Final Solution* (New York, 1953); Karl Loewenstein, "Minsk im Lager der deutschen Juden," in the weekly supplement of the magazine *Das Parlament* (November 7, 1956).

11. J. Graef, *Leben unter dem Kreuz. Eine Studie über Edith Stein* (Frankfurt am Main, 1954).

12. This is the substance of the intimate diary kept by the Auschwitz commander Rudolf Höss and published by Fischer Verlag under the title *Kommandant in Auschwitz* (Frankfurt am Main, 1958).

13. The eminently courageous policy of translating Polish, led by Carl Dedecius, should be noted here. It was less a question of making known a literature, obsessed more than any other by Nazi terror and the universe of the concentration camps, than of giving a human face to a world that Nazi racism and, it should be said, a certain Prussian tradition had habitually scorned.

14. Newspapers such as *Die Welt* and especially *Die Bildzeitung* generated the assassination attempt on the student leader Rudi Dutschke and regularly organize to this day a thinly veiled form of moral persecution against defenseless individuals who are bothersome because of their fame and espousal of popular causes such as Heinrich Böll, Günther Grass, Eberhard Lämmert, Günther Walraff, etc. History will show the part played by this press in the tragic development of Andreas Baader, Ulrike Meinhoff, and their followers.

15. *Über den Wiederaufbau der jüdischen Gemeinden in Deutschland seit 1945,* doctoral thesis in sociology by Harry Maor, an Israeli of German origin, defended at the University of Mainz in 1960, published in 1961.

16. According to Maor, the number of Jews said to be in the capital of the Reich itself in 1945 was 1,418. The publisher Ullstein, married to a non-Jew, had to work as a beast of burden in humiliating tasks just to survive. A few authors of the postwar generation, born in mixed marriages, went through childhood as outcasts, Ilse Aichinger and Günther Kunert, for example.

17. Maor insists that this is the mentality of "those passing through" who seemed to prefer the role of owning bars and seedy clubs.

18. A few of the more important names in the Federal Republic's political and cultural life who succeeded in pursuing a career in the Federal Republic are Herbert Weichmann, Mayor of Hamburg; Joseph Neuberger, Justice Minister in Rhineland/Westphalia; Heinz Karry, Finance Minister of Hesse; Erik Blumenfeld, a CDU deputy; Philip Rosenthal, SPD deputy; Ludwig Rosenberg, General Secretary of trade unions (DGB); the actors Ernst Deutsch, Fritz Kortner, Lily Palmer, Grete Mosheim, etc. The journal *Allgemeine Wochenzeitung des Judentums* was founded by an early re-immigrant by the name of Karl Marx (died in 1966). This same phenomenon of constructive re-immigration took place in the GDR and includes Otto Winzer, Foreign Affairs Minister; Hilde Benjamin, Justice Minister; Albert Norder, Information Minister; Friedrich Wolf, playwright, who became the ambassador to Poland; Alexander Abusch, an important figure in cultural life for many years; Herman Axen and Gerhard Eisler, members of the SED Politbureau; Rudi Singer, director of the National Radio; Deba Wieland, director of the National Press Agency; Grete Wittkowski, President of the State Bank, etc.

19. The procedures used here by these improvised leaders led to some financial scandals and trials such as that of Aaron Ohrenstein, a rabbi in Munich, and of Philip Auerbach, who committed suicide while in prison. These events among numerous others did nothing to better the Jewish image in Germany.

20. According to estimates in the *Encyclopaedia Judaica*, Vol. 7, p. 488, in the 1971 edition, Germany had, in 1966, around 36,000 Jews, the majority of which lived in Berlin, Frankfurt, Munich, Dusseldorf, Hamburg, and Cologne. In addition to the re-immigrants from Israel (the Jored), several hundred Iranian Jews, who arrived in the early 1960s, and several thousand Czechoslovak refugees, following the failure of the Spring of Prague uprising in 1968, should also be included.

21. Symptomatic of this was the republishing of books written by Jews in the 1930s which revealed, to the contrary, a conception of appurtenance to Judaism and of "Jewish" contributions comparable to that of the anti-Semites. Ismar Elbogen, *Geschichte der Juden in Deutschland*, 1935 reedited in 1966; Sigmund Kaznelson, *Juden im deutschen Kulturbereich*, reedited in 1962. See also Hermann Levin Goldschmidt, *Das Vermächtnis des deutschen Judentums* (Frankfurt, 1965). In the same spirit, Europa Verlag of Vienna published in 1968 Albert Massiezek, *Der menschliche Mensch. Karl Marx' jüdischer Humanismus*.

22. See Kurt Sontheimer, *Antidemokratisches Denken in der Weimarer Republik* (Munich, 1962), which gives no importance to Jewish or anti-Semitic problems.

23. Published by Luchterhand, Neuwied in 1966, the book contains articles by Walter Scheel, Klaus von Bismarck, and Hans Mayer and a complete summary of German cultural activities throughout the world up to 1965.

24. Hellmut Diwald, "Der jüdische Beitrag zur gegenwärtigen Internationalität der deutschen Kultur," p. 55: "There is no such thing as a special Jewish contribution to contemporary German culture, nor to its international sphere, rather there is only the contribution of individual Jews, many Jews, important Jews—but the sum of their creativity does not add up to a German-Jewish specificity."

25. *Erinnerungen* was published in 1963 and was a best-seller. The 1969 *Spandauer Tagebücher* can be considered the political testament of a man who could live thereafter on

the royalties from his successful books. One can rightly ask oneself who receives the royalties from the memoirs of other dead and executed criminals, for example the *Goebbels Tagebücher* "rediscovered" and successfully published in 1977.

26. For example, the four volumes of Hitler, *Reden und Proklamationen 1932–1945*, published in Munich by Max Domarius in 1965.

27. Cf. the opposition between Alan Bullock, whose book *Hitler, Eine Studie über Tyrannei*, published in pocket-book form by Fischer in 1964 and A. J. P. Taylor, *Die Ursprünge des zweiten Weltkrieges* (Gutersloh, 1962) or David L. Hoggan, *Der erzwungene Krieg, Die Ursachen und Urheber des zweiten Weltkriegs* (Tübingen, 1961). Though Taylor's and Hogan's books, which are a kind of quasi-rehabilitation of Hitler, were the objects of harsh criticism in scholarly journals (for example, G. Jasper, "Über die Ursachen des Zweiten Weltkriegs" in the *Vierteljahrshefte für Zeitgeschichte*, 1962), these new and very questionable hypotheses received a lot of publicity in fashionable magazines and in the popular press. It goes without saying that the newspaper *National- und Soldatenzeitung*, which had returned to the worst Nazi attitudes, readily referred to these British "historians" to support its reactionary viewpoint. When they are not claiming that Hitler knew nothing about the genocide or Auschwitz, whose horrors have allegedly been vastly exaggerated, the editors of this newspaper, who profit from a very liberal notion of the freedom of the press in the Federal Republic, proclaim that National Socialism did not want the extermination of the Jews but was forced to do it during the war because of the "international Jewish conspiracy." I can hardly give any space in this study to this "revisionist literature," which represents only a small fringe of public opinion. What should be pointed out here is that most of these writings, if they are at all noteworthy, are of foreign origin and could therefore constitute veritable alibis. Typical in this respect is the importance given by Germans to Jacques Benoist-Mechin's book, *Wollte Adolf Hitler den Krieg?* (Oldendorf, 1971). Benoist-Mechin went so far as to claim that the National Socialist Party was philo-Semitic since it had permitted 500,000 Eastern Jews to enter Germany from 1933 to 1938, thus escaping the anti-Semitic madness which reigned in Poland. In opposition to these lucubrations, the very remarkable work of an American historian should be noted. Gerald Reitlinger's *The Final Solution*, which was published as *Die Endlösung. Hitler Versuch der Ausrottung der Juden Europas 1939–1945* and was already in its fourth edition in 1961. Let me finally note H. R. Trevor-Roper, whose book *Hitler's Last Days (Hitlers letzte Tage)* was also published by Ullstein in pocket-book form in 1965.

28. Here are some examples: Helmut Heiber, *Adolf Hitler: Eine Biographie* (1960); Heinrich Bennecke, *Hitler und die SA* (1962); Hans-Bernd Gisevius, *Adolf Hitler. Versuch einer Deutung* (1963); Karl Dietrich Bracher, *Adolf Hitler* (1964); H. D. Röhls, *Hitler—die Zerstörung einer Persönlichkeit* (1965); Friedrich Heer, *Der Glaube des Adolf Hitler* (1968); Ernst Deuerlein, *Hitler—eine politische Biographie* (1970); Wolfgang Hammer, *Adolf Hitler— ein deutscher Messias?* (1970); Werner Maser, *Adolf Hitler—Legende—Mythos—Wirklichkeit* (1971). Maser's book went through many editions until 1974 when it was finally supplanted by Joachim Fest's book on Hitler.

29. Fischer Taschenbuch, Frankfurt, 1977. As far as genocide is concerned, here are some of the unlikely answers published by *Der Spiegel* on August 15, 1977: "He (Hitler) called those who opposed him Nazis. He stuck the Nazis in the gas chambers" (13-year-old). "If a Jew and a German were aryan together according to Hitler, then they had to stand at the market place with a sign around their necks" (15-year-old). "I think he also had Jews killed" (13-year-old). "He let 50,000 Jews be murdered" (15-year-old). "He let the Jews out through the chimney. The Jews were allowed to rot in the gas chamber. Some were allowed to play

games. Russians were allowed to play soccer, and the Jews were allowed to play leap frog in the mine fields" (15-year-old). "He (Hitler) had a friend, and he was Jewish. The Jew lent him money, and Hitler wanted more and more money. But, the Jew said, no, no more money. So Hitler began to hate him and let all Jews be gassed and killed" (16-year-old). "Hitler had very little to do with the extermination of the Jews because he was mainly concerned with violent criminals. It was that dirty crumb Himmler who was mainly responsible for the extermination of the Jews" (15-year-old). "Hitler was himself a Jew" (16-year-old). "His most important achievement was the persecution of the Jews. Many people reproach him for the concentration camps and the persecution of the Jews, but isn't it true that almost all the other countries during this time persecuted the Jews or another minority?" (16-year-old).

30. Some books bearing witness to this uneasiness over the Federal Republic's image are Manfred Koch-Hillebrecht, *Das Deutschenbild—Gegenwart, Geschichte, Psychologie* (Munich, 1977); Gerhard Zwerenz, *Die Westdeutschen* (Munich, 1977); Ulrich Sonnemann, *Der misshandelte Rechtsstaat in Erfahrung und Urteil bundesdeutscher Schriftsteller, Rechtsanwälte und Richter* (Cologne, 1977). At the end of February 1977, the picture of an unknown man giving the Hitler salute during Kappler's burial at Soltau was printed in the international press and widely circulated. This photo became symbolic.

31. Cf. on this subject Dieter Strothmann's excellent dossier in *Die Zeit* (April 28, 1978), 33–37. According to the re-immigrant Herbert Weichmann, former Jewish mayor of Hamburg, the neo-Nazi groups are more a matter for the police than for politics.

32. Sebastian Haffner, *Anmerkungen zu Hitler*, (Munich, 1978). This book's success is explained less by the ideas he defends than by its easy access, the transparency of the style, and its small size (200 pages). It contains seven chapters with clear titles (*Leben, Leistungen, Erfolge, Irrtümer, Fehler, Verbrechen, Verrat*) which form convincing answers to the important habitual questions asked about the Hitler phenomenon.

33. See Klaus W. Wipperman, "Holocaust im Spiegel der Presse," *Tribune* 69 (1979), 22–45.

34. See the statistics of these trials in *Die Zeit*, Nov. 17, 1978. Such was also the case in the important Maidanek trial at Dusseldorf which ended at the end of April 1979 with the acquittal of the accused.

35. See Jürgen Thorwald, "Holocaust—eine Bilanz," *Die Zeit*, (May 4, 1979), 16f.

12

THE "HOLOCAUST" RECEPTION IN WEST GERMANY
RIGHT, CENTER, AND LEFT
Jeffrey Herf

I was in Frankfurt a few years ago to do research on aspects of Critical Theory. But, as with other American Jews working in West Germany for similar reasons, the subject of Germans and Jews was never far from my consciousness. The topic was not a new one for me. My father had fled from Hitler's Germany in 1937. I had opposed the war in Vietnam with arguments drawn from Hannah Arendt's reflections on the banality of evil. I viewed my own "New Leftism" as a logical outcome of a German-Jewish tradition of political and moral intellectualism with which I identified. But living in Frankfurt, while it did not produce a wholly new "Jewish identity" to supplant a secular left-wing identification, did encourage my thinking about relations between Germans and Jews, and Jews and the Left. These personal thoughts coincided with a rather bizarre episode. The American culture industry *appeared* to have made the topic of "Germans and Jews" a huge public discussion for the first time. This essay on the West German reaction to the television film "Holocaust" represents my still uncompleted personal reflections as they intersect with a still uncompleted national debate.

This article had its beginnings in many fruitful discussions with Moishe Postone. It also benefited greatly from suggestions and criticisms by Dan Diner, Sonya Michel, Anson Rabinbach, and Andy Buchwalter.

"Holocaust" was shown on West German television during the last week of January, 1979. An estimated twenty million viewers watched each of the four segments of the program.[1] In the weeks before and months following the telecast, West German newspapers and magazines were filled with material related to the program and its subject. It was not unusual to hear and read that West Germany had engaged in its first widespread public discussion of the Holocaust.[2] My essay will cover some reactions to the program that emerged from conservatives, liberals, and social democrats in the media, and from some voices I thought representative of currents in the left-wing scene. All three, the Right, Center, and Left, displayed blind spots concerning this episode of German history, but they did so for different reasons. The willful myopia of conservatives, especially people whose formative years took place under Hitler, is hardly surprising. They largely seek to "put the past behind us," for they are only too aware of the extent to which it continues to live in the present. Liberals and social democrats, especially in the press and media, are eager to discuss the persecution of the Jews and the attendant issue of *individual* guilt and responsibility among the Germans. But they are reluctant to connect this discussion to suggestions of structural continuities in the nature of the social and class system between the Third Reich and the Federal Republic. The notion that Germany hit a "point zero" *(Nullpunkt)* in 1945 captures this view.

The Left shares neither a conservative impulse to repress the past completely nor a liberal refusal to look at "the problem of continuity" between Nazi and postwar West Germany. Probably no single statement expresses the stance of the Left discussion of fascism better than Horkheimer's wartime dictum: "Whoever does not want to talk about capitalism should remain silent about fascism."[3] Thus, while the Left has had a great deal to say about the relation between fascism and capitalism, it has been less forthcoming on the subject of anti-Semitism.[4] In part, this may be due to the simple absence of large numbers of Jews in the West German Left (and in West Germany in general). But it also appears to stem from some of the rationalist and reductionist biases of Marxist theory *and* from a tendency of young German leftists to leap from the German past to the Israeli and Palestinian present. Both Marxism and politics of identification with the Third World have served as defense mechanisms preventing a distinct left-wing grasp of the anti-Semitic past. At the same time, the reception of "Holocaust" on the Left indicated that bringing the repressed past to the surface could have the desirable effect of fostering a distinctly radical version of coming to grips with the past.

In the immediate aftermath of the "Holocaust" telecast, many commentators in West Germany asserted that the repression of a public discussion of the Nazi past had now ended. It should be kept in mind that numerous books, articles, and documentary films about the Holocaust had been printed and shown in West Germany, so the picture of total and complete amnesia is not an accurate one. But, as the following examples demonstrate, lapses of memory and distortion do exist.

The growth of neo-Nazi organizations in recent years, government officials say, is cause for concern but not alarm. Police estimate that about twenty thousand young people (ages seventeen to thirty) belong to right-wing extremist groups.[5] The attraction of neo-Nazi groups for young people in a country with only about thirty thousand Jews is said to be disturbing evidence of the failure to discuss the Nazi past in the high schools.[6] Neo-Nazi groups have distributed literature in the schools disputing the "facts" of the Holocaust (for example, "No Jews were gassed in Bergen Belsen," or there is quibbling over the numbers killed in Auschwitz). Moreover, these groups have painted anti-Semitic slogans on synagogues, attacked left-wing book stores and offices, and begun to stockpile and train with weapons. There have been several trials and convictions as a result. The case of a Jewish teacher in Berlin who was subjected to anti-Semitic abuse by students became a public scandal after school officials hesitated to bring action against those responsible. The newspaper of the extreme Right, *Die Nationale Zeitung*, readily available on newsstands, regularly displays banner headlines attacking the "lies" being spread about the Holocaust. Explicit anti-Semitism evident in the extreme Right is politically discredited and marginal in West Germany.[7] Whether this would remain the case if unemployment and inflation were to rise beyond the minuscule (by American standards) 2 to 4 percent is an open question.

Less spectacular but, in a sense, more disturbing, is a new respectability that has been lent to West German amnesia by a recent wave of what came to be called "Hitler nostalgia." Unlike the anti-Semitic literature of the neo-Nazis, conservatives such as the British historian David Irving have argued that Hitler's goals in World War II were only tangentially related to the Final Solution and that Hitler had no knowledge of it.[8] Although Irving's thesis was subjected to withering criticism by historians and journalists, his book became a best-seller in West Germany largely because of the support it gave to an old refrain: "If only the Führer knew" about the murder of the Jews, he would have stopped it. The appeal to West Germans, who do not want to break completely with the past, is obvious, for if Hitler didn't know, then neither did the average citizen. Furthermore, Hitler's "idealism" and "positive accomplishments" could be kept separate from Auschwitz, thereby opening the way to a more "balanced" view of Nazism.

Certainly the most spectacular of the recent right-wing respectable revisionists is Hellmut Diwald, a medievalist, whose particular history of Germany incorporated lies and distortions that had heretofore been the exclusive property of reactionary propaganda.[9] The heated controversy which followed publication of Diwald's book focused on his claim that "central questions" concerning the Final Solution "remained unexplained."[10] For example, he wrote that extermination camps did not exist in Germany but neglected to point out that they were manifold in Poland; he argued that the deportations of Jews during the war were due to the need for labor in armaments factories, and he claimed that the ovens built at Birkenau were used to control a typhoid epidemic and that the gas chambers in Dachau were "test models" that were never used. Finally he insisted that the Russian prisoners of war "did not live under worse conditions than the German civilian population" (about 60 percent of them died), and he pointed an accusing finger at the British and Americans for not bombing Auschwitz.[11] In response to the storm of criticism that greeted his book, Diwald said that only when researchers gain access to the "large numbers of documents now in the United States, Soviet Union, France, and England" could the "controversy" be resolved.[12]

The "Filbinger affair," which extended through the first two-thirds of 1978, brought out some of the complexities involved in the relation of West German conservatives to their own activities during the Third Reich. For years Hans Filbinger had been the leading figure of the Christian Democratic Union (CDU) in the conservative region of Baden-Württemberg. He was a staunch advocate of the *Berufsverbot,* the laws prohibiting "enemies of the constitution" from serving in the civil service (from the post office and national railroad to the universities). The Filbinger affair began when the playwright Rolf Hochhuth claimed that several weeks after the end of the war, Filbinger, in his capacity as an officer and judge among German prisoners of war in a British internment camp, sentenced a sailor to death for having called an officer a "Nazi pig." At first, Filbinger said the story was a fabrication and accused Hochhuth of being a terrorist sympathizer. When that failed to silence public criticism, Filbinger admitted that the story was true and defended his actions, saying: "What was right in the Third Reich cannot be wrong today." Filbinger's admirable frankness was political suicide. Had he apologized for the sins of his youth, his career in politics might not have come to an abrupt end. The Filbinger affair demonstrated why conservative politicians would want to "put the past behind" them. It also generated a surprising degree of popular support for a public figure who refused to distance himself from his actions as a loyal civil servant under Hitler.

More than any other issue or event, the debate in parliament over extending or abolishing West Germany's statute of limitations on crimes of murder (known as the *Verjährungsdebatte*) has revealed how the Nazi past became an issue of West German politics today. The telecast of "Holocaust" has been credited with shifting public opinion toward abolishing the traditional statute of limitations, thereby making possible further investigation and prosecution of Nazi war criminals. The debate and its outcome are very complex. For present purposes, the following summary of its importance is adequate. Unlike Anglo-Saxon legal doctrine, German law had, for over a century, contained a statute of limitations which prohibited prosecution of crimes of murder once thirty years had elapsed after the commission of the crime. The West German Constitution, established in 1949, followed this precedent. Hence, if Nazi war criminals had not been charged with crimes as of December 31, 1979 (thirty years after the adoption of the Constitution), and if the statute of limitations was not modified or revoked, those who had successfully avoided punishment up to that date, could not, under West German law, ever be brought to justice. Foreign pressure was exerted on the West German government, especially from Poland, Israel, and the Jewish community in the United States, for it was assumed by those familiar with the history of trials and prosecutions that many ex-Nazis had not been brought to justice. Before the telecast of "Holocaust," West German public opinion could be characterized as disinterested in, lacking information about, and/or considerably opposed to further prosecutions.

The simple facts concerning these legal proceedings are most eloquent testimony to the strength of resistance in West Germany to "coming to grips" with the Nazi past.[13] From 1945 to 1949, the period of what many West Germans would come to call that of "victor's justice," over 5,000 persons were found guilty of war crimes. From 1950 to 1977, a period that encompassed the division of Germany and onset of the Cold War as well as the economic miracle of the 1950s and 1960s, 1,204 convictions were delivered. Of the 84,403 cases opened in 1945, 74,263 resulted in no punishment at all, and 6,432 in convictions of some kind, including 14 death sentences and 164 life sentences at the end of 1977. In a recent talk in New York, Hans Magnus Enzensberger pointed to the incredible disproportion between the resources lavished upon the national police in the "battle against terrorism" and the paltry facilities and staff devoted to investigating and prosecuting participants in the state-organized terror of the Hitler regime.[14]

In addition to the feebleness of the prosecution effort, interminable length of the trials has compounded a record of justice delayed and hence denied. For example, in Düsseldorf, a trial of former officers and guards at the Maidanek concentration camp near Lublin, Poland (in which 1,380,000 Jews, as well as Gypsies and non-Jews were killed),[15] entered its fifth year in 1979. During all this time, the trial aroused hardly any public interest whatsoever. (In the post-"Holocaust" climate, four acquittals—out of eleven defendants—drew a bit more attention, although absurdly lenient sentences for convicted mass murderers have been passed before.)[16]

The West German record in this matter was so regrettable that it moved one German-Jewish journalist to write that the statute of limitations should not be extended on the grounds that to do so would perpetuate the illusion that, although for the past thirty years a persistent effort had been made to prosecute Nazi war criminals, more time was necessary. Such persistence, he argued, was never in evidence. Calling an end to the trials would at least force a simple truth out into the open: Thousands of murderers had gotten away with murder.[17]

Neo-Nazism and the reactionary "revisionist" accounts of the Final Solution, although part of the pre-"Holocaust" climate, were less important that the *Verjährung* debate, which involved the major political parties and put the Right on the defensive. The liberal press during fall 1978 devoted considerable space to the persecution of the Jews by the Nazis and to the postwar story of legal neglect. The admission that "more time" was needed to prosecute ex-Nazi war criminals was, as Broder remarked, damning evidence of just how strong resistance had been even to a coming to grips with the past through the medium of *West German courts,* that is, through the legal system. "Holocaust" was telecast in a climate of growing West German public criticism of the postwar failure to live up to basic liberal principles of justice.

The Debate over the Aesthetic Merits of "Holocaust"

West German criticism of "Holocaust" and resistance to telecasting it in the Federal Republic began in April 1978, when it was first shown in the United States, and continued up to the week preceding the West German telecast in January 1979.[18] Indeed, a right-wing extremist group blew up a TV transmitter in that week. I must confess that, even if the climate of resistance to discussing and/or *doing* something about facing the Nazi past had been different, I would still view objections to "Holocaust" on aesthetic grounds made by West Germans in a different light than identical objections made by a Jewish novelist of the Holocaust such as Elie Wiesel. This blatant double standard often turned out to be an accurate gauge of hypocrisy posing as a defense of culture. Fortunately many West German journalists and critics were also aware of the defensive aspects of aesthetic judgments.

Objections to the program itself assumed different forms. First, "Holo-caust" was the result of a battle among corporate giants of the American media. In particular it was designed to emulate the *commercial* success of "Roots," a program about the oppression of American blacks. It was an obscene and shameless exploitation of suffering for commercial profit. Franz Josef Strauss (the CDU/CSU candidate for Chancellor in the 1980 elections) called it a *"Geschäftsmacherei,"* roughly translatable as a "fast-buck operation."[19] Several directors of regional television networks de-nounced the program as a "cultural commodity . . . not in keeping with the memory of the victims."[20] These moving attacks from the Right on the commercialization of culture found a left-wing analogue in an article in *Konkret,* a monthly journal, which commented on "Holocaust" before it was telecast. The authors argued that the "family drama" format of the program was dictated by the major aim of the producers, which was to capture "the most important group of viewers from an economic stand-point, the American housewife" between the ages of eighteen and forty-two, cutting across all social classes and ethnic groups in the United States. In order to reach a mass market, a program about the Holocaust must offend as few people as possible. Thus, "Holocaust" displays an equal degree of understanding for mass murderers, anti-Semites, and fascists as it does for the Jews and other victims of the Nazis. "Everyone looks good on the screen . . . Auschwitz had paid off well for the American cap-italists."[21]

Second, critics argued that the program trivialized and simplified the most awful events of twentieth-century history. This "destruction of the Jews as soap opera" amounted to a "commercial horror show . . . an imported cheap commodity." This was how *Der Spiegel* waxed indignant over the effort to present fascism "in the format of a family album . . . genocide shrunken to the level of 'Bonanza' with music appropriate to 'Love Story.'. . . Nothing is explained, illuminated . . . it swarms with moralistic charges . . . stale clichés."[22] One conservative director of a regional television network bristled at the mere suggestion that the aes-thetic debate might have something to do with politics. No, he insisted, the "real issue" was that of the "quality" of a program which so crudely juxtaposed "total evil and total good."[23]

Third, the critics found empirical deficiencies in the script. Members of the Hitler Youth were shown wearing summer uniforms at Christmas time. Such errors might "confuse" young viewers in particular.[24] Fourth, telecasting something of such abysmal aesthetic quality was yet another "compulsory ritual in coming to terms with the past," one whose emo-tional energy came from a "well-known German inclination to almost exhibitionistic . . . self-accusation combined in an almost embarrassing fashion with public rituals of penance."[25] *Der Spiegel* went so far as to say that refusing to telecast this "trash" dealing with such a theme would have been an act of courage.

As *Der Spiegel* reported, the pressures from the CDU/CSU on television officials to pursue such a "respectable and courageous" course were strong enough to prevent telecasting the program on the channels normally aimed at capturing a mass audience. Instead, "Holocaust" was telecast on the "third program" channel, normally reserved for "quality" programming. The debate over aesthetics was partly a public manifestation of bureaucratic politics within the media carried out between the conservatives and social democrats. The conservatives, behind the pose of defending *Kultur*, advocated their traditional position concerning the Nazi past: Don't mention it. Social Democrats in the government and media such as Schmidt and Brandt, while not enthusiasts of American television, were strong advocates of the telecast of "Holocaust." Critics from the Left (who were observing the actual fight over whether or not to telecast the program from the outside) found themselves in a dilemma. On the one hand, they favored coming to terms with the Nazi past, but on the other hand, they were critical of the culture industry. Before the telecast, the latter impulse often triumphed over the former.

This was not the case among the cultural liberals and social democrats. Critics of *Die Zeit* and the feuilleton section of the *Frankfurter Allgemeine Zeitung* (FAZ) argued in favor of the telecast. The *FAZ* critics had been highly critical of the program when it was first shown in the United States, but, upon seeing the public reaction it created in West Germany, maintained that objections grounded in the aesthetic quality of the program were a snobbish refusal to admit the educational value it possessed in reaching a mass audience.[26] Precisely those simplifications and melodramatic aspects that had drawn such criticism were, they continued, responsible for the mass impact of the series.[27] Intellectuals would have to "capitulate" to the "eloquence" of TV. Quibbling over minor factual errors could not obscure that "what is central is the truth of the whole" and, taken in its entirety, "Holocaust" grasped this truth.[28] In response to critics who called for more analysis and less sentimentalism, one of the *FAZ* writers defended "Holocaust" as a document of "personal suffering" which no documentary film could express as powerfully. Was not, he asked, such an insistence on "analysis" itself a mechanism of distancing oneself too quickly from the immediacy of horror?[29]

One of the editors of *Die Zeit*, Dieter Zimmer, summarized the aesthetic debate in the following manner: "The wish not to remember these events, especially when the impulse to do so comes from abroad, hides behind a high-minded disapproval of form. The need to repress the past couldn't find a better alibi. . . . The simplicity of the series is its highest quality."[30] Zimmer turned to Adorno's dictum that to write poetry after Auschwitz would be barbaric. Fine art risked turning horror into an object of beauty to be contemplated. Committed art risked turning mass murder into a tool of commercial or political propaganda. All this hand-wringing over cultural barbarism, however, paled into insignificance, Zimmer concluded, when compared to the educational value the program would have in raising the issues of guilt and responsibility in the Third Reich.

After the telecast, the *FAZ* cultural page (a rather amazing amalgamation of shrewd conservative cultural politics) launched some broadsides at the critics of "Holocaust." First, it argued "Holocaust" had been a tremendous success. "After 'Holocaust' one can no longer speak of the fundamental impotence of art."[31] Rather, it had made clear "for the first time in contemporary Germany" how little the population had searched its conscience about the murder of the Jews, how serious the lack of information in the schools had been, how deep the gaps in historical consciousness were. Now, the *FAZ* continued, the "minority" that had attacked the film on aesthetic grounds would have to demonstrate that something other than "gripping triviality" could have exploded thirty years of psychic repression.

One television official who had been instrumental in the decision to telecast "Holocaust" argued that its massive impact had wider implications concerning the issues of art, mass culture, and television. It signaled the "end of the top-down culture" in West German television. "The representatives of the nation of culture (Kulturnation) rose up indignantly against the Hollywood barbarians who appeared to subject even the most shocking event of this century to their utterly shameless marketing strategies. These *arrogant doubters* have been taught a lesson. 'Holocaust' has not only taught us what mass communications can be. After 'Holocaust' German television cannot remain what it has been."[32] What German television "had been" was a medium produced by and for a cultural elite which rested on the assumption that culture would trickle down out of this world of refined discourse to the masses. "Holocaust" was a product of the country of "Mickey Mouse, Donald Duck and Superman" which had succeeded in turning the flow of communication "completely around: it now goes from the bottom up."[33] Although Marion Gräfin Dönhoff, the editor of *Die Zeit*, did not go so far as to say that the program's success negated the intellectuals' criticism of the culture industry, she did suggest that critics of the program had been guilty of an aesthetic purism which, given the importance of aesthetics for National Socialist politics in the past, was "extremely dangerous." "Moral considerations" outweighed "aesthetic purism." Emotional identification with the characters had "finally" created a confrontation with the past that had eluded the efforts of scholarship and documentary films. "Via a detour through Hollywood, what was repressed had been brought to the surface."[34]

Given that both *Die Zeit* and the *FAZ* had defended telecasting the program before it was shown, their euphoria afterward was striking but not unexpected. *Der Spiegel,* which in the previous week had gone so far as to say that not telecasting the program would have been "respectable and courageous," made a quick tactical shift in the week after. "Was this finally the catharsis? Was this, thirty-four years after the end of the war and of the Nazi era, the end of the "inability to mourn?" "Was it, in the 30th year of the German Federal Republic, the first true week of brotherhood?"[35] Heinz Höhne, author of a well-known popular history of the SS, wrote in the same issue of *Der Spiegel:* "It is absolutely fantastic . . . 'Holocaust' has shaken up post-Hitler Germany in a way that German intellectuals have been unable to do. No other film has ever made the Jews' road of suffering leading to the gas chambers so vivid. . . . Only since and as a result of 'Holocaust' does a majority of the nation know what lay behind the horrible and vacuous formula 'Final Solution of the Jewish Question.' They know it because a US film maker had the courage to break with the paralyzing dogma which has always condemned German film makers to failure: namely, that mass murder must not be represented in art."[36] Once the "paralyzing dogmas" of traditional aesthetic theory, especially the attack upon the modern culture industry, were left behind, the way had been opened for facing the past. West German filmmakers and intellectuals, so this line of reasoning went, had been hindered in their efforts to bring the Nazi past to the attention of the West German public by their own critical aesthetics.

Some of the reputed "arrogant doubters" hesitated to give up their "paralyzing dogmas" so quickly. On the contrary, several contributors to the *Frankfurter Rundschau,* a paper editorially close to the SPD, detected in an article entitled "How Several Intellectuals Are Losing their Heads and Demanding the Heads of Other Intellectuals" more than a hint of anti-intellectualism in the post-"Holocaust" euphoria over the possibilities of enlightenment through mass culture.[37] The authors welcomed the discussion of fascism occasioned by "Holocaust." However, they also noted that the contemporary public consciousness did not appear to have been so radically transformed that the candidacy of Karl Carstens (a member of the Nazi Party in the 1940s) for the ceremonial position of Bundespräsident "was made impossible or even received as an obscene provocation." The enormous outpouring of emotion which had few political consequences seemed typical of the German apolitical tradition. The

Rundschau contributors also objected to caricatures of critics of "Holocaust" as apologists for a fascist aesthetics separated from moral considerations, and they resented criticism of intellectuals who did not "join in the euphoria of public catharsis." Trivialization and simplification had not been part of an emancipatory theory of art. Their acceptance would only foster contempt for precisely those "difficult" aspects of art necessary for the preservation of its anticipatory and critical function, those aspects directed against existing mass consciousness. "Holocaust's" impact in West Germany, they wrote, had less to do with its artistic techniques than with the history of West Germany.[38]

Peter Märthesheimer, who was an advocate for "Holocaust" within West German television, argued that it was the psychological mechanism of identification around which the power of the program centered. This artistic technique produced the "unexpected and tremendous response" because it addressed the collective "inability to mourn" of the West German people. Märthesheimer's argument maintained that, although most of the nation did not actively participate in the Final Solution, the absence of resistance and the silence of the majority gave credence to the postwar notion of collective guilt. Faced with the reality of the death factories after the war, most Germans responded to the charge of collective guilt with "individual defenses . . . blindness, deafness, lack of penitence."[39] During the Third Reich, Germans had been relieved of all political responsibility by Hitler, who committed suicide before the nation could direct hatred against him for what he did in its name. Only after the war were individual Germans asked to assume a responsibility which they had avoided during the Hitler era. "In 1945 these people put their soul on ice."[40] Unable to break fully from the psychological childhood that existed under Hitler, the Germans simply repressed it. Because they had not killed the evil father but had believed Hitler to be the good father to the very end, they were unable to separate themselves from him afterward. The "psychopathology of a whole nation" was not to be cured by purely cognitive efforts at "reeducation" on the part of the occupying powers. The real secret of "Holocaust's" impact in 1979, Märthesheimer argued, lay in a narrative strategy that forced the viewer to identify with the Nazis' victims, that is, with the Jews. In sharing the victim's fear, the viewer was freed "from the horrible, paralyzing anxiety that has remained repressed for decades, that we in truth were in league with the murderers. Instead we are able to experience, as in the psycho-drama of a therapeutic experiment, every phase of horror—which we were supposed to have committed against the other—in ourselves . . . to feel and suffer it—and thereby finally in the truest sense of the word to deal with it as our own trauma. 'Holocaust' offered us the role of the patient instead of compelling us to take the role of the analyst, a role which we have been incapable of assuming."[41]

While Märthesheimer's analysis is suggestive, it may be overly generous to the generation that had come of age in the Hitler era. Whether or not the "Holocaust" reception set off the sort of process Märthesheimer describes is not at all clear. In his 1959 essay on coming to terms with the Nazi past, Adorno expressed his reservations about talk of a collective guilt complex or a national psychopathology. "The forgetting of National Socialism should be understood far more as a product of the general social situation than as a byproduct of psychopathology. . . . Indeed, psychological mechanisms of defense against painful and uncomfortable memories serve highly realistic and practical purposes. . . . Those who defend against the memory of the Nazi past make this clear when they point to the . . . damage that would be done to the German image abroad by an all too concrete and stubborn recollection of past events. . . . The destruction of memory is far more the achievement of an all too wide-awake consciousness rather than of the weakness of consciousness in the face of the superiority of unconscious processes."[42] Adorno strongly suggested in this essay and in a talk to the German SDS in 1962 that both anti-Semitism and the social interests that had supported National Socialism continued to exist in the Federal Republic.[43] What the defeat of National Socialism by the Allies had created, Adorno believed, was less a sincere national guilt complex than a wound to the collective narcissism of what was, after all, supposed to have been the "thousand year Reich." As Märthesheimer pointed out, not only was there no successful popular rebellion against Hitler, but after the war the prosecution of ex-Nazis was unpopular at best. In stressing relief of the guilt feelings of those who were *not* "in league with the murderers," Märthesheimer avoids Adorno's point which indicated the obvious advantages of bad memory for those who *were*. For all that, the *Ersatz* solidarity due to identification with the victims in a TV show is preferable to the previous silence.

To sum up, the sanctimoniousness and hostility to "Holocaust" emanating from West German conservatives was fully consistent with the highly practical purposes of amnesia Adorno mentioned. If, as intellectuals of the Left sometimes suggest, West German conservatives focus on crimes against the Jews to divert attention from Hitler's attack on the Left, this "philo-Semitic" tactic did not surface during the debate over the aesthetic merits of "Holocaust." The defense of the program by liberals and social democrats seemed to be perfectly reasonable from the standpoint of encouraging public discussion of anti-Semitism and the Final Solution in West Germany. But it also contained some misplaced sniping at Left intellectuals, whose opposition was sometimes blown out of proportion and was insignificant compared to the Right. Rohrbach's celebration of the American culture industry was probably due more to euphoria than to any serious confrontation with cultural critics. But the basic point made by the liberals, namely, that "gripping triviality" had initiated some kind of public discussion, was true.

The truth of that notion caused problems for commentators on the Left. The so-called "culture industry," "bourgeois public sphere," or "consciousness industry," the same one that flattens all contradictions into one-dimensional drivel, had in fact made many people upset about racism and genocide. One Left response to this most embarrassing paradox was to exaggerate the faults of the program beyond all reason. For example, whatever its shortcomings, "Holocaust" hardly displayed equal sympathy for fascists and their victims. But criticisms of aesthetic shortcomings of the program were not the only or most important mechanisms of defense to come from left-wing critics.

Some Reactions to "Holocaust" on the Left

As I suggested at the outset, the response of leftists to "Holocaust" presents special problems. Unlike conservatives, who simply don't want to bring the subject up at all, or liberals and centrist social democrats, who are quite willing to discuss it but bristle at suggestions that some sort of historical continuity exists between Hitler and post-Hitler West Germany, the West German New Left has devoted a great deal of effort to the analysis of fascism as well as to what it calls the "problem of continuity" between the Third Reich and the Federal Republic.[44] Furthermore, as a movement indebted to Critical Theory in general and Marcusean assertions of the link between memory and emancipation in particular, it might reasonably be expected to demonstrate particular sensitivity to the problem of anti-Semitism and the history of the Final Solution. However, with important exceptions, young leftists have demonstrated their peculiar version of selective memory.

Three factors appear to explain the difficulties that have hindered fuller discussion of anti-Semitism within the West German New Left. First, the small size of the Jewish community in West Germany (about thirty thousand, with heavy concentrations in Frankfurt, Munich, and West Berlin) meant that a German-Jewish dialogue with the Left would be a limited one. In many cities, West German new leftists had probably met few if any Jews. An internal left-wing debate over the nature of anti-Semitism could occur only with some difficulty and abstraction due to the absence of Jews.

Apparently such a discussion did begin in the late 1950s and early 1960s in SDS. Its history has yet to be written.

Second, Marxist analysis of fascism did not place the Final Solution or anti-Semitism at the center of attention. The destruction of European Jewry served absolutely no class, military, or national interest, a fact that is very hard to incorporate into most Marxist historical analyses which hesitate to attribute too much influence to the power of utterly irrational ideologies. Eike Geisel and Mario Offenberg, authors of an afterword to the German edition of Isaac Deutscher's *The Non-Jewish Jew and Other Essays,* wrote the following in regard to defense mechanisms within West German Marxist *analyses* of the camps. Two questions were the subjects of passionate interest in the seminars: "Whether or not the extermination of the Jews was or was not in the interest of capital; who received the profits from the soap which was the end product of extermination. On the theoretical level, the least justice was accorded to the victims . . . all too easily was mass murder endowed with meaning. The coldness of these discussions, their tendency to reify the events was similar to the distancing from horror that was part of the Final Solution itself."[45]

But, in explaining the difficulties of the West German Left in coming to terms with the anti-Semitic past, Geisel and Offenberg concentrate mainly on what they call a "dialectic of anti-Semitism and Zionism," rather than on the small number of West German Jews or the reification of Marxist theory. They argue that "philo-Semitism" was an integral aspect in restoring the political moral image of the West German bourgeoisie after the war. By philo-Semitism, they mean financial contributions to the Jews—and the Jews alone—including financial support for the state of Israel. This "guilt money" was a public relations substitute, they argue, for the program of postwar social change that failed to materialize.[46]

The Left's critique of philo-Semitism was probably given even more impetus by the right-wing Springer press. In 1967–1968, the *Bild-Zeitung* appeared to establish a firm link between domestic reaction and pro-Zionism when it attacked the New Left and praised the victories of the Israeli army in the Six-Day War. (Dayan was portrayed as the new Jewish "desert fox.") Support for the Palestinians and anti-Zionism were part and parcel of the anticapitalist stance of the New Left. The whole mess found a depressing conclusion in 1976 when two West Germans divided Jews from non-Jews among the hijacked airline passengers in Entebbe. At the time, Detlev Claussen, a member of the *Sozialistisches Büro* (Socialist Bureau), wrote that the participation of West Germans in the hijacking was evidence of an anti-Zionism lacking any historical sense, one which was part of the "continuity of German anti-Semitism."[47]

In the week after the "Holocaust" telecast, *Pflasterstrand,* a biweekly journal written by and for the "sponti scene" in Frankfurt and edited by Daniel Cohn-Bendit, published several unsigned statements about the program. They were irreverent and blunt expressions by people whose political experience was primarily that of the mid-to-late 1970s and thus stamped by the issues of *Berufsverbot,* opposition to nuclear power, conditions in German prisons, and the controversies surrounding West German terrorism. Along with discussions that took place in public forums in Frankfurt soon after the telecast, they are interesting documents of some of the trends discussed above.

Four themes are predominant. First, "Holocaust" served contemporary American and Israeli interests. It was located as "a point of intersection of capitalist interests and Zionist *ideology.*"[48] (In the German version of the program the final scene which depicts the lone survivor of the Weiss family about to leave for Israel was deleted.) The capitalist interests which "Holocaust" served were those of the United States, whose own war crimes in Vietnam could be relativized by focusing on the Nazi Holocaust. Along similar lines, the program was "Zionist ideology" not (I assume) because the author believed that it was untruthful, but because it could be used to justify the existence of a Jewish state. Desiring neither to repress the memory of American war crimes or lend support to Zionism, the author cautioned that it was possible to "like" the program for these "wrong" reasons.

Second, the articles argued that the West German media praised "Holocaust" because it suited the ruling ideology of the Federal Republic, namely that National Socialism ended in 1945. While praising the program for its accurate portrayal of the "typical German blockhead," the articles insisted that the same slavish obeisance to authority and the state had continued after 1945.[49] This *continuity* in the structure of the authoritarian personality mirrored a continuity in the "basic structure of fascism which even today exercises an influence on life in our society."[50]

Third, the articles bemoaned the *lack of resistance* among *both* the Germans and the Jews and criticized possible left-wing efforts to elaborate a mythology of resistance where none in fact took place. As for the Jews, they also bore a share of the guilt stemming from their "lack of political consciousness." Only such political consciousness could have saved the Jews.[51]

Fourth, the articles *compared* the Holocaust to the war in Vietnam. "Ten years ago there was a second Auschwitz. It was called Vietnam. Vietnam was genocide, that's clear. The pictures from My Lai look very much like those from the concentration camps. The only difference was that in Vietnam there was resistance"[52] from the victims and within the country of the perpetrators. The continuity of destruction and aggression was evident in other areas today such as "Korea, Indochina, the Soviet Union, Africa, Palestine and the Shah's Iran."[53] These same themes were also articulated at a panel discussion held at the University of Frankfurt. In addition, several left-wing sociologists voiced the following criticisms of "Holocaust" as a media event. First, the program brought forth no information that had not already been more thoroughly presented in numerous documentary films shown on West German television and in the academic literature on fascism. Second, the massive response to the program in West Germany was hardly a spontaneous popular outburst, but a result of a calculated media campaign and of the emotional and melodramatic quality of the program. Third, because "Holocaust" did not discuss the relation between capitalist economics and Nazi politics before 1939 when Hitler destroyed the political Left, it concealed the social and economic roots of the Final Solution. It was this *apologetic* aspect that was underscored, i.e., talking about fascism without mentioning capitalism.

Some comments are in order. First, I cannot judge whether or not the motives imputed to the producers of "Holocaust"—making a fast buck, detracting attention from the crimes of American imperialism, or justifying the existence of a Jewish state—were, in fact, central to the project. In relation to coming to terms with the German past, those motives are irrelevant. The imputation of such motives seemed to me to be similar to the defensive gestures Adorno had referred to in his essay "What Does It Mean to Come to Terms With the Past?" Typical of these gestures, he wrote, was the almost immediate reference to the Allied bombing of German cities in response to the mention of Auschwitz.[54] The suggestion that a program about Auschwitz is really a front for American and Israeli interests struck me as an equally defensive gesture.

Second, the assertion that there is a continuity between Hitler and post-Hitler West Germany and the assumption that West Germany today is, in some sense or another, "fascist" is at best a loose use of the term and at worst obscures the centrality of anti-Semitism and genocide in the Third Reich.

Third, one is struck by the depth of revulsion at everything and anything German which marks the comments on the lack of resistance. The radical critics of the program were deeply alienated from German society past and present. (In this regard, one of the articles referred to "the *two greatest accomplishments of the German nation*" as "the industrialized destruction of the greatest number of people in the shortest possible amount of time—and the subsequent collective repression of these events for the next thirty-four years."[55] The absence of myth-making about resistance is admirable. But the suggestion that the "guilt" of Jews lay in their "lack of political consciousness" (a notion fostered perhaps by the portrayal of the character of Mrs. Weiss in "Holocaust" as an unusually naive person who lacked simple common sense more than political consciousness) was insensitive. It is simply not true that there was no resistance among the European Jews, nor would more "political consciousness" have been an adequate substitute for the weapons and visas which were not forthcoming from the British and Americans.[56]

Fourth, reference to Vietnam as "the second Auschwitz" was most common in the defensive statements. Yet, it must be understood that the American war was a counterrevolution that became a war against the civilian population, one whose viciousness was multiplied by American racism. It was *not* a conscious effort to eliminate the people of Vietnam. Its goal was not a world without Vietnamese. This seems to me to be so obvious that comparisons of the Holocaust to subsequent murderous episodes are, as one journalist rightly claimed, manifestations of ignorance about the Final Solution as much as expressions of outrage at injustice. I had the sense that Vietnam was more familiar, more a constitutive aspect of the consciousness of the authors of the *Pflasterstrand* essays than was the Nazi past.

Several months after the "Holocaust" broadcast, *Der Spiegel* published an article by Jürgen Thorwald, who criticized efforts to compare the Final Solution to other wars and slaughters, such as Vietnam.[57] What set the Final Solution apart as a unique historical event, Thorwald argued, was the worldview of the modern anti-Semite, one which Hitler took to its logical conclusion. It held that a worldwide Jewish conspiracy existed that was the real power behind both "Jewish communism and Jewish capitalism." For centuries, Christian Europe had tried unsuccessfully to convert the souls of the Jews. The messianism of National Socialism lay in the "idealistic and holy" task of eliminating the Jews from the earth, a task that required an elite (the SS) that would sacrifice its conscience in order to bring about a better German future. The Nazis firmly believed that a "higher necessity" demanded the elimination of the Jewish people as an end in itself, beyond any considerations of class, national, or military interest.[58]

The efforts of Thorwald (and others) are not intended to place more emphasis on the Final Solution in history than other episodes of persecution. Nor do such efforts place the Holocaust completely outside the scope of historical explanation. But they do of necessity accord a power and centrality to an utterly irrational ideology which the categories of Marxism simply do not encompass. Since the Holocaust, Jews on the Left in Europe and the United States have been in the position of generalizing the memory of their own history of persecution to others. Left-wing Jews have fought a particularism among Jews that would restrict the memory of oppression to that of the memory of the oppression of Jews. However, there remains a particular history of anti-Semitism which the Left ought to address.

Detlev Claussen's commentary on "Holocaust," published in *Links*, was one hopeful indication that the neglect of the issue of anti-Semitism within the Left may be coming to an end.[59] Claussen argued that the depth of the West German response to "Holocaust" was understandable only in light of the previous failure of West German politics from the Right to the Left to face and root out Germany's racist and anti-Semitic traditions. The official policies of the western occupying powers and the "anti-fascism" of the GDR were no more effective. Anti-fascism was defeated not only in Weimar and the Third Reich, but again in the aborted "de-Nazification" efforts of the postwar era. The only coming to terms with the Nazi past that would have had any practical consequences, namely democratization and public acknowledgment of a racist past, never took place in German politics prior to 1979. Thus, when such an acknowledgment did occur, it did so only as a national catharsis set off by an American television series. Claussen saw this catharsis as giving an impetus to discussion within the Left which would make clear the inseparable connection between the Final Solution in Europe and the founding of the state of Israel.[60] Such a discussion would lead a way out of the sterile formulas of conservative philo-Semitism and identification with the Palestinians. From such a discussion, the Left had little to lose but its mechanisms of defense.

The most promising aspect of the West German Left's response to "Holocaust" was the way it was making its *own past* the subject of public discussion and critical reflection. People asked why West German filmmakers rather than Americans had not made a comparable work. Perhaps the discussions in lecture halls, cafés, and restaurants were concretizations of Habermas' concept of the democratic public sphere. The repressed was brought to the surface of conscious reflection.

Coming to Terms with the Past after "Holocaust"

In the months following "Holocaust," newspapers and magazines were filled with diaries of concentration camp survivors, interviews with former Auschwitz guards, and articles on the history of German-Jewish relations.[61] When four of the eleven defendants at the Maidanek trial were acquitted, there was considerable public criticism of both the decision and the length of the trials. During the parliamentary debates in the spring concerning the abolition of the statute of limitations, reference was made to "Holocaust." Public opinion surveys indicated that the program had fostered public pro-abolitionist sentiment. "Holocaust" and the reaction to it were said to have been a well-timed influence on those members of the parliament who were undecided as to how they would vote.

In parliament, the coalition of conservative parties, the CDU/CSU (Christian Democratic Union-Christian Social Union) opposed abolishing the statute and favored bringing the prosecutions to an end at the close of 1979. The governing coalition of the liberals (FDP, Free Democratic Party) and social democrats (SPD, Social Democratic Party) led by the chancellor, Helmut Schmidt, favored abolition of the statute and continuation of investigations and trials. In July 1979, the SPD/FDP position was victorious, and the statute was abolished entirely. Jewish groups, civil libertarians in the FDP led by Hans Maihoffer, and some left-wing members of the SPD had sought to limit abolition of the statute to cases of mass murder. (As they rightly pointed out, there would have been no debate at all were prosecution of crimes committed as part of the Final Solution not at issue.) The decision of the parliament was thus a legal fiction which treated the Final Solution as a case of simple murder. But it did ensure that prosecutions could legally continue and that no hint of an amnesty would be declared.

However, even the liberal press made it clear that the extension of the statute was a bittersweet victory. The time for coming to grips with the past, if only in a restricted legal sense, had been the 1950s, when memories were still fresh. That this moment was missed then was due, in large part, to the fact that it coincided with the anti-Communism of the Cold War. As if to underscore how halting the parliamentary reckoning with the Nazi past was, Karl Carstens was elected to the position of *Bundespräsident* shortly before the vote in favor of extension took place.

Turning again to the Left, evidence of defensiveness as well as self-reflection continued to emerge. One politically oriented movie theater in Frankfurt, after showing *Exodus* and *The Diary of Anne Frank*, presented a series of documentaries on Palestinian resistance maintaining that the establishment media had focused on the suffering of the Jews but not on that of the Palestinians. In December, another Left cinema showed "Holocaust" again, along with a film on the West German reaction, Alain Resnais' film on Auschwitz, *Night and Fog*, and several more recent West German films on the concentration camps.[62]

"Rock gegen Rechts" ("Rock against the Right") was a demonstration and rock concert organized by a coalition of Left groups and the *Deutsche Gewerkschaftsbund* (DGB, the major organization of West German trade unions) to protest a meeting scheduled by the neo-Nazi *Nationale Partei*

Deutschland (NPD) on June 17, 1979, in Frankfurt. Between thirty thousand and fifty thousand people were estimated to have participated, making it one of the largest demonstrations in Frankfurt in recent years. Although one might think that in the post-"Holocaust" climate the normal hostility directed at such a gathering from the conservative press might be tempered somewhat, such was not the case. On the contrary, the *FAZ*, which had come to the defense of "Holocaust" in the face of criticism from the "arrogant doubters" first gave very little space to the demonstration (making sure to comment that the demonstrators looked very shabby, and drove old, beat-up cars). It then attacked *Rock gegen Rechts* for grossly exaggerating the danger of neo-Nazism in the Federal Republic, for seizing upon the issue to offset the Left's own setbacks and disunity, and for escaping from the problems of the present into the clichés of "anti-fascism."[63] This editorial was consistent with the views of West German conservatives concerning the relation between the Nazi past and the West German present. National soul-searching need not have any political implications for the present. Not surprisingly, the *FAZ* editorial compelled a spokesman for the Jewish community of West Berlin to point out that if the political center did not deal with the issue of neo-Nazism, the far Left might take on an appeal (presumably for young German Jews) which it would not otherwise have.[64]

Conclusion

The German expression *Aufarbeitung der Vergangeheit* translates inadequately into the English "coming to terms with the past." The inadequacy is due to the fact that English does not express the fusion of psychoanalytic and political categories contained in the German. *Aufarbeitung* as a psychoanalytic concept of "working through" implies that the past is never fully overcome unless and until the past that lives on in the present is brought under the control of conscious reflection, thereby bringing about change in the self-reflecting subject.

Adorno understood that the past lives on in the present at the level of society as well as in the individual psyche. In response to the idea that the repression of the past was the product of psychopathology alone, he pointed to the origins of this amnesia in the "general social situation," that is, in the continuity of capitalism before and after 1945. Neither the extension of the statute of limitations nor the broadcast of "Holocaust" broke this continuity, nor were they intended to do so. This said, "Holocaust" did fracture continuity in consciousness in West Germany. It put the Right on the defensive. It was a festival for liberals and a prod to the

Left to give up some of its "defensive gestures" born of theory and practice, gestures that precluded a more fruitful discussion within the Left of National Socialism and the Holocaust.

"Holocaust" may have exercised an impact on the young Left because of the historical moment of its telecast. West German left-wing intellectuals of the 1950s and early 1960s were made aware of the particular role of anti-Semitism and the Jews in German history in two ways which were unavailable to the post-1968 generation: through memories of childhood and youth in the Third Reich, and through the personal and intellectual influence of the German Jews who returned after the war, especially Horkheimer, Adorno, and Bloch. The political climate of repression and left-wing terror of the West German 1970s was hardly conducive to the critical social theory of the returned émigrés. On the theoretical level, Marxist orthodoxy, unable to grasp the force of the irrational in history, ruled out an understanding of the origins of the Holocaust in the German and European anti-Semitic traditions. On the level of political action, identification with Third World movements literally came face to face with the anti-Semitic past that had not been brought to consciousness and mastered. On the basis of these admittedly impressionistic observations, it seems fair to conclude that some young West German Left intellectuals have neither "an all too wide-awake consciousness" nor the "paralyzing anxiety of having been in league with the murderers" standing in the way of looking at Germany's past. The subsequent development of the West German Left suggests, however, that such perceptiveness remains the exception and not the rule.

NOTES

1. See "Holocaust: Die Vergangenheit kommt zurück," *Der Spiegel* (January 29, 1979), p. 18. Also see Andrei S. Markovits and Christopher Allen's excellent and informative report "The German Conscience," *Jewish Frontier* (April 1979), pp. 13–17. The following figures cited by Markovits and Allen point to the dimensions of the reaction to the show: over 40 percent of the television audience watched; over 35,000 telephone calls (four times the number received during the American showing) were received by television stations, and an equal number of letters and telegrams were sent; 20,000 information booklets published by the government to accompany the show disappeared in an avalanche of orders reaching 255,000.

2. Ibid., p. 17. The cover story in *Der Spiegel* is entitled "Die Vergangenheit kommt zurück," and is typical of the mood evident in the West German press that week.

3. Max Horkheimer, "Die Juden und Europa," *Autoritärer Staat* (Amsterdam, 1967), p. 8. The German original is: "Wer aber vom Kapitalismus nicht reden will, sollte auch vom Faschismus schweigen."

4. In a speech at the 1978 Frankfurt Book Fair, George Mosse paraphrased Horkheimer by saying: "He who thinks he has explained National Socialism only by mentioning capitalism is mistaken."

5. See Otto-Jörg Weiss, "Immer wieder tauchen in den Schulen Nazi Parolen auf," *Frankfurter Rundschau.* (February 1, 1979), p. 3.

6. Ibid., p. 3.

7. As for the reaction to "Holocaust" in the GDR, Markovits and Allen are on target when they write: "East Germany . . . has enjoyed the luxury of an easy reckoning with history. Due to its equating fascism with capitalism, the German Democratic Republic has absolved itself of Nazism's legacy. Hence the GDR saw no compulsion to broadcast 'Holocaust,' just as it has refused to pay reparations to individual Jews and to the state of Israel." "German Conscience," p. 16.

8. For a critical discussion and review of Irving's book, see Eberhard Jaeckel, "Hitler und der Mord der europäishen Juden," *Frankfurter Allgemeine Zeitung* (hereafter referred to as *FAZ*), August 8, 1977, reprinted in the useful collection *"Holocaust": Eine Nation ist Betroffen*, ed. Peter Märthescheimer and Ivo Frenzel (Frankfurt am Main, 1979), pp. 151–62.

9. The focus of the controversy is Diwald's *Geschichte der Deutschen* (Frankfurt am Main, 1978).

10. See Diwald's statement in "Grauenhaftes Faktum," *Der Spiegel* (December 19, 1978), pp. 12–13.

11. For reviews of Diwald's book see Eberhard Jaeckel, "Geschichte im Rückwärtsgang," *Die Zeit* (December 1, 1978) as well as Karl Otner van Aretin, "Eine Springprozession durch die deutsche Geschichte: Nicht zu retten: Helmut Diwald's Geschichte der Deutschen," in *FAZ* (January 5, 1979), p. 3.

12. Hellmut Diwald, "Grauenhaftes Faktum," p. 13. The rage of Diwald's critics is apparent in van Aretin's comments on this contention: "There are no documents in the USA, England, or France that have not been accessible to West German historians. The same is true for East German historians (who also have access to their own and Soviet archives) and who have no interest in hiding anything. What is supposed to be in these documents? That Auschwitz was a sanitorium or that the Final Solution was organized by the CIA and the GPU to ruin Hitler's reputation? . . . At this point the good name of the publisher comes into the picture. . . . The firm should have the courage to take this thing off the market. No supplement or addition will save it. It is an incoherent and idiotic book." Karl Otner van Aretin, "Eine Springprozession durch die Geschichte," p. 17.

13. The following figures are taken from "Im Namen des Volkes—Freispruch," *Die Zeit* (November 17, 1978), pp. 9–10. For a more comprehensive discussion see Adalbert Rückerl, *Die Strafverfolgung von NS-Verbrechen: 1945–1978* (Heidelberg-Karlruhe, 1979).

14. "A Determined Effort to Explain to a New York Audience the Secrets of German

Democracy," reprinted and translated in *New Left Review* 118 (November–December 1979), pp. 3–14.

15. See Lucy Dawidowicz, *The War Against the Jews* (New York, 1975).

16. For some examples of lenient sentences see Henryk Broder, "Warum ich für die Verjährung bin," in the daily radical newspaper, *Die Tageszeitung* (April 23, 1979). One defendent was acquitted of the charge of having "cruelly and maliciously" killed Russian civilians in portable gas vans. The decision was based on the recommendation of a professor who argued that because the victims lost consciousness within 60 to 90 seconds after the gas was pumped into the vans, the murders could not be considered to have been cruel and malicious. See also, "Ein Toter gleich zehn Minuten Gefängnis," in *Der Spiegel* (July 3, 1979), pp. 46–55.

17. Ibid.

18. Sabina Lietzmann, "Die Judenvernichtung als Seifenoper," *FAZ* (April 20, 1978), reprinted in *Holocaust: Eine Nation ist betroffen*, pp. 35–39.

19. "Endlösung im Abseits," *Der Spiegel* (January 15, 1979), p. 133.

20. "Gaskammern à la Hollywood," *Der Spiegel* (May 15, 1979), p. 230.

21. Friedrich Knilli and Siegfried Zielinski, "Auschwitz lohnt sich noch," *Konkret* (February, 1979), pp. 34–36. Since the telecast of "Holocaust," Knilli and Zielinski have worked on a film on the West German reaction, held discussions with the American directors of the film, and discussed the West German reaction to it at several American universities in the fall of 1979.

22. See "Gaskammern à la Hollywood," p. 230.

23. Peter Schulze-Rohr, "Keine Frage von Rechts oder Links," *Die Zeit* (June 23, 1978), reprinted in *"Holocaust": Eine Nation ist betroffen*, pp. 46–48.

24. Ibid., p. 47.

25. Ibid., p. 48. After the telecast, *Der Spiegel* devoted much of the February and March issues to issues related to the Holocaust.

26. Karl-Heinz Bohrer, "Holocaust—Eine Prüfung," *FAZ* (September 28, 1979), Feuilleton, p. 1.

27. Sabina Lietzmann, "Kritische Fragen," *FAZ* (September 23, 1978), reprinted in *Holocaust: Eine Nation ist betroffen*, pp. 40–41.

28. "Wenn 'Holocaust' kommt," *FAZ* (January 17, 1979), Feuilleton, p. 1.

29. Karl-Heinz Bohrer, "Holocaust."

30. Dieter Zimmer, "Melodrama als Massenmord," *Die Zeit* (January 19, 1979), pp. 23–24.

31. "Ein Volk begegnet seiner Schuld," *FAZ* (February 1, 1979), Feuilleton, p. 1.

32. Günther Rohrbach, "Ende der von-oben-bis-unten Kultur," *FAZ* (February 1, 1979), Feuilleton, p. 1.

33. Ibid.

34. Marion Gräfin Dönhoff, "Eine deutsche Geschichtsstunde," *Die Zeit* (February 2, 1979), p. 1.

35. "'Holocaust': Die Vergangenheit kommt zurück," p. 17.

36. "Schwarzer Freitag für die Historiker," *Der Spiegel* (January 29, 1979), pp. 22–23. It should be stressed that Hohne was not pointing to a neglect of the subject by West German historians but to their inability to make their research accessible to a broader public.

37. "Wie einige Intellekutelle den Kopf verlieren und den anderer fordern: 'Holocaust' und erste Folgen einer Revision unseres Kulturbegriffs," *Frankfurter Rundschau* (February 5, 1979), Feuilleton, p. 2.

38. Ibid.

39. Peter Märthesheimer, "Vorbemerkungen der Herausgeber," in *"Holocaust": Eine Nation ist betroffen*, p. 12.

40. Ibid., p. 13.

41. Ibid., p. 17.

42. Theodor Adorno, "Was bedeutet: Aufarbeitung der Vergangenheit," in *Gesammelte Schriften, 10.2* (Frankfurt am Main, 1977), p. 558. This essay is a classic statement of the problem of coming to terms with the past.

43. See "Einleitung zum Vortrag 'Was bedeutet: Aufarbeitung der Vergangenheit,'" in *Gesammelte Schriften, 10.2*, pp. 816–17.

44. For a comprehensive West German overview of Marxist and non-Marxist analyses of fascism, see Eike Hennig, *Bürgerliche Gesellschaft und Faschismus in Deutschland: Ein Forschungsbericht* (Frankfurt am Main, 1977) and Anson Rabinbach, "Toward a Marxist Theory of Fascism and National Socialism," *New German Critique* 3 (Fall 1974) pp. 127–53.

45. "Die gegenwärtige Vergangenheit—Zur Aktualität von Isaac Deutschers Schriften zur jüdischen Frage," the postscript to *Die ungelöste Judenfrage: Zur Dialektik von Antisemitismus und Zionismus* (Berlin, 1977), p. 109.

46. While the West German government had made some generous financial compensation to Jews, the record is also one of avoidance and resistance to compensation, a point once again documented in *Less Than Slaves. Jewish Forced Labor and the Quest for Compensation*, Benjamin B. Ferencz (Cambridge, Mass., 1979). Telford Taylor, the chief American prosecutor at Nuremberg, writes in the preface: "I believe that in time, Germans will regret that their industrial leaders did not write a post-war record of generosity, instead of the cold and niggardly one revealed in this book."

47. Detlev Claussen, "Terror in der Luft, Konterrevolution auf der Erde," *Links* (September 1976), p. 44, and reprinted in *Sozialismus und Terrorismus*, a collection of articles. Claussen argued that it was not a defense of Zionism to point out that "it will remain incomprehensive to Israeli citizens, if civilian Jews become victims of terrorism organized by Germans," p. 14. On the relation between West German leftists and the Palestinians, see Hans Joachim Klein, *Rückkehr in die Menschlichkeit. Appell eines ausgestiegenen Terroristen* (Reinbek, 1979). Klein's account was first published in the Paris newspaper *Liberation* and later published in German as a pamphlet. Excerpts appeared in *Der Spiegel* 49–51 (November–December, 1979).

48. *Pflasterstrand: Stadtzeitung für Frankfurt* 47 (February 1–15, 1979), p. 23. "Wir alle wissen es: die Filmproduktion von 'Holocaust' steht mitten im Koordinationkreuz von Kapitalinteressen und zionistischer Ideologie . . ." (Untitled essay).

49. See "In unserer Familie ist die Hölle los," *Pflasterstrand*, p. 25. The article refers to "Diese alltäglichen deutschen Holzköpfe."

50. See "Deutsches Verdrängen," *Pflasterstrand*, p. 27.

51. Ibid., p. 27. "Und die Weiss's (the German-Jewish family) waren unpolitisch, und das war erst ihre Schuld. Denn das enzige, was beide hätte retten können, wäre ihr politisches Bewusstein gewesen."

52. "In unserer Familie ist die Hölle los," *Pflasterstrand*, p. 25.

53. "Deutsches Verdrängen," *Pflasterstrand*, p. 27.

54. "Was bedeutet Aufarbeitung der Vergangenheit?" pp. 556–557.

55. "Deutsches Verdrängen," *Pflasterstrand*, pp. 26–27.

56. See Bernard Wasserstein, *Britain and the Jews of Europe* (New York, 1979) for valuable material concerning what the British did not do to assist Jewish resistance groups that did exist.

57. Jürgen Thorwald, "Aufrechnen bekundet Unwissenheit," *Der Spiegel* (February 5, 1979), pp. 193–195.

58. The literature on European anti-Semitism and the origins of Hitler's worldview is vast. See the work of George Mosse, Hannah Arendt, Lucy Dawidowicz. I have found Norman Cohn's *Warrant for Genocide* (London, 1967) of great help both for its comprehensive bibliography and for a provocative analysis of anti-Semitism which distinguishes it from other forms of racism. For example, whereas white racism is a warrant for enslaving those held to be inferior and powerless (except in physical strength and numbers), anti-Semitism is a "warrant for genocide" because it traditionally conceives of the Jews as organized into an all-powerful and evil world conspiracy. Hence, for the anti-Semite, the Final Solution of the Jewish problem must entail destroying the conspiracy once and for all. Given that all Jews are conspirators merely by being Jewish, the vision of modern anti-Semitism is that of a world without Jews. Cohn traces the history of the idea of a Jewish world conspiracy over an 800-year span of European history, and puts forth a psychoanalytic explanation which sees the Jew as the object of "unconscious negative projections" associated with the "bad . . . evil" torturing, castrating father. This sense of mission bound to ridding the world of evil, accounts for the "idealistic" and "revolutionary" rhetoric associated with the SS.

59. Detlev Claussen, "Geschichte ist Gegenwart," *Links* (March 1979), pp. 10–11.

60. Ibid., p. 11. Dan Diner's *Tausch und Gewalt: Zur zionistischen Struktur israelischer Politik* (Königstein, 1979) is a very important contribution to the contemporary left-wing discussion of the Middle East conflict. It is also a result of much reflection on a Jewish life in both Israel and West Germany and on the "chain of violence that led from Berlin to Palestine."

61. In particular, see the issues of *Der Spiegel*, February and March, 1979.

62. This theater, the *Kommunales Kino*, also ran the following less well known films: *Nackt unter Wölfen*, Frank Bayer, DDR, 1962; *Aus einem deutschen Leben*, Götz George and Elizabeth Schwarz, BRD, 19877 (based on the life of the commandant of Auschwitz, Rudolf Hoess); *Lagerstrasse Auschwitz*, Ebbo Demant, BRD, 1979.

63. "Flucht aus der Gegenwart," *FAZ* (June 19, 1979), p. 1.

64. See Heinz Galinski, letter to the editor in *FAZ* (June 26, 1979). One striking aspect of contemporary discussion of Germans and Jews in West Germany is the extent to which it is one *about* rather than *with* Jews. But there is a small German-Jewish community whose leadership, if Galinski's letter is taken to be typical, has no particular high regard for the Left. He warned the *FAZ* that "all democrats, whatever party they may belong to" should take the issue of extremism of the Right no less seriously than that of extremism of the Left. Failure to do so would enhance the appeal of the Left for those (in the Jewish community) who otherwise would have nothing to do with it.

13

"HOLOCAUST" BEFORE AND AFTER THE EVENT
REACTIONS IN WEST GERMANY AND AUSTRIA

Andrei S. Markovits and Rebecca S. Hayden

Very few television series have ever received the overwhelming and controversial response enjoyed by NBC's "Holocaust." First aired in the United States in April 1978 on four consecutive evenings, reaching 120 million Americans, the film had been purchased by thirty-one countries as of March 1979[1] and telecast by over two dozen by the end of the year. It is fair to say that in the United States, Israel, and most of Europe—the film was shown among others in Great Britain, the Scandinavian and Benelux countries, France, Italy, Switzerland, the Federal Republic of Germany and Austria—public debate on all levels assumed unusually intense proportions, before, during, and after the film's showing. This keen interest—actively and passionately articulated in the family setting, among friends and acquaintances, at work, in the daily press, the popular electronic and print media, and, of course, in various academic disciplines ranging from psychology and literature to sociology and political science—clearly attests to the film's temporary success in highlighting some fundamentally disturbing and unsolved problems of recent Western history.

Nowhere has this painful phenomenon been more manifest—and ultimately of greater importance—than in West Germany and Austria, two immediate successors to the Third Reich. In the following pages we shall give a limited and cursory sketch of what the major effects and implications of "Holocaust" have been on contemporary West German and Austrian public life. While mainly concentrating on the former, we shall

234

summarize pertinent data from the latter where comparisons between the two countries are analytically useful in accentuating differences as well as similarities between them. Thus, following a section in which we shall briefly describe the political, social, and cultural contexts of the Federal Republic of Germany (FRG) and Austria, we shall then turn to discussions of sentiments, attitudes, and opinions before, during, and after the series. Lastly, we shall conclude by looking at some immediate political ramifications of the telecast in West Germany and some related events influencing current public debate.

In trying, at least partly, to understand the inordinate success of an American-made television series of much-debated quality on National Socialism in the FRG, where over nine hundred documentaries about the Nazi period had been shown on television and in cinemas since the late 1940s,[2] we must sketch a few major characteristics leading to this response. Most important in this development is the Cold War. It laid the foundation for the atmosphere of political life in the FRG, where the repression of recent German history has played an integral part.

It was largely because of the Cold War that denazification in all realms of German life was severely impeded, indeed virtually halted. This meant, among other things, a continuation of the old elites in key positions of German economic, political, and administrative structures. Moreover, it necessitated—almost by definition—a denial of the past rather than its mastery (Bewältigung).

A concomitant development—equally the result of the Cold War—was the rapid delegitimation of any system-challenging dissent, especially on the Left. Communism became the foremost national enemy. Its complete discreditation was partly aided by the negative example furnished by the German Democratic Republic's rigid development into a totalitarian society, in and of itself a direct consequence of the Cold War. The Social Democratic Party's (SPD) Bad Godesberg Program of 1959 renounced the party's class character and Marxist tradition in favor of becoming a modern catchall party. This shift effectively blocked any critical opposition that might analyze systematically the recent past and its relationship to the present.

Political one-dimensionality was accompanied by cultural conformity to a society whose only purpose seemed to be material gain. The conditions leading to the much-admired *Wirtschaftswunder* (economic miracle)— sufficient, though not total, destruction of the pre–World War II industrial base; superb labor-market situation in that millions of highly qualified refugees and expellees from the eastern parts of the former Reich competed with the indigenous unemployed for scarce jobs, thereby keeping wages well below West Germany's major competitors—provided an excellent basis for continued silence about the past. An acquisitive consumer society had no use for remembering its recent history. The latent existence of collective guilt was also "paid off" by the newly acquired wealth in generous reparations to Jewish victims of the Holocaust and to the state of Israel.

The youth revolt of the late 1960s led by university students certainly ended the political complacency of German public life. Yet, despite direct challenge to their parents' silence regarding the horrors of the past and the injustices of the present, the students' dissent also failed to come to grips with National Socialism and its legacy in contemporary German life in respect to the "Jewish Problem." It represented a mere negation of their parents' world and of fascism viewed basically as a socioeconomic system. Thus, for instance, many young Germans' uncritical support of the Palestinians as the world's "new Jews" must be seen as challenging their parents' wholehearted acceptance of Israel. Both attitudes stem from unresolved, oppressive guilt feelings regarding the Holocaust, thus representing two sides of the same coin.

Very few people in the FRG had moved beyond silence, guilt, and/or negation of the National Socialist legacy, even by the end of the 1970s. Yet almost thirty-five years had passed since the end of World War II, and the severity of the world economic crisis of the mid-1970s did not leave even West Germany unscathed. The so-called "Hitler-wave" of 1977–1978 interrupted the taboo on National Socialism and saw the mass production of serious literature and documentaries about events in the Third Reich, especially concerning Hitler himself. It was at this new, yet undefined, threshold of West German culture and consciousness that "Holocaust" appeared. Its timing could not have been more perfect.

Austria's post–World War II development parallels West Germany's course in economic successes and substantial social achievements, largely resulting from a modellike welfare state. Yet some crucial cultural, political, and, above all, psychological traits have differentiated Austria's public consciousness from West Germany's regarding the two countries' roles and overcoming of the National Socialist past. Simply put, Austria's annexation by Nazi Germany in March 1938 has been known to the world as "the rape of Austria"[3] rather than as the enthusiastic and widely cheered homecoming for Hitler and Austria's much-awaited return to a united German Reich, providing an excellent moral and psychological alibi to place all the blame and guilt for the Holocaust on the Germans. Thus, whereas the Germans have hitherto largely failed to come to terms with their past but most certainly had to pay for it in the division of their country and in the guilt and shame imposed on them by world opinion, none of these grave costs were exacted from the Austrians. Having regained its complete political independence and territorial integrity in 1955 with the signing of the Austrian State Treaty and the departure of the four occupying Allied powers, the country's subsequent neutrality stipulated by the treaty even enhanced its international prestige and standing. Far from being pariahs in the family of nations and burdened with the possibly unsolvable task of finding suitable answers to the most heinous crime committed in Western civilization, Austrians could, in good conscience, delegate such unpleasant matters to the Germans—their "rapists"—and enjoy their prosperity and relatively conflict-free existence—advantages of smallness and neutrality in a world of giants and power blocs.

Thus, we believe it significant that the Austrians waited for the FRG to air "Holocaust" before going ahead with their own telecast six weeks later. This event, once again, fits the frequent pattern of West Germany having to be a "locomotive" in matters concerning National Socialism and "overcoming the past." Only following the unexpected and overwhelming success of the series in the FRG did the Austrian state-run television feel the need to show the film.[4] It is precisely Austria's relatively guiltless view of its complicity with National Socialism—a special "sociopsychological mechanism of repression,"[5] as one knowledgeable observer called it—which, experts believed, would account for the show's rejection by a majority of Austrians. Most Austrians would see "Holocaust" as an irrelevant, irksome intrusion into a happy present that bore little, if any, responsibility for the past. Yet, the show outdistanced even the German figures in viewers. On the surface, "Holocaust's" telecast in Austria seemed as successful as it did in West Germany. Many of our subsequent points will bear evidence to this effect. Yet, with the benefit of hindsight, one could argue rather persuasively that in both countries—but especially in Austria—the short-term enthusiasm has been replaced by a long-term uncertainty about the truly lasting effects on public consciousness, political awareness, and psychological reorientation. It is to more detailed discussions of these relationships that we now turn.

In sharp contrast to the reactions following the telecast, the debates preceding its showing were largely confined to newspaper journalists, media critics, and the culture pages of the West German press. Significantly, "Holocaust," following the NBC broadcast in the United States, received much greater attention in the West German media and was more widely discussed among interested circles in the FRG than in Austria, where it was hardly noticed. Thus, whereas a large and representative segment of the German and Austrian populations participated in the public reaction immediately following the airing of "Holocaust," the controversy prior to the film's showing could best be characterized as a "highbrow" debate among a select group of intellectuals.

In West Germany, "Holocaust" had the critics in a state of confusion and profound disagreement. Many were opposed to the show, just as others—approximately equal in number—lauded its mere existence and viewed it as crucial for the political education of the West German public, especially the young. Whatever the specific reactions, it became clear from the beginning of the debates that West Germany's intellectuals, journalists, and opinion makers recognized that the highly controversial subject matter of the series made it impossible to judge like any other television show, especially in Germany. One group of critics, largely concerned with *aesthetic* issues of the film, voiced a negative opinion, on the whole. In this view, a subject of such magnitude as the Holocaust is unportrayable by any medium, and its exploitation for commercial purposes not only insults its victims but highlights the obscene dimensions of the exclusively profit-oriented American television industry.[6] Conversely, the writers concentrating on the film's *political* and *pedagogical* implications seemed much more favorably disposed to it in general, and to its telecast in the FRG in particular.

While most arguments against the film centered on its alleged *aesthetic* shortcomings, the arguments in favor of the film focused on its presumed *political* and *pedagogical* value. Many critics felt that the film, while not of high aesthetic quality, was an appropriate vehicle by which audiences could experience the Holocaust emotionally. Critics grudgingly agreed that drama had more emotional power than documentary.[7] They also agreed that trivialized information was better than none, and more positive critics insisted that drama was the only way the Final Solution could be made accessible and emotionally effective.[8] The death of six million is beyond human comprehension, hence empathy; the death of six is not.

Other critics insisted that Germany had a moral obligation to air the show, simply because Germans were the perpetrators of the Holocaust.[9] While some people asked why Germany had failed to make a comparable film, others argued that "Holocaust" had an emotional truth that no German film could have, simply because America did not have the guilt that Germany had.[10]

As noted, the most persuasive argument for the show was the political and pedagogical impact it would have on a mass audience. It was insisted that the average viewer would be reached by this show, and what he/she learned from it was more important than any critic's reaction. If education of the German public was to continue, it was important to know what were people's current knowledge and feeling about the Holocaust. A show such as "Holocaust" would reveal these attitudes.[11]

The importance of audience "mass" rather than critics' "elite" response was taken up by other writers. Because the show was a political, not an artistic, issue, critics should have no influence on whether the film should be shown or not.[12] The series was seen as an intensely political matter, most likely influencing the debates on *Verjährung* (expiration of the statute of limitations on murder in general and Nazi war crimes in particular) and counterbalancing the "Hitler-wave."[13]

Institutions such as the Bundeszentrale für politische Bildung (Federal Center for Political Education), the Landeszentrale für politische Bildung Nordrhein-Westfalen (State Center for Political Education, Northrhine-Westphalia), and the Adolph Grimme Institute had all sent out materials and conducted seminars dealing with the show. These accompanying materials dealt with complementary aspects of the Second World War and Germany's role therein that received little attention in the show. Some of the questions raised in the booklets and papers were the following: (1) What important facts were not developed in the show, such as the German resistance movement, relations of Germany to other nations immediately preceding and following World War Two, the development of the Nazi economy, and the domestic and foreign politics in the Third Reich? (2) What was the reaction of the FRG to World War Two, and what measures had been taken such as reparations and prosecution of criminals and political rehabilitation? (3) What false generalizations could the show trigger? (4) Have people tended to view the events of the war in an ahistorical manner, giving false or exonerating arguments? And finally, (5) Does the show's portrayal of identifiable characters lead to an individualization of guilt?

Some of these issues dominated West German public debate to a hitherto unparalleled degree during and after the film's telecast. It is to this phenomenon that we now turn.

After so much publicity and controversy, the actual showing of "Holocaust" could have potentially been an anticlimax. But the previewing debates and media coverage proved only a minor prelude to the overwhelming reactions accompanying the show and its aftermath. For, while the discussions preceding the telecast were originally conducted mainly by politicians, critics, and television officials, the viewing brought a whole nation into discussion.

West German television officials were doubtful whether the show would attract a large audience. It was feared that the extensive advance coverage of the press could have acted as overkill. Tension was mounting throughout the country as the telecast approached. On January 18, 1979, the Thursday preceding the show (the film was aired on January 22, 23, 25, and 26 in 1979), a television transmitter in Koblenz was bombed during the broadcast of "Final Solution," a documentary shown as background information to "Holocaust." Half an hour later a hole was blown out of the roof of another station in Münster, ruining the antenna cable. Later, telephone calls to television stations confirmed that the two explosions had been planned and executed by extreme Right groups. Security measures were taken by all television stations to prevent further harassment.[14]

The "Westdeutscher Rundfunk" planned to have panel discussions conducted by historians and survivors of the Holocaust after each viewing, and the audience was told that phone calls were welcome. Before the show was even aired, television stations received calls, most of them negative, demanding that the German people be left alone; many threats of physical violence accompanied these initial reactions. After thirty minutes of the first installment, however, the calls gradually changed.[15] Stations were deluged by an increasing number of positive callers. On Monday night, 5,200 calls were recorded, Tuesday, 7,300, Wednesday, 4,852, Thursday, 5,988, and Friday, 6,748, in all, a total of over 30,000 calls.[16] At first there was an equal balance of positive and negative calls, the negative ones usually centering on the theme, "Let's forget the past." Negative callers were also often manifestly or latently anti-Semitic. Typically they insisted that Germans get fair treatment by televising films showing the bombing of Dresden or other atrocities committed by the Allied armies against German POWs and the civilian population.

By the second and third nights, however, these calls virtually stopped, and they became more personal and emotional. The two main themes were total disbelief and shock as to how such atrocities could happen anywhere, especially in a country of such high civilization as Germany, and the question of personal guilt. Many people wept and appeared to need to talk to anyone about their experiences, their shame, their horror. Pictures, diaries, and letters were offered as proof of knowledge about Nazi crimes. One man called to say that he had a picture of a burning synagogue filled with Jews in Bialystok (an event analogous to a scene in the series). One young man said, "If it's true, what was shown, then I want to give up my German passport."[17] An eighty-three-year-old man complained, "Our eighteen-year-old grandson accuses us of being a treacherous people. He doesn't want to have a thing to do with us and wants to move out. We're ruined."[18] Each evening more people called, admitting shamefully that they had not wanted to know what was going on, and that they had purposely remained oblivious to the whole experience. Many callers insisted that because of the show, they were able to talk about World War II for the first time with their families. The amount of family discussion was verified in a survey sent out a week later by the Federal Center for Political Education in which 64 percent of those asked had discussed the show with their families.[19]

Another category of calls consisted largely of factual and specifically historical questions. The most frequently repeated were: (1) Why was there no formal resistance? (2) Why didn't the Catholic and Protestant churches do anything? (3) Why didn't the rest of the world intervene? and (4) Why were the Jews so passive?[20]

The discussion panels were deluged with questions as well and were often criticized by viewers for being too objective, aloof, and impersonal. The original discussion leader, Robert Leicht, a journalist from the prestigious *Süddeutsche Zeitung,* was dismissed for being too remote and blasé. Questions most often asked of the panel by telephone callers were: (1) Why is an American film being shown in Germany, and how accurate is it? (2) Why wasn't the film made by Germans? (3) How could such a thing happen? (4) What did we actually know? (5) What could we have done had we known, and why was there no resistance? (6) Was it really that bad? (7) Why didn't the Jews resist? (8) Why were Jews the Nazis' scapegoats? (9) Weren't people forced to obey orders? (10) What did the churches do? (11) What advice should we have for the generations who weren't involved?[21]

In Austria, where the film was shown with no interruption on four consecutive nights (March 1–4, 1979), the sheer quantity of telephone reactions during the film and subsequent to the only televised discussion following the last installment was beyond all expectations. Proportionate to their countries' respective populations, the 8,227 Austrian callers represent twice the amount recorded in the FRG. Forty-nine percent of the calls were classified as positive, whereas 39 percent expressed an overall negative opinion.[22] More men called than women, and urban areas registered a higher number of callers than rural parts of the country. Positive attitudes increased consistently from the first installment's 44 percent to the fourth's 58 percent. The negative, conversely, decreased from 45 percent to 30 percent. Women had more favorable responses than men, young people more than their elders. As in West Germany, the younger and more educated viewers reacted most positively. Despite the overall enthusiastic and positive telephone responses, there were in Austria, just as in the FRG, some disturbing signs. Thus, one in every five callers expressed overt sentiments of anti-Semitism, with 8 percent of the total voicing openly hostile attitudes toward Jews.[23]

The size of the television audiences was unforeseen and unprecedented in both countries. Never before had the third channel in West Germany gotten more viewers than the other two combined. On Monday night 32 percent watched the show, on Tuesday 36 percent, and by Friday 39 percent (about 15,000,000 viewers) had their television sets tuned into the third channel. The majority of the viewers who called and filled out questionnaires were under thirty, well-educated, or politically interested.[24]

The Austrian figures appear even more impressive than their West German counterparts. The first night attracted 52 percent of Austrian television viewers, which meant that 3.02 million out of a total of 7 million watched the show. The figures for the subsequent installments were 49 percent (2.86 million), 38 percent (2.21 million), and 44 percent (2.54 million) respectively.[25] It is interesting to note that in contrast to West Germany where the figures increased with every installment, in Austria they did the reverse. Two explanations seem plausible for this discrepancy: The lower West German figures at the beginning of the series were largely due to the film's telecast on the "highbrow" third channel. Conversely, many Austrians watched the first installment out of sheer curiosity about the immense intensity of public preoccupation which had been generated and maintained across the border in West Germany since the beginning of 1979.[26]

Reactions in the FRG immediately following the show maintained the intensity that had become commonplace during the telecast. The questions of aesthetics, Hollywood kitsch, and the ability to portray mass horror—so much in the forefront of discussion before the show—were all rendered irrelevant in light of the tremendous viewer response. Obviously mass horror could be portrayed in such a way as to have an emotional effect on millions of people.

In a questionnaire sent out by the Federal Center for Political Education within a week after the showing, 73 percent had a positive response to the show, 20 percent were undecided, and only 7 percent had negative reactions out of 1,800 people questioned. Its emotional effect was undeniable. Sixty-four percent found the show deeply upsetting, 41 percent said the show was an important experience for them personally, 39 percent felt shame that Germans had committed such crimes and had tolerated them as well, 22 percent claimed there were scenes in which they almost cried. Seventeen percent found that the theme was no longer relevant, and only a small 2 percent dismissed the show entirely.[27] In Austria the results were comparable.

Researchers in both countries were particularly interested in the educational and political effects of the film. Had people obtained any new information about the Third Reich and would this knowledge change their political outlook? Also, the tremendous reaction of young people, particularly between the ages of fourteen and nineteen, was noted in both countries. There appeared to be a hunger for information about the Third Reich, especially from students in secondary schools. In the FRG, out of 105,000 requests for accompanying material to the show sent to the Federal Center for Political Education in Bonn, 70,000 were from teachers who claimed their students were demanding information because of the film's impact. Fifty-seven percent of those asked under the age of thirty had a strong wish to learn more about Nazism and the persecution of the Jews. Only 31 percent of those over thirty expressed the same desire.

Interestingly enough, the number of West Germans who did or did not learn something new from the show remained basically equal. Fifty-one percent indicated that they did, whereas 49 percent said they did not. Once again, it was the fourteen- to nineteen-year-olds who were most strongly affected, 69 percent of whom believed that they had learned new facts about Nazism. Overall, however, only 14 percent of the respondents changed their views about the Nazi period as a result of the show. The main fact that seemed most novel—and shocking—to most viewers was the extent of the brutality of the Nazis. This was particularly true of the young women and of less-educated people.[28]

In Austria, some of the following pre- and post-"Holocaust" data shed light on this issue: Whereas only 72 percent believed that millions of Jews were murdered by the Nazis prior to the film's showing, over 80 percent thought this to be true after "Holocaust." Although 47 percent wanted to forget the past before the film, 42 percent still believed this to be desirable thereafter. Forty-eight percent thought it important to make the events of the Holocaust as widely known as possible before the show; this number increased to 55 percent after the program.[29]

It is obviously more difficult to estimate the changes in political consciousness that the show could make. However, some results were pertinent. Before the show was broadcast, 15 percent of the people questioned in the FRG thought that Nazi crimes should continue to be prosecuted, whereas 51 percent believed they should not, with 34 percent expressing no or contradictory opinions on this issue. After the show, 39 percent thought they should be prosecuted and 35 percent did not, with the rest undecided regarding this complicated and politically sensitive issue.[30]

This change, in many ways, represents the most dramatic shift in public opinion that can be directly traced to the film's impact. The marked increase of 24 percent among those West German respondents who wanted the prosecution of Nazi war criminals to continue not only provides ample evidence for the show's direct influence upon public opinion in the FRG, but also highlights "Holocaust's" active intervention in that country's policy-making process: As discussed below, there is good reason to believe that it was partly as a result of this television series that the West German Parliament—after lengthy and passionate debates in which the film received frequent mention—voted on July 4, 1979, to abolish the expiration of the statute of limitations on all murder, thereby permitting the continued prosecution of Nazi war criminals.

Significantly, it is regarding this sensitive topic that the biggest discrepancy between German and Austrian responses to "Holocaust" becomes apparent. Whereas the surveys conducted in the two countries differ substantially with respect to most other questions, thus not allowing point-by-point direct comparisons but requiring a side-by-side presentation of the findings from which certain inferences can be drawn, this issue permits a clear juxtaposition of the results: In Austria, 17 percent wanted the continued prosecution of Nazi criminals prior to "Holocaust," 77 percent desired an immediate and final stop to this practice, and only 6 percent indicated indecision. After the show, the respective figures were 24 percent, 74 percent, and 2 percent. What makes this aggregate finding additionally disturbing is the fact that even the social groups most hostile to National Socialism and Austria's involvement therein—the educated and the young—favor an end to the prosecution of war criminals by a better than two-to-one margin. Only 31 percent of university students want to see justice done by favoring the maintenance—at least on paper— of the law that stipulates the continued prosecution of Nazi war criminals, whereas 67 percent call for an immediate abolition of this statute.[31]

It must be added that, unlike in the FRG, the question of an expiration of the statute of limitations for murder was not a political issue in Austria during the time of the telecast, since in Austria there has been no statute of limitations on any form of murder since 1965.[32] Robbed of its political immediacy, the film failed substantially to alter the minds of most Austrians regarding this important moral question. Precisely because of the absence of a relationship between the film's political implications and their concrete realization in the tangible future via specific legislation—as was the case in the Federal Republic—we agree wholeheartedly with Peter Diem's assessment of the Austrian response to "Holocaust," which he describes as "existent for a short time, but certainly not to the degree and duration as in Germany."[33]

Questions seeking out traces of anti-Semitism were also asked. In West Germany, 15 percent of those questioned before the show said Jews sowed discord, whereas 49 percent thought they did not. After the viewing only 9 percent believed such a myth and 60 percent did not.[34] In Austria, where anti-Semitism enjoyed an even more important historical role than in Germany, and where its legacy in the contemporary political culture may be less tarnished and illegitimate than in the FRG, researchers were particularly interested in "Holocaust's" effect upon this form of prejudice. In addition to the above-mentioned 8 percent increase among those who, following the film's showing, believe that millions of Jews were exterminated under National Socialism (from 72 percent prior to the telecast to over 80 percent thereafter) there also occurred a 5 percent decrease (from 16 percent prior to the show to 11 percent thereafter) among those who doubted the historical accuracy of genocide against the Jews. More disturbing than these rather small changes is the fact that a follow-up survey administered five months after the telecast indicates that the prefilm figures of 72 percent and 16 percent for the two questions respectively had been almost completely "reattained."[35] "Holocaust's" short-lived existence in Austria seems to fit the suspicion regarding the film's impact: a flash-in-the-pan media hype with little lasting substance.

One view in the FRG that was not changed very much by the film was whether all Germans who were adults at the time of the Third Reich bore any kind of guilt. Before "Holocaust" 16 percent felt that this was the case, whereas 53 percent denied it; after the film the respective figures were 22 percent yes, 54 percent no. Prior to the show, 45 percent believed that Germans had a moral obligation to make reparations to the victims of the Holocaust, whereas after the film 54 percent shared such sentiments.[36]

The issue of guilt has a special significance in Austria since one of the most sensitive—hence frequently unarticulated—political topics in post–World War II Austria has centered around the Austrians' role and complicity in National Socialism. The manifest and latent postures on the part of Austrians concerning this touchy subject have had significant political as well as psychological ramifications in Austria's internal development and external relations. Thus, the following figures may be of some interest, especially to Germans, who have long felt that the Austrians have not borne their share of guilt for their active involvement in the Holocaust. Before the film, 44 percent of the Austrians surveyed thought that Austrians shared a responsibility with the Germans for the wrongs committed by the Nazis, whereas 38 percent insisted that solely Germans were to blame. The post-"Holocaust" figures changed to 50 percent and 37 percent respectively. Disaggregating these data into their component parts, it becomes clear once again that age and educational level are the most important discriminating variables. Younger and better-educated Austrians tend to assume more of a responsibility than their elder and less-educated compatriots, who continue to view the Germans as the only culprits for the wrongs committed by the Nazis.[37]

The most distressing reactions in the FRG were the responses to the statement, Nazism was basically a good idea that was poorly carried out.

Before the show 36 percent answered in the affirmative, 30 percent in the negative, and 37 percent were undecided. After the telecast the respective figures were 30 percent yes, 40 percent no, and 30 percent undecided.[38] This question was not part of any Austrian survey.

It is clearly impossible to find out exactly how an entire nation reacted to the show. If a survey is only partly reliable, letters to the editor are even less so because one can assume that only a highly selective group of people write letters to periodicals and newspapers. They are most likely better educated than the average citizen, which already limits the kinds of responses one will obtain. The letters are a good source, however, for learning something about the aftereffects of the show. Most of the telephone calls were highly emotional, immediate responses, whereas the survey had the obvious drawback of being limited to particular questions. Letters, however, expressed all kinds of views, particularly those that arise after some reflection.

Given this hypothesis, the Austrian results are somewhat disturbing since the letters written to Austrian television (ORF) and those published in newspapers all expressed more negative sentiments regarding the film's value and larger implications than did the telephone calls received during and immediately following the telecast. This small indicator corresponds with other occurrences mentioned above, which lead to the tentative conclusion that the "Holocaust effect" in Austria was rather short-lived. The quantity and quality of affective responses decreased with the passage of time. Thus, for instance, the proportion of anti-Semitic reactions and hostile opinions *vis à vis* the movie in particular and its topic in general, which were expressed in letters addressed to ORF, outdistanced in frequency and acerbity similar responses received by telephone. Twelve percent of the letters were anonymous, and the vast proportion of these denounced the telecast in no uncertain terms.[39]

As to the letters written to the Austrian press, two contrasts to the West German situation seem noteworthy. First, the sheer quantity of published letters by any single newspaper, and, of course, by the press as a whole in the FRG far exceeded its Austrian counterpart. Thus, for example, the German daily *Die Welt* published letters concerning "Holocaust" and related matters for months after the show. This again may be construed as a small, but significant sign of the more lasting impact the entire "Holocaust" experience has had in the FRG than in Austria. The second contrast between the two countries concerns press ownership and affiliation, which in Austria—as compared to the FRG—is much more explicitly tied to political parties and interest groups. The ideological cleavages of Austrian macropolitics were intensified by the press coverage of "Holocaust" and its aftermath. Thus, not surprisingly, papers owned by or close to the Socialist Party (SPÖ) had a much more positive attitude toward the film and its implications in their editorials and published letters than their counterparts affiliated with the conservative People's Party (ÖVP) or the Right-leaning Freedom Party (FPÖ). Whereas newspapers close to the latter two political groupings exhibited a lukewarm to negative attitude *vis à vis* "Holocaust" in their editorials, the Socialist and Catholic Church–dominated press voiced the most favorable opinions, with the former stressing political questions, especially by drawing parallels to the ills of our contemporary world, and the latter emphasizing moral and consciousness-related lessons to be learned from the film.[40] Overall, however, it is interesting to note that cutting *across* party-affiliated ideologies in both Austria and West Germany, "elite opinion" as expressed in newspaper editorials, official radio, and television commentaries received "Holocaust" more favorably than "mass opinion" as articulated by telephone calls and letters to the editor.

Regarding West Germany, we have divided the letters collected from daily and weekly newspapers and magazines into four general categories, namely, those offering negative reactions; those relating the show to current political problems; those articulating highly personal responses (including feelings and experiences); and those groping to find ways to deal with the past.

The most common complaint was that the film was unfair to Germans. Repeatedly, people complained about the lack of attention given to the suffering of German POWs at the hands of the Russians.[41] The expulsion of Germans from the eastern parts of the former Reich was cited as another example of injustice.[42] Other letters insisted that the Germans, collectively as a people, were innocent and that it was merely Hitler and the Nazi leadership who were guilty.[43] Others worried that the film portrayed mass torture as a uniquely Teutonic quality, and claimed that the Germans ought to make a film for the Americans about the CIA, My Lai, or the slaughter of the Indians.[44]

Very similar points were raised in Austria as well. Thus, the slaughter of American Indians received frequent mention in this context as did various atrocities committed by the Allies in World War Two, with the bombing of Dresden and the expulsion of Germans from Eastern Europe listed most frequently. A number of letters also mentioned the United States involvement in Vietnam.[45]

Many Germans simply wanted to be left alone. They claimed that any inner healing in both Jews and Germans would be damaged by the renewed hate the film would arouse. Germany had been attacked sufficiently by the world press. Guilt and shame were something that could only be worked out in private.[46] One particularly cynical letter questioned why the Germans were indulging in hypocritical self-blame. It was obvious that the root of the problem was the beast known as man, and that all Europeans were spiritually if not literally guilty.[47] Another bitter letter claimed a counterfilm should be made by the Germans. After all, Europe as a whole was prosperous only because of German wealth. Who, the author asked, was giving jobs to foreign workers by the millions? Who was pouring wealth into other countries via export and mass tourism? He provided his own answer by stating that it was the Germans, of course.[48] A few people called the show a piece of kitsch, but in general, the aesthetic quality was no longer pertinent. Some people were distressed that the film was overly simplistic. Indeed, it was accused of being like a Western with the good guys and the bad.[49] Finally, others were certain that the film would have no effect on those who needed the most help, particularly ex-Nazis. It was all crocodile tears, and there were still many Erich Dorfs at large.[50] One letter criticized the Germans for needing a hero like Joseph Weiss in order to understand the horrors of this particular war and of war in general. Germans always needed a hero whom they could admire, this person concluded.[51]

"Holocaust" triggered intense reactions concerning a vast array of contemporary political problems in the Federal Republic and the world. Issues such as the expiration of the statute of limitations, growing neo-Nazi activities, Israel and the Middle East, Berufsverbot, the "Hitler-wave," and leftist terrorism among many others were all mentioned in conjunction with the show. Many felt that any totalitarian ideology, whether of the Right or the Left, was dangerous, and therefore must be fought.[52] Others hoped that the horror of the film would bring neo-Nazis to their senses.[53] Many people wrote of the "Holocaust of the East," and expressed great fear of the terror of communism.[54] People called for the continued prosecution of Nazi war criminals. Israel was both praised and condemned. Repeatedly, the question was asked whether the FRG was that much different from Nazi Germany. Mentioning the reprehensible practice of Berufsverbot, the plight of foreign workers in West Germany, and the dangers of nuclear power as well as other catastrophes due to the failures of modern science and technology, many writers felt that there were plenty of issues in contemporary West German politics calling for concern, guilt, and active political participation lest the past repeat itself. Other letters pointed to such countries as Uganda, Chile, the Soviet Union, South Africa, Cambodia, and Ethiopia in arguing that totalitarianism and mass murder have not disappeared with the Nazis, indeed enjoy by complicity the tacit approval of all countries, including the Federal Republic.[55]

Although clearly well-meaning, well-informed, and concerned, these voices could be interpreted as yet another attempt to dodge the unpleasant task of facing the past *sui generis*. This interpretation applies to the overall response of the German Left to the Holocaust in general and "Holocaust" in particular. The fact that people once again ignore the horrors of the world does not exclude the absolute necessity that the Nazi crimes be dealt with on their own by the German people, and not in comparison with other crimes against humanity. As one letter said, "It makes one despair, in discussions of our past, to hear over and over that other peoples have committed crimes as well. Who's denying that? And since when is the mass murder of Jews a measuring stick of comparison with other crimes?"[56]

Many letters considered the emotional response the show elicited, and questions of how much one did or did not know. The writers concerned with these issues saw it as irrelevant whether the show was a product of the American television industry or not. Rather, what was important was that the show had portrayed real people, with whom one could identify. People praised the film's nonobjective, nonanalytical, indeed emotional approach.[57] Many confessed that they had in fact known what the Nazis were doing. Some had protested mildly at the time, but all felt that this was insufficient and they suffered from guilt as a result.[58] Others, however, claiming to be objective and pro-Semitic, said they listened regularly to the BBC during the war and had never heard anything about extermination camps. They truly thought the Jews were being transported to work camps, and/or resettled in the East.[59] A good number of letters indicated that all this admission of guilt was self-indulgent and useless, as it came thirty-five years too late. "Even had we known, what could we have done anyway?" was often asked.[60] "Civil courage is what we lacked," said some. "Has that changed at all?" they wondered. Younger writers frequently expressed their outrage that those very same people who were active in the Third Reich were trying to promote democracy today.[61] Others condemned in no uncertain terms all those Germans who saw themselves as victims of the Third Reich—similar to its real victims, like the Jews—and who said that they had no possibility of resisting.[62]

"Holocaust" was seen by many as the first step toward a true *Bewältigung* of the past. Young people claimed that they were not learning enough about the Nazi period in school, and asked that this film be shown as part of the regular curriculum.[63] Others claimed that if youth had really wanted to learn about the past, the materials had always been there. Young people were simply too lazy or uninterested.[64] Many Germans, including politicians and public figures who were asked, hoped that the show would lead to general discussions about the past in schools and families, and that the media and schools would continue the educational process the film had begun.[65] If and when Germany comes to terms with its past, it will be a more humane and democratic society, writers repeatedly argued. One letter claimed that no American product would enable Germans to work out their past. Yet, there were no Germans who seemed interested in making a film like "Holocaust."[66] Finally, most letters from young people demanded more discussions about the past and concrete ways to deal with it, such as, for example, regular trips to Poland and Israel to help surviving victims.[67] But perhaps no letter was as eloquent as that of a seventeen-year-old school girl who said simply, "I cried, cried, cried."[68]

Long after the telecast, "Holocaust" remained a major subject for discussions in the West German press. It also became the starting point for an array of topics dealing with neo-Nazi activity, concern with the German inability to mourn, practical means of working out the past, terrorism, and even media theory. Various magazines ran series on aspects of the war and anti-Semitism,[69] and the different Centers for Political Education were deluged with requests for materials related to the show. This entire episode came to be known as the "Holocaust Wave," a conscious counterattack against the aforementioned "Hitler-wave." This wave rippled into other countries besides the FRG, sparking introspective responses to the war, most notably in France.

Current political activities were being reexamined in the light of "Holocaust," particularly neo-Nazism, which Die Zeit[70] reported was flourishing. Right-wing radicalism had been neglected by media more preoccupied recently with left-wing terrorism. However, "Holocaust" forced authorities not to dismiss the constantly increasing neo-Nazi activities as mere pranks by otherwise well-meaning youngsters. The center of attention was the 1978 annual report on extremist groups and their activities in the Federal Republic, published by the Interior Ministry in July. Receiving front-page coverage in most newspapers,[71] the report, for the first time in years, placed heavier emphasis on Right radicalism than Left extremism in the FRG. The report actually showed a decline in right-wing extremists (from 83 groups observed in 1977 to 76 in 1978). Yet three worrisome signs merited close attention from the German public: the increase of jointly undertaken and well-coordinated measures by numerous groups; their growing use of violent methods; and their increasing attraction to unemployed and disenfranchised youngsters. While these groups are certainly no threat to the present political system in the FRG, West German society must become aware of them to prevent their further proliferation. "Holocaust" may have been the most important catalyst in creating an atmosphere conducive to large-scale debate about this sensitive issue.

A critical eye was cast on current-day West Germany's relationship to its past. One article,[72] for example, argued that West Germany was in a psychological crisis because it had not yet learned to mourn its past. The "Hitler-wave," a supposed objectification of the war experience, was simply further repression of more fundamental, personal feelings. It was not as important to understand Hitler and his deeds as to comprehend why the German people had followed him. By ignoring the Hitler period, the Germans were denying their complete past, which explained the current rejection of many traditional values and cultural aspects. Instead, the Germans had turned into a consumer culture, intent on making money and emulating Americans. Many traditional values, such as the idealization of both aggression and obedience, were indeed questionable, but others, such as creativity and individual initiative, were valid. If all were denied, younger generations would not learn to differentiate the bad from the good. The repressed fear of values had led to current terrorism. Children of those who experienced the war could not identify with their parents and their parents' horrid past, and the subsequent lack of role models led to extremism. It was imperative that Germans relive the guilt and shame of the past so that they would no longer be psychically stunted. Otherwise, the inability to learn from mistakes would continue through the coming generations.

Another critic was even more explicit in linking current terrorism to the Nazi past.[73] "Holocaust" had come twenty years too late, for it was the children of the fifties and sixties who had needed answers to, and evaluations of, the war. Their "Holocaust consciousness" had been twenty years ahead of their time; they had demanded information no one was willing to give. West Germany must mourn a generation that was ignored by its parents, and which, partly as a consequence, resorted to horrid acts of violence. If the show proved to have a lasting effect on West Germany, then its people would feel guilt for their more recent as well as their Nazi past.

Many writers used "Holocaust" as a means to suggest different ways Germans could educate themselves about the past. The periods both before and after the war were of equal importance to the war itself as areas of study.[74] The roots of anti-Semitism and Hitler's ideology must also be studied meticulously. Examples of current-day problems, such as prejudices against foreign workers, should be used so that children would become aware of racism's deeply entrenched existence. This would lead to a greater understanding of history, and the Nazi period would no longer be seen as an anomalous vacuum.

Finally, the West German media's treatment of the topic of fascism developed as a major focus of discussion. One writer found that, on the whole, the media had dealt extensively, and critically, with fascism.[75] He also argued, however, that most of the media's coverage of fascism—until "Holocaust"—was high art, thus reaching only a small, elite audience. On the other end of the spectrum, however, were penny detective novels that celebrated fascist tendencies: a strong death wish, a desire to sacrifice oneself for one's country at any cost, militant anticommunism, and the glorification of heroes and supermen. These cruder outputs of the media had a much larger circulation and dominated the profit-conscious culture industry.

Between these two extremes lay a gray area that had many critics in dispute. Shows on television about neo-Nazism, the film "Hitler: Eine Karriere," and the "Hitler-wave" were seen by some critics to impart information crucial to the understanding of fascism, whereas other writers maintained that a film on neo-Nazi activities, or Hitler's charisma, were grist for the mill of those who already had latent sympathies with fascism. The author demanded that some balance be struck between high and low culture. Mass media, especially in its post-"Holocaust" phase, could no longer be viewed as tasteless or as simply a means to entertain. Television had developed into the best medium for attaining a balance of educational, nonesoteric sources of information about and criticism of fascism.[76]

In most countries "Holocaust" was an exceptionally successful television series. In a select few, such as Austria and West Germany, it developed into a "media event" in the sense that the film itself was merely the core of a whole array of studies, evaluations, and reflections about the country's involvement in the atrocities of the Second World War and the contemporary generation's assessment of the recent and painful past. However, only in the Federal Republic of Germany did the film and the subsequent reactions to it develop a political importance that furnished tangible results for the future of West German society.[77] On July 4, 1979, 255 members of the West German Bundestag—all but one of the SPD delegates supported by a handful of colleagues belonging to the Free Democrats (FDP) and the Christian Democrats (CDU)—voted against the expiration of the statute of limitations for murder, thereby making it possible to continue the prosecution of Nazi war criminals. Listening to the parliamentary debates on the radio, it became clear that "Holocaust" had made an immense impact that was in the process of being transformed into *Realpolitik*. No other book, film, even personal experience, was mustered as frequently as "Holocaust" by the delegates opposing expiration to impress upon the German public and the world the moral urgency of this impending decision for themselves as individuals and for the German people collectively.

Yet, the result would have not turned out as favorably had it not been for a *de facto* bloc vote of virtually all parliamentary members of the Social Democratic Party, which, as is well known, supported the continuation of the present statute making it mandatory for the state to prosecute Nazi criminals well before the telecast of "Holocaust." The same pertains to most members of the conservative opposition who—certainly moved as individuals by the film's horror—failed to alter their well-entrenched position as to the desirability of an expiration of the statute, a position also held well in advance of the television series.

The film, of course, did not bring about the Germans' *Bewältigung* of their past in one fell swoop. No single event of any magnitude has the capacity to change abruptly fundamental historical processes. It would have been completely unrealistic to hope for a miracle. The film, as pointed out in the context of the debate in the Bundestag, also failed to *modify* German political structures. What it has done, however, is to *amplify* already existing traits in today's Federal Republic of Germany by having been part of the normal political process, which seems an excellent guarantor that the events depicted in "Holocaust" will never be repeated on German soil. The film raised public awareness about the Holocaust to hitherto unprecedented levels of frankness and intensity. This phenomenon is the first step in the process leading to a *Bewältigung* of the past. That alone is certainly a greater contribution than any of the film's originators could ever hope of achieving.

NOTES

1. Don Kowet, "The 'Holocaust' Breakthrough," *TV Guide* (April 28–May 4, 1979), pp. 3–6.

2. This figure was mentioned by Siegfried Zielinski, Technical University of Berlin, in a presentation on the reactions to the film "Holocaust," delivered at Wesleyan University on September 27, 1979.

3. Gordon Brook-Shepherd, *Anschluss: The Rape of Austria* (London, 1963).

4. Peter Diem, *"Holocaust": Anatomie eines Medienereignisses* (Vienna, 1979), p. 3.

5. Ibid., p. 3.

6. For some of these criticisms, see Elie Wiesel, "Die Trivialisierung des Holocaust: Halb Faktum und halb Fiktion" in Peter Märthesheimer and Ivo Frenzel, eds., *Holocaust: Eine Nation ist Betroffen* (Frankfurt am Main, 1979), pp. 25–30; Sabina Lietzmann, "Die Judenvernichtung als Seifenoper," *Frankfurter Allgemeine Zeitung* (April 20, 1978); Dieter

Zimmer, "Melodrama vom Massenmord," *Die Zeit* (January 19, 1979); Pankraz, "Pankraz, der Holocaust und die Fernsehserie," *Die Welt* (June 26, 1978); articles in *Pfasterstrand 47* (February 15, 1979) and *Links* (March 1979); Klaus Umbach, "Endlösung im Abseits," *Der Spiegel* (January 15, 1979); Tele-Biss, "Drama aus zweiter Hand," *Die Zeit* (June 2, 1978); Günter Rohrbach, letter to *Die Zeit* (June 15, 1978); Günther Rühle, "Wenn Holocaust kommt," *Frankfurter Allgemeine Zeitung* (January 17, 1979); Siegfried Zielinski, "Die Werbespots nicht einfach rausschmeissen," *Medium* (January 1979), pp. 28–29.

7. Sabina Lietzmann, "Kritische Fragen," *Frankfurter Allgemeine Zeitung* (September 28, 1978).

8. Peter Märthesheimer, "Weniger eine Fernsehserie denn ein Politikum," *Medium* (January 1979), pp. 5–9.

9. Rohrbach, Letter to *Die Zeit* and Märtesheimer, "Weniger eine Fernsehserie."

10. Rühle, "Wenn Holocaust kommt."

11. Tilman Ernst, "Positiver Beitrag zu einem notwendigen Lernprozess," *Medium* (January 1979), pp. 26–27.

12. Heinz Werner Hübner, "Kein Lehrstück, sondern Lernstück," *Süddeutsche Zeitung* (September 22, 1978).

13. Rühle, "Wenn Holocaust kommt" and Ernst, "Positiver Beitrag," pp. 26–27.

14. *Frankfurter Rundschau* (January 25, 26, 27, 1979).

15. Julius Schoeps, "Angst vor der Vergangenheit?" in Märthesheimer and Frenzel, *Holocaust,* p. 226.

16. Ibid., p. 230.

17. Ibid., p. 227.

18. Ibid., p. 228.

19. Uwe Magnus, "Die Reaktionen auf Holocaust," *Media Perspektiven* (April 1979), pp. 226–240.

20. Schoeps, "Angst vor der Vergangenheit," pp. 228–229.

21. "Zuschauer fragen—Verfolgte, Betroffene und Historiker antworten" in Märthesheimer and Frenzel, *Holocaust,* pp. 231–273.

22. *ORF Pressedienst Information* (April 4, 1979), pp. 14–15.

23. For all the above-mentioned information, Peter Diem, *"Holocaust,"* pp. 31–50.

24. Uwe Magnus, "Die Reaktionen auf Holocaust," pp. 226–230.

25. Diem, *"Holocaust,"* p. 17.

26. Peter Diem espoused the following interested hypothesis in this context: Had "Holocaust" been shown simultaneously in Austria and West Germany on the respective first channels without strong competition from the others, more than two-thirds of the combined Austrian and West German populations over 14 would have seen at least one installment. Ibid., p. 75.

27. Uwe Magnus, "Die Reaktionen auf Holocaust," pp. 226–230.

28. For all above information, see Tilman Ernst, "Holocaust und politische Bildung," *Media Perspektiven* (April 1979), pp. 230–240.

29. *ORF Pressedienst Information* (April 3, 1979), pp. 17–18.

30. Ibid., pp. 26–27.

31. Diem, *"Holocaust,"* pp. 26, 27, 77.

32. "Das Common Law kennt keine Verjährung, *Süddeutsche Zeitung* (June 29, 1979).

33. Ibid., p. 77.

34. Ernst, "Holocaust und politische Bildung," pp. 230–240.

35. Diem, *"Holocaust,"* p. 71.

36. Ernst, "Holocaust und politische Bildung," pp. 230–240.

37. Diem, *"Holocaust,"* p. 28.

38. Ernst, "Holocaust und politische Bildung," pp. 230–240.

39. Diem, *"Holocaust,"* pp. 51–54.

40. This assessment is based on study of the following Austrian newspapers: *Die Presse, Arbeiterzeitung, Salzburger Nachrichten, Salzburger Volksblatt, Die Kronenzeitung, Volksstimme, Neues Volksblatt, Kurier,* and the magazine *Profil* during the months March, April, and May of 1979.

41. Letter to Editor, *Rheinische Post* (January 24, 1979).

42. Letter to Editor, *Die Welt* (February 5, 1979).

43. Letter to Editor, Ibid. (February 13, 1979).

44. Letter to Editor, *Der Spiegel* (February 5, 1979).

45. Diem, "Holocaust."

46. Letter to Editor, *Die Welt* (March 3, 1979).

47. Letter to Editor, *Die Zeit* (March 2, 1979).

48. Letter to Editor, *Süddeutsche Zeitung* (February 9, 1979).

49. Letter to Editor, *Die Zeit* (March 2, 1979).

50. Letters to Editor, *Der Spiegel* (February 5, 1979) and *Süddeutsche Zeitung* (February 9, 1979).

51. Letter to Editor, *Die Zeit* (March 2, 1979).

52. "Das denken Deutsche über Holocaust," *Welt am Sonntag* (January 28, 1979).

53. Letter to Editor, *Der Spiegel* (January 29, 1979).

54. Letter to Editor, *Die Welt* (February 13, 1979).

55. Letters to Editor, *Süddeutsche Zeitung* (February 9, 1979); *Der Spiegel* (February 5, 1979); *Die Welt* (March 8, 1979); *Die Zeit* (March 2, 1979).

56. Letter to Editor, *Die Welt* (March 8, 1979).

57. Letter to Editor, *Der Spiegel* (January 29, 1979).

58. Letters to Editor, *Die Zeit* (March 2, 1979) and *Der Spiegel* (February 5, 1979).

59. Letter to Editor, *Die Welt* (March 8, 1979).

60. Letter to Editor, *Die Zeit* (March 2, 1979).

61. Letter to Editor, *Der Spiegel* (February 5, 1979).

62. Letter to Editor, *Die Zeit* (March 2, 1979).

63. Letter to Editor, *Der Spiegel* (January 29, 1979).

64. Letter to Editor, *Die Zeit* (March 2, 1979).

65. "Das denken Deutsche über Holocaust," *Welt am Sonntag* (January 28, 1979).

66. Letter to Editor, *Die Welt* (February 15, 1979). It is interesting and, we think, significant, that unlike German moviemakers, Americans have produced at least three major commercial films about the most trying and divisive trauma of our recent past—the Vietnam War. (The three films are *Coming Home*, *The Deer Hunter*, and *Apocalypse Now*.) No matter what the individual and collective shortcomings of these films may be, they all attempt to deal with a very sensitive aspect of America's recent past. They represent, in a sense, a true *Bewältigung* on a mass level of a collectively committed moral wrong. Moreover, the fact that none of West Germany's brilliant young movie directors like Fassbinder, Herzog, Wenders, or Schlöndorff have even attempted to make a comprehensive commercial film about the German role in World War Two may attest to the Left's and the contemporary intelligentsia's failure to come to terms with the Nazi period collectively with the rest of West German society.

67. Letter to the Editor, *Die Zeit* (March 9, 1979).

68. Letter to Editor, *Der Spiegel* (January 29, 1979).

69. *Der Spiegel, Der Stern, Die Zeit* among others.

70. Gerd Heidenreich, "Der Geist weht Rechts," *Die Zeit* (February 13, 1979).

71. See, for example, *Handelsblatt, Frankfurter Rundschau, Frankfurter Allgemeine Zeitung, Die Neue,* all from July 11, 1979; also, for an excellent analysis, see *Die Neue* (July 13, 1979).

72. Above material taken from Margarete Mitscherlich-Nielsen, "Die Notwendigkeit zu trauern," *Frankfurter Rundschau* (January 25, 1979).

73. Adolf Muschg, "'Holocaust'—Nachgedanke," *Frankfurter Rundschau* (April 7, 1979).

74. Jürgen Thorwald, "Holocaust—eine Bilanz," *Die Zeit* (May 4, 1979).

75. Norbert Schneider, "Für wenige wird viel, für viel wenig angeboten," *Frankfurter Rundschau* (January 25, 1979).

76. Ibid.

77. Due to space limitations we will mention only the crucial debate regarding the expiration of the statute of limitations. However, there have been other noteworthy political events in which the mobilization of consciousness induced by "Holocaust" played a decisive role. Most prominent among them was the "Rock gegen Rechts" (Rock against the Right)

movement, a coalition of approximately 50 civil rights, antinuclear, leftist, environmentalist, and trade-union groups, which mustered well over 50,000 people in opposition to a planned neo-Nazi gathering in Frankfurt on June 17, 1979, the annually observed "Day of German Unity." Not only was the gathering completely successful in that it prevented a handful of neo-Nazis from even showing up in Frankfurt, much less parading their cause publicly, but it also helped infuse an additional political dimension of the post-"Holocaust" spirit into concrete public action. For an excellent account of "Rock gegen Rechts," see articles in the *Frankfurter Rundschau,* June 16 and 18, 1979.

14

HISTORY AS ENTERTAINMENT AND PROVOCATION
THE TV SERIES "HOLOCAUST" IN WEST GERMANY
Siegfried Zielinski

The screening of the NBC series "Holocaust" by West German Television's Third Channel in January 1979 is now history—political and media
history. In the meantime, the four-part series based on Gerald Green's
novel was rerun in November 1982, and since then German audiences
have seen hundreds of hours of programs thematicizing fascism and its
crimes of mass murder against the Jews. These encompassed the most
widely different forms of presentation and dramaturgical concepts: eye-
witness accounts, documentaries, specials, feature films, and even series
whose construction referred back to "Holocaust."

In the meantime a host of cinema films have been made by West German
film "authors," each of whom attempted to get a grasp on the events of
recent history. In Mario Offenberg's "Alptraum als Lebenslauf," Georgia
T. recalls the years of her internment in Ravensbruck death camp. Axel
Engstfeld documents the role of the Nazi judiciary in "Von Richtern und
anderen Sympathisanten" and demonstrates its continuity to a certain
degree in the development of the Federal Republic. These are just two
exceptional examples from the nonfiction genre. Peter Lilienthal, Rainer
Werner Fassbinder, Michael Verhoeven, Ottokar Runze, amongst others,
have all made impressive feature films. "Holocaust" has passed into rock
music and advertising and can be found on the covers of millions of
publications in vastly different constellations of concepts and meanings.
The most abhorrent phenomenon, "concentration camp pornography,"

has come into being or was developed further, for example, as a subject listing on the video film market. In the meantime, the fiftieth anniversary of Hitler's seizure of power has been commemorated at the most diverse levels of cultural and political activity—and not least by a veritable marathon of TV programs on the subject. From October 1982 to January 1983, channels 1 and 2—ARD and ZDF—have devoted one hundred fifty hours of viewing time to this subject alone.

These past five years of works on fascism, both within and outside the medium of television, represent in their effects a context that, naturally, was received only in part by the West German public. When dealing in the following pages with the media event "Holocaust" and some dimensions of its effects, it must be remembered that it is but one element in a process and can only be lifted out of this process for the purposes of analysis. In reality it has long since fused with other factors.

"Holocaust" was unique in the history of television in that the series immediately became the object of socioempirical investigations and cultural discourses. In this respect the Federal Republic was no exception, and many surveys were undertaken, primarily to analyze aspects of the program's effects. My own work on "Holocaust" was done mainly within the framework of a teaching and research project at the Technical University of Berlin, the findings of which are documented in numerous essays and two book publications.[1] I mention our works at this stage in order to avoid repeated references to sources and material contained therein within the text of this essay, and also because collective work inevitably means that one's own conclusions have absorbed those of co-workers with whom one has collaborated in the process of research.

"Catharsis of a Nation" was the somewhat arrogant term applied by *Der Spiegel* to the "Holocaust" telecast in 1979. Others dubbed it a "didactic play" *(Lehrstück)*, whereas some who did not bank on any deeper effects called the visibly hefty emotional reaction of the TV audience "a flash in the pan" (the German word used was *Strohfeuer*—a sarcastic choice of metaphor considering the program's subject). Indeed, there were many variations on these attempts to arrive at a definition, and all had one thing in common: the intent of reducing the significance of this multimedia event to a single category and to bestow on it a clear pedagogical, ideological, or political meaning. The thing simply had to be filed away somewhere, and appropriate labels were readily at hand.

Being concerned with analysis of the mass media, we, too, felt the need to classify the "Holocaust" media event and to define it for purposes of coming to terms with the most atrocious period of Germany's history and, in particular, its reflection in the mass media. This resulted in an analysis of the NBC series and the body of published criticism on it as well as a scrutiny of the many and varied dimensions of its effects. From this it became clear that a single, unequivocal interpretation would fall short of the many-faceted reality. We availed ourselves of the category of contradiction in order to track down "Holocaust" and its functions. At first glance this might appear to be an evasion, but its sophistic character disappears the moment a closer look is taken at the dimensions of cause and effect in the process of the "Holocaust" event. This television film was enacted and produced both with the object of entertaining *and* with the historical and moral purpose of rousing its viewers; it also displayed this ambivalence in its function for West German audiences.

"Holocaust" was a diversion—it made people excited and then calmed them down again—but it also represented a provocation: It triggered discussions and manifest activities. It raised the awareness of the German public regarding fascist anti-Semitism and its ghastly effects. Thus it also possessed a dimension of enlightenment. With the category of contradiction we can move toward a definition of the media event that comprises both its reproductive and productive functions. In this sense "Holocaust" had attributes of a *dialectic of entertainment*. But let us first try to take this odd conceptual construction apart and substantiate it.

The Framework of "Holocaust" in the Federal Republic

"Anti-Semitism . . . is something like the ontology of advertising."[2] What Theodor Adorno expressed by using this metaphor in 1964 had been formulated in various ways in the philosophical fragments gathered in *Dialectic of Enlightenment* together with Max Horkheimer twenty years previously. One of the key "elements of anti-Semitism"[3] that appear again and again is the structural connection between anti-Semitic thinking and behavior and the mechanisms of the culture industry—cultural commodity production, "mass production," "ticket mentality," "ticket thinking," the "lusting" after "property, acquisition," the substitution of judgment with "exchange," the "stereotype," the "cliché." For the two exponents of Critical Theory, these are all attributes and categories that are ideologically coconstituents of anti-Semitism.

By stressing the structural relationship of anti-Semitic stereotypes with the "invariables of advertising psychology,"[4] Adorno's aim in 1964 was quite evidently the strategy of enlightenment that he wanted to see implemented as the basis "in the struggle against anti-Semitism today"—"Only emphatic enlightenment with the whole truth is of any use; strictly foregoing anything which resembles advertising."[5]

In this respect, the TV series "Holocaust" is by no means abstemious.

On the contrary, it is a truly outstanding product of the North American, that is, the capitalist culture, industry, and as such relies fundamentally on advertising psychology. As a generalization one can say that the show's structure exhibits the characteristics of mass production in a particularly pointed and condensed form: in the construction of the plot as a family drama, in the characters' profiles, in the suspense curves of sequences and the separate installments, in the scenes and settings, in the use of music, and so on. The lowest common denominator is the organizing principle of the mass audience. Following this line of thought to its logical conclusion means that in its accumulation of clichés the TV series bases itself on attributes of anti-Semitic thinking—it possesses anti-Semitic elements. For even without the interspersed advertising spots—which is how the series was presented in the Federal Republic and also, for example, in England—its affinity with commodity aesthetics, its construction according to the dramaturgy of advertising, is evident. Admittedly, its subject is lethal anti-Semitism itself. "Holocaust" wants to denounce and condemn anti-Semitism, to show the suffering of its victims and render them comprehensible to the audience, to touch the emotions of the guilty, the uninvolved, the successive generations, and to arouse identification with the victims. In consequence it assails advertising as an accumulation of clichés with its very own strategies. "Holocaust" is not enlightenment, but *antiadvertising*.

But isn't that a tautology? In the age of advanced mass communication, where conditions prevail dominated by Coca-Cola, Disco, Wrigley's, and Levi's—in short, the cultural hegemony of commodity aesthetics—what else can enlightenment be other than antiadvertising? Doesn't one have to submit to the conditions of commodity exchange if one wants to convey anything to the army of consumers? In the face of these conditions, one can withdraw one's desire to instruct and refuse to have any part of them. But wouldn't this mean that one ends up talking to oneself? It is clear at least that it would not be possible to reach those whose everyday experience is dominated by the outward manifestations of commodity aesthetics—those for whom commodity circulation is the actual form of communication in work and leisure. If we take the Adorno/Horkheimer thesis as a starting point, does the quality of the commodity really play a role here? Is a distinction between the TV offerings "Nazi persecution of the Jews" and "Kojak" really significant at all? These are some of the questions—deliberately overstated, of course—that particularly preoccupied certain critical intellectuals before "Holocaust" was telecast, but only marginally afterward because the reaction of the country's inhabitants was so overwhelming. The program was discussed and debated and aroused mourning for a good week in firms, schools, around the dinner table, in pubs, living rooms, churches, and even within the hallowed halls of the German Parliament.

The Adorno quotation cited earlier occurred to me immediately after seeing the original American version of "Holocaust." A few months later, when official rejection of the series was at a pitch here, I thought increasingly of something another writer had said, one who like Adorno had fled to the United States from the Nazis: "The tenet—a work of art is a commodity—would be a tautological assertion if it were not for the fact that there is, nevertheless, something more of function in it, something which constitutes its main value."[6] With Brecht's insistence on the character of art—including industrially reproduced art—as a vehicle of use value and while keeping the "dialectic of Enlightenment" at the back of our minds, it may perhaps be possible to approach the phenomenon of "Holocaust" in the Federal Republic.

There were times one gained the impression from the discussions around and about "Holocaust" that the presentation of Nazi atrocities on the screen had only just begun with this TV series. Of course, the fact of the matter is that it was the first American TV series on this subject to penetrate German living rooms. The tradition of audiovisual expositions on the "Third Reich" and its crimes can be traced back to the period immediately after the liberation of Germany from fascism. The East German DEFA's first film, shot amidst the ruins of Berlin, is concerned not only with the victims but also very much with the guilty perpetrators. "Die Mörder sind unter uns" (The Murderers Are Among Us) by Wolfgang Staudte was premiered in October 1946. The female protagonist is a young Jewess, a survivor of the death camps who tries to settle down in bombed-out Berlin. It took a little longer in the western allied occupied zones. The first feature film to thematicize Nazi crimes against the Jews—amongst other subjects—had its premiere in June 1947—"In jenen Tagen" (In Those Days) directed by Helmut Käutner.[7]

In the former Soviet Occupied Zone—later the German Democratic Republic—the aesthetic treatment of fascism in films evolved into a distinctive subject that runs continuously through the GDR's film and television history. Some of the most important productions are "Ehe im Schatten" (1947), "Affaire Blum" (1948), "Rotation" (1949), "Der Rat der Götter" (1950), "Stärker als die Nacht" (1954), "Der Hauptmann von Köln" (1956), "Sterne" (1959), "Professor Mamlock" (1961), "Nackt unter Wölfen" (1963), "Die Abenteuer des Werner Holt" (1965), "Ich war neunzehn" (1968), "Trotz alledem!" (1972), "Jakob der Lügner" (1975), and "Mama, ich lebe" (1977). This represents only a selection of the feature films made on the subject. In addition, a large number of documentaries, miniseries (like the five-part "Krupp und Krause"), and TV plays have been produced. In accordance with the GDR's attitude toward fascism, this tradition of antifascism signifies neither a foremost nor an exclusive concern with anti-Semitism. Obviously some of the productions concentrate on this subject, like "Ehe im Schatten," "Affaire Blum," "Sterne," and "Jakob der Lügner," all of which, in the meantime, have practically become classics of this genre.

In the postwar West Zones, now the Federal Republic, many documentaries and compilations were produced. The most well known of these, Erwin Leiser's "Mein Kampf" (1960) and "Deutschland, erwache!" (1968), attempt antifascist instruction through the critical interpretation of original audiovisual documents of the Third Reich. In general, though, fictional or dramatic treatments of German fascism remain conspicuous by their absence from the cinematic screen.[8] Of course I am not referring here to the more or less apologetic war films, which enjoyed a veritable boom in the 1950s and early 1960s. Even the modest start that was made with feature films like "In jenen Tagen," "Morituri," "Zwischen Gestern und Morgen," and "Lang ist der Weg" was not continued. For a long time, "Rosen für den Staatswalt" (1959), which deals with the uninterrupted careers of Nazi judges in the Federal Republic, made by Wolfgang Staudte after he switched from the East German DEFA to western production companies, remained a notable exception. The first full-length cinematic production that centers on Nazi anti-Semitism belongs to the "post-Holocaust" era—"David" by Peter Lilienthal. The Berlin Film Festival, which highly acclaimed Lilienthal's film, took place in February 1979, shortly after the telecast of "Holocaust."

The tradition of the Holocaust's treatment on television is a slightly different story. Particularly in the 1960s, when the young Federal Republic was going through its first serious identity crisis, there were a number of dramatizations with an antifascist slant, i.e., Rolf Hädrich's TV play "Der Schlaf der Gerechten" (1965/66), Egon Monk's "Ein Tag. Bericht aus einem deutschen Konzentrationslager. Januar 1939" (1966), Dieter Meichsner's "Wie ein Hirschberger Dänisch lernte" (1969), Aleksander Ford's "Sie sind frei, Dr. Korczak" (1973, as a coproduction with Israel), or "Aus einem deutschen Leben" (1977), directed by Theodor Kotulla. Otherwise, West German TV producers, program directors, commercial film distributors, and the institutions responsible for educational film distribution depended on foreign films but only to a limited extent on those of the DEFA, mainly films from Poland, Yugoslavia, Czechoslovakia, the Soviet Union, and the United States. "The Diary of Anne Frank" (1959) directed by George Stevens must be mentioned here.

The recalcitrance on the part of most of the older generation of film directors regarding dramatic film treatments of fascism and its crimes against the Jews is not difficult to explain since they spent crucial years making their careers in the Nazi propaganda and dream factories. They were the ones to profit from the "elimination" of their Jewish colleagues from the film business or, at the very least, shut their eyes to it. Apparently though, the younger German cineasts have also had great difficulty in approaching the subject. Where attempts have been made, these have taken the form of trauma, as in the Fassbinder film "Ein Jahr mit dreizehn Monden." The figure of the former inmate of Bergen-Belsen, Anton Seitz, a social climber who rises from brothel manager to formidable property agent in Frankfurt, is a clumsy attempt at psychologizing a concentration-camp survivor. Apart from such exceptions, the Nazi genocide, its manifestations and consequences, is taboo.

This situation changed—to begin with, in a negative sense—just before the advent of "Holocaust." In the wake of the considerable boost given by Joachim C. Fest's and Christian Herrendoefer's film about the career of the dictator, the West German media were veritably swamped by a "Hitler-wave." Fascism even became an entertainment attraction in talk and quiz shows, or was used as a trapping in adventure series like "Es muss nicht immer Kaviar sein," which was based on a best-seller by the highly successful writer J. M. Simmel.[9] A boom in Nazi relics was noticeable at the flea markets of West Germany and Berlin. Prices for original editions of Hitler's *Mein Kampf* rocketed. Even the Stars of David that the Jews were forced to wear by the fascists were being hawked for hundreds of West German marks—provided they were the "real thing," of course!

This vogue was in full swing in April 1978 when news about the telecast of "Holocaust" in the United States began to spread. Here of all places, where the market for Nazi nostalgia was flourishing, where they had no compunction about producing Super-8 fascist pornos with swastikas on G-strings and gasps of "Heil Hitler!" between copulations, there was an outcry. Indignation about the commercialization of the Nazi genocide was the main tenor of the critics. Elie Wiesel's evaluation of the TV "Holocaust" as a trivialization of "an ontological event" that resulted in "a soap opera" was adopted by most of the large daily newspapers and broadcasting authorities. This quotation must have appeared hundreds of times or was simply paraphrased.

Precisely because afterward nobody wanted to talk about the initial indignant outburst, it is important to recall those first reactions of published opinion before the "Holocaust" telecast: *Der Spiegel,* which, incidentally, was full of praise for the event later on, was worried about "the German diplomats in the USA, for 'Holocaust' will provoke a new wave of anti-German feeling."[10] The *Frankfurter Allgemeine Zeitung* asked, on the verge of desperation, whether "horror is only comprehensible through banalities?" and retaliated with: "Mistrust of the undemonstrative power of authentic documents is the catch of this miniseries."[11] This in turn supported the imploring argument made by the chief moderator of the news show "Tagesthemen," Claus Stephan, in a telecast that went out on the air after the last installment was shown in the United States: "Not a fraction of the horror of a gas chamber can be conveyed in literal form, with the help of actors: quite the contrary. This artificial, supposedly artistic portrayal obliterates the ghastly truth. Any and every black-and-white photograph of a gas chamber taken after the end of Nazi rule has more effect: silent horror in the face of the murders committed." The *Rheinischer Merkur* moralized: "The most lenient objection to 'Holocaust' is that respect has been sacrificed here to play-acting: respect for reality and respect for the victims."[12] After an initially favorable review, Axel Springer's *Die Welt*, which after all can hardly polemicize much against its own market strategies, was soon complaining that genocide was being portrayed as a "Teutonic phenomenon" and demanding, in the good company of the conservative international law specialist Alfred de Zayas, a revision of American school textbooks because the TV guides in the United States that were distributed when "Holocaust" was telecast did not even take into account "the expulsion of Germans from Eastern Europe."[13]

However, these opinions changed. The hypocritical indignation over the marketing of Germany's past by the Americans was superseded by a political insight: the confrontation was inevitable. And this was due in no small measure to the fact that the Federal Republic was about to celebrate its thirtieth birthday and that international opinion had been following the "Hitler-wave" very attentively. The change of heart was further encouraged by the positive reception of the series in other countries. The United Kingdom's BBC was the first to show "Holocaust" in Europe. Audience response was not high, but the resonance in the press was considerable. Belgium followed suit and then—significantly—Israel, in September 1978. This was the external signal that prompted the final decision in favor of telecasting "Holocaust." Heinz Hübner, the program director of the Westdeutschen Rundfunk, the broadcasting authority had purchased the series, stated: "The film is a political issue, and, if it can be shown in the country [Israel] of those directly affected by the Holocaust, then it is not asking too much of the Germans if it is shown here, too—to those involved in those events and those who came after."[14]

At the end of October 1978, the telecast dates set for "Holocaust" (January 1979) were publicized, and then the public institutions began to prepare almost feverishly for the coming event. Institutions involved in political education commissioned TV guides. The Federal Center for

Political Education devised a nationwide representative survey on the subject. Teacher's unions produced teaching aids. Magazines planned and published special issues. The television authorities themselves produced two comprehensive documentaries designed to prepare the viewing public for the coming film.

These activities reached a first peak on the fortieth anniversary of the so-called "Night of the Broken Glass" ("Reichskristallnacht"). For the very first time—at least to my knowledge—a broad discussion of Nazi war crimes against German and European Jews took place. It was the first time that something akin to deep concern and the attempt to transmit this became apparent in the mass media. Pictures of burning synagogues filled the inside pages of the large daily newspapers or the front cover of illustrated weeklies. The provincial papers from Bavaria to the Frisian Islands published information, in most cases scrupulously collected and compiled, on what happened to the Jewish citizens in that particular region during the years 1938 to 1945. Again and again, the coming event "Holocaust" was the point of reference.

It was in the wake of this publicity, of this media-marathon for an anniversary of grief, that the cautious relegation of the series to the third channel was seen to be absurd. Long before the telecast, the "Holocaust" week had become a social event which no institution having any interest in the workings of West German minds could afford to ignore. The TV magazines of the largest publishing houses, Springer, Bauer, and Gruner & Jahr, did the rest. A week before the telecast they had nearly all the appropriate headlines on the cover of their publications and numerous articles inside: " 'Holocaust' on All Third Channels: The Drama of the Jews!" *(Fernsehwoche)*, "The Series that Moved the World" *(Gong)*, "For America It Was a Spectacle—and for Us?" *(Funk Uhr)*, "The Most Controversial TV Series of All Times Is Coming!" *(TV Hören und Sehen)*, and the like. Just because of the different TV magazines vying with one another and using superlatives, news of "Holocaust" must have reached over 80 percent of the West German adult population. Then there were the introductory television programs. The Arbeitsgemeinschaften der Rundfunkanstalten Deutschlands (ARD) made an attempt to prepare viewers for "Holocaust" with two of its own documentaries on the history and background of Nazi anti-Semitism which were produced especially for this occasion. Political parties, Jewish communities, and Christian church organizations encouraged people to watch the program. Last but not least, neo-Nazi activities (directed at the "6 million—the hoax of the century") contributed to the wide publicity; anti-Semitic leaflets, street-corner agitation, and, naturally, the most spectacular variation: bomb attacks on

Channel 1 transmitters during the second "Holocaust" introductory documentary.

Only against this background of very varied, extremely contradictory circumstances is it possible to account for the fact that almost a quarter of all West German TV sets were tuned in to the first installment of the miniseries in January 1979. What followed during the week "Holocaust" was telecast is unique in the history of Federal Republic television. Although considerably fewer than half of all TV households on the average tuned into the Third Channel,[15] virtually nothing else was talked about at places of socialization in our society: in schools, universities, factories, offices, and living rooms. There was always someone present who had seen "Holocaust" and who provoked discussions and arguments—about fascism, its origins, the persecution of the Jews, guilt, and responsibility. In short, not only what had been seen on TV was discussed but also issues of social and historical relevance that had greater ramifications.[16]

The American TV series about the families Weiss and Dorf succeeded in bringing about a phenomenon where documentaries, curriculae, stage plays, historical novels, poems, and feature films before it had failed. For many days words like Nazi crimes, concentration camps, anti-Semitism, Auschwitz, neo-Nazism, and, finally, the term "Holocaust" itself, pervaded and satiated the daily life of most West Germans. What had formerly been the province of a few educated circles and certain political groupings became a public event of the first order.

A Tentative Evaluation of the "Holocaust" Reception in West Germany

Since the telecast of "Holocaust" the question of its *effect* has been asked time and again and has remained unanswered just as often. Indeed, it would be difficult to offer a satisfactory and theoretically consistent answer to two incongruous premises: On the one hand, it is assumed that a heterogeneous product like the TV "Holocaust"—with regard to its ideological and aesthetic structure—which addresses itself to such a diverse audience could produce a *single* specific effect; on the other, it presumes the *series itself* is the cause of possible or observed effects. Here two simple findings can be advanced as an objection, yielded by several years of study of this national and international television event: The series produced as many dimensions of effect as it assembled different audience groups in front of the TV sets; the effects of "Holocaust" were manifold and qualitatively different—different both on an international level, but also within a given country like the Federal Republic. Furthermore, the series was part of a complex process of public discussion that functioned as a framework and itself interacted with the series: the four episodes of "Holocaust" can only be isolated from this context by an act of force.

For example, our analysis of the viewers' mail to the television authorities after the first telecast of "Holocaust" in 1979 (around nine thousand letters, telegrams, telexes, and postcards) found that the TV studio discussions after each installment played a far more important role with regard to the articulation of specific audience needs than did just the series alone.[17] This finding was confirmed when the series was rerun in November 1982—during prime time, on the first channel but without the mobilizing journalism of 1978–1979. The resonance—or lack of it, to be precise—could in no way be compared to that of the first telecast, which proved that this kind of backup is of crucial importance for the dimensions of qualitative effect of such a TV event.

For these reasons, *the* effect of the bare series "Holocaust" will not be my concern here. My interest lies in certain dimensions of the "Holocaust" event's effect. Among them is the question as to what functions the media event centering on "Holocaust" had for specific social groups and areas, and whether it has helped us in the Federal Republic along the difficult road of comprehending fascism and its crime of genocide against the Jews—with the object of preventing its happening again. The targets of scrutiny are thus behavioral modes, attitudes, and activities that could be observed in the wake of "Holocaust" and that referred explicitly to it. The selection presented may afford a glimmer of the greater whole to become more visible.

Public Agitation, Consternation, and Disavowal of Guilt
One read and heard everywhere that "Holocaust's" most outstanding feat was the "emotional shock" it produced. I must admit that this category means very little to me. Not only is it difficult to verify or substantiate, but my main problem with it is that it is too exclusively located in the emotional makeup of the individual, access to which is very difficult and usually well-nigh impossible.[18] Also, "shock" implies without consequence or paralysis, and "Holocaust" certainly was not without consequences.

Already before the telecast and immediately after, individual and social activities were discernible that were bound to have at least a limited influence. The broadcasting authorities received thousands of telephone calls and letters; newspapers, journals, and public institutions likewise received sacks of mail; intense discussions took place in both the public and private spheres: these are all signs of active thought and reflection processes not usually associated with everyday television consumption. For the viewers themselves, these activities had the function of making public what was occupying their thoughts. All are courses of action presupposing a high degree of excitement and concern while revealing nothing of the actual quality of this reaction. When in January 1980, the topical TV magazine *Report* showed a program about the crimes Germans committed against Soviet soldiers during the last war, a comparable storm of indignation was unleashed. That very evening, the television studios received over two thousand telephone calls, nearly all of which were outraged protests at this supposed "defamation of the Germans."

It is important to note that the agitation over "Holocaust" is certainly not deducible from elements of the series alone, such as presentation of brutal physical violence in the scenes depicting the gas chambers, mass murder, torture, and rape, nor from the appeal to the viewer's pity and the identification proffered with victims and murderers. The very way the whole "Holocaust" *event* was constructed demanded *public agitation:* the controversy over the decision to telecast it or not, the extensive coverage in the TV magazines, the concentration of the other mass media on the event, the compression of the experience into the space of a week, and the splitting of society into two camps—for and against "Holocaust." The nonviewers did not have much to say during that week because practically nothing else was discussed.

This visceral reaction is symptomatic of the gaping hole that must have existed in the minds and emotions of the viewers. "Holocaust's" impact sheds by no means a favorable light on the Federal Republic. On the contrary, it demonstrates the thirty-year-old failure of the mighty culture industry to transmit the experience of fascism and its capital crimes to the mass of the inhabitants of this country—moreover, to transmit them as complex, in a way that does not relegate the problems to an affair of intellectuals and does not bypass the emotions.

On the other hand, the agitation stirred up has been subject to much overinterpretation. It was attributed with a potential for drawing general conclusions about the development of politico-historical consciousness, that is, the assumption of long-term effects. These were hasty conclusions if society as a whole is being considered. Undoubtedly, the most prominent political event coinciding with the reaction to "Holocaust" was the debate about the statute of limitations for Nazi crimes. Results of the survey carried out by the Federal Center for Political Education demonstrate that those opposing limitation increased immediately after the telecast (although 39 percent is still way below half of the total population) but then 14 weeks later, the advocates of retaining limitation (that is, in favor of Nazi crimes no longer being prosecuted) had a relative majority of

41 percent.[19] This development took place *after* Parliament had already voted in favor of abolishing limitation for all cases of murder.

But the agitation caused by "Holocaust" had another dimension that pervaded private and public discussion then as now: the articulation of an overwhelming desire to be finished morally with the subject, in every sense of the word. This desire is shared in different ways by very disparate social groups, and it is attributable to extremely antithetical motives. For example, a large proportion of our parents' generation feel personally accused when reminded of the inhuman crimes of their former leaders and would dearly like to free themselves once and for all from the moral pressure weighing on them. This applies similarly to a section of the postwar generations to whom categories like "historic guilt" appear to mean less and less the younger they are. The two poles these generations represent came together in a striking manner with regard to their reactions to the invasion of Lebanon by Israel and specifically to the case of the massacres of Palestinians at Sabra and Chatila. At last it was time to adjust the balance. At last—or so it seemed—the one side was relieved of their burden and the other had found an opponent, who appeared to them to equal the Nazis' terror: In their eyes the victims had become offenders themselves. And they came so hastily to the historically and morally false conclusion that the Holocaust is *divisible;* the blame could be laid on the Jews for another Auschwitz—Sabra and Chatila. Even if this attitude did not come over so crassly in public,[20] it illustrated very clearly how far we still were, three years after the first telecast and in the wake of 1982's rerun, from understanding the history of the Nazi genocide.

The Mobilization of New Forms of (Self-)Consciousness

Whereas for three decades in postwar West Germany the connection in any positive way to German fascism had been prohibited, it became very apparent that "Holocaust" had had a "liberating" function on this taboo. The growth of a new self-consciousness amongst those who had "gone along" with fascism, who had "taken part," is still for me today one of the strangest effects of the event. Accepted authorities and powerful figures who determine public opinion like the editors of *Der Spiegel* and *Stern*, Rudolf Augstein and Henri Nannen, made loud and perfidiously "honest" confessions (and presumably expected admiration for it): "Did I really know nothing at all about it? Yes and no. We all knew Dachau. Dachau stood for incarceration and Nazi brutality—for all concentration camps. I came home from the war on the eastern front knowing nothing about gas chambers or the systematic murdering. War had made me insensitive. I suddenly realized that all the time my one concern had been my own and my family's fate. I had lost sight of the fate of the Jews" (Rudolf Augstein).[21] "I, at any rate, I knew that in Germany's name defenseless people were being exterminated in the way vermin are extinguished. And unashamed, I wore the uniform of an officer in the German air force. Yes, I knew about it and was too cowardly to resist. Was there anything I could have done at that point in time? That is not the question" (Henri Nannen).[22]

In a kind of way, it became rather socially decorous to have "been around then" and to publish your sincere or just recently concocted struggles with your conscience. It was not the resistance fighters nor the victims who were now put forward as an example but instead, the pitiable fellow travelers. Obviously one of the reasons lay in the massive positive echo this met with in the general public. For many this was a common decisive experience. Long before television's "Holocaust," Elie Wiesel had anticipated this turn of public opinion. In a justifiable overstatement, he alludes to the relationship between public opinion and the victims and survivors of the concentration camps: "It will not be long before they are felt to be unwelcome intruders. The spotlights are now on the murderers. These are presented in film, they are analyzed in detail, they are endowed with characteristic human traits. At first they are viewed objectively, then with sympathy."[23] It is a worthwhile exercise to examine the dramatic construction of the figure of Erich Dorf, the Nazi protagonist of "Holocaust," in the light of this statement.

This phenomenon was also characteristic—albeit in a diminished form—at the level of representative politics. It was not a politician like Willy Brandt, who emigrated because of the Nazis, was active in the resistance movement, and is reviled even today as a "traitor to the people" because of it (and not only by the Nazi press), who threw himself into the moral fray, but it was his party comrade and Federal Chancellor, Helmut Schmidt. As a former Wehrmacht soldier at the front, he shares his biography with the majority of German men now over fifty and thus provides the exemplary model for identification. The most penetrating instance of this took place about seven months after the telecast of "Holocaust." Against the venerable backdrop of the Berlin Reichstag, Schmidt braved the harmless questions of a few American, English, and French journalists. This live television broadcast completely and utterly vindicated all those present, on or off screen. The TV flock of the Federal Republic, which had gathered together for the occasion, listened sympathetically to their chancellor. He told of the scruples and prickings of conscience that he had because of the contradiction between the demands of social duty and knowing why he was required to obey. No one contradicted, delved deeper, or attempted a provocation, neither during the program nor in the press reports that followed. Is it any wonder, then, that criticism of the top politician and West German figurehead, Karl Carstens, formerly in Nazi service, has become so quiet as to be inaudible? The opposite is true. Sympathy with him is going up all the time. After all, he is in office now, and respect is due to that much authority, isn't it? A good illustration is the conservative *Frankfurter Allgemeine Zeitung*'s little résumé of December 1979: "Before the election of the present Federal President, there was some legitimate criticism of a candidate as to whether he was fit for what is, after all, a political office, and there were also the jarring war cries of some of his political opponents. Today, after the first six months in office, neither the office nor its new holder has sustained any lasting injury. Carstens is becoming acquainted with his new duties."[24] In a society that has elevated the *career* to the highest of ethical values, it cannot and must not be reprehensible to subordinate one's duty to resist to the exigencies of one's career.

But "Holocaust" awakened another, positive, variety of new self-awareness in those social minorities who were also victims of the Nazi regime of violence. They are still suffering in the present day because of their identity—Gypsies, homosexuals, the politically persecuted. For the first time in the history of the Federal Republic, their voices have been heard loudly and frequently in public demanding recognition and ideological and material redress. Perhaps this protest was provoked by the fact that the TV series hardly touched on their persecution and suffering. They have started to insist on their rights and to publicize their story—with increasing success.

Removing the Taboos and Playing Down History

The adaptation of the historical Holocaust according to the principles of commodity aesthetics of commercial television production made it possible for the first time to give an international mass audience access to aspects of that horrible reality. After all, more than a quarter of a billion people in thirty-two countries watched "The Story of the Family Weiss" the first time it was screened. In West Germany the audience numbered approximately 12 million. In an international comparison of audience size, however, the Federal Republic was only in sixth place, and in the ratings list of all countries that screened "Holocaust," we occupied only seventeenth place. Nevertheless, for many, especially younger viewers, it was the first confrontation with a part of the history of the European Jews and their tormenters, since this part of German history was one which had hitherto been rigorously excluded from public debate in our institutions of education. The ceremonies of the annual "Week of Fraternity" or commemorations of the *Kristallnacht* (1938), dramas like Peter Weiss's *The Investigation* or Rolf Hochhuth's *The Deputy*, the shamefully few trials of the former concentration-camp butchers of Maidanek, Dachau, and Auschwitz—these were registered by only a fragment of the general public, part of the cultural and political elite. But because of the TV series the word "Holocaust" passed into the common language and replaced to a certain extent terms borrowed from the bureaucratic euphemisms of the Nazis, like "Final Solution." HOLOCAUST became a metaphor for inhumanity.

But this process of lifting taboos was also two-sided, and the negative one has begun to predominate. What Elie Wiesel anticipated after the miniseries's premiere in the United States—that this "ontological event" would be dragged down to the level of everyday normality—has begun to come about in the past years in the most vehement fashion and accompanied by the most incredible phenomena.

In the public consciousness one Holocaust has become many. The TV series unleashed a veritable Holocaust inflation. The metaphor was drained of historical content, and since then has been applied to each and every event manifesting inhuman dimensions of violence: the "Nuclear Holocaust" (although this is one example where the ontological analogy is least controversial), the "Holocaust in Cambodia," the "Armenian Holocaust," the "Palestinian Holocaust," and so on, through to the marketing of the term by the culture industry: Rock music promoters billed a gig of several bands as a "Heavy Metal Holocaust" and the final most degenerate use is the film title "Zombie Holocaust," which is sold on the European home video cassette market by CBS Records—amongst others—a video "nasty" of the cannibalism genre.

One would not feel outraged at these faux pas—to put it mildly—of the culture industry and a few businessmen who think themselves particularly smart were it not for the fact that there are parallels in the public discussions in society. The spectacular remarks of Heiner Geissler, a present minister and general secretary of the Christian Democratic Union (CDU), placing the blame for Auschwitz on those who died there,[25] or the recent characterization of the Nazi pogroms as "still human" compared to the social system of the Soviet Union, also by a CDU politician,[26] were evaluated by public opinion as *individual* blunders, which—and this is part of the contradiction—unleashed a furor of protest, not only from victims. These examples stand at the same time for the loss of adequate consciousness vis à vis the unique individuality of the historic Holocaust, a loss that threatens to become greater as time passes and the warning voices of witnesses are silenced by death. This loss of political and moral culture has already had consequences for everyday life in West Germany. People have become quick to make comparisons with the Nazi era. A few broken windows at young squatters' demonstrations are put on a par with the terrors of the Nazis' "Night of Broken Glass"; members of the Green Party are compared directly with the Nazis; members of the peace movement exhibited a complete lack of historical and moral sensibility by holding nocturnal *Mahnwachen* (warning vigils) on members of Parliaments' doorsteps before the Bundestag's vote on the deployment of new nuclear weapons; the harmless—and justified—occupation of an alternative West Berlin magazine's offices by women's groups was termed a "Rollkommando." The TV "Holocaust" has contributed to fascism's being dragged into the arena of everyday conflicts, and we must be very careful indeed lest in this way it become everyday and banal.

Neo-Nazis: The Double Edge of Increased Publicity

Onlookers in other countries may have gained the impression from the event "Holocaust" in West Germany that the neo-Nazi movement here has expanded and spread. This is not so, but it has not diminished either. What did happen was that it acquired a quality it did not possess two years ago: the movement commands a great deal of public attention and tries to get more in an increasingly militant way. This is one of the most obviously contradictory functions that "Holocaust" helped provoke. Although the general public and the mass media have become more sensitive to what is happening on the extreme Right, the neo-Nazis on the other hand have become more greedy for publicity and attempt to create it by staging spectacular provocations. Only very few of these are ever brought before a court of law. Nonetheless, the Federal Crime Department's list of offences by neo-Nazis exposed in 1979, the year "Holocaust" was first telecast, is menacing: "Fifteen hundred and eighty cases of seizing and impounding literature, 3,400 of distribution of newspapers, journals, posters, and leaflets, 447 of daubings on walls, 24 of desecration of graveyards, 22 of bodily injury, 18 of seizure of weapons, 5 of arson, 3 of planted explosives, 3 of threatened assassination."[27] And this is only part of the extensive catalogue.

Even more brutal is the fact that neo-Nazi militancy has succeeded in intimidating sections of the populace. The following is taken from a report of the German news agency, ddp, on one of the most active neo-Nazi groups, the "Wiking Jugend," in December 1979, and the last sentence sounds only too familiar: "According to security service information, about 30 young people are members of the 'Wiking Jugend' in Berlin, and they wear uniform-like clothes. This clothing is mainly black with high boots. Since the beginning of this year, they have increasingly engaged in violent activities, according to police sources. Thus several fights have been picked by the group. A series of searches of group members' houses resulted in the seizure of warning shot and gas weapons as well as truncheons. The insecurity caused in the general public by this group is being taken 'very seriously' by the police. *However, inquiries were being impeded because persons threatened and molested by members of the group often only gave evidence to the police very reluctantly"* (my emphasis, S. Z.).

All this belongs to the immediate context of the "Holocaust" event. Some of the actions by neo-Nazis in West Berlin even referred directly to it, as when a discussion was interrupted in the "Haus der Kirche" by a "Storm Troop" in the spring of 1979. The double edge of the publicity accorded such actions showed later that the organized right wing was becoming increasingly militant, not even shrinking from murder. Twelve people died and 213 were severely injured in a bomb explosion at the Munich Oktoberfest in 1980 because of a bomb planted by an associate of the Hoffmann Group. "The neo-Nazis have been underestimated" was the unanimous opinion of the press. Those who had given this very warning at the time of the "Holocaust" event were either not taken seriously or branded as out-of-touch left-wingers.

In recent years young people have been showing increasing affinity with the extreme Right. It is they who are affected most by social declassification and isolation. The tightly organized nucleus of the neo-Nazis has successfully recruited new members from various youth subcultures that are particularly vulnerable to fascist ideology, like the skinheads or football rowdies. Since the Federal Republic, too, has begun to feel the impact of capitalism's present structural crisis, the image of their foe has changed— or at least outwardly. The immigrants and particularly the Turkish "guest workers" are the Jews of today. They know full well that this choice meets with broad agreement on the part of the silent majority.

In the fight against the new and old Nazis, it is of crucial importance that another section of youth come to realize what dangers their future may hold. Using their own means of expression, they will certainly achieve more than the most well-meaning institutionalized pedagogy. One outstanding example of many is the "Holocaust" song of the post-punk band "Tank of Danzig":

Holocaust

You read it in a book
You saw it on the TV screen
To you it's a nightmare
To some it's a dream, a dream

Remember Belsen, remember Auschwitz
They try to say they didn't exist

Don't let them put this country in chains
Don't let six million die in vain, in vain

They hide their real character
Behind the German flag
You'd better watch out
They are hiding for a comeback, a comeback

Belsen
Auschwitz
Dachau.

Activation of the Cultural Sector

In the politico-cultural sphere, the functional event of "Holocaust" as enlightenment was fruitful, the most visible effects being in the educational institutions. School students, who had never heard anything about the Nazi genocide, pressed their teachers to deal with the subject in class. Other teachers used the provocative occasion to thematicize a subject that was long overdue. The effects of this were not limited to the immediate teaching situations. More visits to concentration camps were arranged. The desire to talk to survivors of the Holocaust or members of the resistance was voiced. Particularly, the concept of antifascism attained a new status. Working groups of school students constituted for the purpose organized a special antifascist "Day" or "Week," often in the face of resistance by the school bureaucracy and individual teachers. At these events, photo documentations of Nazi atrocities, among other things, were compiled and exhibited, plays staged, discussions held, and other activities arranged.

This movement in the schools, which is continuing, is also not free of contradiction. On the forty-first anniversary of the "Reichkristallnacht" (which, like the following examples, was hardly mentioned in the press) there were individual cases of stiff opposition from school students to the subject being handled in class. Many of my friends are teachers, and they reported cases of massive protest among "their" school kids at the past being "dragged up" yet again. Although remarks like "It was the Jews' own fault" and "Too few were gassed anyway" were rare, it is ominous that their classmates did not put up any opposition; they reacted with uncertainty and disinterest.

A particular occurrence at this time serves to illustrate official reaction to the school students' informative activities. At a West Berlin trade school, the school administration organized the first "Anticommunist Week"—as a necessary counterweight to the antifascist activities, said the director. In the future it will be held annually as "Antitotalitarian Week." In this way, the original opponent is exchanged for the desired opponent in the present—totalitarian theory in practice.

In the domain of the visual and performing arts, "Holocaust" led to the rediscovery of a subject—pictures from the concentration camps and everyday life under the Nazis. Socially committed galleries put together exhibitions with themes like "Children in the Concentration Camps" (Elefantenpress Galerie, West Berlin) or "Resistance: Not Conformism" (Cultural Office, Karlsruhe) which included works used in "Holocaust." The most impressive is "Survival and Resistance," a cooperative exhibition of the West German "German-Polish Society" and the State Museum of Oswieçim-Brzezinka (Auschwitz-Birkenau), which has been touring major cities for months and has met with a great and positive response.

But of far greater significance than the numerous activities emanating from the media event was their content—the way the series was utilized as a starting point. The story of the Weiss and Dorf families disclosed a meaningful way to confront the past in that it dealt primarily with the everyday experiences of the murderers and their victims. Moreover, this was accomplished without totally neglecting the level of high politics. In this way, "Holocaust" succeeded above all in giving the postwar generations an idea of how people lived under fascism. And afterward, this served as a useful point of departure. Since then, there have been many instances of the encouragement of "oral history," of people taking up the search for traces of everyday life under the Hitler regime. Many places in West Germany have thus acquired regular historical signposts. For example, in West Berlin a youth organization, the Stadtjugendring, organizes tours of the city to "famous sites in the history of the Labor Movement, Fascism, and the Resistance." This is an attempt to remedy the fact that for many young people the imposing architectural remains of power and persecution, such as the Reichstag, the Jewish Community Center in the Fasanenstrasse where once the great synagogue stood, the elegant villa in Wannsee where fanatical German bureaucrats decreed the "Final Solution" for the Jews forty years ago, or the execution factory at Plötzensee, have become so much dead matter. In particular, the fiftieth anniversary of the Nazi seizure of power was used as an opportunity to delve into the history of whole districts of Berlin like Kreuzberg, Neukölln, and Wilmersdorf. The results were presented to the public at exhibitions, in brochures, and in films. Streets, sites, and names became known again even though they are not in history textbooks.[28]

One of the most remarkable signs of a modification in cultural consciousness was the thematicization of the long-forgotten and repressed Yiddish culture here. After a number of committed art cinemas—like the Kommunales Kino in Frankfurt or the Arsenal in West Berlin—had organized highly regarded festivals of Yiddish films, Zweite Deutsche Fernseh (ZDF) risked offering such a program in 1983 to a mass TV audience. The genre's history was presented in an introductory film, "Das Jiddische Kino," and in March and April the second channel screened three of the most seminal works: Joseph Green's "Ein Brief an die Mutter" (1938); Maurice Schwartz's "Tewje, der Milchmann" (1939); and "Jidl mit der Fiedel" by Green/Przybylski (1936). This was undoubtedly the first authentic contact with the Yiddish language and culture for the majority of West German viewers.

And forty-four years after the infamous anti-Semitic treatment for the edification of concentration-camp henchmen and the ideological mobilization of the populace, the most controversial and popular figure in recent Jewish-German history made a reappearance: "Joseph Süss Oppenheimer" is the title of a new documentary drama by Gerd Angermann, that ZDF set in contrast to the fascist film interpretation "Jud Süss" by Veit Harlan.[29] Just how sensitive this taboo area is in the consciousness of public institutions is demonstrated by the vacillations over the projected screening date of this program. The original date set was January 24, 1984, but because of Chancellor Kohl's trip to Israel on the same day, the telecast was postponed until February 14. The ZDF press office explained that they did not wish to encumber the "rather sensitive visit of the Chancellor to Israel with even a hint of problems."[30] The widespread identification—Jews = Israelis, which is part of the ideological fundament for the reversal of the victims/perpetrators roles during the Lebanon conflict finds its adequate representation here in the attitude of our state-run television authorities.

In West Germany, probably more than in other countries, the two central categories of content in television communication are opposing ones: information and entertainment. This point of view is shared not only by the producers of aesthetic commodities and the program directors but also by their critics. The mixing of information with entertaining strategies is forbidden, just as entertainers successfully defend themselves against having anything to do with society. Thus, on West German TV, dry political magazines or features coexist with mindless shows and quiz programs, unattractive news broadcasts with detective series or "pure" sport.

This strict division of labor received a provocative challenge from the "Holocaust" event. In the discussion on the pros and cons of telecasting the series, care was taken to point out that there was more to this American family story than adventure, crime, love, tears, and the fascination of horror. The fact that "Holocaust" was consigned to the Third Channel confirmed that the program directors were scared stiff of any wide popular effect it might have. At the same time, this is symbolic of the contradiction within the American TV series itself: An important historical theme has been dismantled, cut up into snacks for easy consumption, which stimulates the famous tingling in the stomach, evokes sorrow, hatred, identification, and at the same time throws up questions, triggers discussion, and activates the gray matter.

This describes a qualitatively new phenomenon in the development of the culture industry, actuated by the American entertainment factory, which is, anyway, the most developed in existence. Marketing is suddenly no longer one-dimensional but ambiguous. The purity of the charge of manipulation brought against everything this factory churns out does not hold good when confronted with a decisive slice of German and world history that has been turned into a commodity. In spite of the commercial packaging of the Nazi mass murder, the subject loses little of its monstrous explosiveness and still provokes proportionate contention.

The "Holocaust" of television is not the only example of this phenomenon and its young tradition. Indicative of this trend are, for example, the TV series "Roots" or "King" and the cinema productions reflecting the Vietnam experience like "The Deer Hunter," "Coming Home," and the most spectacular, "Apocalypse Now." It seems that the culture industry has discovered social contention and reflection as a medium of marketing the goods. It appropriates the social issue, but—and this takes place independently of its intention—by doing this the issue itself becomes effective in a mass context for the first time. The discussion is wrenched away from its confinement in intellectual circles and placed firmly in the area of everyday public debate.

All this could not fail to affect the way that West German television dealt with fascism and especially the mass murders against the Jews. In addition to the standard documentaries, a considerable number of new productions modeled themselves directly on the dramaturgical and aesthetic principles of the NBC series without actually trying to copy it. Both for TV and cinema, the most popular subject became the *biographical film* (or series) that very often used literary autobiographies as a basis for the script.[31] These included: "Die Welt in jenem Sommer" (January 1980), directed by Ilse Hoffmann and based on the autobiographical novel of the same name by Robert Muller, who has never returned to Germany from exile in England; "Kaiserhofstrasse 12" by Ann Ladiges and Rainer Wolffhardt, based on the book by Valentin Senger, telecast December 1980; "Die Kinder aus Nr. 67 oder: Heil Hitler, ich hätt' gern ein paar Pferdeäppel," a feature film set in the milieu of Berlin's "Hinterhöfe" by Usch Bartelmess-Weller and Werner Meyer and which was first shown in 1980 in cinemas and then screened by ZDF in March 1982; "Ein Stück Himmel," an eight-part miniseries based on Janina David's autobiography, directed by Franz Peter Wirth and telecast by ARD April–June 1982; Ottokar Runze's cinema film "Stern ohne Himmel," in which film buffs can detect a sarcastic piece of casting by the director: One of the adult protagonists is played by Malte Jäger, who in 1940 played Karl Faber, the Aryan opponent of "Jud Süss" in the film directed by Veit Harlan. One aspect all these films have in common is the story perspective: All share the child's or teenager's view of the world of victims and their persecutors. Another common aspect is their thematic level: All concentrate on everyday life and on the death and survival of Jewish children and youngsters and the way their "Aryan" contemporaries treat them. For this reason they are of great importance for the younger generations in West Germany and deserve similar promotion to that afforded "Holocaust." But only one other film—a miniseries—has received a measure of that: "Blut und Ehre, Jugend unter Hitler" ("Blood and Honor"), which in the meantime has also been screened in the United States and would certainly have been unthinkable without "Holocaust." It is an exciting piece of TV entertainment about life under the brown dictatorship from the perspective of children and teenagers.

"Holocaust" as antiadvertising, caught between entertainment, which renders its subject harmless, and provocative—professional culture critics did not want to resolve this immanent contradiction in 1979 and opted instead for one side of it or the other. The culture industry has now long since synthesized these antitheses and recognized that with the growing significance of entertainment the need for interpretation and orientation has also grown. At the beginning of 1984, "The Day After" was screened in West Germany, the CBS film about a fictitious nuclear war. Although the voices are not nearly so heated, the same arguments are being put forward in a discussion about the permissibility and ethical integrity of combining commercial considerations with a warning about the nuclear catastrophe, just as was the case five years ago. To take this product of the culture industry and use it as a fruitful point of departure, to develop its effects further as was done successfully in many instances with "Holocaust," would certainly be energy spent in a meaningful way. This would mean the development of a *dialectic of entertainment*, not originating from the products of mass culture themselves, but in the way we utilize them.

Translated by Gloria Custance

NOTES

1. Friedrich Knilli/Siegfried Zielinski, eds., *Holocaust zur Unterhaltung. Anatomie eines internationalen Bestsellers* (Berlin, 1982). F. Knilli/S. Zielinski, eds., *Betrifft "Holocaust"— Zuschauer schreiben an den WDR*. Projektbericht unter Mitarbeit von E. Gundelsheimer, H. Mass, und F. Ostermann (Berlin, 1983). These publications also contain comprehensive bibliographies of international research literature.

2. Theodor W. Adorno, "Zur Bekämpfung des Antisemitismus heute," *Das Argument* 6 (1964), p. 29.

3. Max Horkheimer and T. W. Adorno, *Dialektik der Aufklärung* (Amsterdam, 1968), pp. 199ff.

4. Adorno, "Bekämpfung."

5. Adorno, "Bekämpfung."

6. Bertolt Brecht, *Gesammelte Werke*, vol. 18 (Frankfurt am Main, 1967), p. 201.

7. For a detailed analysis of these two films, see Siegfried Zielinski, "Faschismusbewältigungen im frühen deutschen Nachkriegsfilm," *Sammlung 2. Jahrbuch für antifaschistische Literatur und Kunst*, ed. Uwe Naumann (Frankfurt am Main, 1979), pp. 124–133.

8. I have not included treatments of this subject in other media, i.e., the stage plays by Max Frisch *(Andorra)*, Rolf Hochhuth *(Der Stellvertreter* and his latest *Die Juristen)*, and Peter Weiss *(Die Ermittlung)*. All are of importance for the cultural history of the Federal Republic, and a study of their relationships would be of great value.

9. Cf. my essay on "Fascism as 'Entertainment'" in *Konkret* 8 (1978), p. 42. For the Fest-Herrendoerfer Hitler film, see Jörg Berlin, *Was verschweigt Fest? Analysen und Dokumente zum Hitler-Film* (Cologne, 1978).

10. *Der Spiegel* (July 17, 1978).

11. *Frankfurter Allgemeine Zeitung* (April 20, 1978).

12. *Rheinischer Merkur* (April 28, 1978).

13. *Die Welt* (July 10, 1978).

14. *Holocaust: Der Mord an den Juden als Fernsehserie*, Dokumentation des Evangelischen Pressedienstes (Frankfurt, 1979).

15. By way of comparison, the 11-part TV dramatization of the German classic *Buddenbrooks* by Thomas Mann, which was screened a few months later in 1979, had audience participation averaging 46 percent for the first 7 installments. That is nearly 10 percent more than "Holocaust's" average of 37 percent over four nights.
The survey carried out by the Federal Center for Political Education in Bonn paid particular attention to the conversations and discussions that went on during and after the event. For a summary of the results see Tilman Ernst, "Umfragen der Bundeszentrale für politische Bildung," *Bild der Wissenschaft* 6 (Stuttgart, 1979), pp. 74–80.

17. Knilli/Zielinski, *Betrifft Holocaust—Zuschauer schreiben an den WDR*.

18. In November 1982 the ratings averaged 23 percent, i.e., considerably lower than for the first telecast in 1979. Just how little was done in preparation for the rerun can be seen from the fact that Part I reached a mere 16 percent whereas the last installment did at least achieve 30 percent.

19. Cf. T. Ernst, "Umfragen," and T. Ernst, "'Holocaust' und politische Bildung (Ergebnisse der dritten Befragungswelle)" in *Media Perspektiven* (December 1979), pp. 819–827.

20. To cite just one example, a passage from an interview with the French writer Jean Genet which appeared in the first issue of the magazine *TIP* (West Berlin) in 1984. Both answer and *question* are not lacking in clarity:
"TIP: Could one say that the Palestinians are the Jews of today? Genet: Yes. Today the Palestinians are the martyrs *(Volk der Märtyrer)*, and the Jews are the Nazis *(Nazi-Volk)*."
At the Institute for Media Studies, Technical University Berlin, the press coverage of the war in Lebanon was systematically analyzed over a specific period in 1982. See "Inhaltsanalyse der Berichterstattung in vier überregionalen Tageszeitungen der Bundesrepublik Deutschland über den Libanon-Krieg und die Massaker von Sabra und Schatila," unpublished final report, (TU Berlin, 1983).

21. *Der Spiegel* (January 29, 1979), p. 20.

22. *Der Stern* (February 1, 1979), p. 5.

23. Elie Wiesel, "For Some Measure of Humility," *Sh'ma* 5/100 (October 1975). Cited according to Bruno Bettelheim, "Holocaust—Überlegungen ein Menschenalter danach," *Der Monat* (December 1978), p. 15.

24. *Frankfurter Allgemeine Zeitung* (December 18, 1979).

25. Heiner Geissler said this in front of the Bundestag during one of the debates on the deployment of new American medium-range missiles (Pershing II) by way of a comparison to the present-day peace movement which he made responsible for an eventual World War III.

26. It was the CDU member of Parliament Anton Feyssen from Hildesheim who made this comparison in November 1983 during a public debate. For further details and protest of Heinz Galinski, president of the Jewish Community in Berlin, the *Frankfurter Rundschau* (December 12, 1983).

27. *Die Tat* (December 7, 1979), p. 1.

28. These activities by galleries, youth centers, district cultural departments, artist's associations, etc., were coordinated by the "Berliner Kulturrat," constituted expressly for this purpose. It gave rise to considerable controversy, for the Berlin Senat then refused to supply the funds necessary for a majority of the various activities. Cf. Berliner Kulturrat, eds., "1933 Zerstörung der Demokratie—Machtübergabe und Widerstand, Ausstellungen und Veranstaltungen, Programm 1983" (Berlin, 1983).

29. Cf. Knilli/Maurer/Radevagen/Zielinski, *JUD SÜSS—Filmprotokoll, Programmheft und Einzelanalysen* (Berlin, 1983). For the controversy over the director of "Jud Süss" and the legal trials for "crimes against humanity" against him, see my book *Veit Harlan—Analysen und Materialien zur Auseinandersetzung mit einem Film-Regisseur des deutschen Faschismus* (Frankfurt, 1981).

30. *Frankfurter Allgemeine Zeitung* (December 17, 1983), p. 24.

31. Cf. S. Zielinski, "Aspekte des Faschismus als Kino und Fernseh-Sujet. Tendenzen zu Beginn der 80er Jahre," in *Sammlung 4, Jahrbuch für antifaschistische Literatur und Kunst,* ed. Uwe Naumann, (Frankfurt, 1981), pp. 47–56.

Anti-Semitism: A Reassessment

15

THE JEWS AND THE FRANKFURT SCHOOL

CRITICAL THEORY'S ANALYSIS OF ANTI-SEMITISM

Martin Jay

The posthumous appearance of Max Horkheimer's *Notizen* of 1950 to 1969 in the same volume as a new edition of *Dämmerung,* his aphorisms of 1926 to 1931,[1] amply documents many of the transformations of the theoretical and political positions of the Frankfurt School's leading figure. None is perhaps so striking as that of his attitude toward anti-Semitism and what was once known as "the Jewish question." In the later collection, at least a dozen entries discuss these and related issues, often from the very personal vantage point of a survivor of the Holocaust. In contrast, *Dämmerung* virtually ignores anti-Semitism as a problem in its own right and has little to say about the plight of the Jews in Weimar Germany. The one major exception is an aphorism entitled "Glaube und Profit" (Belief and Profit), which contains a debunking reduction of Jewish identity to class interests: "As the material base of ghetto life was left behind, the willingness to sacrifice life and property to one's religious belief also became a thing of the past. Among bourgeois Jews, the hierarchy of goods is neither Jewish nor Christian but bourgeois. The Jewish capitalist brings sacrifices to power, just like his Aryan class colleague. He first sacrifices his own superstition, then the lives of others, and finally his capital. The Jewish revolutionary in Germany is not different from his 'Aryan' comrade. He commits his life to the liberation of man."[2]

The young Horkheimer's facile dismissal of specifically Jewish problems

287

was shared, at least in their written work, by all his colleagues at the Frankfurt Institute of Social Research, whose director he became in 1930. Indeed, their tendency to subsume anti-Semitism under the larger rubric of class conflict persisted throughout the 1930s even after the Nazi seizure of power and their forced emigration to America in 1934. In their collective project of 1935, *Studien über Autorität und Familie* (Studies on Authority and the Family), no specific discussion of anti-Semitism was attempted in either the theoretical or the empirical sections of the work.[3] Nor were the Jews mentioned in such institute treatments of Nazi or völkisch ideology as Herbert Marcuse's "Der Kampf gegen den Liberalismus in der totalitären Staatsauffassung" (The Struggle against Liberalism in the Totalitarian Concept of the State) of 1934 or Leo Lowenthal's "Knut Hamsun. Zur Vorgeschichte der autoritären Ideologie" (Knut Hamsun. On the Prehistory of Authoritarian Ideology) of 1937.[4] And although anti-Semitism was introduced into Theodor W. Adorno's analysis of Wagner, where it was related to the sadomasochistic dynamics of the composer's worldview, only fragments of that work appeared in the institute's journal, its full publication coming not until 1952.[5]

When Horkheimer did finally compose an essay entitled "Die Juden und Europe" (The Jews and Europe) in 1939,[6] he continued to subsume anti-Semitism under the more general rubric of the crisis of capitalism. The predicament of the Jews, he claimed, reflected the liquidation of the sphere of economic circulation in which they had been particularly active. Moreover, he went on, Nazi anti-Semitic propaganda was directed more at external audiences than internal ones; the German people were themselves not its major target. Not surprisingly, other German Jews more sensitive to the complexities and dangers of the situation, such as Gershom Scholem,[7] were outraged at the essay, which seemed little more than an echo of Marx's controversial remarks in his treatise on the Jewish question of a century before.

In their faithfulness to Marx's own attitude toward anti-Semitism, Horkheimer and his colleagues conformed to a pattern that many observers have noted: the more radical the Marxist, the less interested in the specificity of the Jewish question.[8] Of all the members of the German socialist movement in both the Wilhelmian and Weimar eras, the revisionists were the most attentive to anti-Semitism as a problem in its own right. And of course, the Institute of Social Research had no use for revisionism in any form. Its members tended as well to hold to another pattern that often accompanied this inverse relationship between radicalism and sensitivity to anti-Semitism: Those among them with Jewish backgrounds rarely, if ever, found their ethnic identities significant for their work. Not until the 1950s, when Horkheimer in particular attempted to compensate for his earlier neglect,[9] was this latter pattern reversed. In addition to the *Notizen* published only after his death, and which are mentioned above, he published several essays affirming his commitment to the Jewish community and even alleging that certain aspects of his Critical Theory could be traced to Jewish influences.[10] None of his former colleagues went this far, but it is more than likely that they all shared an awareness of the insufficiency of their prewar attitudes on these issues.

It was, in fact, during the war that their position began to change. Plans were laid for a major project devoted to anti-Semitism,[11] and works written under the institute's auspices, such as Franz Neumann's *Behemoth,* began to pay more attention to the problem.[12] A brief glance at the latter will show, however, how hesitant the shift was at first. Although *Behemoth* was in some ways, particularly in its critical attitude toward the concept of state capitalism,[13] at odds with mainstream institute thinking, its treatment on anti-Semitism seems to have been fairly representative of the general attitude. In the work's first edition, published in 1942, Neumann devoted a chapter to "Racism and Anti-Semitism." He distinguished between totalitarian and nontotalitarian variants of the phenomenon, the former based on "magic and beyond discussion,"[14] the latter preserving "remnants of rationality"[15] and thus open to analysis. The rationality in question was above all that of economics: the distribution of the spoils among strata of the population necessary for the regime's support, the distorted satisfaction of the anticapitalist longings of the German people,"[16] the displacement of the aggressive energies of class struggle, and the justification of eastern expansion. Although Neumann recognized religious sources of anti-Semitism as well as purely social ones, his main emphasis was on its economic rationality. Because of this stress and the concomitant belief that anti-Semitism was manipulated from above rather than spontaneously generated from below, Neumann could reveal that "the writer's personal conviction, paradoxical as it may seem, is that the German people are the least anti-Semitic of all."[17] In this belief, he was at one with his institute colleagues.[18]

In the second edition of *Behemoth,* which appeared in 1944, Neumann appended a section on anti-Semitism in which he acknowledged the new ruthlessness of Nazi policy toward the Jews but still saw it as "only the means to the attainment of the ultimate objective, namely the destruction of free institutions, beliefs, and groups."[19] This view he dubbed "the spearhead theory of anti-Semitism" because of his conviction that the economic goals of the system were still paramount. Many years later, in the last work he was to complete before his untimely death in 1954, Neumann reaffirmed his belief that spontaneous German anti-Semitism was relatively minor.[20]

That reaffirmation, however, appeared in an essay significantly entitled "Anxiety and Politics," which marked a milestone in Neumann's intellectual development because of its belated acknowledgment of the power of the irrational in political life. Neumann's former colleagues in the institute had come to the same understanding much earlier. In fact, the increased integration of psychoanalysis into critical theory coincided very closely with the growing attention they began paying to anti-Semitism during the war. For all their agreement with Neumann's stress on the manipulative nature of Jew-hatred, they did not hold to his distinction between totalitarian and nontotalitarian anti-Semitism, only the latter being amenable to critical analysis because of its rational foundation. Although Horkheimer and the inner circle of the institute never abandoned the economic dimension of their theory, they came increasingly to stress the psychological aspects of the problems they studied, anti-Semitism in particular.

Anticipations of this shift were apparent as early as the fragments of Adorno's Wagner study published in 1939, where the category of sadomasochism, developed in Erich Fromm's contributions to the institute's work,[21] was extensively employed. The first systematic efforts to probe anti-Semitism took place in 1943, when the institute began a massive investigation of American labor's attitude toward the Jews, conducted under the auspices of the Jewish Labor Committee.[22] Although a great deal of raw data was accumulated, much of it damaging to the liberal image of American labor, and several drafts were completed, no results were published because of a number of organizational and theoretical difficulties. The experience of using empirical techniques proved invaluable, however, when the institute's next investigation of anti-Semitism began shortly thereafter, this time under the sponsorship of the American Jewish Committee. In 1944, Horkheimer became the committee's director of scientific research and launched an ambitious program that culminated in the five-part *Studies in Prejudice*, finally published in 1949 and 1950. One of the volumes, Paul Massing's *Rehearsal for Destruction*,[23] was a traditional historical account of Germany's anti-Semitic movements before World War I, which stressed the importance of the economic depression of the 1873–1896 era in stimulating resentment against the Jews. The other four volumes, however, were predominantly psychological in methodology. Two were by non-institute authors and thus merit no comment here.[24] The others were *Prophets of Deceit* by Leo Lowenthal and Norbert Guterman and *The Authoritarian Personality* by Adorno and three members of the Berkeley Public Opinion Study Group, Else Frenkel-Brunswik, Daniel J. Levinson, and R. Nevitt Sanford.[25]

In his introduction to *Prophets of Deceit,* Horkheimer, who oversaw the entire project, argued that because men at present were denied significant political choices, the people themselves did not suffice as an object of study. Instead, those who manipulate them from above must also be scrutinized. Lowenthal and Guterman thus focused on the techniques of demagogic agitators, whose appeals they subjected to a qualitative content analysis using what they called a "psychological Morse code."[26] The specific context was American society, where the potential for mass anti-Semitism seemed sufficiently threatening to justify this careful investigation. Arguing against the assumption that the exposure of deliberate deception was enough to discredit the demagogue, they sought to unmask the arsenal of unconscious devices that accounted for his appeal. Among those discussed was that of the projected enemy, who was conceived of as both strong and weak. The most frequent embodiment of this projection, they claimed, was the Jew, who appeared as both persecutor and quarry in the fantasy world of the agitator. Equated with the "other," the Jew was the victim of a paranoid projection. His gestures and mannerisms were mimicked by the agitator, who made the vulnerable Jew a "symbol on which he centers the projection of his own impotent rage against the restraints of civilization."[27] As we shall see momentarily, these findings perfectly complemented the more theoretical analysis offered by Horkheimer and Adorno (and partly coauthored by Lowenthal himself) a few years before the publication of *Prophets of Deceit.*

In *The Authoritarian Personality,* Adorno and his colleagues turned to the character types who would be most receptive to the appeal of these demagogic devices. Although the most ambitious interest of the study was the generation and testing of a quantitative scale to measure the "authoritarian" potential of individuals (the celebrated "F scale"), the authors also developed a specific "A-S scale" to uncover latent anti-Semitic tendencies as well. In fact, the study began with a specific focus on this problem. And although Adorno wrote that "we came to regard it as our main task not to analyze anti-Semitism or any other antiminority prejudice as a sociopsychological phenomenon per se, but rather to examine the relation of antiminority prejudice to broader ideological and characterological patterns,"[28] *The Authoritarian Personality* still contained a significant discussion of the phenomenon in its own terms. In addition to a long presentation of the procedures of the A-S scale by Daniel Levinson, Adorno himself contributed a chapter devoted to the qualitative analysis of the indirect or "screened" interview conducted on a sample population by the project's staff. Among his conclusions were that anti-Semitism was subjective and irrational in nature, generally grounded in stereotypically distorted experience, rationalized in moralistic, superegoistic terms, inclined to the "mythological" confusion of mental dispositions and physical categories, and often linked to "antidemocratic feeling."[29]

This last formulation with its uncritical acceptance of the norm of bourgeois democracy, combined with the generally psychologistic orientation of the work as a whole, led some observers to believe that the Frankfurt School had abandoned its Marxist past entirely. Moreover, nowhere in the work was an attempt made to see anti-Semitism in essentially class terms, although the motivations behind it were acknowledged to differ according to social background.[30] The study of American labor had convinced Adorno and his colleagues that the problem was no longer confined to one stratum of the social whole. "Sociologically," Adorno wrote, "this syndrome [the authoritarian personality of high scorers on the F-scale] used to be, in Europe, highly characteristic of the lower middle class. In this country, we may expect it among people whose actual status differs from that to which they aspire."[31]

There were, however, frequent suggestions in the work of the Frankfurt School's continued desire to situate the psychological dimension of prejudice in a wider social setting. For example, in discussing the sources of stereotyping and personalization, Adorno wrote: "Ever more anonymous and opaque social processes make it increasingly difficult to integrate the limited sphere of one's personal life experience with objective social dynamics. Social alienation is hidden by a surface phenomenon in which the very opposite is being stressed: personalization of political attitudes and habits offers compensation for the dehumanization of the social sphere which is at the bottom of today's grievances."[32] These instances tended, however, to be lost in the work's more subjective approach. Indeed, as Adorno himself recognized, a satisfactory theory of anti-Semitism "could be approached only by recourse to a theory which is beyond the scope of this study. Such a theory would neither enumerate a diversity of 'factors' nor single out a specific one as 'the' cause but rather develop a unified framework within which all the 'elements' are linked together consistently. This would amount to nothing less than a theory of modern society as a whole."[33]

Although such a general theory was absent from all the volumes of the *Studies in Prejudice,* Horkheimer and Adorno had attempted in 1944 to isolate the "Elements of Anti-Semitism" in a chapter of their joint work, *Dialectic of the Enlightenment.*[34] Published in 1947, this crucial statement of Critical Theory was generally ignored in America because it was written in German. As a result, the objective complement to the subjective approach of the *Studies* was lost to view until the book was rediscovered in the 1960s by young German New Left followers of the Frankfurt School, a rediscovery that ultimately brought it to the attention of an English-speaking audience as well. Horkheimer and Adorno had perhaps counted on its immediate neglect because it was in "Elements of Anti-Semitism" that they voiced sentiments clearly at odds with the liberal orientation of their American sponsors and co-workers. Whereas, for example, *The Authoritarian Personality* refused to investigate the role of the object of anti-Semitism, which had "little to do with the qualities of those against whom it is directed,"[35] the theoretical essay entered the dangerous territory in which the contribution of the Jews was also open for discussion. And instead of making vaguely complimentary remarks about liberal democracy, Horkheimer and Adorno reverted to the more traditional Frankfurt School position that liberalism was itself implicated in the rise of fascism.

The overarching theory they presented was, however, far more than an echo of the reductive Marxist approach that had characterized their work through Horkheimer's "Die Juden und Europa." In addition to the residues of that position, the Freudian categories they were then applying to their empirical investigations were also in evidence. But beyond both was an analysis grounded in the general argument of the book, which stressed the ambiguous implications of the age-old domination of nature in Western culture and the concomitant apotheosis of instrumental reason. To outline the intricacies of that argument is beyond the scope of this essay,[36] but certain of its implications for the issue of anti-Semitism must be discussed.

One problem in doing so, however, derives from Horkheimer's and Adorno's refusal to organize the arguments they presented in a hierarchical fashion. No attempt was made to weigh the relative significance of each "element" in the compound that was anti-Semitism, nor were the causal links among them fully delineated. Instead, Horkheimer and Adorno offered what might be called a decentered constellation of factors juxtaposed in unmediated fashion. Although brilliant and original in many places, the resulting whole was less than fully satisfying.[37] It is nonetheless useful to extract those elements that Horkheimer and Adorno especially stressed, even if a totally coherent and integrated summary of their entire argument cannot be constructed.

Among the most obvious elements in their analysis, and the one perhaps most absent from the *Studies in Prejudice*, derived from the Frankfurt School's early indebtedness to Marx. "Bourgeois anti-Semitism," Horkheimer and Adorno wrote, "has a specific economic reason: the concealment of domination in production."[38] Like Neumann in *Behemoth*, they recognized the function of the Jews as scapegoats for anticapitalist sentiments: "They were the representatives—in harmony with their patriarchal religion—of municipal, bourgeois and finally, industrial conditions. They carried capitalist ways of life to various countries and drew upon themselves the hatred of all who had to suffer under capitalism."³⁹ Although they were sensitive to the fact that "commerce was not [the Jews'] vocation but their fate,"⁴⁰ an acknowledgment that Marx had callously omitted from his earlier diatribe against the Jews, they nonetheless implicated the Jews in—or perhaps, better put, did not exonerate them from—the responsibility for capitalism's triumph and the reaction it engendered. "They are now experiencing to their own cost the exclusive, particularist character of capitalism."⁴¹

But beyond this more traditional Marxist approach, with its echo of Bebel's celebrated characterization of anti-Semitism as "the socialism of fools," Horkheimer and Adorno provided an analysis of the postbourgeois anti-Semitism that characterized fascism per se. Based on earlier Frankfurt School work on the nature of modern authoritarianism,⁴² they argued that fascism represented a more naked form of repression than classical capitalism with its reliance on the mediation of the marketplace: "Whereas there is no longer any need for economic domination, the Jews are marked out as the absolute object of domination pure and simple."⁴³ Fascism is an order of undiluted force led by rulers who "long for total possession and unlimited power, at any price."⁴⁴ These megalomaniacal yearnings produce a certain measure of guilt, however, which is alleviated by claiming that it is the Jews who in fact crave total control.

The long-range tendency toward this type of domination, which went through the classical capitalist stage before reaching its apotheosis in fascism, had to be understood in more fundamental terms than the scapegoat theory would allow. For "anti-Semitism is a deeply imprinted schema, a ritual of civilization."⁴⁵ It is thus to the fundamental dialectic of civilization (or the Enlightenment, as they alternately call it) that Horkheimer and Adorno turned for a deeper explanation.

The essence of that explanation was the equation of civilization with the domination of nature, a domination whose sinister implications were only then becoming fully manifest. "Those who spasmodically dominate nature," they wrote, "see in a tormented nature a provocative image of powerless happiness. The thought of happiness without power is unbearable because it would then be true happiness."⁴⁶ The Jews are singled out for special attack because they are confused with nature itself and thus seen as having "happiness without power, wages without work, a home without frontiers, religion without myth."⁴⁷ But ironically, the Jews are not merely identified with the nature that is dominated and envied; they are also closely associated with the process of civilization itself. As was the case with their being scapegoated for the sins of capitalism, here, too, there was a grain of truth, for the Jews were the "colonizers for progress."[48] From Roman times on, they had promoted civilization and its concomitant domination of nature with "enlightenment as with cynicism."[49] When nature rebelled against its age-old domination, as Horkheimer and Adorno claimed it did with the rise of irrationalist politics, the Jews were inevitably singled out for revenge. But the revolt of repressed nature was itself turned into yet another manifestation of domination; fascism, in fact, "seeks to make the rebellion of suppressed nature against domination directly useful to domination."[50] The ultimate significance of this reversal is that the Jews, who were implicated in the original domination of nature, are sacrificed to the demands of a new type of domination that assumes the guise of a rebellion against its traditional form.

In developing the intricacies of this argument, Horkheimer and Adorno introduced a complicated discussion of the role of mimetic behavior in civilization and its distortion in the fascist mimicry of its Jewish victims. They also analyzed the Christian contribution to the process, which they stressed could not be ignored despite the moribund status of the church in the modern world. But their most interesting argument drew upon the psychoanalytic theory they were then applying to the subjective side of anti-Semitism in their more empirical work: "Anti-Semitism is based on a false projection. It is the counterpart of true mimesis, and fundamentally related to the repressed form; in fact, it is probably the morbid expression of repressed mimesis. Mimesis imitates the environment, but false projection makes the environment like itself."[51] This type of false projection was equivalent to paranoia, but instead of being a personal problem, paranoia had been politicized in the modern world. To many who succumbed to its appeal, fascism provided a mass delusional system that was mistaken for reality.

However, Horkheimer and Adorno went beyond the purely psychoanalytic reading of paranoid false projections by adding an epistemological dimension to their analysis. Projection, they argued, is not in and of itself at fault, for as Kant in particular had shown, all perception contains a projective moment. But a healthy projection preserves the tension between subject and object, neither reducing the former to the latter, as in the case of positivism, nor vice versa, as in idealism. Reflection on the mediated nonidentity of subject and object was, they contended, the key to a healthy, nondominating enlightenment; accordingly, "the morbid aspect of anti-Semitism is not projective behavior as such, but the absence from it of reflection."[52] The domination of nature entailed by a less benign form of enlightenment was thus closely tied to the psychological condition of paranoia and the philosophical tendency of idealism. "Objectifying (like sick) thought contains the despotism of the subjective purpose which is hostile to the thing and forgets the thing itself, thus committing the mental act of violence which is later put into practice. The unconditional realism of civilized humanity, which culminates in fascism, is a special case of paranoic delusion which dehumanizes nature and finally the nations themselves."[53] This argument, which Adorno was later to develop in much greater detail in *Negative Dialectics*,[54] thus situated anti-Semitism at the culmination of a process at once social, psychological, and philosophical, a process which was the dialectic of the Enlightenment itself. The somber implication of this fact that it would take nothing short of the reversal of that process to end persecution of the Jews, was a conclusion far bleaker than that of the *Studies in Prejudice* with its call for increased education for tolerance. "If thought is liberated from domination and if violence is abolished, the long absent idea is liable to develop that Jews too are human beings. This development would represent the step out of an anti-Semitic society which drives Jews and others to madness, and into the human society. This step would also fulfill the Fascist lie, but in contradicting it: the Jewish question would prove in fact to be the turning point of history."[55] In short, once utopia was achieved, anti-Semitism would take care of itself. The inverse of this proposition, however, did not necessarily hold, as Horkheimer and Adorno acknowledged in a final section of "Elements of Anti-Semitism" added after the war's end in 1947. That is, the end of Jew-hatred did not entail the liberation of thought from domination and the abolition of violence. For although "there are no more anti-Semites"[56] now that Hitler has been defeated, the conditions which made fascism possible have not really been changed. The stereotyped "ticket-mentality" that spawned anti-Semitism has survived its decline. Indeed, "the Jewish masses themselves are as prone to ticket-thinking as the hostile youth organizations."[57] The content of fascist propaganda, indeed of fascist action itself, is less important than its source in the paranoid false projection that characterizes the domination of nature. "The ticket mentality as such is as anti-Semitic as the anti-Semitic ticket. The anger against all that is different is teleologically inherent in the mentality, and, as the dominated subjects' resentment of natural domination, is ready to attack the natural minority—even when the social minority is threatened first."[58]

For Horkheimer and Adorno, then, perhaps the ultimate source of anti-Semitism and its functional equivalents is the rage against the nonidentical that characterizes the totalistic dominating impulse of Western civilization. The Jews, in other words, by their very refusal to be assimilated, represent an obstacle to the total integration of the "administered world" or "one-dimensional society," as Marcuse was to call it. In fact, at least Horkheimer came to see the "negative" relation of the Jews to the rest of mankind as a healthy state of affairs. Not surprisingly, this made his reaction to Zionism and the creation of Israel ambivalent, for now the Jews were merely one nation among others: "Jewry was not a powerful state but the hope for justice at the end of the world. They were a people and its opposite, a rebuke to all peoples. Now, a state claims to be speaking for Jewry, to be Jewry. The Jewish people in whom the injustice of all peoples has become an accusation, the individuals in whose words and gestures the negative of what is reflected itself, have now become positive themselves. A nation among nations, soldiers, leaders, money-raisers for themselves."[59] Whether or not this lament, with its echoes of Franz Rosenzweig's much earlier celebration of the Jews as a nonhistorical people,[60] was shared by all his former colleagues, it is clear that Horkheimer was expressing a cardinal tenet of Critical Theory: the prohibition of premature positivity. In his mind, and perhaps in that of certain of his collaborators, the Jews became the metaphoric equivalent of that remnant of society preserving negation and the nonidentical. Indeed, Horkheimer came to argue that underlying the Frankfurt School's refusal to describe the utopian alternative to the present society was the traditional Jewish taboo on naming God or picturing paradise.[61]

The striking disparity between the references to the Jews and anti-Semitism in the two collections of Horkheimer's aphorisms thus mirrored a fundamental shift in the Frankfurt School's attitude. As it moved farther away from the traditional Marxist belief in the proletariat as the agent of positive totalization and more toward the conclusion that the best to be hoped for in the present world was the preservation of enclaves of negation, the attention its members paid to the Jewish question increased. Although assertions of a causal relationship between their own status as Jewish survivors and their vision of a negative dialectics "after Auschwitz" can only be speculative,[62] it is nonetheless clear that at least in Horkheimer's case, the Critical Theorist was understood as "the Jew" of the administered society. And conversely, anti-Semitism became a model of the totalistic liquidation of nonidentity in the one-dimensional world.[63] In "Elements of Anti-Semitism," Horkheimer and Adorno had written that "the fact that anti-Semitism tends to occur only as part of an interchangeable program is sure hope that it will die out one day,"[64] but, when that day would dawn, Critical Theory chose not to say. In fact, for the later Frankfurt School, no hopes could be called sure, although the need to hope was no less urgent.

NOTES

1. Max Horkheimer, *Notizen 1950 bis 1969 und Dämmerung Notizen in Deutschland*, edited by Werner Brede, with introduction by Alfred Schmidt (Frankfurt am Main, 1974). *Dämmerung* was first published under the pseudonym Heinrich Regius in Zurich in 1934. It was translated along with the notes of 1950–1969 under the title *Dawn and Decline* (New York, 1978).

2. *Dawn and Decline*, p. 43.

3. *Studien über Autorität und Familie* (Paris, 1935).

4. The Marcuse article appeared in the *Zeitschrift für Sozialforschung* III (1934) pp. 161–195; the Lowenthal in the *Zeitschrift für Sozialforschung* VI (1937) pp. 295–345. In the latter, footnote 1 on p. 330 quotes a remark Hamsun made about Jews, but makes no comment about it. Lowenthal had written earlier for Jewish periodicals and about Jewish issues, but when he joined the institute, he left this interest behind. Marcuse, in his long career, never discussed Jewish issues or anti-Semitism.

5. "Fragmente über Wagner," *Zeitschrift für Sozialforschung* VII (1939) pp. 1–49; *Versuch über Wagner* (Frankfurt am Main, 1952).

6. "Die Juden und Europa," *Zeitschrift für Sozialforschung* VII (1939). Originally Horkheimer had not wanted to use this title for the essay, only the last ten pages of which actually deals with the Jews. He was persuaded to do so by Adorno, according to the recollection of Gershom Scholem, *Walter Benjamin, Geschichte einer Freundschaft* (Frankfurt am Main, 1975), p. 278. Horkheimer later felt embarrassed by this essay with its frequently quoted phrase, "he who does not wish to speak of capitalism should also be silent about fascism," and chose to omit it from his collection *Kritische Theorie*, 2 vols., ed. Alfred Schmidt (Frankfurt am Main, 1969).

7. Scholem, *Walter Benjamin*, pp. 276–278.

8. This pattern is discussed, *inter alia*, in Robert Wistrich, "German Social Democracy and the Problem of Jewish Nationalism, 1897–1917," *Yearbook of the Leo Baeck Institute* XXI (1976) pp. 109–142; Donald L. Niewyk, *Socialist, Anti-Semite, and Jew: German Social Democracy Confronts the Problem of Anti-Semitism, 1918–1933* (Baton Rouge, 1971).

9. See, for example, "Über die deutschen Juden," in *Kritik der Instrumentellen Vernunft. Aus den Vorträgen und Aufzeichenung seit Kriegsende*, ed. Alfred Schmidt (Frankfurt am Main, 1967), originally published in 1961. For a discussion of Horkheimer's later turn toward Jewish themes, see Eva G. Reichmann, "Max Horkheimer the Jew: Critical Theory and Beyond," *Yearbook of the Leo Baeck Institute* XIX (1974) pp. 181–195 and Julius Carlebach, *Karl Marx and the Radical Critique of Judaism* (London, 1978).

10. In an interview with *Der Spiegel* XXIV (January 5, 1970), Horkheimer claimed that Critical Theory's refusal to name the "other" was derived from the Jewish taboo on naming God or picturing paradise.

11. In 1939 a prospectus was drafted for such a project; it was published in the *Studies in Philosophy and Social Science* (the short-lived English-language successor to the *Zeitschrift für Sozialforschung*) IX (1941) pp. 124–143.

12. *Behemoth: The Structure and Practice of National Socialism, 1933–1944*, rev. ed. (New York, 1944).

13. For a discussion of Neumann's conflict with Pollock over state capitalism, see Martin Jay, *The Dialectical Imagination: A History of the Frankfurt School and the Institute of Social Research, 1923–1950* (Boston, 1973), pp. 162–167.

14. *Behemoth*, p. 122.

15. Ibid.

16. Ibid., p. 121.

17. Ibid.

18. Interview with Leo Lowenthal, Berkeley, California, August 1968. In the 1939 prospectus for a study of anti-Semitism, the institute wrote: "While frank disgust for the anti-Semitism of the government is revealed among the German masses, the promises of anti-Semitism are eagerly swallowed where fascist governments have never been attempted" (p. 141).

19. *Behemoth*, p. 551. This attitude was characteristic of the SPD, to whose left wing Neumann had belonged during the Weimar Republic. See Niewyk, p. 217.

20. "Anxiety and Politics," *The Democratic and Authoritarian State: Essays in Political and Legal Theory,* ed. Herbert Marcuse (New York, 1957), p. 286.

21. For a discussion of Fromm's work with the institute, see *The Dialectical Imagination,* chapter 3.

22. For a discussion of the American Labor Project, see *The Dialectical Imagination,* pp. 224–226.

23. (New York, 1949). According to Ismar Schorsch, "After twenty-five years, Massing's penetrating and judicious study . . . remains unsurpassed." See "German Antisemitism in the Light of Post-war Historiography," *Yearbook of the Leo Baeck Institute* XIX (1974).

24. Nathan W. Ackerman and Marie Jahoda, *Anti-Semitism and Emotional Disorder: A Psychoanalytic Interpretation* (New York, 1950) and Bruno Bettelheim and Morris Janowitz, *Dynamics of Prejudice: A Psychological and Sociological Study of Veterans* (New York, 1950). For a brief discussion of these works, see *The Dialectical Imagination,* pp. 235–237.

25. *Prophets of Deceit* (New York, 1949); *The Authoritarian Personality* (New York, 1950).

26. *Prophets of Deceit,* p. 140. The theoretical underpinnings of the code were spelled out more clearly in Adorno, "Freudian Theory and the Pattern of Fascist Propaganda," in *Psychoanalysis and the Social Sciences,* ed. Geza Roheim (New York, 1951).

27. *Prophets of Deceit,* p. 88.

28. *The Authoritarian Personality,* p. 605.

29. Ibid., p. 653.

30. Ibid., p. 638. Here it is argued that the proletarian anti-Semite is likely to identify the Jew with the bourgeois agent of capitalism, and the bourgeois anti-Semite tends to see the Jew as a "misfit bourgeois" who does not belong to modern society. The study's sample was essentially middle-class, but the earlier labor project had given evidence of the former tendency.

31. Ibid., pp. 759–760.

32. Ibid., p. 671.

33. Ibid., p. 608.

34. *Dialectic of the Enlightenment,* trans. John Cumming (New York, 1972); Lowenthal was the coauthor of the first three of the seven sections of this chapter.

35. *The Authoritarian Personality,* p. 607.

36. For an analysis, see *The Dialectical Imagination,* chapter 8; Susan Buck-Morss, *The Origin of Negative Dialectics: Theodor W. Adorno, Walter Benjamin and the Frankfurt Institute* (New York, 1977), pp. 59–62, 178–180, and Christian Lenhardt, "The Wanderings of Enlightenment," in *On Critical Theory,* ed. John O'Neill (New York, 1976).

37. One of the book's first reviewers, Heinz L. Matzal, found it the least convincing section. See *Philosophischer Literaturanzeiger,* I (1949). In subsequent discussions of the Frankfurt School's work, it has not been prominently featured. Carlebach is an exception, and his attitude is generally hostile. See note 4.

38. *Dialectic of Enlightenment,* p. 173.

39. Ibid., p. 175.

40. Ibid.

41. Ibid.

42. See especially the theoretical introductions to *Studien über Autorität und Familie* and Marcuse's essay cited in note 4.

43. *Dialectic of Enlightenment,* p. 168. They also argued, in a manner anticipating Hannah Arendt's well-known analysis in *The Origins of Totalitarianism* of 1951, that the nineteenth-century Jews had sold their political rights and power for economic security. Accordingly, when the nation-state ceased to protect them in the era of mass politics, they were entirely vulnerable to attack (pp. 171–172).

44. Ibid., p. 169.

45. Ibid., p. 171.

46. Ibid., p. 172.

47. Ibid., p. 199.

48. Ibid., p. 175. In a letter Horkheimer wrote to Lowenthal on July 5, 1946, he talked of the mistrust the peasant had of the urban manipulator of language, which he called partly justified. "This distrust," Horkheimer continued, "is an element of anti-Semitism itself, and the Jew who manipulates language so easily is not free from guilt in the prehistory of what you explain as the fascist handling of language. Here, too, the Jew is the pioneer of capitalism" (Lowenthal collection, Berkeley, California).

49. Ibid., p. 186.

50. Ibid., p. 185.

51. Ibid., p. 187.

52. Ibid., p. 189.

53. Ibid., p. 193.

54. *Negative Dialectics,* trans. E. B. Ashton (New York, 1973).

55. *Dialectic of Enlightenment,* pp. 199–200.

56. Ibid., p. 200.

57. Ibid., p. 207.

58. Ibid.

59. "The State of Israel" in *Dawn and Decline,* pp. 206–207. See also the aphorism entitled "End of the Dream" on pp. 221–222.

60. Franz Rosenzweig, *The Star of Redemption,* trans. William Hallo (New York, 1970).

61. See note 10.

62. For example, see Zoltan Tar, *The Frankfurt School: The Critical Theories of Max Horkheimer and Theodor W. Adorno* (New York, 1977), and Arnold Künzli, *Aufklärung und Dialektik* (Freiburg, 1971). They reduce negative dialectics to Adorno's belated guilt over his earlier rejection of Judaism, produced by his surviving the Holocaust, rather than seeing it as an expression of his (and Horkheimer's) positive identification with the Jews.

63. In "Elements of Anti-Semitism," Horkheimer and Adorno write, "from the outset there has always been an intimate link between anti-Semitism and totality" (p. 172). This critical attitude toward totality, a term that frequently appeared in their other writings in a more positive light, was indicative of a general shift away from what might be called the Lukácsian tenor of their early work. Instead of using totality in a completely positive sense, they began to recognize its ambiguous relationship with totalitarianism. For more on this issue, see Martin Jay, "The Concept of Totality in Lukács and Adorno," *Telos* 32 (Summer 1977) pp. 117–137 and *Varieties of Marxism,* ed. Shlomo Avineri (The Hague, 1977).

64. *Dialectic of Enlightenment,* p. 207.

16

ANTI-SEMITISM AND NATIONAL SOCIALISM
Moishe Postone

What is the relation of anti-Semitism to National Socialism? The public discussion of this problem in the Federal Republic has been characterized by a dichotomy between liberals and conservatives, on the one side, and the Left, on the other. Liberals and conservatives have tended to emphasize the discontinuity between the Nazi past and the present. In referring to that past they have focused attention on the persecution and extermination of the Jews and have tended to deemphasize other central aspects of Nazism. By underlining the supposed total character of the break between the Third Reich and the Federal Republic, this sort of emphasis on anti-Semitism has paradoxically helped avoid a fundamental confrontation with the social and structural reality of National Socialism. That reality certainly did not completely vanish in 1945. The condemnation of Nazi anti-Semitism, in other words, has also served as an ideology of legitimation for the present system. This instrumentalization was only possible because anti-Semitism has been treated primarily as a form of prejudice, as a scapegoat ideology, thereby obscuring the intrinsic relationship between anti-Semitism and other aspects of National Socialism.

On the other hand, the Left has tended to concentrate on the function of National Socialism for capitalism, emphasizing the destruction of working-class organizations, Nazi social and economic policies, rearmament, expansionism, and the bureaucratic mechanisms of party and state domination. Elements of continuity between the Third Reich and the Federal

Republic have been stressed. The extermination of the Jews has not, of course, been ignored. Yet, it has quickly been subsumed under the general categories of prejudice, discrimination, and persecution.[1] In comprehending anti-Semitism as a peripheral, rather than as a central, moment of National Socialism, the Left has also obscured the intrinsic relationship between the two.

Both of these positions understand modern anti-Semitism as anti-Jewish prejudice, as a particular example of racism in general. Their stress on the mass psychological nature of anti-Semitism isolates considerations of the Holocaust from socioeconomic and sociohistorical investigations of National Socialism. The Holocaust, however, cannot be understood so long as anti-Semitism is viewed as an example of racism in general and so long as Nazism is conceived of only in terms of big capital and a terroristic bureaucratic police state. Auschwitz, Belzec, Chelmno, Maidanek, Sobibor, and Treblinka should not be treated outside the framework of an analysis of National Socialism. They represent one of its logical end points, not simply its most terrible epiphenomenon. No analysis of National Socialism that cannot account for the extermination of European Jewry is fully adequate.

In this essay I will attempt to approach an understanding of the extermination of European Jewry by outlining an interpretation of modern anti-Semitism. My intention is not to explain *why* Nazism and modern anti-Semitism achieved a breakthrough and became hegemonic in Germany. Such an attempt would entail an analysis of the specificity of German historical development, a subject about which a great deal has been written. This essay attempts, rather, to determine more closely *what it was* that achieved a breakthrough, by suggesting an analysis of modern anti-Semitism that indicates its intrinsic connection to National Socialism. Such an examination is a necessary precondition to any substantive analysis of why National Socialism succeeded in Germany.

The first step must be a specification of the Holocaust and of modern anti-Semitism. The problem should not be posed quantitatively, whether in terms of numbers of people murdered or of degree of suffering. There are too many historical examples of mass murder and of genocide. (Many more Russians than Jews, for example, were killed by the Nazis.) The question is, rather, one of qualitative specificity. Particular aspects of the extermination of European Jewry by the Nazis remain inexplicable so long as anti-Semitism is treated as a specific example of a scapegoat strategy whose victims could very well have been members of any other group.

The Holocaust was characterized by a sense of ideological mission, by a relative lack of emotion and immediate hate (as opposed to pogroms, for example), and, most importantly, by its apparent lack of functionality. The extermination of the Jews seems not to have been a means to another end. They were not exterminated for military reasons or in the course of a violent process of land acquisition (as was the case with the American Indians and the Tasmanians). Nor did Nazi policy toward the Jews resemble their policy toward the Poles and the Russians which aimed to eradicate those segments of the population around whom resistance might crystallize in order to exploit the rest more easily as helots. Indeed, the Jews were not exterminated for any manifest "extrinsic" goal. The extermination of the Jews was not only to have been total, but was its own goal—extermination for the sake of extermination—a goal that acquired absolute priority.[2]

No functionalist explanation of the Holocaust and no scapegoat theory of anti-Semitism can even begin to explain why, in the last years of the war, when the German forces were being crushed by the Red Army, a significant proportion of vehicles was deflected from logistical support and used to transport Jews to the gas chambers. Once the qualitative specificity of the extermination of European Jewry is recognized, it becomes clear that attempts at an explanation dealing with capitalism, racism, bureaucracy, sexual repression, or the authoritarian personality, remain far too general. The specificity of the Holocaust requires a much more determinate mediation in order even to approach its understanding.

The extermination of European Jewry is, of course, related to anti-Semitism. The specificity of the former must be related to that of the latter. Moreover, *modern* anti-Semitism must be understood with reference to Nazism as a movement—a movement which, in terms of its own self-understanding, represented a revolt.

Modern anti-Semitism, which should not be confused with everyday anti-Jewish prejudice, is an ideology, a form of thought, that emerged in Europe in the late nineteenth century. Its emergence presupposed earlier forms of anti-Semitism, which had for centuries been an integral part of Christian Western civilization. What is common to all forms of anti-Semitism is the degree of power attributed to the Jews: the power to kill God, to unleash the Bubonic Plague, and, more recently, to introduce capitalism and socialism. Anti-Semitic thought is strongly Manichaean, with the Jews playing the role of the children of darkness.

It is not only the degree, but also the quality of power attributed to the Jews that distinguishes anti-Semitism from other forms of racism. Probably all forms of racism attribute potential power to the Other. This power, however, is usually concrete, material, or sexual. It is the potential power of the oppressed (as repressed), of the "Untermenschen." The power attributed to the Jews is much greater and is perceived as actual rather than as potential. Moreover, it is a different sort of power, one not necessarily concrete. What characterizes the power imputed to the Jews in *modern* anti-Semitism is that it is mysteriously intangible, abstract, and universal. It is considered to be a form of power that does not manifest itself directly, but must find another mode of expression. It seeks a concrete carrier, whether political, social, or cultural, through which it can work. Because the power of the Jews, as conceived by the modern anti-Semitic imagination, is not bound concretely, is not "rooted," it is presumed to be of staggering immensity and extremely difficult to check. It is considered to stand behind phenomena, but not to be identical with them. Its source is therefore deemed hidden—conspiratorial. The Jews represent an immensely powerful, intangible, international conspiracy.

A graphic example of this vision is provided by a Nazi poster depicting Germany—represented as a strong, honest worker—threatened in the West by a fat, plutocratic John Bull and in the East by a brutal, barbaric Bolshevic Commissar. Yet, these two hostile forces are mere puppets. Peering over the edge of the globe, with the puppet strings firmly in his hands, is the Jew. Such a vision was by no means a monopoly of the Nazis. It is characteristic of modern anti-Semitism that the Jews are considered to be the force behind those "apparent" opposites: plutocratic capitalism and socialism. "International Jewry" is, moreover, perceived to be centered in the "asphalt jungles" of the newly emergent urban megalopoli, to be behind "vulgar, materialist, modern culture" and, in general, all forces contributing to the decline of traditional social groupings, values, and institutions. The Jews represent a foreign, dangerous, destructive force undermining the social "health" of the nation. Modern anti-Semitism, then, is characterized not only by its secular content, but also by its systematic character. Its claim is to explain the world—a world that had rapidly become too complex and threatening for many people.

This descriptive determination of modern anti-Semitism, while necessary in order to differentiate that form from prejudice or racism in general, is in itself not sufficient to indicate the intrinsic connection to National Socialism. That is, the aim of overcoming the customary separation between a sociohistorical analysis of Nazism and an examination of anti-Semitism is, on this level, not yet fulfilled. What is required is an explanation that can mediate the two. Such an explanation must be capable of grounding historically the form of anti-Semitism described above by means of the same categories that could be used to explain National Socialism. My intention is not to negate sociopsychological or psychoanalytical explanations,[3] but rather to elucidate a historical-epistemological frame of reference within which further psychological specifications can take place. Such a frame of reference must be able to elucidate the specific content of modern anti-Semitism and must be historical, that is, it must contribute to an understanding of why that ideology became so prevalent when it did, beginning in the late nineteenth century. In the absence of such a frame, all other explanatory attempts that focus on the subjective dimension remain historically indeterminate. What is required, then, is an explanation in terms of a social-historical epistemology.

A full development of the problematic of anti-Semitism would go beyond the bounds of this essay. The point to be made here, however, is that a careful examination of the modern anti-Semitic worldview reveals that it is a form of thought in which the rapid development of industrial capitalism, with all its social ramifications, is personified and identified as the Jew. It is not merely that the Jews were considered to be the owners of money, as in traditional anti-Semitism, but that they were held responsible for economic crises and identified with the range of social restructuring and dislocation resulting from rapid industrialization: explosive urbanization, the decline of traditional social classes and strata, the emergence of a large, increasingly organized industrial proletariat, and so on. In other words, the abstract domination of capital, which—particularly with rapid industrialization—caught people up in a web of dynamic forces they could not understand, became perceived as the domination of International Jewry.

This, however, is no more than a first approach. The personification has been described, not yet explained. There have been many attempts at an explanation yet none, in my opinion, have been complete. The problem with those theories, such as that of Max Horkheimer,[4] which concentrate on the identification of the Jews with money and the sphere of circulation, is that they cannot account for the notion that the Jews also constitute the power behind social democracy and communism. At first glance, those theories, such as that of George L. Mosse,[5] which interpret modern anti-Semitism as a revolt against modernity, appear more satisfying. Both plutocracy and working-class movements were concomitants of modernity, of the massive social restructuring resulting from capitalist industrialization. The problem with such approaches, however, is that "the modern" would certainly include industrial capital. Yet, as is well known, industrial capital was precisely not an object of anti-Semitic attacks, even in a period of rapid industrialization. Moreover, the attitude of National Socialism to many other dimensions of modernity, especially toward modern technology, was affirmative rather than critical. The aspects of modern life that were rejected and those that were affirmed by the National Socialists form a pattern. That pattern should be intrinsic to an adequate conceptualization of the problem. Since that pattern was not unique to National Socialism, the problematic has far-reaching significance.

The affirmation by modern anti-Semitism of industrial capital indicates that an approach is required that can distinguish between what modern capitalism is and the way it manifests itself, between its essence and its appearance. The term "modern" does not itself possess an intrinsic differentiation allowing for such a distinction. I would like to suggest that the social categories developed by Marx in his mature critique, such as "commodity" and "capital," are more adequate, inasmuch as a series of distinctions between what is and what appears to be are intrinsic to the categories themselves. These categories can serve as the point of departure for an analysis capable of differentiating various perceptions of "the modern." Such an approach would attempt to relate the pattern of social critique and affirmation we are considering to characteristics of capitalist social relations themselves.

These considerations lead us to Marx's concept of the fetish, the strategic intent of which was to provide a social and historical theory of knowledge grounded in the difference between the essence of capitalist social relations and their manifest forms. What underlies the concept of the fetish is Marx's analysis of the commodity, money and capital not merely as economic categories, but rather as the forms of the peculiar social relations that essentially characterize capitalism. In his analysis, capitalist forms of social relations do not appear as such, but are only expressed in objectified form. Labor in capitalism is not only social productive activity ("concrete labor"), but also serves in the place of overt social relations as a social mediation ("abstract labor"). Hence its product, the commodity, is not merely a product in which concrete labor is objectified; it is also a form of objectified social relations. In capitalism the product is not an object socially mediated by overt forms of social relations and domination. The commodity, as the objectification of both dimensions of labor in capitalism, is its own social mediation. It thus possesses a "double character": use-value and value. As object, the commodity both expresses and veils social relations which have no other, "independent" mode of expression. This mode of objectification of social relations is their alienation. The fundamental social relations of capitalism acquire a quasi-objective life of their own. They constitute a "second nature," a system of abstract domination and compulsion which, although social, is impersonal and "objective." Such relations appear not to be social at all, but natural. At the same time, the categorial forms express a particular, socially constituted conception of nature in terms of the objective, lawful, quantifiable behavior of a qualitatively homogeneous essence. The Marxian categories simultaneously express particular social relations and forms of thought. The notion of the fetish refers to forms of thought based upon perceptions that remain bound to the forms of appearance of capitalist social relations.[6]

When one examines the specific characteristics of the power attributed to the Jews by modern anti-Semitism—abstractness, intangibility, universality, mobility—it is striking that they are all characteristics of the value dimension of the social forms analyzed by Marx. Moreover, this dimension, like the supposed power of the Jews, does not appear as such, but always in the form of a material carrier, the commodity.

At this point I will commence with a brief analysis of the way in which capitalist social relations present themselves. I will thereby attempt to explain the personification described above and clarify the problem of why modern anti-Semitism, which railed against so many aspects of the "modern," was so conspicuously silent, or was positive, with regard to industrial capital and modern technology.

I will begin with the example of the commodity form. The dialectical tension between value and use-value in the commodity form requires that this "double character" be materially externalized. It appears "doubled" as money (the manifest form of value) and as the commodity (the manifest form of use-value). Although the commodity is a social form expressing both value and use-value, the effect of this externalization is that the commodity appears only as its use-value dimension, as purely material and "thingly." Money, on the other hand, then appears as the sole repository of value, as the manifestation of the purely abstract, rather than as the externalized manifest form of the value dimension of the commodity itself. The form of materialized social relations specific to capitalism appears on this level of the analysis as the opposition between money, as abstract, and "thingly" nature.

One aspect of the fetish, then, is that capitalist social relations do not appear as such and, moreover, present themselves antinomically, as the opposition of the abstract and concrete. Because, additionally, both sides of the antinomy are objectified, each appears to be quasi-natural. The abstract dimension appears in the form of abstract, universal, "objective," natural laws; the concrete dimension appears as pure "thingly" nature. The structure of alienated social relations that characterize capitalism has the form of a quasi-natural antinomy in which the social and historical do not appear. This antinomy is recapitulated as the opposition between positivist and romantic forms of thought. Most critical analyses of fetishized thought have concentrated on that strand of the antinomy that hypostatizes the abstract as transhistorical—so-called positive bourgeois thought—and thereby disguises the social and historical character of existing relations. In this essay, the other strand will be emphasized—that of forms of romanticism and revolt which, in terms of their own self-understandings, are antibourgeois, but which in fact hypostatize the concrete and thereby remain bound within the antinomy of capitalist social relations.

Forms of anticapitalist thought that remain bound within the immediacy of this antinomy tend to perceive capitalism, and that which is specific to that social formation, only in terms of the manifestations of the abstract dimension of the antinomy; so, for instance, money is considered the "root of all evil." The existent concrete dimension is then positively opposed to it as the "natural" or ontologically human, which presumably stands outside the specificity of capitalist society. Thus, as with Proudhon, for example, concrete labor is understood as the noncapitalist moment opposed to the abstractness of money.[7] That concrete labor itself incorporates and is materially formed by capitalist social relations is not understood.

With the further development of capitalism, of the capital form and its associated fetish, the naturalization immanent to the commodity fetish acquires new dimensions. The capital form, like the commodity form, is characterized by the antinomic relation of concrete and abstract, both of which appear to be natural. The quality of the "natural," however, is different. Associated with the commodity fetish is the notion of the ultimately lawlike character of relations among individual self-contained units as is expressed, for example, in classical political economy or natural law theory. Capital, according to Marx, is self-valorizing value. It is characterized by a continuous, ceaseless process of the self-expansion of value. This process underlies rapid, large-scale cycles of production and consumption, creation and destruction. Capital has no fixed, final form, but appears at different stages of its spiraling path in the form of money and in the form of commodities. As self-valorizing value, capital appears as pure process. Its concrete dimension changes accordingly. Individual labors no longer constitute self-contained units. They increasingly become cellular components of a large, complex, dynamic system that encompasses people and machines and which is directed by one goal, namely, production for the sake of production. The alienated social whole becomes greater than the sum of its constituting individuals and has a goal external to itself. That goal is a nonfinite process. The capital form of social relations has a blind, processual, quasi-organic character.

With the growing consolidation of the capital form, the mechanical worldview of the seventeenth and eighteenth centuries begins to give way; organic process begins to supplant mechanical stasis as the form of the fetish. Organic theory of the state and the proliferation of racial theories and the rise of Social Darwinism in the late nineteenth century are cases in point. Society and historical process become increasingly understood in biological terms. I shall not develop this aspect of the capital fetish any further here. For our purposes what must be noted is the implications for how capital can be perceived. As indicated above, on the logical level of the analysis of the commodity, the "double character" allows the commodity to appear as a purely material entity rather than as the objectification of mediated social relations. Relatedly, it allows concrete labor to appear as a purely material, creative process, separable from capitalist social relations. On the logical level of capital, the "double character" (labor process and valorization process) allows industrial production to appear as a purely material, creative process, separable from capital. The manifest form of the concrete is now more organic. Industrial capital then can appear as the linear descendent of "natural" artisanal labor, as "organically rooted," in opposition to "rootless," "parasitic" finance capital. The organization of the former appears related to that of the guild; its social context is grasped as a superordinate organic unity: Community *(Gemeinschaft)*, Volk, Race. Capital itself—or what is understood as the negative aspect of capitalism—is understood only in terms of the manifest form of its abstract dimension: finance and interest capital. In this sense, the biological interpretation, which opposes the concrete dimension (of capitalism) as "natural" and "healthy" to the negativity of what is taken to be "capitalism," does not stand in contradiction to a glorification of industrial capital and technology. Both are the "thingly" side of the antinomy.

This relationship is commonly misunderstood. For example, Norman Mailer, defending neo-romanticism (and sexism) in *The Prisoner of Sex,* wrote that Hitler spoke of blood, to be sure, but built the machine. The point is that, in this form of fetishized "anticapitalism," *both* blood and the machine are seen as concrete counterprinciples to the abstract. The positive emphasis on "nature," on blood, the soil, concrete labor, and *Gemeinschaft,* can easily go hand in hand with a glorification of technology and industrial capital.[8] This form of thought, then, is not to be understood as anachronistic, as the expression of historical nonsynchronism *(Ungleichzeitigkeit),* any more than the rise of racial theories in the late nineteenth century should be thought of as atavistic. They are historically new forms of thought and in no way represent the reemergence of an older form. It is because of the emphasis on biological nature that they appear to be atavistic or anachronistic. However, this emphasis itself is rooted in the capital fetish. The turn to biology and the desire for a return to "natural origins," combined with an affirmation of technology, which appear in many forms in the early twentieth century, should be understood as expressions of the antinomic fetish that gives rise to the notion that the concrete is "natural," and which increasingly presents the socially "natural" in such a way that it is perceived in biological terms.

The hypostatization of the concrete and the identification of capital with the manifest abstract underlie a form of "anticapitalism" that seeks to overcome the existing social order from a standpoint which actually remains immanent to that order. Inasmuch as that standpoint is the concrete dimension, this ideology tends to point toward a more concrete and organized form of overt capitalist social synthesis. This form of "anticapitalism," then, only *appears* to be looking backward with yearning. As an expression of the capital fetish its real thrust is forward. It emerges in the transition from liberal to bureaucratic capitalism and becomes virulent in a situation of structural crisis.

This form of "anticapitalism," then, is based on a one-sided attack on the abstract. The abstract and concrete are not seen as constituting an antinomy where the real overcoming of the abstract—of the value dimension—involves the historical overcoming of the antinomy itself as well as each of its terms. Instead there is the one-sided attack on abstract reason, abstract law, or, at another level, money and finance capital. In this sense it is antinomically complementary to liberal thought, where the domination of the abstract remains unquestioned and the distinction between positive and critical reason is not made.

The "anticapitalist" attack, however, did not remain limited to the attack against abstraction. On the level of the capital fetish, it is not only the concrete side of the antinomy which can be naturalized and biologized. The manifest abstract dimension was also biologized—as the Jews. The fetishized opposition of the concrete material and the abstract, of the "natural" and the "artificial," became translated as the world-historically significant racial opposition of the Aryans and the Jews. Modern anti-Semitism involves a biologization of capitalism—which itself is only understood in terms of its manifest abstract dimension—as International Jewry.

According to this interpretation, the Jews were identified not merely with money, with the sphere of circulation, but with capitalism itself. However, because of its fetishized form, capitalism did not appear to include industry and technology. Capitalism appeared to be only its manifest abstract dimension which, in turn, was responsible for the whole range of concrete social and cultural changes associated with the rapid development of modern industrial capitalism. The Jews were not seen merely as *representatives* of capital (in which case anti-Semitic attacks would have been much more class-specific). They became the *personifications* of the intangible, destructive, immensely powerful, and international domination of capital as an alienated social form. Certain forms of anti-capitalist discontent became directed against the manifest abstract dimension of capital personified in the form of the Jews, not because the Jews were consciously identified with the value dimension, but because, given the antinomy of the abstract and concrete dimensions, capitalism appeared that way. The "anticapitalist" revolt was, consequently, also the revolt against the Jews. The overcoming of capitalism and its negative social effects became associated with the overcoming of the Jews.[9]

Although the immanent connection between the sort of "anticapitalism" that informed National Socialism and modern anti-Semitism has been indicated, the question remains why the biological interpretation of the abstract dimension of capitalism found its focus in the Jews. This "choice" was, within the European context, by no means fortuitous. The Jews could not have been replaced by any other group. The reasons for this are manifold. The long history of anti-Semitism in Europe and the related association of Jews with money are well known. The period of the rapid expansion of industrial capital in the last third of the nineteenth century coincided with the political and civil emancipation of the Jews in central Europe. There was a veritable explosion of Jews in the universities, the liberal professions, journalism, the arts, retail. The Jews rapidly became visible in civil society, particularly in spheres and professions that were expanding and which were associated with the newer form society was taking.

One could mention many other factors, but there is one that I wish to emphasize. Just as the commodity, understood as a social form, expresses its "double character" in the externalized opposition between the abstract (money) and the concrete (the commodity), so is bourgeois society characterized by the split between the state and civil society. For the individual, the split is expressed as that between the individual as citizen and as person. As a citizen, the individual is abstract as is expressed, for example, in the notion of equality before the (abstract) law, or in the principle of one person, one vote. As a person, the individual is concrete, embedded in real class relations that are considered to be "private," that is, pertaining to civil society, and which do not find political expression. In Europe, however, the notion of the nation as a purely political entity, abstracted from the substantiality of civil society, was never fully realized. The nation was not only a political entity, it was also concrete, determined by a common language, history, traditions, and religion. In this sense, the only group in Europe that fulfilled the determination of citizenship as a pure political abstraction was the Jews following their political emancipation. They were German or French citizens, but not really Germans or Frenchmen. They were of the nation abstractly, but rarely concretely. They were, in addition, citizens of most European countries. The quality of abstractness, characteristic not only of the value dimension in its immediacy, but also, mediately, of the bourgeois state and law, became closely identified with the Jews. In a period when the concrete became glorified against the abstract, against "capitalism" and the bourgeois state, this became a fatal association. The Jews were rootless, international, and abstract.

Modern anti-Semitism, then, is a particularly pernicious fetish form. Its power and danger result from its comprehensive worldview which explains and gives form to certain modes of anticapitalist discontent in a manner that leaves capitalism intact, by attacking the personifications of that social form. Anti-Semitism so understood allows one to grasp an essential moment of Nazism as a foreshortened anticapitalist movement, one characterized by a hatred of the abstract, a hypostatization of the existing concrete and by a single-minded, ruthless—but not necessarily hate-filled—mission: to rid the world of the source of all evil.

The extermination of European Jewry is the indication that it is far too simple to deal with Nazism as a mass movement with anticapitalist overtones which shed that husk in 1934 ("Roehm Putsch") at the latest, once it had served its purpose and state power had been seized. In the first place, ideological forms of thought are not simply conscious manipulations. In the second place, this view misunderstands the nature of Nazi "anticapitalism"—the extent to which it was intrinsically bound to the anti-Semitic worldview. Auschwitz indicates that connection. It is true that the somewhat too concrete and plebeian "anticapitalism" of the SA was dispensed with by 1934; not, however, the anti-Semitism thrust—the "knowledge" that the source of evil is the abstract, the Jew.

A capitalist factory is a place where value is produced, which "unfortunately" has to take the form of the production of goods, of use-values. The concrete is produced as the necessary carrier of the abstract. The extermination camps were *not* a terrible version of such a factory but, rather, should be seen as its grotesque, Aryan, "anticapitalist" *negation*. Auschwitz was a factory to "destroy value," that is, to destroy the personifications of the abstract. Its organization was that of a fiendish industrial process, the aim of which was to "liberate" the concrete from the abstract. The first step was to dehumanize, that is, to rip away the "mask" of humanity, of qualitative specificity, and reveal the Jews for what "they really are"—shadows, ciphers, numbered abstractions. The second step

was to then eradicate that abstractness, to transform it into smoke, try
in the process to wrest away the last remnants of the concrete mater
"use-value": clothes, gold, hair, soap.

Auschwitz, not the Nazi seizure of power in 1933, was the real "German
Revolution," the attempted "overthrow," not merely of a political order,
but of the existing social formation. By this one deed the world was to be
made safe from the tyranny of the abstract. In the process, the Nazis
"liberated" themselves from humanity.

The Nazis lost the war against the Soviet Union, America, and Britain.
They won their war, their "revolution," against the European Jews. They
not only succeeded in murdering six million Jewish children, women, and
men. They succeeded in destroying a culture—a very old culture—that of
European Jewry. It was a culture characterized by a tradition incorporat-
ing a complicated tension of particularity and universality. This inner
tension was duplicated as an external one, characterizing the relation of
the Jews with their Christian surroundings. The Jews were never fully
part of the larger societies in which they lived nor were they ever fully
apart from those societies. The results were frequently disastrous for the
Jews. Sometimes they were very fruitful. That field of tension became
sedimented in most individual Jews following the emancipation. The
ultimate resolution of this tension between the particular and the universal
is, in the Jewish tradition, a function of time, of history—the coming of
the Messiah. Perhaps, however, in the face of secularization and assimilation, European Jewry would have given up that tension. Perhaps that
culture would have gradually disappeared as a living tradition, before the
resolution of the particular and the universal had been realized. This
question will never be answered.

ERRATA

We hope the reader will understand that sometimes the exigencies of publishing are such that errors will occur in the most carefully edited books. Such is the case now. The interested reader will benefit from placing this sheet after page 314 in the chap-ᵗʳ end notes.

NOTES

ᵗI would like to thank Barbara Brick, Dan Diner, and Jeffrey Herf for their comments on ier version of this essay.

. All Jews in the German Democratic Republic, regardless of their political back-d, receive higher pensions from the government. They do not, however, receive these ᴐns as Jews, but as "antifascists."

2. A rare recent attempt in the West German media to qualitatively specify the Nazi ᴿmination of the Jews was made by Juergen Thorwald in *Der Spiegel* Feb. 5, 1979.

3. For example, see Norman Cohen, *Warrant for Genocide* (London, 1967).

4. Max Horkheimer, "Die Juden und Europa," *Zeitschrift für Sozialforschung* VII (1939), ᴐ. 1–49.

5. George L. Mosse, *The Crisis of German Ideology* (New York, 1964).

6. The epistemological dimension of Marx's critique is immanent to all of *Capital* but as explicated only within the context of his analysis of the commodity. The notion that the ᴀtegories simultaneously express particular "reified" social relations and forms of thought is ᴇry different from the mainstream Marx*ist* tradition in which the categories are understood in ᴿms of an "economic base," and thought is considered superstructural, to be derived from ᴀss interest and needs. This form of functionalism cannot—as was argued above—adequately ᵪplain the non-functionality of the extermination of the Jews. On a more general level, it ᴀnnot explain why a form of thought, which may very well be in the interests of particular ᴐcial classes or other social groupings, has the specific content it does. The same applies to the ᴇnlightenment notion of ideology (and religion) as the product of conscious manipulation. ᴴe popular belief in a particular ideology implies that it must have a resonance, the source of ᴜich must be explained. On the other hand, the Marx*ian* approach, further developed by ᴋács, the Frankfurt School, and Sohn-Rethel, stands opposed to those one-sided reactions ᵗraditional Marxism which have given up any serious attempt to understand forms of ᴜght historically and view any such attempt as "reductionist."

7. Proudhon, who in this sense can be considered one of the forefathers of modern anti-ᵗtism, therefore thought that abolishing money—the manifest mediation—would suffice ᴐolish capitalist relations. Capitalism, however, is characterized by mediated social re-ᴐns, objectified in the categorial forms, one of whose *expressions*, not *causes*, is money. ᴜdhon, in other words, mistook a form of appearance—money as the objectification of the ᵗract—for the essence of capitalism.

8. Theories of National Socialism that present it as "antimodern" or "irrationalist" cannot explain the interrelation of these two moments. The term "irrationalism" tends not to call into question prevailing "rationalism" and cannot explain the positive relation of an "irrationalist," biologistic" ideology to the ratio of industry and technology. The term "antimodern" tends to ignore the very modern aspects of Nazism and cannot account for the attack on some aspects of "the modern" and not on others. In fact, both analyses are one-sided and represent only the other, the abstract, dimension of the antinomy outlined above. They tend to defend prevailing, nonfascist "modernity" or "rationality" in an uncritical fashion. They have therefore left open the possibility for the emergence of new one-sided critiques (this time from the Left), such as those of M. Foucault or A. Glucksmann, which present modern capitalist civilization only in terms of the abstract. All these approaches not only do not allow for a theory of Nazism which provides an adequate explanation of the relation of "blood and the machine," but also cannot show that the opposition of the abstract and concrete, of positive reason and "irrationalism," does not define the parameters of an absolute choice, but that the terms of these oppositions are related to one another as the antinomic expressions of the dual manifest dimensions of the same essence: the social relations characteristic of the capitalist social formation. (In this sense, Lukács, in *Die Zerstorung der Vernunft*—horrified by the unspeakable brutality of the Nazis—fell behind his own critical insights on the antinomies of bourgeois thought which he developed twenty-five years earlier in *History and Class Consciousness*.) Such approaches further retain the antinomy rather than theoretically overcoming it.

9. In order to deal with the question of why modern anti-Semitism found varying degrees of response in various countries and became hegemonial in Germany, we would, of course, have to specify the argument with reference to the respective social and historical conditions. A point of departure in considering Germany, for example, would be the extremely rapid development of industrial capitalism, which heightened its attendant social dislocations, as well as the absence of a previous bourgeois revolution with its liberal values and political culture. The history of France from the Dreyfus Affair to Vichy, however, indicates that a bourgeois revolution prior to industrialization does not seem to constitute a sufficient condition of "immunity" against modern anti-Semitism. On the other hand, modern anti-Semitism was not very widespread in Great Britain, although race theories and Social Darwinism were certainly as prevalent there as on the Continent. One difference could be the degree and manner of the domination of the social abstract at the outset of large-scale industrialization. For example, the form of societalization in France could be conceptualized as being between that of England and that of Prussia, characterized by a particular form of "dual domination," that of the commodity and that of the state bureaucracy. Both are rationalized forms. They differ, however, in terms of the degree of abstractness with which they mediate domination. Perhaps there is a relation between the extent to which institutions of concrete domination, such as the state bureaucracy (including the army and police) and the church, prevailed in early capitalism and the degree to which the abstract domination of capital was later perceived not only as threatening, but as mysterious and alien.

ERRATA

We hope the reader will understand that sometimes the exigencies of publishing are such that errors will occur in the most carefully edited books. Such is the case now. The interested reader will benefit from placing this sheet after page 314 in the chapter end notes.

NOTES

*I would like to thank Barbara Brick, Dan Diner, and Jeffrey Herf for their comments on an earlier version of this essay.

1. All Jews in the German Democratic Republic, regardless of their political background, receive higher pensions from the government. They do not, however, receive these pensions as Jews, but as "antifascists."

2. A rare recent attempt in the West German media to qualitatively specify the Nazi extermination of the Jews was made by Juergen Thorwald in *Der Spiegel* Feb. 5, 1979.

3. For example, see Norman Cohen, *Warrant for Genocide* (London, 1967).

4. Max Horkheimer, "Die Juden und Europa," *Zeitschrift für Sozialforschung* VII (1939), pp. 1–49.

5. George L. Mosse, *The Crisis of German Ideology* (New York, 1964).

6. The epistemological dimension of Marx's critique is immanent to all of *Capital* but was explicated only within the context of his analysis of the commodity. The notion that the categories simultaneously express particular "reified" social relations and forms of thought is very different from the mainstream Marx*ist* tradition in which the categories are understood in terms of an "economic base," and thought is considered superstructural, to be derived from class interest and needs. This form of functionalism cannot—as was argued above—adequately explain the non-functionality of the extermination of the Jews. On a more general level, it cannot explain why a form of thought, which may very well be in the interests of particular social classes or other social groupings, has the specific content it does. The same applies to the Enlightenment notion of ideology (and religion) as the product of conscious manipulation. The popular belief in a particular ideology implies that it must have a resonance, the source of which must be explained. On the other hand, the Marx*ian* approach, further developed by Lukács, the Frankfurt School, and Sohn-Rethel, stands opposed to those one-sided reactions to traditional Marxism which have given up any serious attempt to understand forms of thought historically and view any such attempt as "reductionist."

7. Proudhon, who in this sense can be considered one of the forefathers of modern anti-Semitism, therefore thought that abolishing money—the manifest mediation—would suffice to abolish capitalist relations. Capitalism, however, is characterized by mediated social relations, objectified in the categorial forms, one of whose *expressions*, not *causes*, is money. Proudhon, in other words, mistook a form of appearance—money as the objectification of the abstract—for the essence of capitalism.

8. Theories of National Socialism that present it as "antimodern" or "irrationalist" [do] not explain the interrelation of these two moments. The term "irrationalism" tends not to [call] into question prevailing "rationalism" and cannot explain the positive relation of an "irrati[on]alist," biologistic" ideology to the ratio of industry and technology. The term "antimoder[n]" tends to ignore the very modern aspects of Nazism and cannot account for the attack on som[e] aspects of "the modern" and not on others. In fact, both analyses are one-sided and represen[t] only the other, the abstract, dimension of the antinomy outlined above. They tend to defe[nd] prevailing, nonfascist "modernity" or "rationality" in an uncritical fashion. They have therefo[re] left open the possibility for the emergence of new one-sided critiques (this time from the Left), such as those of M. Foucault or A. Glucksmann, which present modern capitalist civilization only in terms of the abstract. All these approaches not only do not allow for a theory of Nazism which provides an adequate explanation of the relation of "blood and the machine," but also cannot show that the opposition of the abstract and concrete, of positive reason and "irrationalism," does not define the parameters of an absolute choice, but that the terms of these oppositions are related to one another as the antinomic expressions of the dual manifest dimensions of the same essence: the social relations characteristic of the capitalist social formation. (In this sense, Lukács, in *Die Zerstörung der Vernunft*—horrified by the unspeakable brutality of the Nazis—fell behind his own critical insights on the antinomies of bourgeois thought which he developed twenty-five years earlier in *History and Class Consciousness*.) Such approaches further retain the antinomy rather than theoretically overcoming it.

9. In order to deal with the question of why modern anti-Semitism found varying degrees of response in various countries and became hegemonial in Germany, we would, of course, have to specify the argument with reference to the respective social and historical conditions. A point of departure in considering Germany, for example, would be the extremely rapid development of industrial capitalism, which heightened its attendant social dislocations, as well as the absence of a previous bourgeois revolution with its liberal values and political cul[t]ure. The history of France from the Dreyfus Affair to Vichy, however, indicates that [a bour]geois revolution prior to industrialization does not seem to constitute a sufficient con[dition of] "immunity" against modern anti-Semitism. On the other hand, modern anti-Semitism [was not] very widespread in Great Britain, although race theories and Social Darwinism were certainly as prevalent there as on the Continent. One difference could be the degree and manner of the domination of the social abstract at the outset of large-scale industrialization. For example, the form of societalization in France could be conceptualized as being between that of England and that of Prussia, characterized by a particular form of "dual domination," that of the commodity and that of the state bureaucracy. Both are rationalized forms. They differ, however, in terms of the degree of abstractness with which they mediate domination. Perhaps there is a relation between the extent to which institutions of concrete domination, such as the state bureaucracy (including the army and police) and the church, prevailed in early capitalism and the degree to which the abstract domination of capital was later perceived not only as threatening, but as mysterious and alien.

17

"THE JEWISH QUESTION" RECONSIDERED

NOTES ON ISTVÁN BIBÓ'S CLASSIC ESSAY
Ferenc Feher

István Bibó was one of the most important non-Marxist, leftist theorists of Eastern Europe in the last forty years. The need for this presentation of his *[illegible]* of itself, indicative of the extent to which original ideas are *[illegible]* and suppressed by governments and official apparatuses of Eastern Europe. Bibó (1911–1979) was born into a Protestant Hungarian family and was brought up in Hungary, Vienna, and Switzerland. He studied history and other social sciences and from youth on belonged to the Transylvanian branch of Hungarian social theory, which is characterized by an affinity to Cartesian rationalism and a firm but realistic Hungarian patriotism which, in contrast to the often shortsighted and foolhardy chauvinism of the Hungarian motherland, learned how to live between world powers without blind illusions or servile self-abandonment. Very early he developed a sense of the so-called social question which, in Hungary, was identical with the problem of the peasantry and agrarian reform. This is why he was very close to the movement of populist writers of the thirties, without sharing that romantic-anticapitalist irrationalism which (in spite of, or together with, their social radicalism) led some of them to an alliance with fascism and infected nearly all of them with anti-Semitism.

Bibó's central value was democracy, and though always *en garde* against the theory of the dictatorship of the proletariat, he felt a certain sympathy with Communists of the Popular Front mold. During the war he participated in what Hungarian resistance there was; Bibó himself was later to criticize it as consisting of *salon* conversations spiced with anti-German witticisms. His first creative period was between 1945 and 1948, when he published a series of important studies containing a fairly coherent theory of a new democracy. His concept of democracy differed from both people's democracy, a camouflage behind which Communist party dictatorship reigned supreme, and parliamentary pluralism in the classic liberal tradition. In Bibó, both the theoretically generalized Swiss experience of his youth (direct democracy) and a socially radical impetus were still at work. Of course, this theory brought him into frequent collisions with the Hungarian Communists who, despite their numerical insignificance, were a repository of most important powers immediately after 1945. To begin with, the state security police was in their hand, and they always "had the ears" of the omnipotent Soviet military, which remained a legitimate occupying force until 1948. It is a miracle of sorts that Bibó nevertheless continued to enjoy the approval of the Hungarian Communists, as evidenced by his remaining unimprisoned and unscathed, though he was a proscribed person in political and ideological circles during the terrible years between 1948 and 1953. This treatment was at least partly attributable to his personality. Anyone who met Bibó would have recognized his unselfish personal integrity and total absorption in the ideas that radiated from his schoolteacherlike being. It is possible that the Communist leaders, mostly ruthless, pragmatic Machiavellians, considered him a harmless dreamer rather than a rival. They made a mistake. The time was soon to come when Bibó showed that he could act as a statesman, perhaps better than those who had to rely on the bayonets of an occupying army and who immediately fled when the storm then conjured up finally broke out. In 1956, under Imre Nagy's second pluralistic government, Bibó became a minister of state without portfolio, a representative of the leftist Peasants' Party, which existed more in statements than in reality. He also worked out a *Program*, a draft for negotiations between the Soviet world-power and a new Hungary born in anti-Stalinist revolution. The draft was a masterpiece of political realism. Had the Soviet leaders had any intention other than crushing the Hungarian rebels by armed force, they would have found it a highly reasonable document. But they did not, so Bibó (who heroically smuggled out a *Memorandum* to the United Nations' Hungarian session) was arrested and sentenced to life imprisonment. Fortunately Bibó spent *only* six years in prison; for the remaining fifteen of his life he lived as a recluse in the secrecy of his study, where he wrote important studies on the international organizations. These were circulated at home as manuscripts, were smuggled out by friends and supporters, and appeared in print abroad. I had the opportunity to meet him a few times in his last years; his unpretentious personal dignity, his shabby clothes, and the visible poverty borne with indifference provided a reassuring contrast with the pretentious display of prosperity by the corrupted Kadarist intelligentsia.

The Political Aspect

The essay "The Jewish Question in Hungary" was written and published in 1948.[1] As far as "official" publications are concerned, it was Bibó's "swan song." There was good reason indeed to write a study of this problem. Five hundred thousand Hungarian Jews had been deported and gassed, mostly in Auschwitz in 1944, making Hungary's the third greatest quota of the Holocaust after the Polish and Russian contingents. In addition, although the deportation was a German action led personally by Eichmann, the "transportation expert," there was a marked official Hungarian co-responsibility for it. Parts of the Hungarian ruling classes, especially its forces of coercion, had been deeply infiltrated and corrupted by the Gestapo and other Nazi secret services; they frantically tried to remain voluntary allies even after March 1944, when Hitler occupied Hungary. Their most significant contribution to the alliance lay in domestic anti-Semitism: the gendarmerie confined rural Jewry in hastily improvised ghettos, reduced them to inhumane conditions, prepared lists of persons to be deported, and actually drove them with bayonets into wagons whose destinations could be no mystery to anyone after such preliminaries.

Bibó also documents amply that the Hungarian army and the gendarmerie persecuted Jews even *prior* to the German occupation, sometimes acting contrary to the instructions of their superior officers. The armed forces had for decades been a political weapon in the hands of the Hungarian ruling classes, and served mostly to keep the extremely poor and rebellious peasantry in check rather than as a law-enforcement agency. They handed over tens of thousands of Jews from the northern part of Hungary to German authorities with scarcely any doubts that they were to be gassed in Polish camps. Hungarian national responsibility in the Jewish question was undoubtedly enormous. True enough, Hungary was not the Soviet Union, and some of the main perpetrators were publicly tried and hanged as murderers of Jews, not just as "war criminals" in general.

There was good reason, then, for Bibó, the Cartesian democrat, to analyze the catastrophe that brought extinction to the majority of Hungarian Jews and stood as a moral and political test for *all* Hungarians— one that they failed. This is the conclusion of Bibó's investigation. But what explains the choice of the point of time, 1948? If we take into consideration that this was the period of the gathering storm, of a Communist takeover so clearly approaching that even people with incomparably less political foresight and talent than Bibó saw it coming, we may rightly guess that "The Jewish Question in Hungary" was rather a *parable* with multifarious "moral" lessons. (Parable and its allegorical didactics alone were left for a public analyst of social ills at that time of mummified parliamentarism, not *oratio recta.*) What were the "lessons to be drawn" from this parable? Firstly, that all social problems can result in catastrophe if a nation cannot work out a democratic model of resolving them: somewhat too general, but an unmistakable and highly topical warning at that time. Secondly, that parliamentary forms are not in themselves sufficient for this purpose; a more direct democracy, radical movements, a general tendency of equalizing socially and culturally underprivileged strata are needed as well. A third lesson: A type of "communication model" has to be politically developed (we will return to this below) in which all interests, all opinions, occupy a legitimate role, however hysterical or ideologically distorted they may be; the sole exception is that which tends to oppress all other interests and opinions, a restriction that applied above all to Nazi or pro-Nazi political forces.

One may object that while these "lessons" are undoubtedly sublime and worthy of universal consideration, they are too abstract in the case of the *particular* subject matter of Bibó's study. Yet I believe that the choice of the Jewish question in Hungary as the subject was far from random. Bibó, as a profoundly thinking radical democrat, had a norm: *It is always the relation to the "persecuted par excellence" that will decide whether there are democratic standards, expectations, and the like* in a nation or society, whether it "deserves" to be democratically governed or despotically ruled. This is obviously not a "definition of democracy" but rather a "borderline value," and one that can be used in an operative sense. It is precisely in this sense that in Bibó's assessment the Scandinavian countries and Holland *as democracies* pass the test brilliantly whereas Hungary, as a traditionally antidemocratic country, failed in its entirety, not only as far as its ruling classes are concerned, although they of course bore the brunt of responsibility.[2]

There is a crucial constituent of Bibó's model of radical democracy which he, being unphilosophical by nature, would have simply called objectivity or the principle of *audiatur et altera pars,* but which in the wake of Habermas one is inclined to term, as a system, domination-free communication. Although a man of the Enlightenment, Bibó is guided neither by excessive anthropological optimism nor by pessimism, but rather by *resignation.* It is precisely this resignation that leads him to the conviction that if one intends to achieve the goals of radical democracy, there is no other option left but objective and domination-free communication among *all* standpoints. For as frail as human beings are morally and psychologically, it is an option that still stands some chance and is worth trying. Hence the peculiar but important feature of Bibó's study, one which will inevitably disturb the biased Jewish reader but which is, nevertheless, an integral part of his intention. His addressees are not only Jews and philo-Semitic democrats or socialists but to some extent also the anti-Semite, who has to be convinced of his/her "optical distortion."[3] Of course, Bibó is skeptical enough to realize that not just *any* communication will result in healing the wounds or resolving millenial conflicts. As a determined man of the Enlightenment, he is ready to formulate the guidelines to the conditions under which (and under which alone) communication between the parties will be successful.

One should seek to remind oneself and all others of the concrete human content of everything that is Jewish and its fundamental identity with all other human conditions. The non-Jew should raise the question whether, behind the overestimation of offences caused by Jews cannot be found a refusal to recognize the human equality of Jews. . . . He [the non-Jew F. F.] should communicate and indefatigably repeat all the facts regarding the horrendous amount of Jewish suffering; he should speak of all the human insults which, in the form of the usual negative moral judgments and moral denigration of Jews, add to their physical torments and human losses. . . .

What could a non-Jew say to a Jew? The non-Jew should state his responsibility felt for Jewish sufferings without asking anything in return, especially not that Jews should forget and forgive what they have suffered. . . . The utmost he can ask them to do is not to isolate their cause from that of others, but to identify their sufferings with those of all who suffer, their humiliations with those of all who are being humiliated, their seeking for justice with the endeavors of all others who seek justice. What can a Jew say to a non-Jew? He could speak of the reality of Jewish experience and its direct human content . . . he *should* speak of the horrible facts of Jewish suffering in the distant and near past . . . he should not, however, try to convince non-Jews of the validity of his ideas about the causes of anti-Semitism in which non-Jews figure in an all too unpleasant and Jews in an all too pleasant light. . . . Finally, can there be anything productive said by a Jew to another Jew with regard to the struggle against anti-Semitism? . . . My hunch is that no Jewish moral preacher can start with anything but that which is the beginning and the end of all meaningful influence: Give up being confined to your own subjective experiences and do not mistake your own mental products for reality. . . . But these fundamental theses can be made concrete for Jews only by other Jews.[4]

In describing Bibó as a defender of Jewish equality *in his capacity as a democrat,* we must also counter Sartre when he writes: "Nevertheless, the

Jews have one friend, the democrat. But he is a miserable defender. To be sure, he proclaims that all human beings have equal rights. . . . But his very declarations show the weakness of his position. He has chosen . . . the spirit of analysis. He has no eyes for the concrete syntheses presented him by history. He knows neither Jew, nor Arab, nor Negro, nor bourgeois, nor worker, only man. . . . He resolves all collective entities into individual elements . . . for him, individual is nothing but the sum total of universal traits. It follows from this that his defence of the Jews saves the Jew as man and annihilates him as a Jew."[5] In spite of his Cartesian education, which is the very hotbed of the analytical spirit, Bibó is a different type of democrat and a genuine and worthy defender of Jews. Firstly (in marked contrast to the tacit presumption of his own definition of the anti-Semite) he is not a "philo-Semite," he is not a sentimental protector of Jews who remains on the whole unaffected by general human suffering while exclusively involved in his "pet victim." This one-sidedness is the reason that the philo-Semite cannot provide a universal-synthetic world explanation. However, Bibó can, and he understands "Jewish destiny" in terms of this universal explanation. Secondly, unlike Lenin, another defender of Jews, Bibó is not obsessed with the idea of assimilation but rather suggests a variety of solutions. Finally, he is "vaguely socialist," and the adjective is not meant pejoratively. At least in his youth, his ideal was the transcendence of capitalism, not through any dictatorship, but rather through what he calls "consensual revolution" and "revolution based on agreement"—a kind of socialist 1688. At the same time he refrains from tying this ideal to any particular socialist doctrine.

The following is a brief presentation of the stages in Bibó's account of the "Jewish question" in Hungary in the twentieth century. The first phase is initiated by the collapse of the Hungarian Soviet Republic and the establishment of the aggressively conservative dictatorship of Admiral Horthy—a dictatorship decorated with a pseudoparliamentary system. In characterizing the "status" of anti-Semitism during Horthy's regime which began its deplorable tenure with a brutal white terror against Communists, Socialists, and nonleftist Jews, Bibó terms the Jewish question a *social* problem. On the one hand, Horthy "punished" the Hungarian Jewry for its allegedly unpatriotic behavior during the war and especially during the revolutions. He did this by excluding them, first practically, then later (through the continuous, even if partial, introduction of the "Nuremberg laws") *formally* and "legally" from public life. On the other hand, his regime did not touch upon the wealth and, as a result, the social influence of Jewish capital. This is a true description but a questionable use of terminology in that it is intrinsically connected with Bibó's most dubious category, "Jewish experience," which I am going to analyze (and criticize) later. For the moment I would only add that anti-Semitism can always be just as "projective" as "social." The distinction simply means this: Anti-Semitism can sometimes be in the forefront of social life, even in countries where there are practically no more Jews. (Poland in 1968–1969 is an example of this.) In such cases anti-Semitism as an active and widespread feeling is obviously a projection of hatred, anxiety, inner confusion, and turbulence in the society in question, and stems from different sources. These "malfunctions" cannot be articulated in a manner adequate to their genuine nature but are projected onto the Jew as a universal and traditional symbol of the "origin" of social ills.

There is, however, another type of anti-Semitism for which there is some factual material to corroborate the "validity" of its fantasy which is centered on hatred and persecution. This is the type of anti-Semitism that constantly refers, for instance, to the unusually high percentage of Jews in the secret police of certain Communist countries, or the unusually high percentage of Jews among the wealthy bankers and industrialists of a certain capitalistic country. I would argue against Bibó that whereas anti-Semitism *cannot* be exclusively social, in that it must entail, by the very nature of this attitude, "projective" elements as well, it *can be* purely projective without any social frame of reference.

The second phase started in 1941, when Hungary joined Nazi Germany in its war against the Soviet Union (and symbolically its Western allies). It ended in 1944–1945 under German occupation when the Nazi organizations of the "final solution," widely assisted by various types and groups of Hungarian Fascists, murdered nearly 600,000 Hungarian Jews in Polish and Austrian annihilation camps, on the Eastern Front, in pogroms and massacres in so-called "front operational territories." For an accurate understanding of the situation and within it, the denouement of Jewish collective Calvary, it is necessary to consider the following factors. First, Hungary's ruling strata was Anglophile rather than pro-German and only when they had to accept as necessity (in the second part of the 1930s) Germany's prevalence and superior military power in the area, did they turn toward Hitler instead of Great Britain and France. In regard to Jews, this meant an increasing concession to Hitler's racist policy: the continuous but never wholehearted introduction of Nuremberg laws, on the one hand, and a (not morally motivated) hesitation to cross the threshold of a "final solution" on the other. It is this hesitation that saved the Budapest Jewry, decimated as it was in the ghetto, yet intact as a main body. They were kept as "exchange objects" and "tokens of goodwill" for the negotiations with Churchill. Secondly the Hungarian landed gentry, the backbone of Horthy's dictatorship—of the army, administration, and police forces—had been intermarried with Jewish money for at least three generations. Radical Nazism, with its widely extended Nuremberg legislation, would have placed this very stratum into the traps of "Aryan laws." Hence it had good reason to fear Nazism proper. Finally, Hungarian Nazism, insignificant in number, loud and vulgar in its demagogy, was much too plebeian and much too radical (in the sense that Roehm's SA meant radicalism within Nazism) for the Hungarian ruling classes.

Bibó lives up to his own norms: For him, the second phase, the Holocaust of the Hungarian Jewry, is the absolute criterion for the moral decay of Hungarian society. This, not territorial losses, is the greatest catastrophe, for it was in this that Hungary as a whole nation became co-responsible for fascist crimes. He speaks of collective *responsibility* (and as a strict moralist, rejects out of hand the efforts of those who would suggest silence in order to protect the "Hungarian reputation"), *but not of collective guilt*. As a theological category applied to social bodies, collective guilt can only cause unjust acts and outbursts of unacceptable revenge rather than mete out just punishment. Collective responsibility means the exact and rational assessment of varying levels and extent of responsibility. At the same time, and in perfect harmony with the distributive justice of his rationality, Bibó defines the exact portion of responsibility for the Horthyist ruling classes. They were no murderers in the Nazi sense (even if they were indulgent toward Nazi crimes in the Hungarian army, gendarmerie, and so forth, for which they bear full responsibility). But they made concessions to Nazi racism.

The third stage, which began in 1945, was largely an open matter to be decided in the future. The crucial question was the following: What are the *Jewish perspectives*? According to Bibó's method, *in uno actu*, this was a question for Hungarian democracy, namely, that of the vitality and commanding validity of democratic norms in Hungarian society or their total absence from it. Once again, then, the parable about the future and the chances for democracy was *not accidentally* written on the fate of the "persecuted *par excellence*," the Jew.[6]

At this point, Bibó, the historian and sociologist, the skeptical realist of political theory, gives an answer far superior to Sartre's radical and rigorous, but exclusively moralizing option. The Sartrean text is lucid and leaves no doubt about the *only* solution open to a Jew:

> Jewish authenticity consists of choosing oneself *as a Jew,* in other words, of realizing the Jewish condition. The authentic Jew abandons the myth of universal man: he is aware of himself and wills himself in history as a creature, historical and damned; he ceases to escape from, and be ashamed of, his own next of kin. He has understood that society is wrong; he substitutes a social pluralism for the naive monism of the inauthentic Jew; he

knows that he is *excluded*, untouchable, shameful, proscribed and he reclaims himself *as such*. All of a sudden, he renounces his rationalist optimism: he sees that the world is fragmented by irrational divisions, and by accepting this fragmentation, in that he proclaims himself Jew, he appropriates some of its values and dividends; he chooses his brothers and his equals: they are the other Jews; he "bets" *(parie)* on human greatness by accepting a life which is by definition unliveable—for he takes his pride from his humiliation.[7]

Sartre's tragic colors, the *grandeur* of his morphology, fit one situation specifically: the historical hour of the Warsaw ghetto uprising. It was then that, for the first time, the millennial underdog struck back, thus testifying against being subhuman; that a community of Jews in the process of *becoming authentic* chose themselves, their existence, this scandal of moral world order (and by the same act: their obliteration) and thus also chose human greatness and dignity. All these old-fashioned words for which alone it is worth living are in this case adjectives of a *borderline* situation. (Whereby I do not at all deny the *moral* relevance of Sartre's precept in more "daily" situations.)

But what would be the *sociologically generalizable* options? Here we have to listen rather to Bibó, the skeptical realist. His first remark seems to be entirely negative: There is *no primacy* of Jewish emancipation as compared with the general process of human emancipation (by which, we already know, he means a "certain type" of socialism). Anti-Semitism cannot be eliminated from a "Jewish" position. But the negative statement can be formulated positively as well, even if it is not, or but rarely, formulated by Bibó: A "new world" is needed in order that Jewish humiliation, Jewish suffering, together with all other types and classes of humiliation and suffering, should disappear. Bibó stresses very emphatically that this methodological viewpoint does *not* mean the acceptance of the Communist recipe which tells us to remain silent about the Jewish question. Jews were one group of victims among many, and do not deserve any distinguished place in the narrative of sufferings.

For Bibó, the Jew remains the victim *par excellence;* his Calvary the story about the limits of human nature, and what is beyond. But more important is what Bibó has to say about the "Jewish ways out" of a situation created by the Holocaust. Emphasis is laid on the *plural*. Bibó does not belong to the type of friends of Jews for whom there is one, and only one, salutary solution. His nondoctrinaire socialism rests (without a philosophical elaboration of the problem) on the recognition of a plurality of human needs, and he consistently applies his principle to the Jewish problem. I wish to emphasize how unusual the pluralism of needs is in this particular case. *Generally speaking,* within a liberal (or even liberal-conservative) state of affairs, problems like assimilation or emigration and the like are easily resolved and—until they collide with other (state or group) interests— have no dramatic dimensions. But in the particular case of Jews, precisely because they became either the universal scapegoat, the prime target of projective hatred, or the scandal of civilization— its shame personified— passions tended to extinguish calculative reason and everyone believed themselves in possession of one absolute remedy: a "final solution" or an "ultimate liberation." To give Sartre's paraphrase, in this regard both open enemies and false friends of Jews strive for the actual extinction of the Jew, in one way or the other, but always through the application of *one* exclusive recipe.

Bibó's pluralism starts with the analysis of *assimilation,* and understandably so: Without any special knowledge in the field, I think it is fair to say that up until the Holocaust, the empirical majority of Jews chose (or at least experimented with) assimilation. However afterward, and precisely because of what happened, assimilation, once seemingly so smooth a process, became a problem even for the assimilated. At this point, Bibó's unmatched "sociological realism" comes to the fore: In the wide literature on the problem there is practically no one to compare with him when it comes to the analysis of its *practical options.* His hypercritical mind immediately avoids the usual, and totally sterile, bifurcation of alternatives—the eternal pitfall of this debate—into assimilation or not assimilation. He knows perfectly well that an infinite amount of argument can be mobilized equally for and against, with the result that the problem cannot be solved on an abstract level. Instead, he raises two other highly relevant questions: *What kind* of assimilation and assimilation *to what?* Here he distinguishes between *organic* and *rational* assimilation. The first is an unattainable ideal and a dangerous one. It stems from an irrationalist mythology and almost inevitably results in zenophobia. Since Bibó is an enemy of racism (he is unable to look for the reason for it among the genes) and yet seeks to fathom the causes of such an aggressive mythology, he introduces a distinction which I find unsatisfactory from a scientific and philosophical standpoint, but productive as far as its sociological yield is concerned. The distinction is between *connate* or *ethnic* manifestations, which are (or have become) *instinctive* and *communal patterns of behavior* (ways of "social procedures," language, rules regarding games, prestige and honor, human contacts, models of behavior, communal goals, ideals, discipline, and so on). Assimilation *cannot* in fact be based on the first set of characteristics and if it is, if the goal of those to be assimilated or the requirement of the assimilating community is the attainment of such an "organic merger," then the result can only be a new flare-up of irrational hatred against the "irreparably alien." Bibó is unambiguous concerning what he means by *rational* assimilation:

> The line of demarcation between these two groups of communal character traits is, of course, fluid. This much is certain, however, namely, that it is, first of all, the second group of characteristics that provides the bulk of qualities to which one can and should assimilate. To become assimilated does not mean to "eject" all characteristic or recognizable features; to become undiscriminable, "organic." All this is not the essence, but is at best a late and collateral phenomenon accompanying assimilation. Assimilation should not prevent someone from retaining his characteristic nose, characteristic cuisine, characteristic style of life, characteristic set phrases, alien expressions—in other words, all those physical and ethnic manifestations of life, which have no or very little sociological relevance. Assimilation means participating in the life process of a real and active community; getting acquainted with, practicing and accepting its patterns of behavior, conventions, requirements.[8]

Here I shall note only the most important theoretical conclusion to be derived from this viewpoint. In a rough typology, the *conceptions of nation* can be divided into two, diametrically opposed types: the *contractual* and the *organic*. (For the latter, it would be more appropriate to use the word *patria* or *Vaterland*.) The first is based, at least in principle, on the free decision of citizens—despite all the intricate implications of contract theories and even if contract does not exclude by its very character collective egoism, jingoism, and the like. At least it guarantees constitutionally certain fundamental rights with regard to national affiliation, including immigration and emigration. It is a highly rational, although not "businesslike" relation in which emotional elements, unselfish dedication, taking risks, and in moments of danger, even sacrificing one's life are also not absent. In the second, the opposite prevails in an emotionally intensified way (sometimes heightened to hysteria). This is why for irrational and tyrannical reasons this relation is often problematic. The requirement of *patria* is (and herein lies the opposite element) that the state subject should accept its historically given status as something "deeper" than the self-chosen attitude which is "alien" (in Eastern-Central Europe: mostly "Jewish," "individualistic," "suspicious," "inorganic," and the like). It was not by chance that I used the term "state subject" instead of citizen. Even after the countries in question achieved some kind of a constitution, they remained for a variety of historical reasons "organic," and *in this sense, intolerant and half-feudal* toward those living within their borderlines.[9] When Bibó argues *against organic* Jewish assimilation, he also argues against "patria" and for a free "contractual" type of nation. This commitment is especially valuable, since it does not come from some "suspicious," "inorganic," "alien" element but from an enthusiastic Hungarian patriot for whom the Hungarian (and Protestant-Transsylvanian) past is precious and who is absorbed by its reliquiae and lingo.

On this basis, it can also be made clear *to what* Jews should assimilate if they choose to do so. First of all, to the *language* and the *"elementary norms of habit"* of the new community. Further, to its *basic "network of solidarity."* In Bibó, the impartial democrat, this is meant as a critique of what is popularly called "Jewish clannishness." The latter is, by the way, so far from being an exclusively Jewish characteristic that its most extreme and dangerous examples were provided by German minorities in Czechoslovakia, Poland, and Hungary during the Hitler regime. They opposed their justified and often violated minority rights to the legal and political existence of the "mother" state. Finally and very importantly, Bibó stresses in his typical "moralizing" way not only the responsibility of the assimilant but (unlike the majority of works dealing with the problem) the responsibility of the *assimilating community* as well. There the basic category is *reciprocity:* The receiving community has to give material and spiritual "accommodation," and above all, *protection* for those assimilating to it.

Once again, Bibó becomes a severe moral and political critic of his own community. He argues that it was to be predicted from the beginning, that is to say, from the late nineteenth century onward, that Jewish assimilation in Hungary (one may add in Eastern Europe in general) would not succeed, so "unbalanced" or lacking in democratic norms was the inner life of the Hungarian community. Hungarian life and assimilation to it produced hundreds of thousands of "half assimilants" (Sartre would say: inauthentic Jews). They were people who left the (originally religious) Jewish community without appropriating or aspiring to appropriate another and subsisting, economically sometimes very prosperously, in a cultural no-man's-land. And when the Hungarian Jewry was abandoned to the mercy of the Nazis—for which, as we know from Bibó's analysis, all strata of the Hungarian community were equally responsible even if they did not share in it equally—this community betrayed the principle of reciprocity on which alone non-organic-rational assimilation may rest.

Bibó draws the obvious and oft-repeated conclusion that Zionism thrives on the ruins of misconceived Jewish assimilation. Though such a conclusion may not have been unique, the conditions under which it was formulated and spelled out, however, testified to a unique courage. Bibó defends the right to Zionist organization, even against the Communists in 1948 (!), the year when Stalin's myrmidons murdered Shlomo Mikhoels, the head of the Soviet Jewish cultural community, executed twenty-four leading Jewish cultural activists and intellectuals in the so-called "Jewish Crimean conspiracy trial," and destroyed the whole of Jewish cultural autonomy in the Soviet Union. Bibó may have been unaware of these facts, but it could not have escaped his attention—he was politically too sensitive for this—that hostile winds had started to blow from the Soviet Union toward the Eastern European Jewry.

While Bibó is not uncritical of Zionism, the *second* massive "Jewish way out" of the post-Holocaust, he does not feel himself entitled either on moral or scholarly grounds to criticize the idea itself. For him, the brunt of reprobation must fall on its manner of realization. Zionists ought to understand, he writes, that an overzealous recruiting would discredit precisely one of the greatest merits of the doctrine, namely, that it is conceived as a free and contractual nationalism. Should it be driven beyond its limits and transformed into an "organic" principle (which is obviously counterfactual, given that the majority of even the surviving Jews did not choose Israel), it would lose all its emancipatory thrust.

Bibó does not rule out a third, collective way out of the psychological-intellectual misery of the post-Holocaust: not Zionist emigration nor rational and contractual assimilation, but rather *ethnic separation within a confederative system.* Not only does he consider this ethnic separation to be perfectly in harmony with the Jews' fundamental human rights (in sharp contrast with the Soviet Union, which degraded this tendency into a symbolic ghetto for Jews), but he was also capable of an impartial and distanced analysis of its preconditions and traps. Basically, Bibó sees two preconditions for such an ethnic separation, neither of them absolutely obligatory and both very likely: *lingual separation* and *massive relapse into religion.* The first needs no further commentary. The second, in addition to the difficulty it raises for the "enlightenment process" so dear to Bibó, is complicated by another factor. If Bibó refrains from generalizing about religions, he does note that religious *neology,* rather than having emancipated Jews, presented them with a problem. While no longer a binding moral formula regulating life in its entirety, religion still divides Jew from non-Jew. Thus while Bibó is not denying the legitimacy and the relevance of ethnic separation, he does warn against a number of difficulties provoked or intensified by it in view of the "consensual" transition to the type of vague "democratic socialism" he had chosen.

Finally, to complete this overview, Bibó mentions another significant if ungeneralizable way out, namely the life-style of what he calls the "dissimilant." This type is overwhelmingly characterized by *negative* features. (Actually, this is the one closest to Sartre's authentic Jew.) It is *not* rooted in any national community; it is *not* assimilated, although it is also *not* Zionist or ethnic separatist. In the majority of cases, the sociological equivalent of this "dissimilant" is a cosmopolitan intellectual with an awareness of all the traps stemming from being Jewish. It is indicative of Bibó's impartial theoretical "magnanimity" that even if he regards this type as transitory, and even if, as a sociologist and political theorist, he has a predilection for generalizable options, he still includes this over-whelmingly intellectual phenomenon in this typology.

As I continue the Jewish story in Hungary (as Bibó could not) and turn to its fourth and fifth stage, I do so with less skill and breadth of information—and inevitably with less impartiality. Nevertheless, the story must be recounted up to the present. The *fourth* stage begins with the Communist takeover in Hungary in 1948 and ends with the 1956 revolution. In this period, on the *Communist side,* that ever prominent feature of Hungarian communism, namely the hypertrophic presence of Jewish elements, was even increased. This occurred at the most sensitive and conspicuous points of social life, in the Politbureau and in the AVH, the dreaded secret police, both leading positions of the ideological apparatus. While not wishing to advocate any kind of *numerus clausus,* I would still call this situation a malignant hypertrophy. As early as the 1919 revolution, the number of Jewish Communist *and* social democratic people's commissaries and dep-uty commissaries was so overwhelming (nearly exclusive) that the white terror could easily equate communism (or socialism in general) with Jewry. In the great purges of the 1930s Stalin usually preferred as sur-vivors non-Jews to Jews, but in the Hungarian case, even *his* omnipotence proved to be futile: *All* contending factions, the whole reservoir of Hun-garian communism, consisted mainly of Jews. It is thus that Rákosi came to power, a classic case of half-assimilation and "clannishness," whom Berija called the "first and last Jewish king of Hungary."

Stalin's allegedly unlimited power over all Communist parties in every area once again proved to be a myth. When it came to Jewish predomi-nance, the otherwise cowardly and pathologically servile Rákosi was in-flexibly obstinate. Bibó may not have known, but Rákosi had to know what happened to Jewish activists in the Soviet Union. Nonetheless, it remained strict party policy that as long as he had absolute power (up until June 1953) no data about the increasingly anti-Semitic overtones of Soviet political life was to reach the ears of the sensitive Hungarian "general public." It is most telling that while Rákosi was pushing other Communist leaders (Beirut, Gottwald) into having *their own* show-trials—not wanting to remain alone (in the company of his Bulgarian colleagues)—when it came to the Slansky trial with its unmistakably anti-Semitic character, the trial itself was dealt with at length while the aspect of anti-Semitism was toned down to a minimum. It was only the "Jewish doctors' plot" in early 1953 that forced Rákosi to realize that he could not go any farther with his

Jewish-centered policy without seriously endangering himself. He hastily concocted a Hungarian "Jewish plot" (partly among secret police officers who had outlived their usefulness), but when Stalin died, the "Jewish plot" collapsed. Rákosi's unchallenged rule came to its end as well.

This cynical wisdom had a predictable conclusion: In spite of the marked presence of Jewish intellectuals in the opposition preparing the ground for the revolution between 1953 and 1955, the 1956 revolution was the first moment after 1945 (apart from three pogroms between 1945 and 1947) in which anti-Semitism publicly appeared on the streets. This happened simply because many Hungarians, even those demanding a democratic or vaguely socialist transformation, tended to see Rákosi's rule as a "Jewish regime." To what extent a system with an overwhelming Jewish presence in its police, press, and leading political bodies could be termed "Jewish rule" had already been raised in the hour of preparation by the hypersensitive Bibó. But the case has to be reopened now in retrospect.

It would be perhaps too cheap to point to the carefully distributed presence of Jews among the victims of the show-trials (two of the five executed in the Rajk trial alone were Jews). Bibó has a *rational* (measurable and generalizable) criterion for what sensibly can be called "Jewish rule." Is such a rule advantageous and profitable for the *whole* (or at least the overwhelming majority) of Jews as an *ethnic* group as opposed to others? This is the question, the answer to which decides whether a rule is Jewish or non-Jewish in character. If we raise this question, the following facts immediately come to mind. First, Jewish martyrdom, the Holocaust in general and its Hungarian version in particular, became anathema at the moment that the Communist party seized political power. Second, and more important, the Hungarian government, this allegedly "Jewish dictatorship," showed an astounding ambivalence regarding the past. On the other hand, they did sign the peace treaty, thereby acknowledging *formally* their responsibility for deeds of former pro-Nazi governments. This was a demand of the victorious allies that they had to meet. They also produced halfway open, halfway covert propaganda about "Hungarian responsibility" for participating in the war; for certain Hungarian atrocities such as those, for instance, committed for the most part in the Ukraine by Hungarian soldiers against Ukrainian peasants. But the acts committed by Hungarians and Germans against *Hungarian Jews* became nonevents not only in the press. The Hungarian government, reeking of Jewish clannishness, disclaimed any and all responsibility for the surviving Jews.

So in this allegedly Jewish rule, the surviving Jewish community (steadily diminishing from 200,000 in 1945 to the present 60,000 or about) whose members, according to a popular myth, even had money under their skin, were, if not employed by the Communist party top hierarchy, double pariahs of a society, and at any rate poor.[10] It is highly characteristic of the outcome of Bibó's radical-democratic expectations, that in the dark night of the early 1950s everything promising turned to its deplorable opposite and that there was not a single oppositional intellectual, Jew or non-Jew, who would have mentioned, during the "Hungarian Spring" of 1953–1956, this burning shame of national life.

Kádárism, as a *fifth phase* of the Jewish question in Hungary in the twentieth century, brought new elements to this complex problem. The Kádárist "consolidation" can be summed up as a mélange of *Leninist "philo-Semitism,"* a *carefully measured political numerus clausus,* plus a continuation of the total suppression of any public discussion or analysis of the problem. In other words, it is a dogmatically assimilationist system that functions without superfluous dogmatic escapades and without oppressing a community whose presence after 1956 in Hungarian society became rather more "projective" than "social." On the other hand, it shows all the inner contradictions and impotence of a "philo-Semitic" regime based on conservative coercion and manipulation.

But in order to understand the whole intricacy of the Kádárist position, one has to take into consideration that it was precisely during Kádár's advent to power in 1956–1957 that final shape was given to *Soviet anti-Semitism.* William Korey, in his excellent and uniquely documented book *The Soviet Cage,* gives the story of the officially supported and even officially organized Soviet anti-Semitism. But one of his remarks shows that he is perhaps not fully aware of all the implications of his own story. The remark reads:

> The twin aspects of Soviet policy of Jews stand in fundamental contradiction to one another. On the one hand, there is the attempt to bring about the forcible assimilation of Jews through the elimination of specific Jewish institutions and the obliteration of references to Jewish tradition, especially Jewish martyrdom. On the other hand, there is the enforcement of patterns of discrimination, based precisely upon the nationality identification in passports and questionnaires. And the patterns of discrimination are accompanied by a propaganda campaign which stimulates and strengthens local sources of anti-Semitism, including those sources which give effect to and, indeed, extend the patterns.[11]

The historical *locus* of this policy can only be correctly understood with a brief sketch of the phases of Soviet anti-Semitism. Judged by the most authoritative sources (such as Korey's book or Schwartz's more naive but very valuable and amply documented essay published during Stalin's lifetime, in New York: *Antisemitism v Sovietskom Soiuze*), there can be hardly any doubt about the fact that Jews felt the Leninist period and its immediate aftermath as their emancipation from a Czarist rule that had openly incited pogroms. They were represented in all segments of the country's life and in political and intellectual strata were even overrepresented. In the 1930s, despite the fact that Stalin's personal anti-Semitism became increasingly visible in the internecine party strife against Jewish opponents, nothing basically changed. The bloodbath was so universal that Jew and non-Jew alike felt threatened.

The negative turn, in a doubly paradoxical and deeply tragic way, came in the anti-Hitler war and it was initiated *from below, not from the top*. There is overwhelming evidence to support three facts. First, it is beyond doubt that the Nazi occupation, which was at first accepted by wide strata at least with uncertain hopes, for the first time after a quarter of a century's oppression by Cheka and GPU methods, gave vent to traditional Russian (Ukrainian, and so forth) anti-Semitism. The usual identification of the Soviet regime with Jewry was widespread in occupied territories. At least in two republics, Lithuania and the Ukraine, significant groups of the population participated in the mass extermination of Jews, the situation best described in terms of Bibó's morphology of the Hungarian attitude to Jews. Secondly, it seems to be irrefutably documented that the partisan movement was either indifferent toward the fate of Jews (but even in this case they did not tolerate, or hardly, Jews in the Ukrainian and other partisan groups) or were directly hostile, even menacing toward Jews who lived in so-called "family camps" in the endless Russian and Ukrainian forests and who had formed their own partisan groups. In addition, there is no substantial evidence of the Soviet government's having put any kind of special pressure on its own partisans to include or even protect escaping Jews even though they were dependent on them, at least as far as armament supply was concerned. Thirdly, it has been proven beyond the slightest doubt that throughout the war the Soviet press systematically suppressed all evidence of the Holocaust. The story of this unprecedented genocide was merged into a suffering *en general*. But there was a deeper implication still behind this silence: The Soviet government actually made a compromise with popular anti-Semitism and started to "assimilate" some of its elements into its own, official, politics.

> In the autumn of the same year, 1944, Stalin called a meeting in the Kremlin that was attended by members of the Politburo and Central Committee Secretariat, republic and regional first Party secretaries and leaders of the defense industry, the Army and the state security organs. The topic under discussion was the "Jewish question." In his opening remarks Stalin expressed his support, though with certain reservations, for a "more cautious" policy towards the appointment of Jews to leading positions in state and

Party institutions. All those present understood perfectly well that he was talking about the gradual exclusion of Jews from important jobs. A more detailed speech was given on this occasion by G. M. Malenkov, who demonstrated the need for "heightened alertness" in relation to the Jewish cadres. Soon after this meeting Party committees at various levels received a memorandum signed by Malenkov (later known in party circles as the "Malenkov circular") which listed those jobs that it was thought undesirable to give to Jews. At the same time, certain limitations were imposed on the admission of Jews to institutions of higher education.[12]

The next phase came between 1948 and 1953, following a short postwar armistice between Jews and authorities during which Jewish culture seemed to flourish. Its point of departure was the above-mentioned physical elimination of the best Jewish militant intellectuals (all pro-Soviet and emotionally Communist) in the so-called "Crimea trial" and it reached its peak in the "doctors' plot," where there is evidence of both incipient "popular" pogroms and a mass deportation of Jews prepared (or planned) by Stalin. Considering Stalin's ways of settling "social ills," this is surely more than a mere fairy tale.

As in so many spheres, here too Krushchev put an end to Stalinist practices on the one hand, and introduced elements of a conservative consolidation of the system on the other. However, there is a far greater continuity in Krushchev and his successors in regard to the Jewish problem than in many other fields. The new system, combining forcible assimilation and discrimination *without* plans (or fantasy images) for mass extermination, works in a number of ways. The first is the separation of Soviet Jewry (some two million people) from the bulk of the population by official designation, the most important of which is the designation "evrei" (Jew) in the Soviet citizen's identity card, "internal passport," a label based on and checked and rechecked by very far-reaching, "Nuremberg-like" investigation of one's ancestors. As a result, Soviet Jews constitute only *de jure* not *de facto* a nationality group; they only "enjoy" all the disadvantages of forcible official separation from all other (e.g., Russian, Ukrainian) nationalities.

Secondly, an elaborate system of *numerus nullus* and *numerus clausus* is built on this forcible separation. *Numerus nullus* prevails in political leadership, among the higher ranks of army and navy officer corps and the KGB, the Foreign Ministry, and diplomatic services.[13]

Thirdly, there is a practice started under Krushchev, but intensified ever since, that the Soviet mass media regularly publish articles and satirical drawings and the rubric "Zionist"—which publicize precisely the same (or very similar) anti-Semitic stereotypes as the Nazi *Stuermer,* for which

Julius Streicher, the only "ideological" defendant of the Nuremberg trials, was justly executed. More than being simply derisive in a hostile manner and inciting to anti-Jewish hatred, the "anti-Zionist" propaganda puts the Jew into the context of an "infernal international conspiracy."

Only against this background can Kádárism and its policy on the Jewish question be assessed objectively. In this regard, Kádár, a man for whom it is a matter of genuine inner bathos that he feels himself a "Leninist," can enjoy the satisfaction that he is more "Krushchevite" than Krushchev himself. When it came to the Jewish question, Lenin, a man devoted to forced assimilation, was nevertheless a philo-Semite. Krushchev was an anti-Semite. Kádár's philo-Semitism is immediately visible within the Hungarian scene, where overt manifestations of both Soviet and anti-Soviet anti-Semitism are coercively suppressed.[14] And Kádárist philo-Semitism is not simply cautious silence during periods when the dirty flood of old-time and anti-Jewish propaganda is flowing copiously from the Soviet, Czech, and Polish mass media. Korey mentions a series of public acts of the Hungarian leadership: the ample Hungarian press coverage of Eichmann's trial, which was either a nonevent in the Soviet Union or a mere pretext for attacks against Adenauer; the very careful wording of the Hungarian standpoint following the 1967 Israeli-Arab war, which made it unmistakably clear that the Hungarian government's pro-Arab foreign policy would not mean tolerance toward militant anti-Semitism in the disguise of anti-Zionism (and in fact did not). Hence it was not accidental and indeed was a warning to the Hungarian leadership, at that time increasingly in disfavor with Breshnev, when on February 3, 1972, Pravda referred to the "intrigues of Zionism" supposedly increasing in Hungary.[15]

On the other hand, the Kádárist case study demonstrates that without democratic safeguards the best intentions of "higher authorities" will not eliminate the Jewish question. More profoundly still, it testifies to the impossibility of eliminating the Jewish question (even its "projective" version) through philo-Semitism pure and simple. Following both Leninist convictions and political shrewdness (Lenin clearly urged that the situation not be turned into a social conflict, a situation that in turn became, because of the small number of the Jews, only projective), Kádár did everything he could. He went to the limits of his possibilities, something that cannot be said for the overcautious Hungarian leadership. The omnipresent agents of the Hungarian secret police not only noted, they also *understood* what a certain lecturer of "Marxism-Leninism" meant when she allegedly said that all revisionists are Zionists (the person in question was "seriously warned," a doubtful support for Jews, to say the least). There is also no *numerus nullus* in Hungarian political life, which in itself is always an absolute indicator of anti-Semitic hatred. However, there is a cautious *numerus clausus* at the top, which is there in order to avoid the bad "popular press" of the Rákosi leadership.

But there is one revealing fact that cannot be explained away by the notion of "complying with Soviet wishes": The Jewish question remained, even historically, anathema for Hungarian cultural life. With the exception of a few books, the last twenty years have seen hardly any publication about the fate and history of Hungarian Jewry. No sociology of the Hungarian Jewish community is tolerated. There is, to be sure, a rabbinical instruction whose freedom of activity and level is unparalleled in "real socialism," but this fits the general pattern of Kádárist tolerance toward religions. No public utterance of the fact that the Jewish problem has existed since 1945 is admitted in the Hungarian press. Even if Hungarian Jews could, with a historical delay, accept a part of German recompensation for their (or their relatives') suffering, no legislative act has ever been passed during Kádár's nearly quarter of a century leadership to make up for the negligence of the "Jewish king," Rákosi: namely, to declare publicly that Hungarian Jewry was Hungary's prime victim and greatest homogeneous war casualty and as such, the nation owes at least some symbolic compensation to their surviving relatives and offspring.

Why the silence if Kádárism is a philo-Semitic regime? Simply because of Soviet pressure? I do not think so. Some of the reasons are obvious. Kádárism, as all Eastern European dictatorships, is most hesitant to admit the existence of *any* inner social tension. It is even less ready to tolerate public and democratic debate about the sore points of social life, let alone give in to *autonomistic* tendencies. (Of course, because of the silence imposed upon them, no one knows whether there are such in the very small Hungarian Jewish community.) But there is another reason for my firm conviction. Historically, Kádárism finds itself at the point at which the Soviet leadership was during the war. In spite of the lack of anti-Semitic tendencies, it has to yield to the pressure of a new anti-Semitism from below, which is increasingly militant but which is not necessarily anti-Kádárist. To make the sociological formula complete, let me emphasize that I do not mean the simple, spontaneous popular anti-Semitism that exists in pubs and football stadiums, not do I refer to antediluvian vestiges of the Horthy times. There is now in Hungary a new anti-Semitism of the *middle classes* (among them intellectuals) which is multifaceted and, as anti-Semitism always is, aimed at different targets. On the one hand, it is vehemently anti-Marxist and antisocialist, and in the usual manner of anti-Semitic radicalism, produces hybrid monsters of imagination by coupling incompatibles: Oppositional intellectuals are linked with the regime they are opposed to on the grounds that they are both nominally Marxist, or at least socialist and, by implication, Jewish. On the other hand, as I mentioned, this increasing new wave of anti-Semitism is not necessarily anti-Kádárist. Partly it considers the dissidents (an unusually high number of whom are, according to long-term Hungarian traditions, Jewish) to be "alien elements" and is totally mistrustful of them. In January, 1977, Hungarian dissidents organized a collective action of solidarity with Charter 77, whose organizers and signatories alike were, in fact, for the most part Jews. A celebrated Hungarian intellectual, known for his critical opinions, was asked in a confidential circle of friends in Paris why he did not join them. He answered: "I do not join such Jewish actions." Kádárism is regarded in part by many nationalist and anti-Semitic middle-class people as providing a maximum of comfort in Eastern Europe. For them, servility is Hungarian and "trouble-making" is alien, in other words, Jewish.

It does not take any special acumen or analytic training to see that we are confronted here with a classic—and multifaceted—case of *projective* anti-Semitism. In part it is the hostility felt because of their own social impotence, which is naturally projected onto those who took the risk. As with all projections of this sort, it is conceived in bad faith and needs the *traditional* scapegoat for purposes of rationalization. What comes through the filters of a distorted attitude is equally an act of bad faith: an intended dissent which does not have the guts for it. A classic self-manifestation of this is the following. The "national problem" (that is, independence) is an unresolved problem; it cannot even be resolved under given Eastern-European conditions. Nevertheless, let us support the government (which is at least halfway patriotic and defends some of the national interests) rather than joining these "uprooted" ones who are constantly involved in Czech, Polish, and other alien affairs. Understandably so, since they are alien themselves, in other words, Jews. This is a classic projective attitude that satisfies the need for hatred arising from one's feeling of impotence and gives the false self-assurance of being a "critical" element. It also guarantees the peace with a government ill at ease about this tendency (of which they, reading confidential police reports of intellectual conversations, know incomparably more than I), but which is not foolish enough to admit its existence and produce a new tension with the "critical" intelligentsia, which is one of its pillars.

One may ask if this whole complex is of any importance? Is its detailed analysis not the result of a Jewish persecution complex fantasizing about dangers from all directions? Undoubtedly, in itself and in its present dimensions, it is not of primary importance. But it is a *symptom* and a *latent danger*. It is a symptom of the inner weakness of opposition in Hungary; the projection of fears in the form of hatred against the "alien," who is also the weaker, is a well-known and amply explained analytical formula. It is a *latent danger* as well, which can become actualized, as it did, for instance, in Poland in 1968 and 1969, when precisely the strata and this attitude were mobilized in a hysterical flare-up of anti-Semitism against non-Jewish, rebellious intellectuals. István Bibó, one of the most clear-sighted Hungarian political minds that ever existed, was aware of the meaning of this symptom and of this latent danger. When he was asked by friends how he could imagine the first steps of his possible comeback to Hungarian ideological life, he was said to have answered: "Reprint my 'Jewish Question in Hungary.' Unfortunately, it has not lost its relevance."

The Methodological Aspect

The highest compliment that can be paid to István Bibó (and a correct locating of his intellectual achievement) is to say that he has only one competitor: Sartre's *Reflexions sur la question juive*.[16] The basic difference between them is this: History is totally nonexistent in Sartre. In his truly immortal essay, one of the great gestures of this great life, whose absence we have to feel so painfully now, he gives the philosophical morphology of the *modern* state of Jewish affairs from the aspect of a leftist-radical existentialism. For Bibó, the whole complex can only be understood in terms of *historical sociology*. As a result, their scenarios have very *different* *protagonists*. In Sartre, it is the anti-Semite who is the focal point. The Jew is only his product, his derivative (in his/her inauthentic Jewish being). With Bibó, it is the confrontation of Jew and non-Jew that creates the whole complex, and in a nonindividualistic sense, a collision of collective entities or ethoses. Both standpoints are in harmony with their respective authors' historical backgrounds. For Sartre, a French thinker for whom the great revolution separated the millennial period from the present (which is called by Bibó by its popular name, Middle Ages), the whole pre-1789 problematic is "textbookish" and irrelevant. Only what happened from the Dreyfus affair to Petain and Laval is relevant. (Here, of course, one must try to understand the terms of a methodology, not accept its explanation.) For Bibó, an Eastern European, specifically a Hungarian, where "Middle Ages," semifeudalism, fragmented emancipation, unresolved national (and national minority) problems, imperfect pluralism, and sham constitutionalism grew from those "Middle Ages" into the present—this was an impossible approach. It is thus that Bibó, who (in spite of his careful academic training) remained a "philosophical somnambulist," came closer to or rather better prepared the ground for, certain fertile solutions than did his competitor, one of the greatest philosophical minds of this century. (Which again does not mean, as will be seen below, that at crucial points I am not going to criticize Bibó, relying on Sartre.) The main terms of Bibó's standpoint are the following. First, according to him, there is no general definition of Jew in the modern age. The definition is dependent on the approach to the problem; for a racist, it is a *racial,* for a Hassidic mystic a *religious,* for a Zionist a *national* problem. Bibó's suggestion is (and in this regard he is influenced by Marx) that history and its products have to be understood in terms of *conflicts.* It is conflict that produces social strata (or classes) and separates competitive ethoses, not the other way round. This is why he understands what is Jewish by analyzing the conflict of Jew and non-Jew as collective entities. This is why he makes an inventory of the usual explanation of the Jewish problem (historical materialist, historicist operating from the *fact* of the traditionally developed hostility between Jewish and Gentile, psychoanalytic-projective) but rejects all of them as insufficient and one-sided. Bibó establishes a three-scale method of investigation and distinguishes between two periods of the problem. "I consider the correct hierarchy [of the steps of search for explanation] to be, first, a grasp of the social development and positional changes of Jewry as a social community, the conditions of its being intertwined with other communities, with surrounding society, and the mutual impact of individual and communal patterns of behavior stemming therefrom. Finally all this should be placed in the universal process of social evolution."[17] There is no need to be petty regarding minutiae (such as the somewhat misty content of "social evolution"), nor do I want to be an orthodox advocate of historical materialism. This methodological program is historicist and collectivistic enough for me to fulfill one fundamental function: It clearly distinguishes between two epochs (the Middle Age and the modern, overwhelmingly described by Bibó as capitalist), the first of which is *nonuniversalistic,* the second *universalistic.*

In my opinion, the difference between these two categories which I introduced into Bibó's train of thought has a crucial bearing on the understanding of the Jewish problem. I call the period (a "world-epoch") universalistic in which values, patterns of behavior, moral prescriptions, systems of needs and habits, *tend* to spread in all countries and geographical regions, in which cultures coexist through an interrelation of mutual "exploitation" in that they transplant (sometimes in a confused *mélange*) the others' good into their own soil and in which practically everything that is "valuable" in the other must somehow be fitted into "our own," even if it contradicts many of "our" life premises. Nonuniversalistic is its opposite. Rigidly separated cultures live side by side between which there is no commerce, not even tacitly tolerated osmosis, but rather, for reasons of principle, a relation of mutual and total exclusion.[18]

This is all the more important since Bibó points out that whatever may accurately be called *medieval* (Christian and Moslem) *anti-Semitism* and what can be better described as the "problematic intertwining" of three cultures (Christian and Moslem with Jewish) full of conflict often violently acted out, is to be understood by starting out from the fundamental social fact that it was *ritual community* (not a national or tribal state) that provided the key social organization pattern of the period.

> Ritual communities had in the whole of medieval Europe a crucial importance, and the Middle East still lives in such, from Morocco to India. The determining impact of these communities has been previously felt all over the world, and in the Middle East is still more important in many places than any kind of national and racial line of demarcation. It encompassed and organized incomparably more aspects and manifestations of human emotional and volitional life and communal solidarity than did the state, which has represented for a very long time a mere power structure. In this respect, rite means, not European religious confession or denomination in the present meaning, but rather a community which determines, beyond religious aspects, convictions of confession and the whole of human—individual and collective—way of life: its social morals, everyday habits, or what, to use a fashionable term, we would call human *ethnic* characteristics.[19]

While this extraordinarily deep insight into medieval social organizations provides a basic clue for the understanding of Jewish social destiny (and a great many other problems), it also "conjures up" unexpected mysteries of social development that I cannot even try to fathom here. But in order to grasp the specificity of medieval Jewish life, it is necessary to introduce the above-mentioned category of "nonuniversalistic." The Jewish social situation from the Diaspora (beyond which, Bibó is right, only Jewish mystics push the question any further) to the period of emancipation can be fully understood in terms of a nonuniversalistic ritual community where emphasis is laid on both noun and adjective. Jewish, Christian, and Moslem cultures, all three, lived in nonuniversalistic ritual communities in which the interrelationship between state (the relatively separated political sphere) and ritual community, and as a result, the interrelationship between these coexisting cultures, was most different. As I shall be giving a somewhat more detailed analysis of the Jewish situation, a few remarks should suffice regarding the other two.

First, only for brief historical moments could Christian and Moslem cultures unite political culture, state, and the whole of ritual community (for reasons only partly clear to me and which cannot be enumerated here). This separation had different implications for the two ritual communities. Within Islam, to sketch the situation, political despotism had mostly been combined with a contemptuous indifference toward the inner moral and religious habits of the conquered. This is what Bibó called the "less ideological," the "less complicated" character of the Moslem establishment. It is in this indifference that he locates the source of relative intolerance accorded the Jews by the Moslems for many centuries. In (Western) Christianity the separation between state and church (spiritually representing the whole of ritual community) meant, on the one hand, the introduction of plurality and individual freedom into the system, for which it paid with its intensified religious-ideological character. The latter made it impossible for Christianity to show the same neglect and indifference toward Jews as the Moslems. This explains the paradoxical situation that for centuries Jews suffered more at the hands of the "religion of love" than from martial Islam. Secondly, not being universalistic did not mean that these cultures were not "spreading" and conquering; it only meant that they were *not reciprocal*. As opposed to many Asian cultures (which never or hardly ever trespassed on their geographical-racial borderline) both Moslems and Christians aspired to exclusivity. This meant, however, in the case of Moslems, only political rule, in the case of the latter the exclusive domination of Christian norms and habits (up to the extermination of the alien, the "pagan" one). It will become clear again from all this, I think, why Jewry under Christian rule inevitably had to suffer from violence ("outbursts of anti-Semitism," as one would say with modernization) whose systematic recurrence would have perhaps, without religious reform blunting the edge of religious zeal for exclusivity, led either to total religious assimilation or the equally total expulsion of all Jews from the sphere of Western Christianity. Before turning to an analysis of the Jewish ethos between the Diaspora and the beginnings of emancipation, one factor crucial for Jewish destiny should be understood with regard to Christianity. For this latter, ideologically overheated, ritual community of Christianity, which was exclusivistic but not universalistic, in other words, which only wanted to eliminate the heathen, not to assimilate it in a true "give-*and*-take" process, the religiously alien did not simply provoke the shock one normally feels when confronting the unusual. It was eternal scandal and constant provocation.

I shall now offer a sketchy typology of the "medieval" Jewish ritual community, with all the necessary deficiencies of such a broad overview. First, it was a strictly monotheistic universe, something accepted as their (imperfect) forerunner by both Moslems and Christians. But this was a dangerous proximity. The Jew could not simply be regarded as an "erring pagan" with his many deities, who could be reformed by authoritarian instruction. The Jew was perverted and perverting (especially for the Christian), since once having reached the closest possible vicinity to Truth (they had Christ who *is* Truth), they turned against it and crucified the Redeemer. Not condescending contempt, as was the case with the pagan, but rather hatred was the Jews' lot for this perversion and obstinate wickedness in the eyes of Christianity. The Church, true enough, did not simply reduce matters to the notion that "the Jews crucified Christ," but the Christian community never could overcome its hatred at the very sight of a people that had Jesus Christ as its own and could not but crucify him. In addition, the only Jewish God was an incorporeal being who had never turned into blood and flesh (as had the Christian God). Thus we find both the traditional Jewish inclination for abstract speculation (which was strictly confined to religion, and never harbored elements of enlightenment) and the conflict with a popular and sensuous, though equally speculative, Christianity.

Secondly, Jewish ritual community was based on a religion that was a *religion of legality* (in the Kantian sense of the word), *a religion of customary prescriptions, not of conscience and inwardness.* One of the possible interpretations of the Jesus tragedy (which, for instance, returns in Bach's *Johannes Passion*) is that Jesus, as a powerful subject of morality who declared himself to be the incarnation of the "new law" and who introduced unheard-of categories such as charisma, the "strength of belief," and so forth, was an unbearable provocation for the Jewish religion, which observed rules devoid of subjective overtones of conscience. This is, however, in itself a source of conflict, of hostility between the Jewish and Christian ritual communities. Even though the latter turned Jesus Christ's subjective moral roster into the foundation of a new collective ethos, it always preserved the individual's subjective relation to the collective morality (herein lies one of its great emancipatory missions). As a result, it could react with nothing but hatred and suspicion to Jewish "submission without dedication," whereas the whole attitude was for Jews (even for Jews who decided to let themselves be Christianized) irrational, inhuman, and absurd. On the other hand, Jewish ethos acquired very early the collective wisdom *not* to transform their religious legality into a political one. They gave up all political aspirations for nearly two thousand years. The "law" they had (and in the name of which they demanded the crucifixion of "Rex Iudeorum") was and remained a religious law without political implications, and its inner-worldly consequences did not transcend in principle the walls of the ghetto. To a great extent this wisdom contributed to Jewish survival. It created the millennial stereotype of the "cowardly" Jew who cannot lift a finger in his/her own defense (and as such provoked a great many aggressive acts), but did not make its obliteration a necessity either.

Thirdly, Jewry turned out to be *indomesticable* as far as its *religion* was concerned. Here it is immaterial how many Jews converted to Christianity under duress. The only objective way to assess this is to take the opposite route: to understand the miraculous fact that the ritual community, small as it remained in number, still survived. Of course, there were good reasons for this miracle. Jewish religion was not only just as exclusivistic in its eschatological beliefs, just as dogmatic in its "epistemology" as the Christian, it had in addition a *vivid and flamboyant messianic spirit*, whereas the "messianic spirit" (given the Advent of the Messiah as an event *in the past*) was sparkling as a *future perspective* only in Christian sects. At this point, the previously mentioned "wisdom of survival" prevailed once again in the Jewish ritual community: The Jewish religion was not a converting one. Of course, there were solid external reasons for it not to be. It is sufficient to read Singer's *The Slave* to see what mortal danger a Jewish community was exposed to if it tolerated converts (let alone if it incited to conversion). But this argument is not absolute, for many sects fought and converted until their complete physical extinction. The spirit of the Jewish ritual community shaping the individual psyche of Jews for nearly two thousand years was a strange mixture of utter submissiveness outside the (spiritual or actual) walls of their ghetto and passive but daring stubbornness to the point of death when it came to the ultimate principles of the religious community.

Fourthly, Jewry as a ritual community was an "unsettled" one. They showed no specific affinity to any area, ethnic group, nation, or the like. The Jew was *the alien par excellence*. This was a collective trait of Jewry as ritual community which so deeply determined traditional Jewish intellect and inclinations that it remained a trait with an unusually high number of Jews far after the assimilation process started. This remained so even after the ritual community as such disintegrated and no longer shaped (at least not necessarily) the individual Jew's psychology. Goebbels's infernal but always sharp intellect grasped at least one aspect of something actually existing when he coined the slogan of hatred about "Jewish-Bolshevik plutocracy." Jews, in great number feeling the fascination of alienness— even decades after getting out of the ritual rootlessness—found the two channels through which one could "find roots" without being nationally affiliated: money and socialism.

Finally, as a combined upshot of the various already mentioned factors (inclination to abstract thinking, coercively circumscribed social existence which excluded Jews from many professions, self-determination through religion) there came about a *limited rationalism and pragmatism* as a characteristic feature of Jewish ethos. Here I would briefly mention two aspects. There is a limited rationalism inherent in Jewish ritual community, although the latter strives to keep critical reason within the boundaries of religious tradition. We should not overestimate the "natural" Jewish affinity to Enlightenment. If we think of the unceasing conflicts between the greatest Jewish intellects and the ritual community (say, from Maimonides to Spinoza), we get the same picture. Further, Jewish "calculative-pragmatic" rationalism easily finds its way into the financial world. This is the basis of Sombart's story about the Jews' role in triggering capitalism (if we now abstract from his famous distinction between "organic" and "inorganic" capital, which was to play such a somber role later). As is evident, all this is but a reformulation from a different angle of what has been said above.

From these constituent parts there emerges a circumscribed, distinct, and isolated Jewish existence in a historical cosmos, whose *differentia specifica* is that it does not entail *tolerance* and a *reciprocal learning process*, even as a norm. As a result, the cosmos surrounding the Jews feels not only alienness, which in a universe lacking tolerance and reciprocity as a norm is irritation in itself. This world also has the perception of a ritual community, which is, first, self-conscious, even proud (in its own disguised way) of its distinctness. Secondly, this community is close enough to Christian ethos (I now leave the Moslem out of consideration deliberately) to contain some of its basic categories, but in a transformed, or according to Christian lingo, distorted way. For this reason, it does not need "instruction," but requires "harsh measures" to keep its perversion in check. Finally, this irritating and ideologically self-conscious ritual enclave has no political-military means to defend itself, which makes it an easy prey and provokes aggression.

All this has to be said in order to criticize the weakest point of Bibó's conception. According to him, the conflict between Jews and non-Jews has three equally important, constitutive elements: (1) medieval anti-Jewish religious bias, (2) the "disturbances" of modern development (which is a euphemism for the antinomies of capitalism and, for the last sixty years, the conflicts within the new society calling itself socialism), and (3) the (non-Jewish) experience collected about Jews. Now it is the third category that I partly want to transform in its meaning, partly clarify as far as its conceptual status is concerned, and partly reject.[20] In my opinion, the category of "Jewish experience" has a certain limited explanatory relevance for the clarification of the nature and roots of *medieval* anti-Jewish feeling, but is *not* something distinct from what Bibó calls religious anti-Jewish bias. The latter is based—within a universe in which, let me repeat, tolerance and reciprocity are not even norms—on the perception and statement of the others' alienness, and this alienness is in itself the substance of anti-Jewish religious bias *and* of "Jewish experience." These are not two distinct factors *but one*. The Christian ethos, which is exclusivistic but not universalistic and which operates in terms of a dogmatic epistemology knowing only "true believers," "heretics," and "pagans," perceives that the Jew is alien. This very act is the negative experience about Jews *in itself* in a world in which ritual communities do not tend to appropriate all values of the others, but on the contrary, deliberately exclude certain values of the other ritual communities.[21] Alienness is in itself the basis of hierarchy and (negative) judgment and doubly so in the case of a ritual community that is submissive and obedient politically, but provocatively obstinate as far as its "false" religious ideas are concerned. This will be made the *universal scapegoat* for "worldly ills." In this unified role, where perception of alienness and its negative-biased judgment are two aspects of one act, the term "causation" can be accepted. In all pre-Enlightenment ethoses from which norms of tolerance and learning from alien experience are absent, the statement of the other's alienness is *cause* for an instantaneous hostility toward him or her on varying levels of intensity. This is true if we conceive of "cause" as an explanatory principle that feeds back the individual behavior to what is regarded as right, and wrong, in the given ethos. Even in the present world, we are witness to outbursts of a type very similar to medieval anti-Semitic pogroms such as those against expatriate Chinese communities, these Jews of Asia, by pre-Enlightenment (Indonesian, Malaysian, Vietnamese, and so forth) "ethos" that are *caused* by exceptionally intensive feelings of hatred against the alien.

When we come to the second world epoch, the universalistic-capitalistic one, Bibó's explanation about the Jewish experience as a causative principle loses all its relevance and takes on dangerous, namely racist, connotations.[22] The reason for this is simple: The new period is characterized by emancipation and the disintegration of ritual communities, also by the universal acceptance of tolerance and a reciprocal learning process *at least as a norm*. (We need not dwell on the well-known fact that this norm is violated daily.) But in this new universe, in which ritual communities no longer exist and individualization proceeds to an unprecedented extent, common value and need systems cannot be perceived or stated in social entities, nor can any "common moral substance" be found. The feeling of being alien is no longer justification for outbursts of violence against the alien, not even in the eye of one's own (national, ethnic) community.

At least this is the case in post-Enlightenment communities and "normal"—that is, nonfascist—periods whereas, as I have argued, it *was* justification indeed in the previous world epochs. Perhaps it is not too far-fetched to assume that racist ideologies serve (especially in countries in which nation is more an organic than a contractual body) as substitutes for this missing homogeneity of disappeared ethoses based on ritual community. Also, they serve by implication, as (false) lines of division between the allegedly superior and allegedly inferior collective entities. Only if one accepts (which Bibó most certainly does not intend to do) these false and mystical (racial) "substances" which are distinct and stand in a moral hierarchy in each ethnic-national group as compared to the other(s), can one speak of the "Jewish experience" as a *cause* of anti-Semitism. If, however, one accepts the universalistic character of the modern world epoch, in which no distinctive value cosmos can be ascribed to any national body whose constituents would not at least be claimed by all others, can "experience" of any type serve as a cause of a generalized negative stereotype, regardless if the point of departure is an individual or a collective experience? If medieval "Gentiles" stated correctly that Jews were "alien" in every aspect of their confession and ritual community based on this confession, that was not only factually true but it also implied a relative justification for the hostility against them, given the structure of rationality in any pre-Enlightenment, nonuniversalistic world order. In that sense, it was cause. If the young Goebbels stated that Gundolf unjustly rejected him as a *doctorandus* because he had excellent intellectual capacities (which was a factual truth, as many Jews had the misfortune to "experience" on their skin), and *therefore* Jews are unjust and a malignant tumor in the social body to be eliminated; if anti-Semitic groups state correctly that Jews have a predilection for intellectual work, that they are regularly overrepresented in intellectual fields, and *therefore* are lazy and should be sent to camps "to teach them mores," the premise is not a cause but *a pretext for destructive generalization and projection.* (It is not accidental that in our universalistic epoch people are as touchy as they are about *any* kind of generalizations.) As a result this latter attitude is not accompanied by *aversion,* our usual reaction to what we feel to be simply alien, but by *hatred.*

It is my firm conviction that Sartre was absolutely right when he characterized the anti-Semite in the following way: "This commitment [that of the anti-Semite against the Jew] is not provoked by experience. . . . The (Jewish) experience is very far from generating the notion of the Jew; on the contrary, it is the notion that explains the experience. . . . So it is the *idea* made of Jews which seems to determine history, and it is not historical data from which the idea was born."[23] And this morphology is not a sentimental gesture of philo-Semitic magnanimity, it is not a wreath placed on the statue of the persecuted. Sartre, the thinker, is of much too hard a core to resort to shallow and simple emotional gestures. While Bibó was superior to him in drawing the broad historical outlines of the problem, he missed, in his traditional rationality, the whole complexity of modern life that Sartre grasps in one firm gesture with his central protagonist, the anti-Semite. As I mentioned, here Bibó commits the Jewish mistake; he tacitly identifies the anti-Semite with all those who are not philo-Semites and who have no positive stereotype of Jews (even though this is fairly inconsistent personally, for he was not himself philo-Semitic in the sentimental sense of the word). But the "man of aversion" is the average hero of nonuniversalistic ethoses and has very little to do (if anything at all) with the modern anti-Semite. The latter is the *rightist radical* who lives in the chosen passion of hatred against the Jew and for whom this "vision" is central and the focal point of illumination he sheds on his universe.

I would like to emphasize three components of Sartre's detailed characterization. The first is the following: "The anti-Semite has chosen hatred, for hatred is a religion."[24] But the anti-Semite is not only a man of hatred, he is also a man of fear: "This is a man who is afraid, of course, not of Jews but of himself, of his consciousness, of his freedom."[25] And finally and perhaps most importantly: "Of course, all the enemies of the Jew do not demand his death publicly. However, the measures suggested by them and which aim at his humiliation, debasement and communication are the derivatives of that assassination they are inwardly contemplating: these are symbolic murders. Only the anti-Semite has his own image of himself: he is a criminal for good motives. It is not his fault, at any rate, if it is his mission to reduce Evil by Evil. . . . He knows that he is evil, but since he does evil for the sake of goodness . . . he considers himself to be the holy evil."[26]

In analyzing this remarkable phenomenology, one is entitled to disregard the *sociological aspects*. They are secondary to Sartre's main intentions, sometimes mistaken or exaggerated and often "too French" to be generalizable (although they are superior to those of Bibó at least in one respect: they clearly show that anti-Semitism does not occur only when democracy is missing, but that the problem is more complex). The chief merit of Sartre's phenomenology is the transcendence of the usual level of discussing anti-Semitism in socialist theory. Up until his essay, the general level (if not necessarily the wording of the arguments) was determined by Bebel's dictum that "anti-Semitism is the socialism of fools." This formulation suffers from the following ills. First, it reduces the whole complexity of the problem to the poverty of intellectual content, which, in the wake of the undeniable fact that intellectuals of the rank of Hamsun, Céline, and so on, joined militant anti-Semitism, is no longer tenable. Second, "low intellectuality" does not account for the heat of the hatred; the dedication to the evil cause; the Hegelian twist of serving the "good" through evil means; the operatic invention and artistic design of mass annihilation. Nor does it, thirdly, explain the wide *sociological diversity* of those having joined anti-Semitism as a militant way of life, from the genuinely poor in spirit to the intellectually sophisticated. Sartre's formula accounts for all these factors. When he describes anti-Semitism as a *belief* (a noninstitutionalized religion), a religion of the Grand Inquisitor (a religion of the "fear of freedom"), a religion inextricably bound up with evil, he actually inverts Marx's thesis of *religious alienation*. In Marx's conception, "man" finds human species being, his/her "best part" in religion in an alienated form. But, irrespective of alienation, the intention is aimed at the good.

What does the anti-Semite find in the religion of hatred, or fear of freedom? A *new demonology,* the myth of the infernal in an increasingly atheistic epoch. As in many other aspects, the awakening of religion, here too, has not brought emancipation in itself, since mundane emancipation has not come true. István Bibó is right when he emphasizes that even if Christian prejudice is responsible for anti-Semitism (more precisely, it is an integral part of this religion), the essence of Christianity cannot be exhausted by this prejudice. The justified (and nonapologetic) character of this remark is never more clear than when one considers Sartre's argument about the anti-Semite's "negative religion"—demonology to the end. By this I mean the move *to the extreme,* to the moment when Hitler, in a pagan escapade, cuts the umbilical cord that up until then still somehow tied anti-Jewish feeling to the religion of the God-Son, to the religion of love. It is in this moment of pagan freedom that the "final solution" is conceived and executed.

What made the Jew, the representative victim of the Christian ethos, once again the victim *par excellence* in an epoch that is increasingly atheist? We gain *sociological* insight into this in reading Bibó and we obtain an ultimate *philosophical* explanation by interpreting Sartre's theory about the "negative religion" of the anti-Semite: These two outstanding presentations of one of the greatest human tragedies do not contradict each other. For Bibó, the sociological reasons are the following: First, Jewish affinity to "alienness," to nonaffiliation with any national community, persists (at least in a considerable part of Jewry) despite assimilation, and especially when its first waves fail. Hence the stereotype of "homeless," "rootless," sometimes that of the "born traitor" (in the Soviet version: the cosmopolitan); second, its *urban* character imposed on Jewry by the Christian community; its forcible exclusion from the Christian village turns into an advantage in that it becomes involved in *haute finance* and is overrepresented in intellectual professions. Hence the stereotype of the "lazy" or the "scheming" Jew who "has money even under his skin." Finally, Bibó, the genuine democrat, reproaches the Jew (because of a deep solidarity with the persecuted) for suffering his lot too obediently. From this submissiveness stems the dangerous stereotype of the easy prey that tempts aggression. For Sartre, we know it already, there is no "Jewish experience": It is the anti-Semite who creates the (inauthentic) Jew in his image and whose "religion of hatred" creates Jewish experiences. As a result, sociological evidence is for Sartre irrelevant. But as far as historical tendencies are concerned, his answer does not fundamentally differ from that of Bibó. The believer in the "religion of hatred," the rightist militant of "religious atheism" simply takes over the universal scapegoat of positive religion for his own negative religion, demonology. There will be no end to these practices, both Sartre and Bibó state (the latter at least in one period of his life) except in a "classless society," which makes regular outbursts of hatred (no matter whether of "social" or "projective" character) a negligible human by-product.

The Contemporary Artist

What is the actual background (broader than the Hungarian scene) against which these thoughts were put down on paper? First and foremost is the feeling that the moderate hopes that great analysts of the Jewish question such as Bibó or Sartre raised more than thirty years ago have altogether waned. As a radical Jewish observer of Jewish affairs (and without even claiming special knowledge in this field), one can say with resignation that unfortunately we are living in historical times in which there is once again a "Jewish question." What are its constitutive elements?

First, there is once again a region of the globe in which anti-Semitism (in its pre-Auschwitz form) has in barely disguised form become *official policy*, namely, in the Soviet Union and its Eastern-European satellites. The forms of this vary from country to country.[27] "Soviet" anti-Semitism ranged from practically open discrimination through "internal passports" (a system complemented with more covert forms of discrimination) to a kind of "philo-Semitism" that represses both Jewish self-articulation *and* overt anti-Semitism, while constantly reproducing anti-Semitism against its own will. In some of these countries (Poland, Lithuania, the Ukraine) traditional "popular" anti-Semitism benefits from overt and covert official support, making a "tacit coalition" with it and taking increasingly aggressive form. From Korey's book we know that the petition of twenty-six Lithuanian Jewish intellectuals against anti-Semitic policies in 1968 was not signed because of a fear of pogrom. That this fear is far from being unfounded has also been documented by Korey: the existence of at least one pogrom is known to have occurred in Plunge, Lithuania, in 1958.[28] Press releases on "Zionists" in Poland in 1968–1969 testified not only to a *Stuermer*-like tone of the "socialist" media, but also to the existence of an unpleasantly detailed knowledge of certain people's Jewish past who survived the Holocaust and who wanted to erase it from their memory but who could not skip out unnoticed from the grasp of this "omniscient mind." An additional grave sign of deterioration and a further degradation of inner democratic norms lies in the fact that we can find a "mirror symmetry" between official and oppositional anti-Semitism. Despite the great Russian intellectuals such as Sakharov, Medvedev, Nekrasov, Yevtushenko, and Sinyavksy, who have kept alive the Tolstoyan tradition of stigmatizing anti-Semitism as Russian malady "above" and "below," in Solzhenitsyn's attitude and statements (with all due regard to his unforgettable contribution to Russian emancipation) there are signs of a hopeless bigotry similar to that of the Soviet leaders he hates most. Nor is this all. The new development of the last ten or fifteen years, with its so-called link between "anti-Soviet" Zionist (that is, Jewish) agitation and "world Zionism"—this relapse into the lingo and misty but emotionally arousing hints of the Black Hundred and the "Protocols of the Elders of Zion" about Jewish aspirations for world domination, which transforms a nationalism (Zionism), uncritically accepted in the case of Arab states, into "racism"—cannot but pave the road to events that perhaps even those who prepare the sociopsychological conditions for them do not intend.

Second, it is clear that one great hope of world Jewry has withered away in the last decade, namely, the hope that with the establishment of Israel as the Jewish state, anti-Semitism would abate and Jews, regardless of whether they lived in Israel and were its citizens, would be treated not as specimens of a race and targets of hatred but as (actual or possible) members of a national community. To my knowledge, one aspect of Entebbe, so illuminating in this regard while emotionally played up, has rarely (if ever) been analyzed. Even if we look beyond the dismal sight of "German revolutionaries" isolating Jews from non-Jews (in order not to evoke the sight of earlier National-Socialist "German revolutionaries" in SS uniform) at the Entebbe airport, we cannot disregard the fact that they were looking for *Jews* (specimens of a race), not for *Israelis* (citizens of a state). Needless to say, had they done the latter, this would not have made the action any more humane or acceptable. My point, here, however, is that Entebbe was a spectacular practical success for Israel as a state and a just as symbolic and spectacular denial of its hopes that Israel's very existence would channel racist hatred back into the normal framework of nationalist conflicts.

One might well ask whether this is indeed the question for the agenda, rather than its contrary. As Edward Said has asked: Should we not see Zionism with the eyes of its victims[29]—is this not the duty of democrats and socialists, Jewish or non-Jewish? I think it is appropriate to state the following as my personal conviction. The Palestinian case must be solved within the framework of an autonomous state of their own. No jingoism, no oppression is acceptable on the part of Israeli military or civilian authorities. A state born out of moral indignation and sympathy for the eternal underdog, created by the surviving remnants of pogroms and gas chambers, simply undermines the bases of its own existence (more than other states) if it becomes oppressive and retaliates against the fascist actions of terrorist commandos toward children by bombing women and children in refugee camps.[30] All this makes Israel both responsible for its own oppressive policy and co-responsible for some of the deeds of the American strategy on which it has perforce to rely in its "struggle for life." Certainly it exposes the State of Israel (and with it a considerable part of the remaining world Jewry) to new and grave dangers. Yet, having said this, let me immediately add a pessimistic prediction. While there is no peace without solving the Palestinian question, there must be serious doubts whether, with its solution, there will be peace and reconciliation (or, formulated differently, whether powers interested in tension, not in peace, would ever allow eventual peace). It is hard not to detect a new upsurge of general anti-Semitism which is projective in character and multidimensional as far as its goals are concerned, but which is unified in one sense—its pro-Palestinian emancipatory fervor is mostly a pretext for pushing various policy objectives.

Before I proceed to analyze this unholy alliance, let me point out the undeniable features of false zeal on the part of the highly different advocates of the Palestinian cause (particularly since I would like to avoid any "counterconspiracy" theory against world Jewry). Needless to say, these are the remarks of a layman, not of an expert. First, whatever the serious (stupid and selfish) mistakes of various Israeli governments and pressure groups, forgotten is the fact (which plays a crucial role in the emergence of the whole Palestinian problem) that Israel accepted and the Arab countries rejected the original UN decision regarding the situation in Palestine. It has also been forgotten that the War of Independence in 1948 was a result of this negative Arab attitude, and that at least a part of the Palestinian population left voluntarily as a protest against the Israeli victory. (Others were forced to leave.) This circumstance does not, of course, change the misery of those living for thirty years in refugee camps and no one has the right to make a hierarchy between "first class" and "second class" sufferings. But at the very least it modifies the false formula of innocent victims versus aggressive "Zionist imperialists." More importantly, however, hardly any of the "Zionist imperialists" have been as pernicious, brutally exploiting, and cynically manipulating toward the Palestinians as have most of their Arab "brothers." Apart from the fact that they received their most bloodletting from *Jordanians, not Israelis,* and apart from the rough treatment they got from the Syrians in Lebanon, they are also constantly kept at arm's length and on the front line as living objects of demonstration for Zionist brutality. No Arab country has made any real effort to solve the Palestinian problem *within its own reach,* for the simple reason that they would forfeit their most powerful means of general blackmail.

Secondly, it is undeniable that although Palestinians suffer injustice, Israel *fights for its physical existence.* It is a fact so well known that it needs no corroboration that in 1967 the aim of the Arab invaders was to push Israel into the sea—in other words, a new Holocaust. (What is more, the statements have been repeated up until the present.) In 1973 they had more common sense than to advertise their aims prior to victory, but the fact that the PLO and other Arab "hard-liners" never accepted Israel's right to existence speaks for itself. And I do not think that anyone has the moral right to suggest that the victims of the Holocaust should remain passive since "things will turn out to be less serious than they seem to be." Things seemed to be less serious in 1938 than they later turned out to be. Such advice, often given to Israel, is particularly hypocritical on the part of a world which, at the end of the war, made gentle hints to the victim who perished by the millions in Nazi camps that he passively let himself be destroyed without sufficient resistance. Third, practically all analysts terming Israeli nationalism (Zionism) a racist ideology show a suspiciously naive and uncritical attitude toward the *projective and highly insincere character* of Arab nationalism. It would be cheap (although an undeniable fact) to refer to the directly Nazi stereotypes (provided by Nazi experts employed by Nasser's Egypt) of Jews as a way of combating this Arab nationalism. The problem is more complex. Nevertheless, it comes to mind that the highly heterogeneous Arab forces—sometimes one another's most bitter enemies and living in the constant convulsion of palace coups, conspiracies, and counterconspiracies of cliques of officers, feudal autocracies, and modern half-totalitarian tyrannies of various molds, but never in democracies—*need their enemies and have no need whatsoever for their own main ally and token victim, the Palestinian.* On the one hand, the unmanageable impulse toward peasant revolution latent in the Palestinian organizations is a danger for authoritarian governments of *all* kinds. Arab governments, in irreconcilable internecine strife, need the Palestinian "cause" as a lever and a means of blackmail—they do not need the Palestinians. But they do need Israel, precisely in the sense that the militant anti-Semite needs the Jew in Sartre's morphology. For what would unite them, at least symbolically, if this so salutary enemy disappeared? This is, by the way, the *only* but not satisfactory counterargument to Arab plans for a new Holocaust. This is an unsatisfactory guarantee, for this was precisely the dilemma of the militant anti-Semite at the time of the *Kristallnacht* pogrom in 1938, a dilemma that was most radically solved in the hope for new prospective targets. Finally, one must point to a curious aspect, namely, the frequently overheated tone and unconcealed hatred of the anti-Israel discourse. Often, as in the case of many German Left extremists, it is crystal clear that their vehemence against "Zionist imperialism" is simply old-fashioned anti-Semitism *à rebours*.

How could these facts, known to every Israeli schoolboy and schoolgirl (but sometimes even appearing in more sophisticated discourses too), escape the attention of so many analysts? If we now disregard those who are simply bought (by Arab or by Soviet money or by both) and whose number is not necessarily small and if we ask ourselves seriously how three million people (together with their—diminishing—"know-how" superiority) can be presented as "mortal danger" to 100 million having inexhaustible financial resources and sophisticated weaponry, then we either have to assume an anti-Jewish world conspiracy, which is a figment of understandably feverish Jewish minds, or we have to look elsewhere for explanations.

In my opinion, the real reasons can be found in a historically accidental meeting and alliance between two power factors, both using anti-Semitism in its projective form, but both doing so for different reasons. The causes and character of *Soviet* anti-Semitism have been analyzed briefly here. Obviously, it was not Soviet anti-Semitism that motivated Soviet intrusion in the Middle East. On the contrary, economically and strategically motivated Soviet intrusion used a means which made its movements in the area easy and unresisted and which attracted possible allies of different molds—a means that long since has been a handy tool for channeling social contradictions into the harmless pipelines of social demagogy at home. Militant *Arabic* anti-Semitism, as I have analyzed it, was a relatively late development as compared to the Jewish situation under Christian domination, which makes it even more important to understand its particular character. The change from an attitude that tolerated Jewish presence with contempt but generally without pogroms and excessive violence, into one in which anti-Jewish bathos and commitment seem to be the major cementing force between highly divergent, seemingly incompatible forces cannot be accounted for either by the Jewish ritual community's turning into a political one or by the Palestinian question. (Not even if one adds the problem of Jerusalem as a religious center.) Nor is it an easy task to explain how this anti-Jewish attitude can be motivation enough to strike a bridge between *Soviet* aspirations and many Moslem dictatorships (such as Qadhafi's), which were originally and ideologically vehemently anti-Communist.

I think that the Islamic-Arabic world (obviously these are not identical concepts) is now living through its great crisis because it possesses (in the form of oil wealth) the adequate means to become industrialized at the same time that its traditional social structures (subjected to the most divergent political forms of rule, some of them modernizing, some of them deliberately preserving its archaic character) resist the simple transfer of Western (or Communist) ways of life. In terms of this essay, the Moslem Arabic world does not want to become universalistic. It is this tendency, what observers have otherwise called the upsurge of *fundamentalism*, that finds its most clear and extremist manifestation in Khomeini's rightist radicalism. Now Israel, in the wake of the Jewish community's drastic change into a Western-rationalistic political entity, is in part the tip of a dart, sensitive on their own skin and, more importantly, a target for the projection of hatred for all nonuniversalistic fundamentalists intending to preserve Islamic order intact in its archaic or somewhat modernized form.[31] It was not the aim of this essay to give "practical suggestions" to peoples of a region as to what to do or not to do, only to make remarks on the margin of a classical essay. Its author never forgot that the attitude to our civilization's persecuted *par excellence* is the test of the validity or nonvalidity of our democratic norms, not to speak of radical convictions.

NOTES

1. István Bibó, "A zsidokerdes Magyarorszagon" (in what follows I am going to refer to the title only in English: "The Jewish Question in Hungary") in István Bibó, Harmadik út; politikai és történeti tanulmányok. Sajtó alá rendezte és a bevezetöt írta: Szabó Zoltán. London, 1960.

2. It is precisely in this sense that Sartre, in his *Reflexions sur la question juive* (1946) to which I return repeatedly, expresses deep doubts regarding the democratic character of the French pluralist liberal democracy. Very understandably, he takes into consideration not so much the main representatives of Vichy but that "general opinion" which, while deeply shocked by the fate that befell the Jews, nevertheless told the Jews not to be "selfish" by placing "their interests" (i.e., their physical survival) before "general French national interests," which could only be left unimpaired if Jews were swiftly shipped to extermination camps. Sartre's description has very strikingly "Hungarian" *couleurs locales*, which demon-

strates that the problem is not simply identical with the existence of certain democratic parliamentary institutions.

3. While I totally agree with Bibó's impartiality, I think that his definition of the anti-Semite differs from that of Sartre's substantially and here I agree with Sartre, not with Bibó. This insufficient definition (which tacitly accepts the Jewish prejudice that anyone who is not philo-Semitic is anti-Semitic) causes certain theoretical confusions to which I am going to return. But I agree with Bibó's deeper intention: to "convince," "reeducate" (not to terrorize) the "man of prejudice."

4. I. Bibó, "The Jewish Question in Hungary," pp. 298–300.

5. Jean-Paul Sartre, *Reflexions sur la question juive* (Paris, 1954), pp. 66–68.

6. Was Bibó aware of the fact that he had joined a long and respectable line of democrats who applied the same parable to their own age and society, that Lessing had been the first to do with his *Nathan the Wise*? There is no answer to this in his written work.

7. Sartre, *Reflexions*, pp. 169–170.

8. I. Bibó, "The Jewish Question in Hungary," p. 303.

9. For a "rough typology" the United States and Switzerland serve as the best examples of the first, and Eastern-European countries and Germany for the second type. But it would be a mistake to simplify matters into a division between democratic (or liberal) and backward-half-feudal countries. For reasons, amply analyzed by Tocqueville, overcentralized France with all its democracy had *patria*- rather than *nation*-character and movements which constantly reemerged on the French political scene.

10. The fact that Jewish religious instruction was destroyed and that Zionist organization was no longer tolerated, should not be mentioned here. In this regard, Jews only shared the niceties of a general situation.

11. William Korey, *The Soviet Cage* (New York, 1973), p. 174.

12. Roy Medvedev, *All Stalin's Men* (Oxford, 1983), p. 146.

13. In all this, one can rely on Korey's book, which draws its data partly from the analysis of (available) statistical publications and partly from the statements of dissidents, such as Roy Medvedev, the courageous Leninist defender of Jewish rights.

14. Not long ago, at a conference of Hungarian émigrés, I heard the allegation against Kádár that he selected the victims of the post-1956 trials according to their Jewish or non-Jewish origin, protecting the latter. I cannot reject this charge out of hand, as some people did at this conference, for the simple reason that *no one* is acquainted with the statistics of retributions except the Hungarian leadership, hence no one knows the real proportions. However, I doubt the validity of the accusation.

15. Korey, *The Soviet Cage*, p. 153. Probably it was also a belated answer to an incident in which the Hungarian leadership behaved ambiguously according to Moscow standards. In December, 1970, after the death sentences in the Leningrad hijacking trial, G. Lukács and members of his Budapest School, nearly all Jews, protested to the Hungarian Political Bureau against the death penalty in a collective letter, a fact with which the Soviet authorities had to be acquainted and which the Hungarian leadership answered to in an evasive and noncommittal way.

16. Here I am not going to discuss, even briefly, the Jewish mystical conceptions. They

are either specific branches of one tree, mysticism in general, or, if they assume a special "Jewish substance."

17. István Bibó, *The Jewish Question*, p. 262.

18. To my mind, there is no doubt that this distinction can be best explained by historical materialism, whatever the limitation of this doctrine. It is capitalist production aimed at universalization that creates the all-pervasive cultural universalization of the period.

19. I. Bibó, *The Jewish Question*, p. 263.

20. Let me make it very clear that it is not Jewish bias that motivates me in this criticism. I do not deny at all that if we take human groups, one of them exclusively Jewish, the other non-Jewish in their practical-moral intercourse, we shall find as many negative, repulsive, inhumane, and so forth, features on the Jewish side as on any other non-Jewish one.

21. As far as sexual ideals, monogamous or polygamous marriage, marital virtues, and equality (at least before God), and so forth, are concerned (to mention only some of the concrete values of the ethoses in question), there can be no doubt about the different role these values play in different ethoses. Some of them are accepted in all, and interpreted in a similar way, others are only part of one or the other, some are exalted as bases for hierarchies.

22. Needless to say, all this happens in spite of the author's intentions. Bibó simply falls victim here to an exaggerated impartiality.

23. Sartre, *Reflexions*, pp. 14–18.

24. Sartre, *Reflexions*, p. 22.

25. Sartre, Ibid., p. 64.

26. Sartre, Ibid., pp. 59, 60.

27. There was, of course, a "Jewish question" in the Arab countries that disappeared with the "de-Judification" of these countries and which is, to my knowledge, complete. There is also gathering evidence of the flare-up of anti-Semitic measures in Iran in which a rightist-radical government oppresses all sorts of minorities anyhow.

28. Korey, *Soviet Cage*, p. 174. And if one argues that this was not an officially organized action (which is a certainty), perhaps not even encouraged by the authorities and maybe even punished by them, the fact still remains that the Soviet press, while always making such a strong case about "anti-Soviet" crime, for instance, at the time of the Plunge pogrom about crimes of embezzlers, almost all with Jewish names, kept perfect silence about the fate of pogromists.

29. Edward W. Said, "Zionism from the Standpoint of its Victims," *Social Text* 1 (Winter 1979), 7–58.

30. As a general principle, one can state that while politics has moral principles and moral implications, politics is *not based on morality*. But the status of Israel as a state is special even more so than was the status of the United States which had been "philosophically deducted" from natural law and the principles of Enlightenment. (This latter circumstance was, by the way, not at all without influence on later American policy and created a constant frame of reference for democratic, even for radical-socialist, aspirations.) Israel was born of a collective feeling of retrospective responsibility for the Holocaust on the part of a "public opinion" which remained unconcerned (or irresponsibly optimistic) about Jewish fate until it

was too late. Jews can argue that a belated and worldwide pang of conscience is not *their* moral situation, it is something alien imposed on them and that they want to behave "normally," i.e. with the normal egotism of national bodies. Yet they cannot change the fact that many a pragmatic *ruse de guerre* (such as the use of "counterterrorist" "hit-teams"), is not permitted them without Israel losing its basis of existence, something which is not the case for other luckier nations employing dirty methods. In this regard, it is very interesting that, whereas there was some formal protest against the "illegal" character of this action, no one protested seriously against Eichmann's kidnapping, which corroborates negatively my thesis about the moral foundation of the State of Israel. One would think that it is especially prohibitive for Israel to have close relations with a fascist state such as South Africa. Undeniably, this is a special burden on the shoulders of the average Israeli citizen who would behave as an average member of any average interest group, not as a moral principle personified. But one has to say in the spirit of the protagonist of this study, István Bibó: Such acts are beyond morality and for that reason, even politically unacceptable in the special case of Israel.

31. Needless to say, I do not want to make *any* statement at all regarding Islam's (as a religious doctrine) capacity to elaborate or at least to tolerate ways of life that tend to a universalistic world order.

BIBLIOGRAPHY

Adorno, Theodor W. *Negative Dialectics*. Translated by E. B. Ashton. New York: Seabury Press, 1973.

Alson, Jacob, Benjamin R. Epstein, and Nathan C. Bolth. *Germany Nine Years Later*. Unpublished manuscript. B'nai B'rith, 1954. A report of the Anti-Defamation League of B'nai B'rith of a study tour undertaken at the invitation of the Federal Republic of Germany.

Améry, Jean. *At the Mind's Limits: Contemplations by a Survivor on Auschwitz*. Translated by Sidney and Stella Rosenfeld. Bloomington: University of Indiana Press, 1980. Translation of *Jenseits von Schuld und Sühne*. Stuttgart: Klett Cotta, 1966.

———. *Widersprüche*. Stuttgart: Klett Cotta, 1971.

Andernacht, Dietrich, and Eleonore Sterling, eds. *Dokumente zur Geschichte der Frankfurter Juden, 1933–1945*. Frankfurt am Main: W. Kramer, 1963.

Anders, Güther. *Besuch im Hades*. Munich: Beck, 1979.

Arendt, Hannah. *The Jew as Pariah*. New York: Grove Press, 1978.

Aschheim, Steven E. *Brothers and Strangers: The East European Jew in German Jewish Consciousness, 1800–1923*. Madison, Wisc.: University of Wisconsin Press, 1982.

Benjamin, Jessica, and Anson Rabinbach. "Germans, Leftists, Jews." *New German Critique* 31 (Winter 1984), pp. 183–194.

Berghahn, Marion. *German-Jewish Refugees in England: The Ambiguities of Assimilation*. London: Macmillan, 1984.

Biale, David. *Gershom Scholem: Kabbalah and Counter-History*. Cambridge, Mass.: Harvard University Press, 1979.

Bier, Jean-Paul. *Auschwitz et les nouvelles littératures allemandes*. Brussels: Editions de l'Université Bruxelles, 1979.

Bossmann, Dieter, ed. *Was ich über Adolf Hitler gehört habe. Auszüge aus 3042 Aufsätzen von Schülern und Schülerinnen aller Schularten der Bundesrepublik*. Frankfurt am Main: Fischer, 1977.

Broder, Henryk. *Deutschland erwacht*. Cologne: Kipenheuer und Witsch, 1978.

———. "Gegen meinen Willen in die Geschichte verknotet." *Konkret* (April 1981), pp. 55–57.

————. "Für Juden gibt es hier keine Normalität." Interview in *Der Spiegel* 17 (1981), pp. 39–55.

————. [Henryk M. Broder], "Ihr bleibt die Kinder Eurer Eltern." *Die Zeit,* no. 10 (February 27, 1981).

————. "Alice Schwarzer und der Antisemitismus." *Profil* 51/52 (1982), pp. 62–69.

Broder, Henryk M., and Michel Lang, eds. *Fremd im eigenen Land. Juden in der Bundesrepublik.* Frankfurt am Main: Fischer, 1979.

Claussen, Detlev. "Im Hause des Henkers." In *Die Verlängerung von Geschichte,* edited by Dietrich Wetzel, pp. 113–125. Frankfurt am Main: Verlag Neue Kritik, 1983.

Coser, Lewis A. *Refugee Scholars in America: Their Impact and Their Experiences.* New Haven: Yale University Press, 1984.

Cuddihy, John. *The Ordeal of Civility: Freud, Marx, Levi-Strauss and the Jewish Struggle with Modernity.* New York: Basic Books, 1974.

Dahl, Peter. "Dicht Daneben, Lieber Henryk." *Konkret* (April 1981), p. 53.

Dawidowicz, Lucy S. *The War Against the Jews 1933–1945.* New York: Bantam Books, 1976.

"Deutsche, Linke, Juden." Special issue of *Ästhetik und Kommunikation* 51 (June 1983).

Deutscher, Isaac. *The Non-Jewish Jew and Other Essays.* New York: Hill & Wang, 1968.

Dinnerstein, Leonard. *America and the Survivors of the Holocaust.* New York: Columbia University Press, 1982.

Diwald, Helmut. *Geschichte der Deutschen.* Frankfurt am Main: Ullstein, 1979.

Eichberg, Henning. *Minderheit und Mehrheit.* Braunschweig: Westermann, 1979.

Engelmann, Bernt. *Deutschland ohne Juden.* Munich: Goldmann, 1979.

Fest, Joachim. *Hitler.* Translated by Richard and Clara Winston. New York: Harcourt Brace Jovanovich, 1974.

Fleischmann, Lea. *Dies ist nicht mein Land. Eine Jüdin verlässt die Bundesrepublik.* Hamburg: Hoffmann und Campe, 1980.

Freed, Leonard. *Deutsche Juden heute.* Munich: Rütten & Loening, 1965.

Freimark, Peter. "Das Institut für die Geschichte der deutschen Juden in Hamburg und die deutsch-jüdische Geschichtswissenschaft heute." *Revue d'Allemagne* 18 (July–September 1981), pp. 589–596.

Friedman, Saul S. *No Haven for the Oppressed: United States Policy Toward Jewish Refugees, 1938–1945.* Detroit: Wayne State University Press, 1973.

Gay, Peter. *Freud, Jews and Other Germans: Masters and Victims in Modernist Culture*. New York: Oxford University Press, 1979.

Gershon, Karen, ed. *Postscript. A Collective Account of the Lives of Jews in West Germany since the Second World War*. London: Gollancz, 1969.

Ginzel, Günther Bernd. "Phasen der Etablierung einer jüdischen Gemeinde in der Kölner Trümmerlandschaft 1945–1949." In *Köln und das rheinische Judentum. Festschrift Germania Judaica*, edited by Jutta Bohnke-Kollwitz, Willehad Paul Eckert, Frank Golczewski, and Hermann Grieve, pp. 445–461. Cologne: J. P. Bachem Verlag, 1984.

Glesermann, Abraham. "Kritik heisst, über die eigene Schande zu reden." *Konkret* (April 1981), p. 54.

Goldmann, Nahum. *Le paradoxe juif*. Paris: Stock, 1976.

Greffrath, Mathias, ed. *Die Zerstörung einer Zukunft. Gespräche mit emigrierten Sozialwissenschaftlern*. Reinbek: Rowohlt, 1979.

Grosser, Alfred. *Germany in Our Time*. New York: Praeger, 1971.

Grunfeld, Frederic V. *Prophets Without Honour. A Background to Freud, Kafka, Einstein and Their World*. New York: Holt, Rinehart and Winston, 1979.

Halperin, Irving. *Here I am: A Jew in Today's Germany*. Philadelphia: Westminster, 1971.

Heenen, Susann. "Deutsche Linke, linke Juden und der Zionismus." In *Die Verlängerung von Geschichte*, edited by Dietrich Wetzel, pp. 103–112. Frankfurt am Main: Verlag Neue Kritik, 1983.

Heilbut, Anthony. *Exiled in Paradise: German Refugee Artists and Intellectuals in America from the 1930s to the Present*. New York: Viking, 1983.

Henry, Frances. *Victims and Neighbors: A Small Town in Nazi Germany Remembered*. South Hadley, Mass.: Bergin & Garvey, 1984.

Hilberg, Raul. *The Destruction of the European Jews*. Chicago: Quadrangle Books, 1961.

Horkheimer, Max, and Theodor W. Adorno. *Dialectic of Enlightenment*. Translated by John Cumming. New York: Seabury Press, 1972.

Huyssen, Andreas. "The Politics of Identification: 'Holocaust' and West German Drama." *New German Critique* 19 (Winter 1980), pp. 117–136.

Jackman, Jarell C., and Carla M. Borden, eds. *The Muses Flee Hitler: Cultural Transfer and Adaptation 1930–1945*. Washington, D.C.: Smithsonian Institution Press, 1983.

Jacobmeyer, Wolfgang. "Jüdische Überlebende als 'Displaced Persons.'" *Geschichte und Gesellschaft* 9 (1983), pp. 429–444.

Jay, Martin. *The Dialectical Imagination. A History of the Frankfurt School and the Institute for Social Research 1923–1950*. Boston: Little, Brown, 1983.

"Juifs et Allemands—Une communauté de destin?" Special issue of *Revue d'Allemagne* 18 (July–September 1981).

Kaplan, Marion. "To Tolerate Is to Insult." *New German Critique* 31 (Winter 1984), pp. 195–200.

Katcher, Leo. *Post-Mortem. The Jews in Germany Today.* New York: Delacorte, 1968.

Kersten, Hermann. *Ich lebe nicht in der Bundesrepublik.* Munich, 1964.

Knilli, Friedrich, and Siegfried Zielinski, eds. *Betrifft "Holocaust"— Zuschauer schreiben an der WDR.* Berlin: Volker Spiess, 1983.

———. *Holocaust zur Unterhaltung. Anatomie eines internationalen Bestsellers.* Berlin: Elephanten Press, 1982.

Kugelmann, Cily. "Was heisst jüdische Identität?" *Alternative* 140/141 (December 1981), 234–240.

Kuschner, Doris. "Die jüdische Minderheit in der Bundesrepublik Deutschland." Ph.D. dissertation, University of Cologne, 1977.

Lamm, Hans, ed. *Vergangene Tage. Jüdische Kultur in München.* Munich, 1982.

Lanzmann, Claude. "From the Holocaust to the *Holocaust.*" *Telos* 42 (Winter 1979–1980), pp. 137–143.

"Legacy of the German Refugee Intellectuals, The." Special Issue of *Salmagundi* (Fall/Winter 1969/70).

Maor, Harry. "Der Wiederaufbau der jüdischen Gemeinden in Deutschland." Ph.D. dissertation, University of Mainz, 1961.

Marcuse, Herbert. "Nachwort." Walter Benjamin, *Zur Kritik der Gewalt und andere Aufsätze.* Frankfurt am Main: Suhrkamp Verlag, 1965.

Märthesheimer, Peter, and Ivo Frenzel, eds. *Im Kreuzfeuer: Der Fernsehfilm "Holocaust."* Frankfurt am Main: Fischer, 1979.

Mendes-Flohr, Paul, and Jehuda Reinharz, eds. *The Jew in the Modern World: A Documentary History.* New York: Oxford University Press, 1980.

Meyer, Alwin, and Karl-Klaus Rube. *Phantomdemokraten oder die alltägliche Gegenwart der Vergangenheit.* Reinbek: Rowohlt, 1979.

Mosse, George L. *The Crisis of German Ideology.* New York: Howard Fertig, 1964.

———. *Germans and Jews: The Right, the Left, and the Search for a "Third Force" in Pre-Nazi Germany.* New York: Howard Fertig, 1970.

———. *Toward the Final Solution: A History of European Racism.* New York: Howard Fertig, 1978.

———. *Masses and Man: Nationalist and Fascist Perceptions of Reality.* New York: Howard Fertig, 1980.

———. "Gedanken zum deutsch-jüdischen Dialog." *Chronik der Ludwig-Maximilians-Universität München 1982/83* (Munich, 1983), pp. 45–58.

Neveux, Jean-Baptiste. "Hochschule für jüdische Studien à Heidelberg." *Revue d'Allemagne* 18 (July–September 1981), pp. 597–600.

Oppenheimer, Walter. *Jüdische Jugend in Deutschland.* Munich: Juventa Verlag, 1967.

Piccone, Paul, and Russell Berman. "Recycling the 'Jewish Question.'" *New German Critique* 21 (Fall 1980), pp. 113–128.

Piwitt, Hermann P. "Lernen wir, unbefangen zu sein." *Konkret* (April 1981), p. 58.

Rabinbach, Anson. "Anti-Semitism Reconsidered." *New German Critique* 21 (Fall 1980), pp. 129–142.

Reichmann, Eva. "Der Bewusstseinswandel der deutschen Juden." In *Deutsches Judentum in Krieg und Revolution 1916–1923,* edited by Werner Mosse. Tübingen: Mohr, 1971, pp. 511–612.

Reitlinger, Gerald. *The Final Solution. The Attempt to Exterminate the Jews of Europe, 1939–1945.* 2nd rev. ed. London: Vallentine, Mitchell, 1968.

Richarz, Monika, ed. *Jüdisches Leben in Deutschland. Selbstzeugnisse zur Sozialgeschichte 1918–1945.* Stuttgart: Deutsche Verlags-Anstalt, 1982.

———. "Jüdische Kultur." In *Kulturpolitisches Wörterbuch. Bundesrepublik Deutschland/Deutsche Demokratische Republik im Vergleich,* edited by Wolfgang R. Langenbucher, Ralf Rytlewski, and Bernd Weyergraf. Stuttgart: Metzler, 1983, pp. 347–351.

———. "Jews in Today's Germanies." *Leo Baeck Yearbook* 30 (1985), in press.

Rürup, Reinhard. *Emanzipation und Antisemitismus.* Göttingen: Vandenhoeck & Ruprecht, 1975.

Sartre, Jean-Paul. *Anti-Semite and Jew.* Translated by George J. Becker. New York: Schocken Books, 1965.

Scholem, Gershom. *On Jews and Judaism in Crisis: Selected Essays.* New York: Schocken Books, 1976.

Schönbach, Peter. *Reaktionen auf die antisemitische Welle im Winter, 1959/1960 (Frankfurter Beiträge zur Soziologie).* Frankfurt am Main: Europäische Verlagsanstalt, 1961.

Schultz, Hans Jürgen, ed. *Mein Judentum.* Stuttgart: Kreuz Verlag, 1978.

Schwarzer, Alice. "Wir sind Kinder unserer Eltern." *Konkret* (May 1981), pp. 46–47.

———. "Sind wir alle Antisemiten?" *Emma* (August 1981), p. 57.

Sievers, Leo. *Juden in Deutschland.* Munich: Goldmann, 1979.

Simmel, Ernst, ed. *Anti-Semitism: A Social Disease.* New York: International Universities Press, 1946.

Sperber, Manès. *Churban oder Die unfassbare Gewissheit.* Vienna: Europa Verlag, 1979.

————. *The Achilles Heel.* Translated by Constantine FitzGibbon. London: A. Deutsch, 1959.

Theweleit, Klaus. *Männerphantasien.* 2 vols. Frankfurt am Main: Verlag Roter Stern, 1977.

Wasserstein, Bernard. *Britain and the Jews of Europe 1939–1945.* Oxford: Oxford University Press, 1979.

Weil, Frederick. "The Imperfectly Mastered Past: Anti-Semitism in West Germany since the Holocaust." *New German Critique* 20 (Spring/Summer 1980), pp. 135–153.

Wetzel, Dietrich, ed. *Die Verlängerung von Geschichte. Deutsche, Juden und der Palästinakonflikt.* Frankfurt am Main: Verlag Neue Kritik, 1983.

Willis, Ellen. "The Myth of the Powerful Jew." *Village Voice* (September 3, 1979), pp. 1, 12.

Wolffsohn, Michael. "Leben im Land der Mörder." *Die Zeit* 22 (May 27, 1983), pp. 9–10.

Wyman, David. *The Abandonment of the Jews, 1941–1945.* New York: Pantheon, 1984.

Zipes, Jack. "The Return of the Repressed." *New German Critique* 31 (Winter 1984), pp. 201–210.

ABOUT THE AUTHORS

Jean Améry (1912–1978) was born in Vienna, where he studied literature and philosophy. He emigrated to Belgium in 1938 and participated in an anti-Fascist resistance group. In 1943 he was arrested by the Gestapo and imprisoned for two years in a concentration camp. After the war he settled in Brussels and soon became known as one of the most important social philosophers in Europe. He wrote numerous essays and books and was awarded the German Critics' Prize in 1970 and the Lessing Prize in 1977. Among his best known works are *Wider-Sprüche, Lefeu oder der Abruch,* and *Jenseits von Schuld und Sühne,* from which we have taken a chapter for the present volume.

Jean-Paul Bier is a professor of German literature at the University of Antwerp in Belgium. He received his doctorate from the Université Libre de Bruxelles and was the director of the Fonds National de la Recherche Scientifique. His major speciality is German literature of the twentieth century, and he has written numerous articles on Hermann Broch, Günther Eich, East German literature, and Austrian literature. His most notable book is *Auschwitz et les nouvelles littératures allemandes,* the first chapter of which he has revised and expanded for the present volume.

Paul Breines is a professor of history at Boston College, specializing in modern European intellectual history. He has published many articles on European political thought and has served on the editorial board of *Telos.* With Andrew Arato, he is coauthor of *The Young Lukács and the Origins of Western Marxism.* He is presently working on a study of images of violent Jews in American pulp fiction.

Detlev Claussen is a professor at the Institut für Soziologie at the University of Hannover. He studied philosophy and sociology at the University of Frankfurt from 1966 to 1971, during which time he was a member of SDS. He specialized in international relations and became editor of the magazine *Neue Kritik,* and since 1975 he has served on the editorial staff of *Links.* He has writen widely, including *Spuren der Befreiung—Herbert Marcuse* and *Grenzen der Aufklärung* and is currently completing a project on anti-Semitism.

Dan Diner is currently teaching at universities in Frankfurt am Main and in Israel. He received his doctorate in political science at the University of Frankfurt and has been active in German-Jewish relations for the past ten years. In addition, he is on the editorial staff of *Links* and writes for publications in Germany and Israel. Two of his books are: *Israel in Palästina* and *Keine Zukunft auf den Gräbern der Palästiner*.

Ferenc Feher received his doctorate from the University of Budapest and wrote a dissertation entitled *Dostoevsky and the Crisis of the Individual* under the supervision of Georg Lukács. In 1977 he was forced to leave Budapest after participating in dissident groups for a long time. He emigrated to Melbourne, Australia, where he teaches politics at La Trobe University. He has published extensively on aesthetic and political theory and among his most important books are: *Dictatorship over Needs* (with A. Heller); *Doomsday or Deterrence* (with A. Heller). He edited G. Lukács's, *The Specificity of the Aesthetic* and (with R. Miller) *Khruschev and the Communist World*. Another coedited work is *Legitimation in Communist Countries* (with T. H. Rigby).

Atina Grossmann is an assistant professor of history at Mount Holyoke College, where she teaches Modern European and Women's History. She has published articles on the sex reform movements and the "New Woman" in Weimar Germany and is coeditor of *When Biology Became Destiny: Women in Weimar and Nazi Germany*. She is currently working on a book called Women, Family, and the Rationalization of Sexuality: Sex Reform 1925–35.

Rebecca S. Hayden received a B.A. from Weslyan and an M.A. from Boston University. She has collaborated at both institutions with Andrei Markovits on articles dealing with the Holocaust and German/Austrian politics. She has recently completed a year of teaching in Germany as a Fulbright Scholar.

Jeffrey Herf is a visiting research associate at the Center for International Affairs at Harvard University (1985–1986), and Assistant Professor of Political Science at The College of the Holy Cross. From 1981 to 1985 he taught at Harvard University and has been a research associate of Harvard's Center for European Studies. His book, *Reactionary Modernism: Technology, Culture, and Politics in Weimar and the Third Reich* was published by Cambridge University Press in 1984. He is the author of articles on social theory, modern German history and politics, and international affairs. He is completing a book on national identity and neutralism in West Germany since the 1960s.

Martin Jay is professor of history at the University of California, Berkeley. Aside from publishing numerous articles for leading journals in America and Europe, he has written four significant books: *The Dialectical Imagination, Marxism and Totality, Adorno,* and *Permanent Exiles.* He is currently working on the problematic of vision in twentieth-century French thought while serving as senior editor of *Theory and Society.*

Andrei S. Markovits is associate professor of political science at Boston University and a Research Associate at the Center for European Studies at Harvard University. His research and teaching interests include comparative labor movements, social democracy and the welfare state, the politics of Fascism, and the situation of Jews in Austria and the Federal Republic of Germany since 1945. He is the author of over thirty articles and several books, among which are *The Political Economy of West Germany* and *The West German Trade Unions.*

Moishe Postone is a research fellow at the Center of Psychosocial Studies in Chicago. He studied history at the University of Chicago and sociology at the J. W. Goethe-Universität in Frankfurt am Main. He has written articles on Marxian theory, contemporary German politics, critical theory, and anti-Semitism. He is presently preparing a reinterpretation of Marx's mature works for publication.

Toni Oelsner (1907–1982) studied sociology and history at Frankfurt University from 1931 to 1934. Then she did research on Jewish emancipation and lectured for Jewish organizations until 1939, when she emigrated to the United States. She continued to work on the social history of Jews in Germany until her death in 1982. Among her most important publications are *Three Jewish Families in Modern Germany,* "The Place of the Jews in Economic History," and *The Economic and Social Conditions of the Jews of Southwestern Germany in the Thirteenth and Fourteenth Centuries.*

Anson Rabinbach teaches European history at The Cooper Union for the Advancement of Science and Art in New York. He is a founder and coeditor of *New German Critique.* The author of numerous articles in modern European history, his books include *The Crisis of Austrian Socialism: From Red Vienna to Civil War 1927–1934* and *The Austrian Experiment: Social Democracy and Austromarxism.* He is currently completing a book on the perception of work, fatigue, and energy in modern Europe.

Manès Sperber (1905–1984) was born in Poland and moved to Vienna during his youth. He studied psychology in Vienna and moved to Berlin during the 1920s, when he became one of the leading disciples of the psychologist Alfred Adler. Sperber joined the Communist Party and broke with Adler and psychology to join the anti-Fascist resistance. In 1933 he emigrated to Yugoslavia and then in 1934 to Paris. By 1937 he had left the Communist Party because of the Moscow show trials. During the war he worked with the resistance in France and Switzerland. After 1945 he settled in Paris, where he wrote his famous novel trilogy *Eine Träne im Ozean* and his autobiography *All das Vergangene*. Aside from these works he has written outstanding psychological and political studies such as *Individuum und Gemeinschaft* and *Die Achillesferse*. In 1973 Sperber won the Goethe Prize, in 1974 the Prize of the City of Vienna, and in 1983 the Frankfurt Book Fair Prize.

Yudit Yago-Jung was born in 1946 in Germany, where she lived until 1970. She then moved to Israel for three years and from there she emigrated to the United States in 1974. In 1976 she received her Ph.D. from Frankfurt University. She recently completed a book entitled State or Revolution: The Search for National Identity in the Jewish Workers' Movement. Presently, she is a psychoanalyst in private practice in New York.

Siegfried Zielinski is a professor at the Technical University of Berlin. He specializes in mass media research and the study of anti-Semitism. He conducted a research project on the reception of the American television film "Holocaust," and he has also done some important studies of the film *Jüd Süss*. Zielinski published a study of the "Holocaust" reception with Friedrich Knilli entitled *Holocaust zur Unterhaltung*. He has also written extensively on contemporary German theater and postwar German films in both East and West Germany.

Jack Zipes is professor of German and Comparative Literature at the University of Wisconsin at Milwaukee, and one of the coeditors of *New German Critique*. He has written extensively on contemporary German literature particularly on the theater and the novel, and he has also reported on German politics and questions pertaining to Germans and Jews. In addition he has specialized in the study of folk and fairy tales and has published several books on this topic such as *Breaking the Magic Spell: Radical Theories of Folk and Fairy Tales*, *Fairy Tales and the Art of Subversion*, and *The Trials and Tribulations of Little Red Riding Hood*.